THE
UNNECESSARY
WAR

THE UNNECESSARY WAR

Whitehall and the German Resistance to Hitler

by

PATRICIA MEEHAN

SINCLAIR-STEVENSON

First published in Great Britain in 1992
by Sinclair-Stevenson
an imprint of Reed Consumer Books Ltd
Michelin House, 81 Fulham Road, London SW3 6RB
and Auckland, Melbourne, Singapore and Toronto

This paperback edition published by Sinclair-Stevenson in 1995

A CIP catalogue entry for this book
is available from the British Library.

ISBN 1 85619 550 3

Typeset by Rowland Phototypesetting Limited
Bury St Edmunds, Suffolk

Printed and bound in Great Britain by
Clays Ltd, St Ives plc

Contents

Acknowledgements

I am greatly indebted to the following for information, hospitality and access to documents: Frau Adelheid Gräfin zu Eulenberg; Frau Lore Kordt; Frau Dr Clarita von Trott zu Solz; Signora Fey Pirzio Biroli von Hassell; Miss Hilde Waldo; Dr Georg V. Bruns; Peter and Christabel Bielenberg; Dr Hellmut Becker; Dr Otto John; the late Dr W. A. Visser 't Hooft; Herr Reinhard Spitzy; Mrs Martha C. Johnson (formerly Mrs E. A. Bayne); Mr Warren Magee; the Hon David Astor; the late Lady Vansittart; the late Lord Kaldor; the late Hon Sir Con O'Neill; Mrs Pamela Turner. I am particularly grateful to the Hon David Astor for his generous support and invaluable criticism.

Crown copyright material in the Public Record Office is reproduced by permission of the Controller of Her Majesty's Stationery Office.

I gratefully acknowledge the following for permission to reproduce photographs: Popperfoto: 1, 5, 8, 39; Frau Lore Kordt: 2, 23, 24, 25; Associated Press: 3, 12; *The von Hassell Diaries 1938–1944*, Hamish Hamilton Ltd, 1948: 4, 35; Bundesarchiv: 6; the Hulton-Deutsch Collection Ltd: 7, 10, 13, 14, 15, 17, 18, 19, 20, 21, 26, 27, 28, 30, 36; the Trustees of the Imperial War Museum, London: 9, 34; World Council of Churches: 11; Public Record Office: 16, 29; the von Weizsäcker family: 22, 38, 40; Bildarchiv Preussischer Kulturbesitz, Berlin: 31; Bundespresse-und Informationsamt, Bonn: 32, 33; Clarita von Trott: 37.

Every effort has been made to trace the copyright holders of quoted material and photographs. If, however, there are inadvertent omissions these can be rectified in any future editions.

Introduction

President Roosevelt once asked me what this war should be called. My answer was – 'the unnecessary war' . . . .

Winston S. Churchill

It is perhaps difficult for the pure historian to write contemporary history. It cannot be written on documents only – above all on diplomatic ones. I know too much of what lies behind them, too much of what does not appear.

Lord Vansittart
former Head of the Foreign Office

S HORTLY after the signing of the Munich Agreement, in a broadcast to the United States, Winston Churchill declared:

> If the risks of war which were run by France and Britain at the last moment had been boldly faced in good time, and plain declarations made, and meant, how different would our prospects be today. . . .

Had the German dictator been confronted by a 'formidable array of peace-defending powers':

> This would have been an opportunity for all peace-loving and moderate forces in Germany, together with the Chiefs of the German Army, to make a great effort to re-establish something like sane and civilised conditions in their country.

And he spoke of how the 'whole population of a great country – amiable, good-hearted, peace-loving people' could be 'gripped by the neck and by the hair' by a tyranny bent on war.[1] In November, 1945, in the flush of victory, Churchill returned to this theme in a speech in Brussels. He told his audience: 'President Roosevelt one day asked me what this war should be called. My answer was "the unnecessary war".' He then echoed almost exactly the words he had used in his message to America in October, 1938:

> If the Allies had resisted Hitler strongly in his early stages . . . the chance would have been given to the sane elements in German life, which were very powerful – especially in the High Command – to free Germany from the maniacal system into the grip of which she was falling.[2]

2

In these two speeches, separated as they were by a great war, Churchill linked directly Hitler's confrontation by a 'swift and resolute gathering of forces' which would force him to recoil, and the German opposition waiting in the wings who would thereby have been given the opportunity to free Germany from the 'maniacal' Nazi system. Hitler's enemies at home could have achieved what his enemies abroad could not do short of war.

The German Opposition had looked to Britain, the moral leader of Europe, to present a firm front against the dictator, as Churchill himself well knew. They were not seeking subversive action against Germany by a foreign power. They rejected totally any intervention from abroad outside the vital sphere of international diplomacy. The overthrow of the Nazi régime had to be accomplished by the Germans themselves. What they were asking was no more than many British people were asking at that time – for 'plain declarations, made and meant'. In the years before the war, leading members of the Opposition had come to Britain at the risk of their lives to warn the government of Hitler's intentions and to advise, from their inside knowledge, what steps might most effectively be taken against him. It was these men and those whom they represented in Germany that Churchill would have had in mind when he made those two speeches in 1938 and 1945. He had been one of those to whom they had confided their message. They knew where Churchill stood and longed for him to be taken into government. Those who came to London did not hesitate to press for this. It was not a sentiment calculated to advance their cause with the British political establishment.

Certainly the British Government could not be expected to take at face value approaches from those who claimed to be Hitler's enemies. But certainly the Foreign Office, which as will be seen was the conduit for almost all information originating from Opposition sources, had a duty to probe this unknown area discreetly and critically; yet with a positive attitude and an open mind. Goebbels' presentation of a strong and united Germany was (and indeed still is by many) accepted on the British side. Yet in the years before the war information was flooding in to the Foreign Office from reliable British sources – diplomats, industrialists, bankers, journalists, academics – proving just the opposite. The record is there in the files. It is a picture of economic chaos, military weakness and increasing public disaffection. It certainly warranted a close examination of the whispered reports of forces of opposition which were advancing the possibility of overthrowing the régime.

The leading personalities of the Opposition were men of substance and proven integrity in their own country. Some of them were known in diplomatic and establishment circles in Britain. They shared the same social background: that of aristocrats, landowners, diplomats, high-ranking officers, senior administrators. They were not anarchists or cloth-capped revolutionaries. They were quite alien to a world of *coups d'état* and assassinations. They forced themselves to enter it because of the overwhelming evil with which they were faced. To have ignored and dismissed the advice and appeals of such men (supported as these were by exceptional intelligence from within the German Reich), argues a certain selective deafness. Yet all indication of a substantial and influential Opposition element inside Germany had been vigorously discounted during the years of appeasement. Even after the end of the war, the existence of what the Foreign Office always referred to (with careful punctuation) as '"good" Germans' was suppressed.

In September, 1938 the anti-Nazi Opposition had come breathtakingly close to achieving their end. The British Government were informed that they were armed, poised and ready to act at the moment when the Allies should deliver their *ne plus ultra* over Czechoslovakia. A new democratic government of distinguished citizens, all dedicated anti-Nazis, was ready to take over. There was to be no dangerous vacuum of power. It was the moment of maximum opportunity. It was aborted through the impetuous, ill-judged and unforeseen flight of an almost pacifist British Prime Minister to wait upon the Führer at Berchtesgaden. Too late, when the crisis had passed, Lord Halifax, the Foreign Secretary, conceded that the voices from Germany had been correct and should have been heeded. The Opposition did not abandon its efforts after the disaster of 1938, even after the outbreak of war. They intensified their contacts with the British during the 'twilight war' of 1939–1940. As long as battle was not actually joined, and blood shed, there was still hope that the ultimate catastrophe might be averted. But the circumstances which were so favourable at the time of the Czech crisis could never be re-created.

It was the diplomats of the German Foreign Office, under State Secretary von Weizsäcker, who were the spear-head of the most formidable secret war against the Nazis and their aggressive preparations. Every possible opportunity was taken to inform and to warn their opposite numbers in Britain. Information came from the innermost sanctum of Ribbentrop's Ministry of Foreign Affairs. Invaluable political-military intelligence was passed to the British who did not have to lift a finger to get it. Every milestone on Hitler's road to war was mapped out for them in advance. But these voices of Hitler's opposition were not welcome in Whitehall. The line laid down by Chamberlain was that one day Hitler would be brought to heel and made to change his policies which after all were only an extreme pursuit of German interests. This might mean certain concessions but in the end the aggressor would be pacified and a new and better relationship could be established with a sanitised Third Reich.

The German Opposition were seen as a hindrance to these plans – mere malcontents on whose toes Hitler had no doubt trodden. They were rocking the boat which Chamberlain himself desired to steer into calmer waters through appeasement. It was a matter of those who were anxious to reach an accommodation with the German government not welcoming the unconventional activities of those who wanted to destroy it. Admittedly the Prime Minister had the last word and Chamberlain pursued his course singly and single-mindedly. (Collier, Head of Northern Department, minuted that '. . . in matters of foreign policy we live under a dictatorship, just like Germany or Italy . . . .'[3]) Nevertheless, it was the function of the Foreign Office, as the professionals and experts in foreign affairs, to advise. As Permanent Secretary at the Foreign Office, Sir Robert Vansittart had been the lone voice against appeasement and the advocate of listening to the German Opposition. Once he had been 'kicked upstairs' by Chamberlain, and once his successor, Sir Alexander Cadogan, had fallen dutifully into line, the hopes of the Opposition for British co-operation were doomed.

In their clandestine visits before the war, the representatives of the Opposition sought urgently to impress upon the British that Nazism was not merely a particularly reprehensible form of nationalism. It was a system which aimed at European domination at the least. In appealing for a firm stand on the part of the Western democracies, they were pleading for the peace and freedom of Europe and ultimately the world. But the British maintained the attitude that the German Opposition were attempting to force them into provocative declarations which they did not wish to make, simply in order that the Germans themselves might be rid of a domestic tyrant. When war came, the detached attitude towards the domestic brutalities of the German government was made abundantly clear. In his Final Report to the Foreign Secretary, after the outbreak of the war to which his own ineptitude had contributed so much, Sir Nevile Henderson, last Ambassador to the Third Reich, summed it up:

> It would be idle to deny the great achievements of the man who restored to the German nation its self-respect and its disciplined order-liness. The tyrannical methods which were employed within Germany itself to obtain this result were detestable, but were Germany's own concern. Many of Herr Hitler's social reforms, in spite of their complete disregard of personal liberty of thought, word or deed, were on highly advanced democratic lines . . . typical examples of a benevolent dictatorship. . . .

So long as National-Socialism remained an article for internal consumption, continued Sir Nevile, the government of Germany was the affair of the German people.[4] (Or, as the Prince of Wales put it more pithily to the Prince of Hesse: 'It's nobody's damned business what Germany does to Germany.')

This nice distinction was also made by the historian, Arthur Bryant, who was asked by R. A. Butler, the Minister of State at the Foreign Office, to prepare a paper on war aims: 'Our real quarrel is not with the form of government by which the Germans choose or submit to be ruled, but with the violence and the lack of good faith shown by that government in its dealings with others. . . .'[5] In the House of Commons Sir Archibald Sinclair, the Liberal leader, was even more precise:

> It is not for us to chastise another people for its own misgovernment or to go to war on behalf of Pastor Niemöller and the German Jews. The German people must find ways to set their own house in order and we must recognise the rights of self-government in their own country. . . . The objection to Hitlerism is that conquest and tyranny over other nations is implicit in it. . . .[6]

But to suppose that the two aspects of Germany – the internal and the external – could be considered separately, and that Germany stewing in its own juice was not a danger, was to ignore the Nazi rallying cry: 'Today Germany! Tomorrow the world!'

Although the outbreak of war had vindicated all the Opposition's warnings and advice, the Foreign Office showed no signs of revising its attitude, which had been reinforced by the replacement of Halifax by Eden as Foreign Secretary. Churchill told Fabian von Schlabrendorff who visited him at Chartwell in 1949, ten years to the day since his previous visit while in Britain as a secret emissary of the Opposition, that he had come to realise that 'during the war he had been misled by his assistants about the considerable strength and size of the German anti-Hitler resistance.'[7] Between the two visits, Schlabrendorff himself had been cruelly tortured by the Gestapo and had escaped the scaffold by a miracle.

Eden's implacable enmity to the Germans as a whole and to the Opposition in particular admitted of no alternative to total defeat and indefinite subjugation. The one war aim which was to be clearly and unequivocally enunciated was that of 'Unconditional Surrender'. This became officially 'our first war aim' and was declared the overall objective of the war by the Joint Chiefs of Staff in the final *Sextant Report*. The policy, so casually thrown off by Roosevelt at Casablanca in January, 1943, and backed, to his later regret, by Churchill, was wholly inimical to the efforts of the Opposition. One of the leading Opposition figures, former Ambassador Ulrich von Hassell, wrote that its announcement destroyed at a stroke the work of six years. They were left with nothing to offer their countrymen, after the overthrow of Hitler, but a leap in the dark. Freiherr Hans Herwarth von Bittenfeld (later the German Federal Republic's first ambassador to Britain) had no doubt that many more general officers would have joined the resistance, but that they could not accept the responsibility for an action the outcome of which was so uncertain for the future of the country:

> If the Allies had issued a statement that the overthrow of Hitler would affect the settlement, however minimally, it would have had a profound impact. . . . I discussed this issue with Stauffenberg. We were deeply depressed by the Allies' silence.[8]

Yet it was rash for the Allies to assume that Hitler's German enemies would never achieve his removal. By 1944 there had already been some half-a-dozen serious plots against the Führer's life. All had been narrowly aborted through circumstances outside the control of those involved. Always some malignant power seemed to intervene on Hitler's behalf. It did so again on 20 July 1944. But this time an actual explosion took place the sound of which reached the outside world. Stauffenberg's attempt came within a hair's-breadth of succeeding.

In the course of an interview with an intelligence officer at the end of the war, the former Chancellor Franz von Papen asked his interrogator what Britain would have done if the attempt had succeeded. The officer was somewhat nonplussed. He could only reply, vaguely: 'I suppose we should have stopped the war.'[9] But the war could not have been stopped, like a football match, by blowing a whistle. Unconditional surrender could hardly have been demanded, in 1944, from an enemy still undefeated in the field. Nor would any new non-Nazi government, seeking the support of the nation, have been able to submit to such a demand. And would British and American public opinion have countenanced the continuation of the war against such a government offering terms: particularly the sort of terms which the Allied governments were well aware the Opposition would offer? It was discussed in Cabinet what line the Foreign Secretary should take in the House in dealing with the attempt against Hitler and it was agreed that 'at this stage the less said the better.'[10]

Indeed, the relief in Whitehall at the failure of the plot was considerable. There was, it was found, a bright side to the subsequent purges in which thousands perished. The historian John Wheeler-Bennett, a member of the Foreign Office Political Intelligence Department, summed up the advantages:

> It may now be said with some definiteness that we are better off with things as they are today than if the plot of July 20th had succeeded and Hitler had been assassinated. . . . By the failure of the plot we have been spared the embarrassments, both at home and in the United States, which might have resulted from such a move, and, moreover, the present purge is presumably removing from the scene numerous individuals which might have caused us difficulty, not only had the plot succeeded, but also after the defeat of a Nazi Germany. . . .
> The Gestapo and the SS have done us an appreciable service in removing a selection of those who would undoubtedly have posed as 'good' Germans after the war. . . . It is to our advantage therefore that the purge should continue, since the killing of Germans by Germans will save us from future embarrassments of many kinds.

This bloodthirsty effusion was accepted, *nem. con.*, by Central Department. Roberts minuted: 'It all seems sensible and calls for no special comment.'[11]

The remaining months of the war resulted in vast numbers of deaths – among the soldiers on all fronts; among the civilians in the obliterated cities of Germany and under the hail of V-bombs on Britain; and among the Jews in the death camps in Eastern Europe. And Yalta was still to come, with its consequent monumental transfers of human beings to and fro across Europe. It is difficult to agree with the Foreign Office view that the survival of Hitler was a good thing.

Why did Hitler's opponents in Germany – alive – constitute such a threat that their 'removal from the scene' by the Gestapo was so welcome in Whitehall? Wheeler-Bennett declared that these people would have 'posed' as '"good" Germans' after the war. *Posed?* The Gestapo certainly were taking them for the real thing. Had the *coup* been successful and a new government emerged in Germany, the Foreign Office might indeed have found itself in considerable 'difficulty' and 'embarrassment' particularly in the eyes of the Americans. The new government would have counted among its members those leading Oppositionists, now being executed, who had sought British co-operation. The British might then have found themselves facing the charge (as it was expressed in a Foreign Office minute some years later) that but for their refusal to listen, war might have been averted, or ended at an earlier date.

That the Foreign Office was more than a little uneasy about aspects of its past record, which it was felt would be better left undisturbed, is demonstrated by the lengths to which it was prepared to go to prevent that record being exposed to public scrutiny. The advent of peace found the Foreign Office fighting a rearguard action in a secret war for its own reputation.

In June, 1944 the Minister of State, Richard Law, announced in the House of Commons the forthcoming publication of *Documents on British Foreign Policy*, a series of selected Foreign Office documents covering the years between the two wars. The Minister made clear that the purpose of publishing these documents was:

> . . . to show to the world and to the historians of the future what was our foreign policy; it is not the intention to try to explain how that foreign policy was arrived at, or how the foreign policy which in fact we had might have been improved. . . .[12]

When the first volumes appeared they met with some sharp criticism. *The Times* objected strongly to the absence of departmental minutes – 'such a valuable part of earlier collections.'[13] These minutes – mostly handwritten – are added to a file as it circulates among senior advisers. They are a true record of attitudes, judgments, contrary opinions, personalities and prejudices. E. L. Woodward, the official historian, claimed considerations of constitutional propriety for their omission.[14] But a minute of his own reveals that his motive was less a lofty concern for propriety than a matter of protecting colleagues: 'I thought that the publication of minutes would be – on the whole – misleading and therefore unfair to the writers, many of whom were still in the service.'[15] The Foreign Office had good reason to congratulate itself on that quality in its official historian which, it was felt, 'is very important from the Office point of view – discretion.' Like the former Permanent Secretary Vansittart, the authors of such minutes knew that history could not be written out of diplomatic documents alone; that 'too much lies behind them, too much of what does not appear.'

The Foreign Office, as will be seen later, would dearly have liked to rearrange the history of pre-war foreign policy by withholding certain documents from publication. But what also lay concealed behind diplomatic documents – in the unpublished minutes – was the record of the attempts by the anti-Nazi Opposition inside Germany secretly to establish fruitful contact with Britain with the aim of avoiding war or of curtailing it. This was buried in the archives together with the record of the British response, embargoed for fifty years. By the time the rule of access to State papers was relaxed to thirty years (in 1968) denigratory representations of the German Opposition had already been established by certain complaisant historians, with connections with the Foreign Office, to whom no unwelcome fact was sacred. These accounts did not reflect the facts about the relationship between the Opposition and the British. Indeed, the Foreign Office and its chroniclers succeeded in creating the impression that there was nothing to tell.

The most venomous language of these writers was reserved for those German diplomats who had been in direct contact with the Foreign Office: Ernst von Weizsäcker and the brothers Erich and Theo Kordt. These three, being stationed abroad, had escaped the purges of 1944. The versions of events produced by these and other key members of the Opposition, whether given in courts of law or published in books of memoirs, could be – and were – readily discredited as the work of former Nazis anxious to whitewash their past. The Foreign Office kept the lid firmly on the evidence which would have corroborated their claims. And even perjury was not a stumbling block when there were secrets to be kept.

In their efforts to distort or suppress the truth wherever or whenever it emerged, members of the Foreign Office were in effect passing judgment upon themselves. Evidently this was a chapter of contemporary history better left untold.

It is the intention of this book to supply that missing chapter. This is not a history of the German Opposition – which was more extensive than appears here – only of its British connection, which continued to the bitter end. The pursuit of that connection beyond the outbreak of war testifies to the very real existence of those 'peace-loving forces' who in 1938 were denied their opportunity. The story has been re-constructed from many disparate sources but primarily from the files of the Foreign Office. The inevitable absence of documents on the side of the German conspirators is made good by the recorded reactions in minutes and memoranda which, though negative, attest positively to the Opposition's endeavours.

The German Opposition had foreseen the horror which an unchecked Hitler would bring first to Germany and then to the rest of Europe. It was exactly such an image which they so forcefully attempted to bring to the attention of the leaders of the outside world. They failed. Few of them survived to see the bitter end when at last, at immense cost, Hitler and his régime were finally obliterated and his enemies had 'created a desert and called it peace.' They had feared defeat less than the victory of Hitler, the 'arch-enemy of the whole world.' When the 'unnecessary war' broke out, Carl Gordeler, the Opposition leader executed in February, 1945, who had been in constant touch with the highest levels of British diplomacy before the war, wrote:

Influential Englishmen and Americans were informed before this war that Hitler would start it. They considered us, the Germans who warned them, to be men without national feeling. They overlooked the fact that we love our country dearly and want both its greatness and its honour. . . .
We do not wish to diminish the responsibility which we as Germans will have to bear, but the guilt for the tragic events rests not with the Germans alone. . . .[16]

— I —

Whitehall and Wilhelmstrasse

[The Foreign Secretary] said he was very lazy and disliked work. Could he hunt on Saturdays? I said there was a lot of work but much of it could be done at home or in the train.

Diary of Oliver Harvey
Private Secretary to Lord Halifax

According to my observations at that time, the official world in London was not ready to act as it should have been.

State Secretary von Weizsäcker
Head of the German Foreign Office

O N 12 September 1938, the First Lord of the Admiralty, Duff Cooper, wrote a personal letter to the Foreign Secretary, Lord Halifax. It should be borne in mind, he urged, how important the hunting and shooting side of life was to the men of Goering's type who now played so big a part in Germany:

> If one of them were to go to England, how much might be accomplished by well-prepared entertainments of this kind. A big shoot at Chatsworth, for instance, or at Belvoir, might produce a wonderful effect.

Some of these people, concluded the First Lord, 'belong to a world so different from that to which we are accustomed, that a real effort of imagination is required if we are to make a useful approach to them.'[1] Evidently imagination thus exercised found that common ground for an approach existed in the surroundings and language of the sporting life. The Germans had used this expedient themselves. A year earlier, a personal invitation to Halifax – as Master of the Middleton foxhounds – to attend a hunting exhibition organised by Goering had brought together the German Chancellor and the British Foreign Secretary in private talk. Now, in September, 1938, Goering was 'jovially' offering Halifax, through the British Ambassador, 'the four best stags in Germany' if Britain disclaimed an interest in Czechoslovakia. Meanwhile, the Prime Minister, soon to fly to call on Hitler at Berchtesgaden, was marching towards the sound of gunfire in Scotland. 'I have had three days on the moor,' wrote Chamberlain to Halifax, 'two of them really good ones, and I feel a new man.'[2]

What Duff Cooper seemed to be striving for was some frame of reference into which those Germans whom Halifax rather delicately referred to as 'the crazy persons who had managed to secure control of the country' might be fitted. But there were other Germans who needed to be fitted into a frame – the professional diplomats of the Foreign Ministry in the Wilhelmstrasse. It was here that a real effort of imagination by their opposite numbers in Whitehall was required. They did not belong, as the Nazi leadership did, to a world 'so different' from the British experience: but it was a world turned upside down. In London the British Foreign Office, representative of a great power – supreme in its prestige, respected for its centuries of experience in diplomacy, effortless in its superiority – reflected, in its refusal to be unduly alarmed, the lethargic attitude of government and public. In Berlin, men in the same diplomatic mould, respecting the same conventions, also upper class in their origins, were working in quiet desperation; infiltrated by secret police; emasculated by a Head of State who despised their profession. They were forced, in their efforts to subvert Hitler's aggressive foreign policy, into devious and perilous expedients totally foreign to their background and training. So set was Whitehall in its ways and blinkered by its prejudices that both the imagination and the will were lacking for these circumstances to be turned to constructive advantage in the cause of the prevention of war and the elimination of the public enemy, Hitler. 'We ought to have been aided before the outbreak of war,' Ernst von Weizsäcker, then Head of the Foreign Office, declared years later. 'Such régimes as this one . . . can only be abolished with help from abroad.'[3]

Neither successive Foreign Secretaries nor their professional advisers in the Foreign Office could plead ignorance. The Nazis had been put clearly in their sights by the despatches received from the Embassy in Berlin. Sir Horace Rumbold was ambassador from the 1920s until Hitler came to power in 1933. He had monitored the earliest stirrings of National Socialism, taken its measure and reported accordingly with style and wit. His despatches were brilliantly prophetic and his advice was to prove both timely and accurate. As early as 1933, he took the Foreign Office step by step through *Mein Kampf* to show how closely Hitler was following his blueprint. 'This despatch,' wrote Rumbold, years later, 'made a considerable sensation but was pigeonholed in due course. Neither MacDonald nor Baldwin could face the facts.'[4] When in 1928 Sir Robert Vansittart had been seconded to Downing Street as Private Secretary to Prime Minister Baldwin, his Chief at the Foreign Office, Lord

Tyrrell, had instructed him: 'Your real job will be to get him interested in foreign affairs. You may not find it easy. . . .' It was not. Vansittart admitted later that he failed to 'attune the Prime Minister to aliens.'[5]

In March, 1938, a few days after Hitler's march into Austria, the 'Mein Kampf despatch' was retrieved from its pigeon-hole by Sir Maurice Hankey, Secretary to the Cabinet, who sent it to Sir Horace Wilson, Chamberlain's *éminence grise*, with a handwritten note:

> I think you would find it worth your while, as I did, to glance through the attached prophetic despatch by Rumbold of five years ago. It shows in the light of after events, how closely Hitler had adhered to *Mein Kampf* and perhaps provides some guide to the future.[6]

When Sir Horace Rumbold reached retiring age in 1933 Vansittart, Head of the Foreign Office, regretted that the ambassador had not been born five years later – 'given time, he might have frightened the Cabinet.' It seems unlikely! The retiring diplomat received the customary smooth letter of appreciation from the Foreign Secretary. His despatches 'would be of great and permanent value to His Majesty's Government in determining their policy towards Germany. . . .'[7] The author of this letter, Sir John Simon, was later to become – with Lord Halifax and Sir Samuel Hoare – a member of Chamberlain's 'inner Cabinet' which so wholeheartedly pursued appeasement to its disastrous conclusion. Rumbold's despatches certainly were to play no part in determining their policy towards Germany.

Rumbold's successor, Sir Eric Phipps, made a cautious start but after a few months' residence in Berlin was walking firmly in Sir Horace's footsteps. The Ambassador's advice was uncompromising: unless Hitler was checked, the inevitable consequence of his aggressive policies would be war. If Hitler perceived no real opposition abroad, the tempo of his preparations would increase. A vigorous and united policy on the part of other Powers would impress the Chancellor: Germany was still sufficiently conscious of her weakness to be halted in her tracks by demonstrations of concerted opposition abroad. Hitler was putting everything into rearmament; the economy could not stand the strain of the military preparations. Already the sacrifices being imposed upon the nation in pursuit of this rearmament, together with the pervading presence of the secret police, were exposing symptoms of disaffection of which the Nazi Party itself was well aware. The image abroad of a nation both strong and united, insisted the Ambassador, was spurious.[8]

Rumbold and Phipps between them built up for the Foreign Office an identikit picture of Nazi Germany on which the government could base its foreign policy. It is difficult to see the necessity (however apt) for shooting parties in great houses. Alas, in the crisis years, the Berlin Embassy was to fall into the hands of an ambassador of very different calibre of whom the Head of the Foreign Office was to write: 'Sir Nevile Henderson is a national danger in Berlin.'

Those members of the anti-Nazi Opposition inside Germany who survived the war have left on record in their memoirs the sense of urgency, of desperation, of time running out, during these years. In the British Foreign Office the atmosphere was altogether more relaxed.

In February, 1938, the personal crisis between Eden and Chamberlain over Italian policy came to a head and Eden resigned. The new Foreign Secretary, Viscount Halifax, was hardly the man for the moment. His biographer, Lord Birkenhead, described him as a man not interested in Europe, who accepted the post of Foreign Secretary without enthusiasm because Chamberlain had asked him to and he thought it was his duty. But he had his reservations, as his Private Secretary, Oliver Harvey, noted in his diary:

> He said he was very lazy and disliked work. Could he hunt on Saturdays? I said there was a lot of work but much of it could be done at home or in the train and we agreed that he needn't see as much as A. E. used to do.[9]

Hunting in the winter, cricket in the summer and some gentleman farming made the weekend the most important part of the week for the Foreign Secretary. A few months before the outbreak of war Cadogan, Head of the Foreign Office, wrote of his Chief:

> Even in times of crisis Halifax goes off to Yorkshire on a Friday afternoon. When he's in London he's at a loose end and doesn't know what to do with himself so ruins everybody else's day.[10]

'It is difficult,' he complained, 'to conduct affairs with Halifax in Yorkshire and the PM in Scotland.'

The one diplomat who shared the pressing anxiety of the Opposition inside Germany was Sir Robert Vansittart. Appointed to be

Permanent Head of the Foreign Office in 1930, Sir Robert was to serve under three Prime Ministers and five Foreign Secretaries. He assumed his important post with no illusions: like Rumbold he had taken the measure of Nazi Germany from its very beginnings, and he knew what ought to be done. He subscribed to the dictum of a former Foreign Secretary, Sir Edward Grey, who – also faced with the threat of German military strength in 1912 – advised the Government not to rely on foreign policy to protect the United Kingdom. If the country's strength was allowed to fall below that which might be suddenly brought to bear against it, 'you are setting foreign policy a task which you ought not to set it.'

Although an ardent Francophile and no lover of Germany, nevertheless Vansittart recognised that there was a genuine opposition to the régime in high and influential places inside Germany of which advantage could and should be taken. That opposition, in turn, fixed their hopes on Vansittart. They knew they had sympathisers in Britain but it was Vansittart who had – if not actual power – very powerful influence. The Nazis themselves were aware of his rôle as a key figure in British foreign policy-making, and of his antagonism. In March, 1935, Vansittart received a private message from Sir Eric Phipps, Ambassador in Berlin (and also his brother-in-law), that Hitler would like to meet him personally because he was convinced that the Permanent Secretary was his enemy. Vansittart's reply to Phipps began with an uncharacteristic protestation of friendship towards Germany. He knew, he told Sir Eric, that in Germany lack of success in relations with Britain was attributed to himself, and that he was accused of being anti-German. This was not so. He had always regretted the imprudence of the 'rough usage' of Germany at Versailles. But the material and moral military preparations taking place in Hitler's Germany were facts. Unless these facts were changed, words were not going to change his own attitude. He concluded: 'These are not only my own feelings; they are the frame of mind and attitude which I expect from those who work with me in the Foreign Office.'[11] Vansittart's expectations of his colleagues were not to be fulfilled either by those above him or those below.

Vansittart once wrote in despair: 'It seems as if nobody will listen to me or believe me. I will never know why.'[12] Certainly a contributing factor was what the official historian, E. L. Woodward, described as the 'Edwardian over-elaboration' of his style, which certainly made considerable demands upon the reader. Yet when he took up his appointment as Head of the Foreign Office, Vansittart circulated to the staff an appeal for an improvement in what he described as the forbidding nature of official prose. 'It is a minor ambition of mine,' he told them, 'that we should be as readable as possible.' Better writing might give a better chance of a hearing and this was particularly important in papers destined for the Cabinet. 'Our sentences often feel like a fortnight without the option of a fine.'[13] Alas, Vansittart could not more precisely have described the effect of his own style on his colleagues, on his Chief and on Cabinet Ministers. Sir Warren Fisher, Head of the Civil Service, actually inveigled Lady Vansittart to tea in his office in the hope of enlisting her help in persuading her husband to curtail his memoranda. 'I want you to tell Van not to write these long papers for the Cabinet. They don't like it. . . .'[14] That the medium and the message were equally unwelcome is shown by an entry in Cadogan's diary in which he comments on the Head's absence from the office on one occasion:

> Afraid he is writing a paper. I only hope it won't be another in his usual German-scare style, simply urging rearmament and disclosing the complete bankruptcy of our foreign policy. And I hope it won't be in his usual style, which brings discredit on the Office.[15]

Although it is true that Vansittart's memoranda called for attentive reading (his handwritten minutes were usually short and pithy) one is tempted to enquire what else his colleagues had to do that was more important than weighing the advice of the Permanent Under-Secretary. The conclusion which suggests itself is that the reader's block was caused as much by resistance to the message which the paper was bound to contain, as by the convoluted style in which it was enclosed.

As Minister with responsibility for League of Nations affairs, Eden had come within range of Vansittart's forceful personality and had no intention of sharing power when his turn came as Foreign Secretary. And he could count on powerful allies. Vansittart's persistence in his unpopular policy on Germany had reached the point of over-kill. Far from making any impact, he had alienated his political masters to such a degree that he was to be removed beyond the spheres of policy-making. Persistent warnings about the German menace were unwelcome, and Ministers were well aware of Vansittart's opinions on this score. When Eden endeavoured to address this subject in Cabinet, he was acutely conscious of the exchange of amused glances among his colleagues – 'His Master's Voice', they seemed to be saying.[16] A vain man, Eden avoided these embarrassing encounters by withholding material on Germany which came to him from Vansittart, even though it was based on intelligence of the highest quality.

But relief for Eden arrived at last. In December, 1937, Chamberlain pounced. He wrote gleefully to his sister:

> After all the months that S. B. [Stanley Baldwin] wasted in futile attempts to push Van out of the FO it is amusing to record that I have done it in 3 days. . . . I hope to announce it after the House has safely dispersed. . . . Van will be removed from active direction of FO policy and I suspect that in Rome and Berlin rejoicings will be loud and deep.[17]

A sinecure was created – a siding into which Vansittart could be shunted. He was given the title of Chief Diplomatic Adviser to the Government, although the last thing Chamberlain wanted from anyone was advice. The adage that no man is a prophet in his own country was amply demonstrated in Vansittart's case by the reaction inside the German Embassy towards his change of rôle. There at least his considerable gifts were recognised. To the German diplomats (among whom admittedly there was a strong anti-Nazi element) the whole affair was a mystery. It is doubtful whether Counsellor Theo Kordt, who had such close and secret contacts with Vansittart, realised to what extent his 'promotion' meant exile from policy-making. Counsellor von Selzam (also in the anti-Nazi Opposition) reported to the Foreign Ministry in Berlin:

> Vansittart is one of the most outstanding members of the British Foreign Service, a man of quite extraordinary ability and experience, praised for a magnificent memory for facts. It is scarcely imaginable that Chamberlain would wish to forgo the co-operation of such a man, even if the two had different views regarding various questions of foreign policy.

The Embassy promised to report again when more information was available, but they couldn't quite get to the bottom of it. The Chargé d'Affaires, Woermann, reported: 'So far no reliable knowledge of the exact origin of the changes has leaked out. One thing is certain, and that is that the changes in the Foreign Office have a Cadogan angle and a Vansittart angle. . . .'[18]

What the German Opposition could not know was to what extent the 'Cadogan angle' meant that they had lost a receptive ear in the most important position in the Foreign Office. Not only was Cadogan unsympathetic to the point of antagonism to the concept of Germans against Hitler; the fact that those Germans continued to use Vansittart as their point of contact ensured that, in the Foreign Office, their cause was doomed.

The change of attitude at the top of the Foreign Office can be seen in a private letter to Henderson in Berlin, which Cadogan wrote a few months after his promotion, at the time of Hitler's march into Austria. Compared with the customary uncompromising attitude of Vansittart, it has the overtones of a lovers' tiff: 'If, with a professed desire to help them, we begged the Germans to tell us what, in their view, was wrong and how they would wish to see it put right, and if they refused, I still don't see that we should have done much harm.'[19] Cadogan's diary gives a glimpse of the Foreign Office under its new management, when Vansittart had become Yesterday's Man:

> He sends in minutes to the Secretary of State snarling at some of Nevile Henderson's telegrams, which Halifax hands gloomily to me. I keep them for two or three days and then hand them back to Halifax and say: 'I'm very stupid: I can't remember what you told me to do about this'. He looks unutterably sad and says, 'I think we might burn it now'.[20]

In his unfinished autobiography, *Mist Procession*, Vansittart wrote: 'Mine is a story of failure. . . . I have achieved little but seen much. I can recall no major issue on which my advice was taken.' After events had justified his premonitions he had hoped, he wrote, to be occasionally consulted but it was not to be.

It is sad that Vansittart should be best remembered not for his tireless efforts to protect the nation from the inevitable result of weakness and compromise in its foreign policy, but for what was to become known as 'Vansittartism'. In retirement, during the war, he turned his literary talents to what can only be called racist attacks on the whole German people and its history in language worthy of Goebbels himself. In the book *Black Record* he pandered to the basest of public opinion in a manner unworthy of a former Head of the

Foreign Office. Cadogan's comments on Vansittart's book are an indication of how little chance the anti-Nazi Opposition had with the British Foreign Office. He minuted: 'I confess to a suspicion that *Black Record* may be correct. . . . I have never thought it wrong but always thought it silly.'[21] Churchill was repelled by the bloodthirsty prose and did not share the sentiments. 'I definitely disagree with your line on this,' wrote the Prime Minister when Vansittart criticised him for making a 'fallacious' distinction between 'Nazi' and 'German'. 'I contemplate a reunited European family in which Germany will have a great place. We must not let our vision be darkened by hatred. . . .'[22] But Vansittart's vision did become darkened, to such an extent that, as will be seen, he abandoned and calumniated his former German diplomat colleagues with whom he had shared the secrets of opposition. The grossness of the attacks on the German people – 'The Nation of Beasts: bestial, bloodthirsty, foully different from all other breeds – the German' – was grist to the mill of the delighted Goebbels. The Propaganda Minister found it excellent material for stiffening the people's will to resist.

It was a tragic irony that the man who had fought Nazism so tenaciously and so single-handedly from the very beginning should in the end be incorporated into the Nazi war effort. Goebbels conferred upon him the supreme accolade:

> This Vansittart is actually worth his weight in gold for our propaganda. We should erect a monument for him somewhere in Germany after the war with the inscription: 'The Englishman who did most for the German cause during the war.'[23]

By the spring of 1937 both 10 Downing Street and the Berlin Embassy were under new management. Berlin at that time was, without doubt, in Vansittart's words 'the most important post of all.' Nevertheless it was allowed to become a victim of a game of diplomatic musical chairs.

Early in 1937 the post in Paris became vacant. Sir Eric Phipps, who after nearly four years in Germany had an expert knowledge of the Nazi régime, was allowed to have it. Now, at this critical time, a new man would have to start at the beginning in Berlin. There appears to have been no question of selecting the man for the job, but rather of who was due for a change. (As Churchill once said about the appointment of ambassadors: 'The doctrine of Buggins' turn is very powerful.') Vansittart's choice fell upon Nevile Henderson, then Ambassador to Argentina. The most critical diplomatic post in Europe – or indeed the world at that time – was bestowed upon a diplomat on the grounds that he was a good shot; and that 'he has done his stint in South America: he shall have his reward.' The new Ambassador was to prove, in Vansittart's own words, a national disaster. In the years that followed, it must have added greatly to Vansittart's anguish at Henderson's inept performance in Berlin that he himself was responsible for putting him there.

Henderson's first public act in Germany caused scandal at home. A dinner was given in honour of the new Ambassador by the Anglo-German Fellowship in Berlin. In his speech, Sir Nevile deplored the fact that in England far too many people 'have an entirely erroneous conception of what the National Socialist régime really stands for. Otherwise they would lay less stress on Nazi dictatorship and much more emphasis on the great social experiment which was being tried in Germany. . . .'[24]

Even Cadogan eventually had to admit that 'Nevile Henderson is completely bewitched by his German friends'. In the light of his report on the Nuremberg Party Day in September, 1937 this seems a fair description. The impressionable diplomat was quite swept off his feet. Alas for Sir Nevile: Nuremberg was never going to be quite such fun again. The lyrical description which Henderson sent to the Foreign Office shows how the British Ambassador had fallen under the spell:

On Hitler's arrival at the far end, and as he entered the stadium, the 300 huge searchlights surrounding it were turned up into the air, each throwing a broad blue beam some 20,000 feet or more into the sky, where the lights converged to make a square roof which a chance cloud made even more realistic. The effect, both solemn and beautiful, was something like being inside a cathedral of ice. . . .

At the word of command 32,000 standard-bearers then advanced from out of sight at the southern end up the main lane and over the further tiers and down the four side lanes. The standards were illuminated by lights on the shafts of a certain proportion of them, and the spectacle of these five rivers of red and gold, one broad and four smaller, rippling slowly forward under the dome of blue lights through the massed formations of brown shirts, and absolutely silently, till, about a hundred yards from where we were sitting, suddenly the tramp of feet was heard, was indescribably beautiful.[25]

The final social function which Henderson attended at Nuremberg was a supper party given by Himmler himself at the SS camp on the outskirts of the town. The Ambassador's report read like a contribution to *The Tatler*:

> Each of the guests received a bowl of SS china filled with sweets, the china being made in a special SS pottery run, so I understand, on voluntary lines. . . . Among the guests of honour were the two Mitford girls whom, as vamps of Hitler, I would have been glad to meet, but I failed to make their acquaintance. . . .[26]

The Head of the German Foreign Office, Ernst von Weizsäcker, remained well-disposed towards the British Ambassador personally, although deploring his professional performance. Weizsäcker was described by one of his colleagues after the war as having been 'very upset' and to have repeatedly referred to Sir Nevile Henderson's tactically and psychologically wrong attitude towards Ribbentrop, the Foreign Minister.

There was some ineffectual discussion at the Foreign Office about Henderson's future after the rape of Czechoslovakia, which he so signally failed to predict (though Vansittart had). The Ambassador was recalled to London for an indefinite period. But in spite of Vansittart's insistence that 'the Nazis are convinced that they can make our Ambassador in Berlin believe anything that they wish him to believe', by 23 April 1939 Sir Nevile was back at his post. 'Last year,' wrote Vansittart, 'the embassy had only a faint conception of what was really going on in Germany and I don't suppose that 1939 will be very different in that respect.'[27] But the last thing anyone wanted from the Chief Diplomatic Adviser was advice. 'Whosoever left Henderson at Berlin,' wrote the historian A. J. P. Taylor, 'would have made war inevitable, if it had not been inevitable already.'[28]

Between the Austrian *Anschluss* and the Munich Conference – Europe's last chance – Britain's representative in Nazi Germany had nothing more to offer than a petulant despair:

> The Germans are impossible. All foreigners are impossible: it is a matter of degree. But the Germans are worse than most, in their present uplift. What an unsatisfactory and disheartening job this is. I am very tired of it all.[29]

There could scarcely have been a greater contrast than that between the relaxed and clubbable atmosphere of Whitehall and the dangerous and oppressive conditions in which their opposite numbers in the Wilhelmstrasse strove to maintain some semblance of diplomacy. According to a British observer with friends in the German Foreign Ministry, it was no exaggeration to say that an atmosphere of terror weighed upon its officials.

Hitler detested the Foreign Ministry. He considered it legalistic, conservative, defeatist and cosmopolitan. Its members should only be given those tasks, he declared, which it had already been decided not to carry out. He saw it as an obstruction to his expansionist plans. He therefore set up a rival establishment – on the other side of the Wilhelmstrasse – with Ribbentrop, whom he had chosen as his adviser on Foreign Affairs, as its head. For Ribbentrop, foreign affairs consisted simply in the furtherance of Hitler's ambitions. A former colleague testified at Nuremberg that he knew extraordinarily little of the tenets of National Socialism; he was bound personally to Hitler himself, on whom he had a hypnotic dependence (as did Hess). Theo Kordt, a member of the Foreign Office, described him as being capable of crime but incapable of insubordination. Weizsäcker said: 'Hitler had goals, even if they were mad, whereas Ribbentrop had only one single aim, to please Hitler'. Ambassador Rumbold reported to London in June 1933 on the establishment of this 'duplicate' Foreign Office of Ribbentrop. It was known, wrote the Ambassador, that Foreign Minister Neurath and his colleagues in the Wilhelmstrasse resented the state of affairs, and many wondered why Neurath did not resign: 'I venture to think that he is playing a patriotic part in remaining in the Government lest worse befall. . . .'[30]

The Foreign Office was not only isolated in its own sphere. On Hitler's personal order, other departments of government were forbidden to maintain any contact with the Wilhelmstrasse. State Secretary von Weizsäcker and the Chief of Staff of the Army, General Halder, both intimately concerned with matters of war and peace, were forced to meet out-of-doors and under cover of darkness: not because they were anti-Nazi conspirators (which in fact they were) but because Hitler had expressly forbidden any relationship between the Foreign Office and the Army. To flout the orders of any Nazi leader was a dangerous undertaking. It is almost impossible to comprehend – with the normal life of Whitehall in mind – that under the Nazi régime members of the administration could quite simply be shot out of hand. But there is no shortage of evidence. Ribbentrop made clear to members of the Foreign Office the dire consequences of opposing his orders. More than one former member testified after the war that Ribbentrop declared that if he found anyone interfering with his orders he would personally shoot him in his office. Though such summary execution might not have taken place on the premises, there is no doubt that it was within Ribbentrop's power to have a threat carried out elsewhere. Hewel, Ribbentrop's own liaison man with Hitler, once related how he 'almost met his doom' by an adverse comment to Goebbels about Hitler's views. Goebbels had flown into a rage and Hewel had to beg him not to give him away to the Führer, who 'would merely have pressed a button and called Rattenhuber, the Chief of his Security Service, and had me taken away and shot.'[31] In 1936 Schacht, Minister of Economics, sent a message to Eden, then Foreign Secretary, warning against the impossibility of economic or political agreement with Germany until 'civilisation' had been restored. All sense of personal security, he said, had disappeared. 'At any moment the door may be opened and members of the Nazi secret police may walk in and shoot me down.'[32] All this may smack of melodrama but Hitler had already established, in the 'Night of the Long Knives', the principle of murder with impunity as a method of political control.

Anyone in a position of influence inside the structure of government knew that success in thwarting Nazi policy could only be attempted by tortuous methods of careful circumlocution. It was necessary firstly to endorse the policy in principle (and in the language of the Party), and then to enter a *caveat* that perhaps the policy might not properly serve the cause. 'One writes for fools and in competition with fools,' the State Secretary told his son. As Weizsäcker explained: it was no use to say that war would be immoral; one had to say: 'We are going to lose that war.' How the system worked in the Foreign Office was described by a member of the Political Division in the witness box at Nuremberg. Weizsäcker, he said, would formulate directives to overseas posts according to the instructions of the Minister, Ribbentrop, and in the approved language. The State Secretary's colleagues, however, knowing his mind, would interpret these instructions, where possible, according to what they knew his real wishes to be. (Even the Weizsäcker family correspondence was sometimes conducted in code. Hitler was 'Pfeiffer' and the Party was 'the Pfeiffer family'. A dash after a sentence indicated that it actually meant the opposite.)[33] Alas, this silent battle against the régime was to have unfortunate repercussions for former diplomats in the face of the uncompromising attitudes of the post-war period. Early in 1947 Weizsäcker was visited by two members of the Anglo-American Commission which was working on the publication of captured German Foreign Office documents. These were to be presented chronologically and without commentary. The former State Secretary found this a very questionable undertaking. Facts might be revealed but not motives. Ribbentrop had expressly forbidden advice or argument in diplomatic papers. Even private notes often showed the fear of the Gestapo; some, on the other hand, were deliberately composed to mislead the Gestapo. Irony was often difficult for the outsider to distinguish. There was a danger therefore, thought Weizsäcker, that the envisaged publication might obscure historical truth rather than reveal it.[34] However, British Foreign Office files show that historical truth was not entirely in the forefront of the enterprise. The matter became more pressing for Weizsäcker when he found himself standing trial by the Americans. He warned the Court that they should be very careful how they used documents from the Third Reich because nobody at that time ever achieved their aims except in the language current at the time and with arguments suited to the man to whom they were addressed: 'That is why the story of what Germans did for peace at that time will always be full of gaps insofar as documents go'.[35] Even the British editor of the collection of captured German diplomatic documents was obliged to acknowledge the existence of this special 'Party' language. He explained in the Foreword:

> Translation presented peculiar difficulties particularly since, under Hitler, there was no one style of diplomatic German as there had been under Bismarck. Some of the writers use the 'Nazi German' which conveys only a foggy impression.[36]

Externally, also, the customary language of diplomacy no longer fulfilled its purpose in dealing with Germany. A British Foreign Office informant related a confidence made to him at a party by 'a prominent German official':

Germany no longer has an 'aerial' for diplomatic language. We do not understand words like: 'Your action will cause certain repercussions and may prompt us to take certain measures which in turn will produce certain results'. We can only understand if somebody says: 'If you don't stop doing this I will hit you on the head'. Then we will listen.[37]

But no threats could be effective unless there was the power – and the will-power – to back them up. If that was lacking, the currency of diplomatic exchange merely became devalued, as Dr Schmidt, Hitler's interpreter (and a covert anti-Nazi), privately pointed out to a British friend early in 1939. In the past, said Schmidt, 'when His Majesty's Government "took a serious view" of some matter, such a phrase was translated into German as meaning that action would follow, but in recent months even small nations had been able to ignore British protests. . . .'[38]

When receiving foreign ambassadors, State Secretary von Weizsäcker was inhibited about what he said, just as much as by what he wrote. Code-breaking by German intelligence had reached such a degree of efficiency that the Foreign Office in Berlin could read at least half the telegrams passing between foreign diplomats and their governments. It was impossible for Weizsäcker to have any confidential conversation with representatives of governments whose cyphers he knew to have been broken by his own government. In some cases he went so far as to ask that his name should not be mentioned in any of their despatches. Weizsäcker told his son that M. Coulondre, the French Ambassador, 'did not seem to understand my game and I could not tell him anything because we have the French code, and whatever I told M.C. will be on Ribbentrop's desk tomorrow morning'.[39] The British Embassy code, however, had not been broken by German intelligence, which was in one way unfortunate. Had it been, Weizsäcker would have been aware of the misinformation which Henderson, with his propensity for appeasement, was sending home. The diplomats of the Opposition were all too aware that their British colleague had no real appreciation of what was happening in Germany. Henderson was too obtuse to pick up the hints which were Weizsäcker's only way of transmitting critical information. This is clearly illustrated by the account in their respective memoirs of Hitler's march into Prague in March, 1939. The State Secretary had been forbidden to give any advance information to any foreign diplomats. However, he was able 'to give a hint at the last minute to the British Ambassador' though the conversation was 'difficult'. Nevertheless he thought the Ambassador had understood. But Henderson's own record shows that he quite failed to grasp the State Secretary's urgent hint that the German Army was going to march and sent a negative report to the Foreign Office. In his memoirs Weizsäcker wrote that 'I was afraid that the march to Prague might cost Henderson his post because of his failure to foresee it. I felt I was not to blame for this. . . .'[40]

An instance of the acute disability under which the German State Secretary laboured occurred during the visit to Europe of President Roosevelt's representative, Sumner Welles, in February, 1940. Orders had been given that the subject of peace should not be raised with the American diplomat. When he received him, Weizsäcker informed Welles of the embargo and then proceeded to break it, but not without first drawing his visitor into the middle of the room. Although he had long ago had his room checked for hidden microphones by his friend Admiral Canaris' counter-intelligence experts, he was taking no chances. How little the implications of this incident were borne in upon Sumner Welles is shown by the fact that he had no hesitation in relating it in his book, *A Time for Decision*, published during the war. This betrayal of Weizsäcker's confidence could have cost him his life. The State Secretary himself read the account with some consternation; however, through some fortunate chance the book escaped Ribbentrop's notice.

Weizsäcker would occasionally 'jam' conversations in his room by turning on the radio. He took it for granted that all his telephone calls were monitored and adapted his language accordingly.

But Ribbentrop had problems too. In spite of his close relationship with the Führer, he had no automatic right of access and had to employ his liaison officer, Hewel, to maintain contact with Hitler's Chancellery. All Ribbentrop could do was to make sure that he was at the right place at the right time. Weizsäcker described how his Chief used to follow Hitler and his entourage from place to place. He would then settle down somewhere about half an hour or so away, since Hitler did not always want to have him around. There he would stay, on his toes and ready to appear on the scene at any moment, while Weizsäcker was left alone in Berlin to cope with foreign ambassadors, and having to guess what was being planned in the field of foreign policy.[41]

In this Byzantine world of the Wilhelmstrasse, with the Gestapo behind every arras, there were two foreign diplomats with whom Weizsäcker shared complete confidence and to whom he could speak freely: an Italian, Ambassador Bernardo Attolico, and a Swiss, Carl J. Burckhardt. All three were united in their dedicated pursuit of peace, and on the means to attain it. Both the State Secretary and the Ambassador suffered equally in living and working under a dictatorship. They saw their respective leaders as a disastrous partnership, urging each other on to aggressive adventures, and they did not wish to see a close relationship between the two countries. It was due to Attolico's personal influence that in 1939 Italy at times acted more as a brake than a spur to Hitler. Attolico died in 1942 but his voice could still be heard in Weizsäcker's defence through the memoranda which Burckhardt made of their conversations. Carl Burckhardt was a distinguished Swiss historian and former diplomat who was a friend of Weizsäcker of many years' standing. In 1937 he was appointed League of Nations High Commissioner for Danzig. Burckhardt's prestige was such that he was even vouchsafed an occasional audience with Hitler. He was also *persona grata* in Paris and London (Duff Cooper described him as 'one of the most interesting and charming men you could meet') and was an unimpeachable source of information about Germany. On a memorable occasion, as will be seen, he acted dramatically on Weizsäcker's behalf with the British. Confidences between the State Secretary and the High Commissioner were shared on the occasions when his diplomatic duties brought the latter to Berlin. These meetings took place either at Weizsäcker's house or strolling safely out of earshot in the *Tiergarten*. There were no secrets between them about the extent and the efforts of the Opposition inside the Foreign Office. For private correspondence the two friends used a sort of code, a form of Nazi-speak intelligible only to each other.[42]

One of the harshest voices which was persistently raised in the British Foreign Office against the Opposition was that of G. H. Harrison, First Secretary at the Berlin Embassy before the war. Nevertheless he admitted that the German Foreign Ministry had always been to a considerable extent anti-Ribbentrop and anti-Nazi: he had seen many instances of this during the various crises leading up to the war, 'but they are of course powerless to do anything.'[43] Though powerless in the formal sense – Weizsäcker did not, unlike his opposite numbers Vansittart and Cadogan, play any part in the formulation of foreign policy – much was done surreptitiously to protect individuals or groups from the barbarity of the State. More importantly for the rest of the world, the Opposition was able to convey, from the heart of the German establishment to the heart of the British, information of the most critical kind which could be used as a weapon against Hitler's aggressive policies.

The two prime movers in the effort – through early intelligence – to engage foreign diplomacy in the fight against Hitler were the brothers Theo and Erich Kordt, members of the foreign service who were personally and professionally close to Weizsäcker. Born into a Catholic family in the Rhineland, sons of an architect, both entered the foreign service in the early 1920s. Their upbringing and their experience abroad, both as students and later as diplomats, set them early on the path of opposition to National-Socialism.

During the years when Hitler was still in the wings consolidating his power, the elder brother, Theo, was Private Secretary to the Head of the Foreign Ministry, Baron von Bülow. After President von Hindenburg had dismissed Chancellor Brüning and put von Papen in his place, the way was open for Hitler. In 1934, a year after Hitler's seizure of power, Kordt was alerted to the possibility of positive active opposition to the new régime. Admiral Canaris, the enigmatic head of the Abwehr (the Intelligence Department of the War Ministry), visited him in Athens where he was now First Secretary. The Foreign Office and the military, claimed Canaris, were moving closer together, towards a radical opposition which alone could prevent catastrophe. He asked for Kordt's help.[44]

Within a year or so Canaris evidently considered the time had come to approach the younger brother. Just before the occupation of the Rhineland, Erich Kordt was approached at a friend's house by Canaris. Kordt knew of the intended move into the Rhineland, which was still a secret confined to a few Nazi leaders. Without actually mentioning the plan, Canaris referred obliquely to its possible consequences. Kordt responded. The connection was made. Thenceforth, recorded Kordt in a memoir after the war, Canaris continued the style of conversation which he had used at their first meeting:

Sometimes he would suddenly appear beside me in a large gathering. He would give me his hand as if by chance, while already looking in another direction, and speak softly, and with oblique references, to me.

This style seems to have rubbed off on Kordt himself. A friend once said that Erich reminded him of the Admiral in his way of speaking.[45] He was certainly modelling himself on an expert.

Erich Kordt had by now become, in his own words, the most important source of information for the Wilhelmstrasse on Hitler's future plans. What was of unique value to the Opposition was his special relationship with Ribbentrop.

In 1934, against professional advice, Hitler appointed Ribbentrop Special Commissioner for disarmament questions. Erich Kordt was assigned to him by State Secretary von Bülow as official aide and unofficial watchdog. His instructions were to relay privately to the Office all information concerning the new Commissioner's activities. This task would be eased by the fact that his brother Theo was working in von Bülow's office. It was the hope of the Foreign Office that Ribbentrop would be given enough rope to hang himself. Erich Kordt was ordered by his Chief (somewhat to his consternation): 'At no time conceal or correct the incompetence and errors of the new Commissioner.' Kordt accompanied Ribbentrop on visits to London, Paris and Rome where his inadequacies as a serious diplomat were widely perceived. He managed to provoke contempt and ridicule, recorded Kordt, 'even in Italy.' The professional diplomat was appalled by the quality, both of style and content, of the reports Ribbentrop sent to Hitler but these did not result, as Kordt hoped and expected, in any loss of standing with the Führer. Back in Berlin, Ribbentrop would hover in the anterooms of the Chancellery, picking up clues to Hitler's current ideas and then presenting them as his own at conferences in which seven or eight participants, with Hitler in the middle, walked up and down the great room of the Chancellery. Inevitably there were clashes between Ribbentrop and his aide, and Kordt endeavoured to extricate himself from the attachment. However, when Ribbentrop was appointed to the London Embassy in 1936, Kordt was assigned as First Secretary. From this advantageous position he was able to influence the staffing of the Embassy and to install colleagues of his own persuasion, known to him for their opposition to Nazi policy.[46] As the Gestapo also had its men planted in the Embassy, the work of diplomacy must have been attended by the most peculiar difficulties. But his most important achievement was the succession of Weizsäcker, at that time Political Director, to the key position of Head of the Foreign Office. He became the inspiration and protector of the young diplomats of the Opposition already grouped round Erich Kordt. Ribbentrop did not relinquish control of his Berlin Bureau on his posting to London but divided his time between the two capitals, to the chagrin of the British Foreign Office who did not consider this was the correct way for an ambassador to fulfil his function.

In spite of Ribbentrop's disastrous record as ambassador he still retained Hitler's confidence. In February, 1938, in the upheaval following the Fritsch crisis, Neurath was re-assigned to head a phantom Advisory Council and Ribbentrop was appointed to succeed him as Minister for Foreign Affairs. He was now able to extend his baleful influence beyond the Ribbentrop Bureau to the whole of the Foreign Ministry. One of Vansittart's prime informants, Philip Conwell-Evans, who had many old friends in the German Foreign Office (including Erich Kordt), reported on return from a visit to Berlin:

> I was also able to see that Ribbentrop is proceeding to revolutionise the German Foreign Office, which has hitherto been a very efficient institution, well-manned by able and upright officials. One experienced person after another – all persons known to me – is 'falling out of favour' as the phrase goes, and young men from Himmler's guards are being brought in.[47]

These young thugs monitored all correspondence and eavesdropped on the work of the Office – though it is difficult to see what they could have made of it all. Their constant presence made the normal conduct of affairs extremely difficult, particularly for the members of the Opposition who were attempting to 'sabotage' the dangerous foreign policy. The professional diplomats of the 'old school', however, were able to take steps to outwit and outflank Ribbentrop. Erich Kordt had been brought back from the London Embassy to be Head of Ribbentrop's Secretariat, a position which gave him unique access to the machinations of the Führer and his Foreign Minister. Kordt was able to engineer another supremely valuable appointment for the Opposition. There was in the Foreign Office a brilliant interpreter, Dr Paul Otto Schmidt. During the visit of Anthony Eden and Sir John Simon to Germany in 1935, Kordt assigned him to the Führer as personal interpreter. Hitler had not been well-served in this sphere, often having to rely on the inadequate Ribbentrop. The Führer was so impressed by Schmidt's expertise that thenceforward he insisted that he should be present at every meeting with foreign visitors. It was with some difficulty that Schmidt successfully resisted being transferred to Hitler's entourage, which would have cut him off from his Opposition colleagues in the Foreign Office. Schmidt was able safely to transmit invaluable information to Kordt without dangerous subterfuge by the simple device of openly dictating his notes in Kordt's presence in the office.[48]

With the Opposition network established in Berlin, attention was turned to the London Embassy, now left vacant by the elevation of Ribbentrop. It was a key factor in Opposition planning. The inside information being collected in the Wilhelmstrasse must be passed down the line to Whitehall so that the British Government should be kept accurately informed of evil plans being concocted in the Chancellery. Leaders of the Opposition inside and outside the Foreign Office realised that a successful revolt against Hitler would have to be timed to coincide with a major crisis in foreign affairs when Nazi aggression posed an imminent threat of war. A firm stand by the British at the right moment would either cause Hitler to fall back under a crushing diplomatic defeat from which he could not recover, or expose him to the nation as being ready to plunge it into war. It was essential that up-to-the-minute information should be available in London. The new Ambassador must at least be someone who would not get in the way. The Ambassador in Tokyo, Dr Herbert von Dirksen, had found the Japanese climate unsuitable for health reasons and was returning home. He was a career diplomat and not an ardent Nazi and his passive attitude would allow an active Counsellor to pursue his own plans without interference. His appointment to London was arranged.

But the most important move – for the Opposition – was the posting from Athens of Erich Kordt's brother, Theo, to the Embassy in London. An unassailable intelligence link between Berlin and London was now in place. Had there been any lively minds in Central Department of the Foreign Office keeping events in Germany under special scrutiny, the possible implications of this game of diplomatic musical chairs might have been picked up. That one brother should leave the Embassy and take his place at Ribbentrop's elbow in Berlin, and that the other should replace him in London, might have suggested some form of collusion. And that these appointments could only have been made with the authority and approval of the State Secretary would have strengthened speculation. In Whitehall there was a passing show of interest in the new diplomatic appointment in February, 1938 though hardly commensurate with the unsettled climate of the times. The British Legation in Athens put the Foreign Office in the picture about their German colleague:

> Dr Theo Kordt, the Counsellor of the German Legation here, who has been appointed Counsellor in London, is a colourless person, although he gives the impression of being capable. In appearance he is rather the English caricaturist's idea of the middle-aged, middle-class German unrelieved by any of the modern German's athletic tendencies. The epithets the casual observer would apply to his wife are perhaps 'portly' and 'dowdy'. There may be recondite reasons for the choice but on the surface it seems an unsuitable one.

A Foreign Office wag minuted:

> Chosen, perhaps, because he cannot be caught bending!

A later minute recorded the Counsellor's arrival in the rather arch style much favoured in internal Foreign Office communications:

> I regret to have to confess that Herr Kordt's appearance at his *visite de cérémonie* today did not belie the description of him. If his wife also accords with Athens' estimate of her, she is possibly less to be pitied than if she were beautiful or dashing.[49]

These minutes are interesting because their derisive tone and schoolboy humour reflect an attitude in the Foreign Office towards the Germans – a mixture of dislike and contempt – which surfaces frequently in the files. It was a state of mind which undoubtedly militated against any serious consideration of the existence of a strong anti-Nazi element in influential places whose ardent desire was to co-operate with British diplomatic colleagues to achieve the elimination of Hitler and his régime. Yet it was this same 'colourless', middle-class German who was later, in a dramatic encounter and at the risk of his life, to offer directly to the British government the very real possibility of preventing the catastrophe of the Second World War.

An incident related by Beverley Baxter, the journalist and Member of Parliament, discloses something of the pressure beneath the new Counsellor's composed exterior. Baxter was a fellow-guest with Theo Kordt at a private luncheon at the home of another member of the German Embassy. Exasperated by the diplomat's seeming reluctance to extend the conversation beyond mere platitudes, Baxter tried to raise the temperature by declaring that if their two countries should go to war again, 'the curse of history will be upon us.' To his astonishment, Kordt sprang to his feet, threw up his hands and cried: 'Every word of what you say is true. The curse of history and the curse of God would be upon our peoples.' Baxter could scarcely believe his eyes: it was, he wrote, a strange and unexpected moment.[50]

By March, 1938, the Foreign Office Opposition group was well in place at home and abroad. Weizsäcker had established secure appointments for the exchange of intelligence with members of the Opposition in the High Command and the Abwehr through his trusted liaison officers. The diplomats would know *where* Hitler intended to strike: the military would know *when*. The Foreign Office could not, as Weizsäcker himself said, 'shoot with files' but it provided the indispensable source of information about Hitler's policies on which future active opposition could be based. There were urgent and cogent reasons why those members of the Opposition who, as public servants, held key positions in the State should remain at their posts. The overthrow of the Nazi régime for which they were working would almost certainly result in some armed conflict between the Army and the SS. But massive civil disruption could be avoided if the major structures of the administration of the country remained firmly in place and in the hands of non-Nazis. Where the Foreign Ministry was concerned this was particularly important. If the country should be already at war when the moment came it was essential that experienced diplomats of established reputation both at home and abroad should be immediately available to handle such matters as peace treaties. From time to time Weizsäcker was tempted to ask to be relieved, but the entreaties of those working against the régime prevented him from doing so. It would probably not have been possible, anyway. Resignation under a dictatorship was a liberty which public servants were not permitted. Also, many persecuted individuals and groups owed their safety or their lives to Weizsäcker's judicious and unobtrusive manoeuvring (as they testified after the war). The withdrawal of his protection would have had tragic consequences. Weizsäcker knew there could never be any giving up. He told his colleagues: 'People like us must not abandon the ship. Our nation needs us now more than ever before, even if we are only forgotten soldiers.'

Confirmation of the importance of State Secretary Weizsäcker staying in place was received from an unexpected quarter during the war. In 1942, Burckhardt, now Vice-President of the International Red Cross in Geneva, had occasion to travel to London. He called on Churchill, whom he knew, and Germany was naturally discussed, though with some severity on Churchill's part. But quite suddenly, in the middle of the conversation, his attitude changed and with an expression of friendly interest Churchill enquired how Herr von Weizsäcker was and what he was doing. Burckhardt related this conversation to Kessel, the Red Cross liaison officer at the German consulate, on his return to Geneva. He had the distinct impression, he added, that the Prime Minister was glad to hear that Weizsäcker was still at his post. Kessel, an active member of the Opposition, immediately travelled to Berlin to relay his news to his friends. As it was felt that only Churchill could end the war with a just peace (i.e. with a non-Nazi government after the overthrow of the régime) this news was, according to Kessel, 'tremendously important to us.' It was more than ever essential that Weizsäcker should remain at the Head of the Foreign Office.[51] Nevertheless the strain was very great. Weizsäcker was a professional diplomat of the old school, an upright man from a family with a tradition of public service. His father had been Prime Minister of the old kingdom of Würtemberg. He was not bred to underground resistance movements. Evidence of this strain found its way into the records of the British Foreign Office. In January, 1939 Orme Sargent wrote to Ogilvie Forbes at the Berlin Embassy:

> We hear from secret sources that Weizsäcker had a tremendous row with Ribbentrop . . . and retired for a period on leave. . . . We should be glad to know if you can cast any light on this report. Will you please burn this letter when you have read it.[52]

Ogilvie Forbes replied that he could not confirm this but that it would not surprise him, as the position of senior Foreign Office staff from pre-Nazi days was becoming increasingly difficult. Erich Kordt described Ribbentrop as 'a high-grade psychopath whose presence can only be borne with great nervous strain and considerable expenditure of energy.' Weizsäcker may only have been half-joking when he said at his grandson's christening that he liked to visit the baby every Sunday because 'he wanted to see a reasonable human being at least once a week.' He commented to his son, Karl Friedrich, upon the untimely deaths of various diplomatic colleagues, instancing the ambassadors Hoesch and Koester and State Secretary von Bülow: 'these people are all dying of desperation. I think *angina pectoris* is the disease of the time. Hitler is consuming all these people.'[53]

Burckhardt once asked Ambassador Attolico, who also strove for peace under the yoke of a dictator, how he would define Weizsäcker's aim. He replied: 'His aim is the same as mine: prevent, prevent, prevent.' Even to plot uprisings, to conspire, needed less strength and courage than 'to wrest the impossible from hard reality day by day, defeated yet starting anew time and time again, apparently approving of what one abhors. . . .'[54] When Burckhardt saw his old friend early in the summer of 1939 he reported to the British Foreign Office that he did not think that Weizsäcker could stay the course much longer. But Weizsäcker was still at his post when war broke out. In 1943 the Casablanca declaration of the formula of Unconditional Surrender, which struck a body blow to the work and the hopes of the Opposition, coincided with an upheaval in the Wilhelmstrasse. Ribbentrop's mole inside the Foreign Office, Luther, dropped some indiscreet remarks about the sanity of his Chief and was removed to a concentration camp. In the reshuffle ordered to cover up the affair, Weizsäcker, in despair, accepted the post of Ambassador to the Vatican. At least from there he felt he might still pursue the possibilities of peace. As the train taking him to Rome was leaving, he told his son: 'I am not going as Hitler's ambassador. I am going as the representative of those in Germany who will still be there when Hitler is gone.'[55]

The primary concern of the diplomats of the 'old Foreign Office' in the Wilhelmstrasse was the prevention of war and the preservation of peace. But it was not to be peace at Hitler's price – a price the Western democracies seemed all too ready to pay. In the desperate circumstances created by the malign régime under which they lived, these diplomats were prepared to see the disappearance of the Head of State, either through disgrace or assassination. Only then could any lasting peace and international stability be achieved. They were to look to their colleagues in the British Foreign Office for co-operation in the diplomatic field, where crucial pressure could be brought to bear on the dictator. They were to look in vain.

— II —

The Other Germany

If we succeed in liberating ourselves, the world will realise what decent Germans have suffered and borne, and how many of them have died a cruel death for German honour and the freedom of the world.

Carl Goerdeler

I thank God that in this island home of ours, we have never been put to the test.

Winston S. Churchill

IN 1937, somewhere between the appointment of Sir Nevile Henderson to the Embassy in Berlin and the arrival of Neville Chamberlain at 10 Downing Street, Himmler, the Head of the SS, addressed a stern lecture to a group of generals. This was Germany after four years of Nazi rule:

> It is absolutely essential for you, as well as everyone in a responsible position, to understand the vital importance of the internal battle-ground, which in case of war will mean life or death for us. . . .
> We must have more concentration camps. At the beginning of the war, mass arrests on an unprecedented scale will be necessary. Many political prisoners will have to be shot out of hand. Utter ruthlessness is essential. Any way in which we neglect the internal battlefield will lead to catastrophe. Thirty divisions of the Death's Head units of the SS are to form the nucleus of the considerably larger force we shall need to guarantee internal security and full control of the people. . . .
> Unless we can manage, by hook or by crook, to keep that fourth one – the Home Front – in check, the three other fronts: those fighting by land, sea and in the air, will once again get the stab in the back.
> To solve this problem, and to solve it ruthlessly, is the order the Führer has given me, and he has given me unlimited powers to carry it out.[1]

At the Party Rally at Nuremberg a few months later, the new British Ambassador was to regard the SS as a sort of theatrical entertainment, an adjunct of the Party which liked dressing up. But the troops which Himmler planned to unleash upon the population at the outbreak of war were a formidable force. A report which Lord Melchett of ICI received from his confidential source in Germany stated:

It is impossible to over-emphasise that the SS are the only *long-service* troops which Germany possesses, in training and experience certainly superior to the young conscript Reichswehr and in equipment at least as good as the best in the army. They are also politically much more reliable.[2]

That Hitler should contemplate the diversion of such a valuable fighting force to the home front in the event of war proves how seriously he took the threat of another kind of 'war on two fronts' in which one enemy would not be a foreign power. When war did break out, the threat was still there. Hitler told his generals: 'I shall destroy everyone who is against me. Externally, no capitulation; internally, no revolution.'

The very existence of the Gestapo and the fact that so many of the resources of the country had to be diverted to internal security is proof enough that Hitler had not recaptured all the votes which had gone against him in 1933. The then Ambassador, Sir Horace Rumbold, monitored at the time what he described as 'the hurricane nature of the Nazi appeal to the country'. Goebbels' final effort was, Sir Horace thought, almost worthy in its way of the theatrical director Max Reinhardt:

> Saturday was to be the long-awaited day, the Day of Resurrection for National Germany. 'All along the threatened frontiers from Silesia to Memel, from one end of the Corridor to the other' bonfires were to blaze as a signal 'that the nation was at last awakened'.

In spite of all they could do, the Nazis failed to secure their overall majority. Out of a 90% poll they drummed up less than half the votes. The opposition held on. The Social Democrats, forbidden to hold meetings or publish their views in the press, retained almost all the 7 million votes won the previous November. The Communists, with everything against them, had managed to hold 5 out of the 6 million votes *they* had previously polled. The Centre Party, also obstructed electorally, showed their immunity to Nazi propaganda. Rumbold felt that 'one cannot help admiring the steadfast loyalty of the other parties to their principles at a moment when self-interest seemed to point either to abstention from the polls or to acquiescence in the "great new movement" alleged by Dr Goebbels to be "sweeping like a tempest from the Danube to the Baltic".'[3]

Although the 17 million votes cast for the Nazis far eclipsed those cast for any other single party, nevertheless 20 million other voters denied them their absolute majority. But the Enabling Act which followed swiftly on the election eliminated parliamentary government and ensured that those voices would henceforth not be heard. Intelligence gatherers abroad would have done well to note the existence of this reservoir of dissent suppressed but not eliminated. Churchill himself acknowledged, much later, that indeed it would be astonishing if, among 80 million Germans, there should be only one pattern of thought. The distinguished émigré writer, Sebastian Haffner, reckoned that the loyal population supporting the régime had but a small numerical superiority over the disloyal. The latter was to become something quite new to Germany – 'the silent, dangerous, malignant, snarling disloyalty towards the State and Authority; a deaf ear and utter indifference towards all "national" slogans, a menacing, waiting hatred. . . .'[4]

Within a year of the elections, Sir Eric Phipps, who had succeeded Sir Horace Rumbold as Ambassador, sent home a chilling description of the citizen of Hitler's Reich:

> The individual has been deprived of his liberty and any action which he may take in opposition to the designs of the Government is labelled high treason and is punishable by death. More important still, the Nazi conception presupposes the willing acquiescence of each individual in a system in which he is merely a cog in a vast machine. . . .[5]

The Ambassador later reported that nothing had so enhanced Hitler's prestige as the behaviour of the ex-Allies since he had taken power. For many Germans, the processions of foreign dignitaries who came to pay their respects to the Führer and the failure of other powers to oppose any of his moves, however audacious, seemed to indicate that perhaps it would all come right in the end. In the meantime, one just had to keep one's head down. Nevertheless, some in Germany found it difficult to be so forgiving. Fabian von Schlabrendorff, who in 1945 escaped almost from the foot of the scaffold, looked back with some bitterness on his compatriots of the Nazi years. The German people, he wrote after the war, could be divided into three groups – the Nazis, the non-Nazis and the anti-Nazis. The non-Nazis were almost worse than the Nazis: 'Their lack of backbone caused us more trouble than the wanton brutality of the Nazis.'[6] Opposition had to be uncompromising from the very begin-

ning; to yield a little here and there could only end in abject surrender. This was a heroic doctrine but Schlabrendorff had earned the
right to affirm it.

In October, 1934 Phipps was able to report that the most unsatisfactory feature from the point of view of the régime after its first
twelve months in office was 'the obstinate and taciturn opposition
of the intelligentsia which had so far proved intractable':

> A very widespread opposition exists but it is confined to those classes
> which prefer normally to express it with ink and paper rather than
> those violent arguments which is what the Nazis understand. Thanks
> to censorship of the Press it remains imperceptible to the un-
> initiated. . . .

This Opposition camp was made up of Communists and intelligentsia, Church, landowning classes, aristocrats and to some extent
the armed forces, he wrote.[7]

There were other reports, too, which showed that the Nazi régime
was mistaken in 'pre-supposing the willing acquiescence' of the individual to assume his place as cog. As long-term residents in Germany, closer to the daily life of the people than were the Embassy
staff, the British consuls were particularly well-placed observers. In
a report in 1937 the Consul at Stettin sought to correct the impression
that the Germans were a 'well-conducted and contented people':

> The freedom of the people exists in being allowed to praise as fully
> and as loudly as they like all steps taken by their leaders, and this is
> done very widely by a certain class of people. But everybody is fully
> aware that any criticism will without fail lead at once to arrest and
> under these circumstances it is not surprising that the German people
> give the impression, especially to foreigners on a short visit, of con-
> tentment with the present régime.[8]

The British Foreign Office was in a position to be better informed
about Germany than were the Germans themselves, whose knowledge of what was happening in their own country, or in its relationships abroad, reached them if at all filtered through strictly controlled
media. The Foreign Office was not dependent only on ambassadorial
despatches, excellent though these were in the early years of the Nazi
era. During the years leading up to the outbreak of the Second World
War, the Office was flooded with information about Nazi Germany:

the reality, not the image portrayed in the German newsreels and documentaries, or by the admiring British visitors who were fêted and sent home to tell flattering tales of Hitler. Reliable intelligence was supplied to – indeed pressed upon – the Foreign Office by British businessmen, industrialists, bankers, academics and journalists. The cumulative effect of all these reports as the Nazi years progressed was of a country steadily deteriorating behind its stage-managed façade; economically broken-backed and near bankruptcy; militarily unready; its citizens terrorised and increasingly disaffected, and some of the most influential members of society conspiring to overthrow the government. Reading the Foreign Office papers one cannot escape the impression that all this information, far from being collated and studied, was allowed to run into the sand. Certainly it had no effect on foreign policy. The received idea of Nazi Germany – then as indeed now for many people – was that of Goebbels' myth of a country happy, healthy, united and strong; of a nation of ardent Nazis shoulder to shoulder behind their adored leader.

In November, 1936 the Foreign Secretary, Eden, received a personal letter from Nigel Law, a former Foreign Office colleague, now a businessman. He had just returned from a visit to Germany with an impression, he told Eden, 'so definite as to outweigh those other impressions, of which we hear so much, obtained by travellers on pleasure, equipped with but an imperfect knowledge of the country and its language.' Law attached a lengthy report which covered in much detail the gathering economic difficulties of the Third Reich. But he also gave a stark account of the life of the ordinary citizen in the year when the Nazi capital was crowned by the staging of the Olympic Games, an event which impressed and delighted so many foreign visitors:

> To return to the individual and the uncertainty which surround him. Night and day he feels himself spied upon. [He] anxiously looks behind the door before answering your question and then decides, after all, that it is wiser not to reply. . . .
> People no longer read the papers: they are bored with the repetition of speeches and the accounts of parades. They contain no other news and, as someone said to me: 'We have no information on which to base ideas of the future and it is wise and more pleasant not to think. The problems of each day are enough. . . .'
> To sum up, I found a depressed people without hope for the future and obsessed by fears. Trembling when a uniformed Nazi rings the

bell to collect the *Winterhilfe* lest he has come to enquire into some unwitting transgression of a new and unknown law; trembling lest they may have said something unwise, and fearful lest the threatened attack by Russia may be realised. . . . But how the Germans will distinguish Bolshevism from their present régime I do not know. No foreigner will notice the difference.

Eden hastened to commend Law's report to the Prime Minister, Stanley Baldwin, for his attention as being that of 'a very competent English observer.'[9]

Just before he retired in 1933, the British Ambassador Sir Horace Rumbold had written: 'These men [the Nazis] have succeeded in creating an atmosphere of terror which is increased by the difficulty, for Germans, of obtaining authentic information about what is going on. . . .' In five years nothing had changed. Sir Auckland Geddes, himself a former Ambassador, vouched for the German author of the following in August, 1938:

> The face of the land has been altered by the introduction of a reign of terror in every sphere, which prevents any free expression of opinion and rests upon a comprehensive system of spies and informers. If in any particular case information is given by a member of the Party or by a spy, his evidence alone is enough to send the suspected person to a concentration camp.
> Still worse is the complete lawlessness which prevails under the pretext of 'equal rights for all', resulting in the imprisonment in concentration camps of thousands of people on account of personal enmities. Defence in the courts is refused to a person unless it is approved by the supervisor or the informer involved in the case, and a member of the Party cannot be called to justice before the courts without special permission. . . .[10]

A vivid impression of how the system of terror worked was sent to London by the British Legation at Copenhagen. The writer, whose identity could not be divulged even to the Foreign Office, was described as a non-German who had been living in Berlin for many years and was *persona grata* in high places. In spite of this, he had himself twice been summoned to police headquarters on the grounds that 'too many people came to see him.' Even the meeting of a small group in a humble home, he wrote, could be constructed as either real or attempted conspiracy and the mere suspicion 'set the terror machine in motion.' He described its effects:

Nazi skill in the use of terror consists precisely in the fact that while everyone knows and must know that barbaric terror is applied, they are kept nevertheless in ignorance as to *where, when and on whom*. An atmosphere of secret horror is thus created, the reality of which no-one doubts, but against which all reaction is impossible, since it cannot be focused on, or directed against, any definite object.

The small circles or groups were more numerous, continued the writer, than one could imagine. Their members had devised a form of protection which had become almost instinctive:

The façade cannot be perceived. What goes on behind it cannot be divined. I have myself several times seen how, at the slightest suspicion or alarm, the scene has shifted literally in a split second from free comment and criticism to a kind of ultra-Nazism with the appropriate gestures, terms and accents. . . .[11]

Christabel Bielenberg, the British wife of a German lawyer who was an active member of the Opposition, describes vividly in her book *The Past Is Myself* the extraordinary lengths to which those opposed to the régime went to protect themselves in ordinary social circumstances, such as a wives' tea party. In the presence of any 'stranger' – even if introduced by one of their own circle – an 'appropriate' façade was maintained. On one occasion, the indiscreet English wife of a German diplomat ignored the presence of a woman she did not know, but who was in fact the sister-in-law of Hitler's lawyer. Subsequent disaster was averted by 'eight respectable ladies' willingly perjuring themselves and swearing that the fatal words complained of had never been spoken: it was all a misunderstanding.

That such caution even in intimate domestic surroundings was vital is demonstrated by the story of the Solf circle, which did not have such a happy ending. Frau Solf was the widow of a former Foreign Minister and Ambassador who until his death in 1936 had been a stern opposer of Nazism. She was a member of a circle of like-minded people who wished to oppose and counter the oppression and degradation of human beings by the régime. Some were members, active or retired, of the German Foreign Ministry. In all good faith, one of their number invited a young man to a tea party attended by members of the circle. The talk was unguarded. But the young man was a Gestapo agent. All those present, and other members who were not, were arrested. Most of them were executed.

Three years earlier, in 1940, Frau Solf had managed to send a letter
to a friend in England – a major-general. It found its way to the
Foreign Office through Lord Ismay. It is a poignant echo from the
'other Germany':

> You know my ideas and ideals – and therefore you can imagine *what*
> and *how* I suffer. It is not easy for a mother to send sons to war. But
> to send *my* sons in *this* war is a torture. . . .[12]

The distinguished émigré, Sebastian Haffner, described the 'uncanny
twilight quality' of life caused by the existence of these hundred
thousand little airtight circles 'into which one steps as into a strange
land'; and only after giving a password. The millions of disloyal
people formed an 'immense glowing mass of grief and hatred that
smoulders restlessly beneath the surface.'[13]

For those with an eye for such things, there was a perceptible
ratio between the extent of disaffection among the citizens and the
escalating extravagance of the annual Party fiesta at Nuremberg. The
Nazi year had its liturgical calendar, commencing with the day of
the seizure of power on 30th January through Memorial Day, Hitler's
birthday, Labour Day, Mother's Day, Party Day, Harvest Thanks-
giving and finally 9th November anniversary of the Munich *Putsch*.
There was even a special Bureau for the Organisation of Festivals,
Leisure and Celebrations whose function was to create occasions for
National Socialist demonstrations. The Party Day was the ultimate
celebration. Hitler, who never had any precise policies to enunciate,
used the occasion literally to woo the German people. He himself
was carried away by his own oratory: inebriated, as Disraeli said of
Gladstone, by the exuberance of his own verbosity.

The peak of the celebration was always at night. The blaze of
torches and searchlights blotted out the Führer and his audience from
each other, thereby creating an intimacy which the vast stadium and
the illumination of the serried thousands would have killed: 'Not
every one of you can see me and I cannot see you. But I feel you
and you feel me,' he yearned out of the darkness. 'That you found
me long ago and that you believed in me has given your lives a new
meaning.'[14]

It seems a pity to break the spell, but the fact is that the German
people did not assemble spontaneously to acclaim the manifestations
of the Third Reich and their Leader. When Mussolini came on a state

visit in 1937, for instance, there was an enormous gathering in the Maifeld in Berlin, where Führer and Duce were to address the faithful. It was to be one of those 'spontaneous' demonstrations which Goebbels was so good at organising. In advance of the Duce's arrival, he dictated to the people of Berlin what their emotions were to be:

> He will, we are certain, be welcomed in Berlin with rejoicing and jubilation and will be encompassed with the love and affection of the whole people.
> From Monday, September 27th until Wednesday, September 29th inclusive, Berlin must be a sea of flags. The flags of Fascist Italy will flutter beside those of the Third Reich. All Berlin will pay homage to the two men who, rising from the lowest ranks of their people, have truly become the leaders of their people. In Berlin these festival days will reach their zenith at a great demonstration on the Maifeld, when the Duce and the Führer will speak. . . .
> On the Führer's instructions all businesses in Berlin, except those of vital importance, will on this day remain closed. A holiday in the schools has already been announced.
> Four-and-a-half million Berliners shall have the opportunity of witnessing an event which counts amongst the most brilliant and most significant in the history of the capital.[15]

There was no chance of this enforced holiday being used for any frivolous and unofficial purpose. A British colonial officer, who was on holiday in Berlin at the time, wrote a report for the Foreign Office. He had been shown the operational orders which had been issued to every factory, department store, bank, office, etc. and he watched how they were carried out. At 4 p.m. the day before, all works and shops closed their doors and next morning the whole of business and industrial Berlin marched in orderly battalions to the Maifeld, every worker carrying a water bottle and a haversack with one day's ration which he had to provide for himself, although he received his full wages for the day: 'This was the spontaneous and enthusiastic monster welcome to the Duce. . . .'[16]

'All very interesting and impressive,' a director of Siemens, who had been present, told the British Consul in Leipzig, 'but how different and more real our feelings would have been if the festivities had been in honour of, say, the King of England!'[17] In its report of the occasion, *The Times* did Goebbels proud:

The general public struggled behind cordons of black uniformed Nazi guards to catch a glimpse of the Duce wherever he drove in the lavishly decorated streets and cheered with enthusiasm. . . . The Berliners gave a demonstration of genuine friendliness which must have gone far to convince the Duce that the Rome–Berlin Axis is ratified by the German nation. . . .[18]

Goebbels' proclamation to the Berliners had concluded with the words: 'The regulations of 1st May regarding the payment of wages shall be applied on the days designated.' Workers were paid as usual; a demonstration was just a day's work in another place. The government compensated the employers for lost time but only on a percentage basis. This was the reality behind the enthusiastic crowds which German newsreels presented to the world and 'The Thunderer' to its readers. When the Italian Foreign Minister, Ciano, came to Berlin to sign the Pact of Steel in 1939, the Party had some difficulty in drumming up enough public enthusiasm. The Labour Front was called into action and industrialists were begged to send their workers on to the streets, although this was a time when mobilisation of manpower was at its peak. The Nazis had, in fact, invented 'rent-a-crowd'.

But the most striking – and significant – example of this cosmetic enthusiasm was that reported by the Ambassador, Sir Nevile Henderson. It was at the time of the Austrian *Anschluss*. Hitler had declared from the balcony of the Hofburg in Vienna:

As Führer and Chancellor of the German Nation and of the Reich, I hereupon report to History the entrance of my homeland into the German Reich.

Surely this historic moment would have been rapturously acclaimed in Berlin. Goebbels was taking no chances. The British Ambassador reported to London:

All factories and places of business are to be closed at 1.00 p.m. Hitler is arriving back at 5.00 p.m. Dr Goebbels has addressed a proclamation to Berliners saying that no-one may be absent from the streets and that the Chancellor is to have a reception such as the capital has never seen.[19]

The Minister of Propaganda was rewarded with some wonderful visual images of the Führer's popularity to spread around the world.

If Goebbels' proclamation had been reproduced in the British press and cinemas against those images, they could have been put into their true perspective. International bankers were in a special position for taking the German pulse. In 1938, Hambro's Bank reported to the Foreign Office a palpable tension in Berlin. There was none of the applause that used to be given when leaders spoke nor was there any cheering of troops on the move. Criticism was more free and open than ever before:

> Our general impression is: among the bulk of the people dislike of the régime is steadily growing, and while it will probably not show itself in open opposition, the Nazi Party are conscious that they no longer have the bulk of the people behind them.[20]

The Consul-General at Frankfurt, Smallbones, sent a long report on discontent in the Rhineland but added that it never reached higher levels because adverse reports were unpopular. He also reported cases of insubordination among the troops. This highly significant piece of intelligence was confirmed from Vansittart's sources, who reported indiscipline and insubordination among reservists.[21] He hastened to inform the Foreign Secretary:

> The German General Staff is in ever-increasing anxiety about the moral decline of the combatant forces. General Halder, who followed Beck as Chief of the General Staff, alluded in a recent conversation to a condition of ruinous dissolution (*ruinose Auflösung*) from which the German Army was suffering.[22]

This assessment was dismissed in the Foreign Office. Whitehall knew better. The German Army had done very well in its occupation of the Sudeten areas – hardly a military campaign! – and the SIS claimed that the High Command was very impressed. But indications that all was not well with the Army had already been received. As Hitler's aggressive intentions towards Czechoslovakia were becoming increasingly manifest, the British Military Attaché had been told by one of his contacts that 'the spirit of the people generally and most of those called up is bad, and there is everywhere terror at the prospect of a catastrophe. . . .'[23] As the crisis deepened public opinion began to get out of hand – even Goebbels' hand.

Reports from British consuls confirmed that Hitler did not have the nation with him in this crisis. This evidence of the instability of the régime, far from stiffening the attitude of the Western Allies, was dismissed as spurious by the British Foreign Office. On a despatch from the Consul-General in Hamburg, who reported that people were dissatisfied and apprehensive about war, Mallet minuted, on 15th September: 'All this dissatisfaction will be immediately changed into far greater triumph and devotion to the régime if Hitler gets his way again without war.'[24] That this turned out to be very far from the case can be seen in a despatch from the Consul-General in Munich. One of the most noticeable facts, he reported in the first days after the signing of the Munich Agreement, was the abandonment under the stress of anxiety of the usual reticence in regard to the criticism of the régime. Members of the Consulate had had it whispered to them that the Party consisted of a gang of upstarts and that 'Herr Hitler himself is a madman or the devil incarnate.'[25]

The fatal disregard of all the evidence of the instability of the Nazi régime owed much to the attitude of the British Ambassador, Sir Nevile Henderson, who always enjoyed the confidence of the Cabinet in the face of any conflicting evidence from other sources. In July, 1938 he wrote to Cadogan, Head of the Foreign Office:

> You may be hearing, especially through secret sources – which it can be taken for granted are anti-Nazi and to that extent unreliable – that dissatisfaction against the régime is growing in Germany and that Germany itself and Austria are seething with discontent.
> It is true, but its effect should not be overestimated. . . . Some people, who allow their wishes to be father of their thoughts, foresee in this the possibility of the weakening of the régime and the reinforcement of the theory that Germany is unprepared for war. . . .[26]

Goebbels, however, did not share the British Ambassador's calm appraisal. In the wake of the Munich crisis Hitler's standing with the nation was dangerously low. Hitler himself was furious that credit for the resolution of the affair had been given by the German people to the British Prime Minister, who was being loudly applauded by them as their saviour. They had to be turned back towards their Leader. Within two weeks of the Conference, Goebbels addressed 4,000 workers, assembled on the Maifeld. The British Embassy sent home a summary:

> On October 11, Dr Goebbels addressed an audience of 4,000 workmen on the Maifeld. He began by saying that many of the German

people did not realise the burden and responsibility borne by the Chancellor in the recent crisis. And he had determined, when it was over, to lose no opportunity of expressing to the German people the Chancellor's thanks for their steady bearing. . . .

Dr Goebbels went on to say that the Chancellor's policy would not have been possible with the German people as they were between 1918–1933 because he can only take great decisions in full reliance on their bearing and discipline, which must be such that foreign countries can never, in the decisive hour, play off some opposition section of the people against the Government.[27]

That Goebbels selected an audience of workers and was prepared to sacrifice so many precious man-hours of production to deliver this combination of cajolery, defensiveness and apprehension, is a measure of the Party's anxiety.

But the proof that the Party was out of touch with the mood of the nation was given by the public reaction to the events of 9th/10th November, 1938: the notorious pogrom known as the *Kristallnacht*. Aware of the tension and shock in the country which had been brought to the brink of war, the Party leaders looked for a suitable distraction to relieve the tension. What would be more popular than some lively harassment of the Jews? A nationwide demonstration was arranged for the anniversary of the 1923 *putsch*, which though it had failed, marked Hitler's entry on to the political stage and which he celebrated every year. The name of Munich had more potent associations, after all, than the signing of international agreements which would never be kept. According to instructions from Gestapo HQ the demonstration was to be a controlled affair – no looting or theft – but synagogues were to be burned and thousands of Jews, particularly well-to-do ones, were to be arrested. But on the eve of the anniversary a young Jew murdered a member of the German Embassy in Paris. All constraints were now off. Heydrich ordered his SS on to the streets in civilian clothes to foment violence. When it was all over, Buchenwald concentration camp was unable to cope with the number of victims. The atrocity did not, however, have the revivalist effect on the population for which it had been staged: in fact, quite the reverse. The British Consul in Frankfurt, who had lived in Germany since 1930, sent home a striking description of public feeling:

The action against the Jews . . . has aroused passionate resentment
and compassion not only among members of the Christian churches,
in the army, the civil service and all classes of the population but it
may even bring about a split in the Party itself.[28]
I am persuaded that if the government of Germany depended on the
suffrage of the people, those in power and responsible for these out-
rages could be swept away by a storm of indignation, if not put up
against a wall and shot. . . .[29]

This was confirmed by Vansittart's informant, Group Captain
Christie, who was a frequent visitor to Germany. He sent a powerful
account of public reaction:

> The Jewish pogroms that occurred in November have caused as great
> a revulsion of feeling among the German people as they have done in
> England, and Hitler and the régime have suffered a further loss of
> prestige.
> I was in Berlin at the time and can testify to the universal horror felt
> by the German people, and I was again in Berlin and in Essen in
> December, when I found similar proof of the general abhorrence felt
> by the mass of the people and the industrial leaders. . . .
> There is no doubt that Hitler has felt the pressure of German public
> opinion in regard to his latest treatment of the Jews. The German
> people are not fully aware of the evil forces dominating their Govern-
> ment but recent happenings have shaken them deeply. . . .[30]

It is worth adding the contemporary record of a German, all too
aware of those evil forces, in the fight against which he was to
sacrifice his own life. The former ambassador Ulrich von Hassell
noted in his diary:

> I am writing under crushing emotions evoked by the vile persecution
> of the Jews. . . . Not since the World War have we lost so much
> credit in the world. But my chief concern is not with the effects abroad
> . . . I am most deeply troubled about the effect on our national life,
> which is dominated ever more inexorably by a system capable of such
> things. . . .
> These days are marked by a deep sense of shame which has weighed
> heavily on all decent and thoughtful people since the hideous events
> of November. There is talk of little else.[31]

Indeed within the Party itself there seems to have been an uneasy
feeling that perhaps things had gone a little too far. The notorious

Jew-baiter Julius Streicher testified at his trial in 1945 that: 'It was remarkable that the indignation at what happened during those demonstrations expressed itself even in Nuremberg – even among the Party members.' He himself had felt obliged, he said, in the prevailing atmosphere, to make a public speech protesting at so much sympathy being shown to the Jews.[32]

In his book *The Nemesis of Power* Wheeler-Bennett, who never allowed the truth to get in the way of his preferred opinions, quoted from a letter which the Opposition leader, Carl Goerdeler, had sent to a friend in America following upon Munich and the *Kristallnacht*. 'You can hardly conceive,' Goerdeler had written, 'the despair that both the people and the Army feel about the brutal, insane and terroristic dictator and his henchmen.' Never, pronounced the British historian, was wishful thinking more eloquently expressed, never a less accurate picture portrayed for foreign consumption. Contentment, satisfaction and relief were the salient factors of German thought at this moment, both among the people at large and among the Army. 'Their Führer had saved them from war and had given them additional honour, glory and security.' As for the pogrom itself, this had evoked only qualified reprobation, occasioned by the looting and damage to property which offended the German sense of law and order, rather than the persecution of the Jews.[33] How happy Goebbels would have been had this been a true picture of the situation.

Goerdeler had also reported to the Foreign Office in London. Throughout all parts of Germany, he wrote, the cruel and senseless persecution of the Jews was deeper and deeper resented: 'The feeling of the masses, because of these terrible happenings, has never been so bitter against the Nazi régime.'[34]

Festering discontent in a dictatorship must be controlled by a constant flux of activity and excitement. There must never be time for calm reflection. Even in the early days of the régime, Sir Horace Rumbold reported that he and his fellow-diplomats in Berlin were 'bewildered by the whirlwind development of Hitler's internal policy.' After the Great War, the defeat of 1918, the political turmoil which followed, and the psychological trauma of the appalling inflation, what the German people sorely needed was internal peace. They were not to get it. In his personal report to his friend the Foreign Secretary, in June, 1937 the former diplomat Nigel Law underlined the significance of the fact that

There is no leisure in Germany. If you are not working you are marching or singing or attending meetings of your particular 'front' – arbeiter-front or whatnot. There is no time even to fish; the sale of fishing apparatus in the shops has fallen almost to zero. Therefore community grumbling has been abolished.[35]

Ambassador von Hassell wrote that the people were 'weary to the point of nausea' by the 'officially inspired' popular demonstrations. Goering's own cousin, an engineer at the Herman-Goering Werke, told a member of the British Embassy staff that the people were 'sick of parades', with shops and businesses closed and traffic stopped, and workers and school-children sent on the streets to cheer. Such was the thoroughness (or desperation) of the organisers, apparently, that children were threatened with detention if they did not sing, because their shrill voices made the most noise. The workers were instructed to shout 'Sieg Heil' every few minutes.[36]

After their narrow escape from war in September, 1938 and the apparent accommodation with foreign powers reached at Munich, the German people could have hoped to find themselves in calmer waters. This feeling is well described by a British-born informant who had lived all his life in Germany and sent reports through the American Bankers Trust Company in Paris 'when opportunity of a safe hand offered.' In December, 1938 his *Memorandum respecting the Present State of Mind in Germany* was forwarded by the Ambassador in Paris to the Foreign Secretary, Lord Halifax. The author must have been a person of some standing as Halifax instructed that his paper should be circulated to the Cabinet:

> The Radical Nazis are well aware of the fact that the German population at large has never had a moment's respite since 1914, and that the last five years under Hitler have been a tremendous psychological strain . . . and that there is now a great desire on the part of the population to relax and enjoy life. . . .
> It is evident that Hitler's decision not to consolidate Germany's position has created tremendous disappointment in the major part of the German population and primarily among the leaders of banking and industry, which has resulted in quite a noticeable passive resistance. . . .

The author stressed the effect that the falling away of public support for the régime at home would have on foreign policy: 'All this will only make the Radical Nazis move much faster and all my German friends agree that 1939 will be a very hectic year. . . . One can only fervently hope that Great Britain, France and the United States will do everything in their power to rearm as quickly as possible, as this is the only way to make Germany stop and think. . . .'[37]

The Munich crisis had brought forth in Germany a public vote of diminishing confidence in Hitler and a reluctance to endorse his foreign policy. The economic problems were becoming uncontrollable. There was one way out for the dictator which would force the people to follow their Leader. He placed the Fatherland in danger. As the events of the 'hectic year' of 1939 passed the point of no return, Consul-General Smallbones sent his last report on Germany from the safety of the British Consulate in Basle. In the course of it he described the mood in which, away from the newsreels, the German people entered the war. The Foreign Secretary, Halifax, thought the despatch of sufficient interest to be sent to the King and circulated to the Cabinet:

> There is no doubt that the Hitler régime is highly unpopular with vast numbers of Germans at present, to the point that many would risk their lives to fight it openly. In the last few days before my departure, such sentiments were openly and loudly expressed in public beer-gardens.
> But whatever the hardships suffered and the consequent discontent, we should be under no illusion that a revolt in Germany is imminent. The Party is so organised that combined action is next to impossible. Nazi friends of mine have made it quite clear to me that in the case of war they are prepared and expect to kill at sight whoever shows the slightest sign of hostility to the régime. . . .[38]

When the Gestapo moved into the territories of occupied Europe they could use the skills which they had perfected during those years when every nation in Europe except Germany itself had been at peace. The knock on the door at night; the arrests for which there was no legal remedy; the forced labour and the disappearances; the concentration camps and the executions – all that was to become the pattern throughout Europe.

In the summer of 1937 Colonel Hotblack of British military Intelligence informed the Foreign Office that 'there was all the material for a civil war lying about in Germany'.[39] He was not aware that such a war had already been in operation there for some time, conducted clandestinely and without firearms. The security forces were massively committed to an endless struggle against what Haffner described as a 'jack-in-the-box' opponent – who stands up again just when he seems to have been struck down. In a country which ran on propaganda and in which all forms of communication were controlled, the opponents of the régime had to devise a means of disseminating their message to their fellow citizens.

The Popular Front ran a short-wave station: *Deutscher Freiheitssender*, mounted on a truck and kept continuously on the move to avoid Gestapo jamming. The British Consul-General in Hamburg reported in March, 1938 the rumours that the Gestapo were having difficulty in suppressing a Communist portable short-wave transmitter. The programmes were devoted to exposing Nazi terrorism. Each nightly transmission was preceded by the message:

> We stand for all those who are opposed to Nazi terrorism and warmongering. We stand for all those who are striving for the peace of the world and civic liberties in a truly democratic Germany.

The transmission always ended: 'You will hear us tomorrow in spite of the Gestapo.' The broadcasts continued nightly even in the early part of the war. Workers in a Berlin armaments factory used the station to broadcast to the people of Berlin:

> This war is not a just war, not a patriotic war, nor a war of liberation. It is an unjust war. It is not a just war because it is not a war for the honour of Germany, of our people, but for the suppression of other peoples and for the conquest of foreign territories. . . . Down with Hitler! Let us all join in the fight of the German people for peace and freedom. . . . The enemy is in our own country! The overthrow of those who have caused this war is the task of the German people.[40]

The production and dissemination of illegal literature was conducted on such a scale that a special department was set up by the security forces to combat it. Much of the material was printed abroad and smuggled into the country. Official statistics for 1937 recorded 120,286 confiscations. In 426 of these cases, it was recorded, 'firearms had to be used.'

A rare contemporary account of how such subversive material

was produced is contained in an anonymous open letter to the Commander-in-Chief, General von Brauchitsch, written by the father of three sons, one of whom had already fallen in Belgium, and another in Russia. The letter, written late in 1941, was a personal attack on Hitler and ranged over the whole history of Germany under his rule. The author challenged both the inception of the war and its conduct. He concluded with a message to 'the gentlemen of the police': a pseudonym was used not out of cowardice but because further letters would be appearing 'as long as one of us remains alive.' The methods used were then set out to prove the uselessness of trying to trace the source:

> *To the fingerprint experts*: the impressions on the papers, the sheets, envelopes, stamps are not those of the writers. All work was done with gloves.
>
> *Photo-chemical department*: nothing that is found comes from us. We are experts in photo-chemical matters.
>
> *Criminal investigators*: Papers and envelopes, stencils and dyes, come partly from government offices and partly from old stock. Nothing was purchased recently. Never from individual shops. The stamps were procured four weeks ago, not in Berlin and from various offices. The typewriter is not very far from Tirpitz Ufer [headquarters of the Abwehr]. It is still there. The keys have been changed, of course. The duplicator lies in the water between Nedlitz and Glienickerbrucke. Neither individuals nor firms nor other addressees are known to the writers. They were copied completely at random from advertisements, newspapers, magazines; also from lists of addresses and telephone numbers.
>
> The edition is of a size to suit its purpose. It was assumed that several hundred would come into your hands. That still leaves enough in circulation. The actual posting is done partly by messengers, partly by orderlies, none of whom had any idea what they were carrying.[41]

Some of the most powerful material which passed from hand to hand was not illegal in its origins; it had been uttered on the only public platforms which existed in the Third Reich: the pulpits of the great cathedrals. From these, voices were raised against the doctrines and practice of National-Socialism in uncompromising terms. Copies were made and spread throughout the country; even the occupied countries were able to hear what was being said aloud in Germany. Some of these sermons were reprinted in Britain in the form of leaflets and dropped over Germany by the RAF.

The British Minister in the Vatican forwarded to the Foreign Office the text of such a sermon by Bishop von Galen (known as 'The Lion of Münster') delivered in his cathedral on 20 July 1941. The Bishop spoke openly of 'our enemies within this country.' He did not hesitate to name the Gestapo again and again. They had seized all religious houses in the Province and put their occupants on to the streets. A protest to the President of the Province of Westphalia had received the answer that the Gestapo was a completely independent body with which he could not interfere. The Bishop read out to the congregation the text of a telegram of protest he had sent to the Führer himself, begging him 'to protect the freedom and property of German citizens against the arbitrary measures of the Gestapo.' He had sent similar telegrams to Goering, to the Ministry of Home Affairs and to the High Command of the Army. The persecutions had continued. These punitive measures of the Gestapo against innocent men, condemned without charge or defence, 'undermine the security of the Reich, saps the feeling of justice and destroy confidence in the administration of the State.' The Bishop adjured his Catholic flock:

> Against the enemy within our own country, who tortures and strikes us, we cannot fight with weapons. There remains one kind of struggle: strong, persistent, dogged endurance. At this moment we are not the hammer but the anvil. . . . If [the anvil] is firm and hard it usually lasts longer than the hammer. . . . Obedience to God and conscience may cost you or me our lives, our freedom, but let us die rather than sin.[42]

To have been present when such words were publicly proclaimed from the pulpit must have been an electrifying experience.

Bishop von Galen was not the only churchman to speak out so forthrightly against the régime but through his towering personality he became a legend in his lifetime. When Münster suffered its first air-raid, he reminded his congregation of the tinkling glass of the pogrom of the *Kristallnacht*. The effect which his sermons had, even on Hitler, was described in a letter sent by the Secretary of the World Council of Churches in Geneva, Dr Willem Visser 't Hooft, to the representative of the International Missionary Society in London, William Paton. It was intercepted by the British censor and sent to the Foreign Office. Himmler wanted the Bishop shot but Hitler, fearing the effect on the thousands of workers in Westphalia, would not consent. The Catholic bishops' public stand against the 'euthanasia' of the unfit had caused the policy to be halted. Hitler had now reined in the most radical elements of the Party and decreed that for the time being no further measures should be taken against the Church.[43]

R. H. S. Crossman, Head of the German Section of the Political Warfare Executive, commenting on the violent conflict which had arisen between the Gestapo and the Catholic and Protestant clergy, thought that it was 'to our interests to intensify it.' The Christians were to be thrown to the Gestapo lions. In propaganda broadcasts, 'we should do everything possible to report fully the Christian Opposition in Germany and Europe and thereby to promote violent attempts by the Gestapo to crush it.'[44] (The rationale behind the proposal was obscure, but so was much that came out of PWE.) In this context of religious opposition to the state it is interesting to recall that in 1938 the Archbishop of Canterbury was asked to put his name to a statement, to be issued by leading churchmen in Europe and the United States, on behalf of Martin Niemöller, the Evangelical pastor and former war hero consigned to a concentration camp for condemning the régime from the pulpit. The Archbishop felt it necessary to consult the Foreign Secretary – he did not want 'to rock the boat.' The Foreign Office reminded Lord Halifax that Hitler had not taken at all well his references to the religious question when he had visited him the previous November. There would be 'embarrassment' if the Archbishop signed. No doubt the Archbishop would refrain from associating himself with the manifesto if strongly advised by His Majesty's Government.[45]

A letter written by the widow of a clergyman who had died after ill-treatment in a Gestapo prison was passed to the Foreign Office by Lord Ponsonby. It was a harrowing account of what life was like under the régime for those who opposed it. The letter touched no hearts in Whitehall. Sir Orme Sargent pronounced: 'Very prejudiced and exaggerated, I should say.'[46]

One of the most tragic manifestations of 'the other Germany', because of the youth of those involved, was the White Rose organisation based on Munich University. Discussion was translated into positive action as a direct result of Bishop von Galen's sermon, a copy of which was thrust by an anonymous hand through the letterbox of the Scholl family in Ulm. Hans Scholl, a medical student in Munich, was so inspired by its language that he began a movement in which his sister Sophie joined him, directed at fellow-students all over Germany. He and his companions produced pamphlets and leaflets which attacked the moral obloquy of the régime, called for passive resistance against the war and urged German youth to 'avenge and atone for' Germany's crimes against the world. They also looked to the regeneration of Europe in a new spirit. The pamphlets were hand-carried with great danger all over the Reich and even as far as Vienna. On 18 February 1943 Hans and Sophie took two suitcases of leaflets to the University in the early morning. After scattering them throughout the building, they went to the top floor and threw the remainder down into the street. They were immediately arrested and after the usual Gestapo interrogation condemned to death in the People's Court by the same judge, Freisler, who was later to condemn those responsible for the attempted assassination of Hitler in July, 1944. The brother and sister, with some of their companions, were beheaded, but many buildings in Munich carried the slogan: 'The spirit lives'.[47]

Not all material circulating clandestinely in Germany was anonymous. Early in 1940 the Foreign Office had sight of another example of subversion, this time from outside Germany. In May, postal censorship in Gibraltar intercepted a document which was on its way from the Jewish Congress in Geneva to the Jewish Congress in New York. A covering letter indicated that it had already been circulated inside Germany. The document was an open letter to his workers, written at Christmas, 1939 by Friedrich Thyssen, the steel magnate. He had been one of the major industrialists who had staked Hitler in 1932 but as the years passed bitterly regretted his mistake. He became increasingly open in his opposition to the régime and to the persecution of the Jews and had refused to vote in the Reichstag in favour of the war. He had fled to Switzerland and in his absence been deprived of all rights and property. The long letter to his workers was a passionate denunciation of Hitler personally and every aspect of his criminal madness while admitting openly his own guilt in having been seduced by Hitler's promises and his sheer 'mediocrity' which these clever tycoons had thought to exploit. The war must be stopped, but no Nazi must have a hand in making peace. A new administration must be formed – 'there are responsible men in Germany who are ready to undertake these duties.' As for the future:

Never again a party, nor an army, nor a single man – be he a prophet or a genius. Never again Strength through Joy, uniforms for children, a private army, nor SA nor SS, nor Gestapo and purity of Aryan blood, and 'Lebensraum'. Never again a Great Germany and 20 different kinds of marks. Never again swastikas, pogroms, concentration camps, torture chambers, splendid buildings, flags and Autobahnen. Never again professors and judges who say 'Yes' to every crime against civilisation. . . . Employers and workers, stand together against the enemy of Germany – against Adolf Hitler and his war![48]

How this document of some 2,500 words was smuggled into wartime Germany is not known. That this should have been accomplished and that it should have been circulated inside Germany argues the existence of a network of willing hands. Many of them had been opposing Hitler in the workplace before Thyssen had seen the error of his ways.

In vigorous contrast to Goebbels' claques in Berlin, the men of the great ports of Hamburg and Kiel gave the Führer's pronouncements little respect. In March, 1936 at the famous shipyards of Bloehm and Voss, 5,000 workers were assembled in the main building to listen to a relay of an important speech by the Leader. They walked out in the middle of it. At Germania-Werft, 6,000 workers were brought together in similar circumstances to listen to the voice of Hitler. They shouted and barracked during the speech and when it was over, they came to blows with the Storm-troopers manning the gates.[49] Schacht himself sent word to England of this widespread subversion among the workers. On his way back from a visit to India in the summer of 1939, he stayed in Switzerland with Hugo Stinnes, son of the famous tycoon of the 1920s. Speaking about oppositional attitudes and activities in Germany, he told Stinnes of the passive resistance in factories – such as the leading producer of synthetic fuel, rubber and nitrogen: Leuna-Werke. The most effective resistance was in the mines – in the Ruhr and the Sudetenland. The Gestapo were powerless to check on men underground, although the decline in output was all too obvious. Although Goering had lengthened the working hours and increased the labour force by thousands, coal production in May, 1939 was actually less than at the same time the previous year. In Austria too, said Schacht, particularly in Vienna, the workers were slowing down production. Stinnes recorded Schacht's information in a paper which his doctor, who had been present during the conversations and was a trusted friend, conveyed to the Foreign Office in London.[50] As late as December, 1944 an intelligence source reported to SHAEF that there was much unrest in Krupps, which was a centre of anti-Nazi activity among the workers. In the predominantly Catholic Ruhr, the source reported, there was close connection between clergy and workers and what was described as 'spiritual sabotage'. There had been arrests of Krupps workmen and engineers, together with seventy Catholic priests.[51]

A US Intelligence Survey compiled immediately after the war states that the underground activity of trades unionists, Socialists and Communists was on a national scale. (When the *Daily Mail* printed an article about the re-birth of the Miners' Union, the Foreign Office sniped: 'We shall no doubt hear lots more about these old trades unionists with fiery glints in their eyes who have never been anything but anti-Nazis and have never lost faith in their own ideas.')[52]

But the problem for the leaders among the workers was that to stand aside from Nazi organisations was impossible. With every form of organised human contact taken over by the régime, simply to display no positive participation in the manifestations of the State was in itself to imply inner opposition and potential resistance and therefore to invite suspicion. Also, only by belonging to workers' organisations could the Opposition in the labour movement keep in touch with the everyday world of work. But these former trades unionists trained themselves in the techniques of passive resistance and of go-slow. They could become 'Trojan horses' and carry these techniques into the labour force. The most remarkable success for this plan of campaign was demonstrated by what happened on the West Wall. The problem for the authorities in combating industrial subversion was that widespread arrests would interfere with production. Nowhere was this more crucial than on the fortifications in the West which were to be the answer to the German problem of a war on two fronts. The engineer, Dr Todt, was in overall charge of the operations and the Todt organisation brought together a massive army of forced labourers from all levels of society – professional men as well as artisans – from all parts of the country and from the left and right of the political spectrum. They were dragged from their jobs and their homes to work in appalling conditions on what was seen to be a preparation for war. It was an ideal field for sabotage and there were among the workers many who had been trained in conspiratorial work – the Trojan Horse ploy. By creating this vast army of disaffection, the Nazis reactivated what they believed they had crushed out of existence: the power of organised labour. The trained agitators organised concerted action against the bad working conditions in the form of go-slows and frequent complaints. Dr Todt cynically told them to send their complaints to the Saarbrucken Radio station: it was assumed that a few ringleaders would do so, who could then be identified and arrested. Instead, thousands wrote in. As the organisers had foreseen, there were no massive reprisals: manpower could not be locked up in concentration camps. The work had to go on. The western barrier was essential to Hitler's strategy: to keep out the invader in the West while he struck in the East. The rejection of further demands by the workers was met by a strike along the whole length of the Siegfried Line, from Gersweiller to Saarbrucken, on 11 June 1939. The government gave in within a week. In the teeth of the dictatorship the workers managed to achieve some improvement in wages and working conditions. But go-slows and sit-down strikes continued to bedevil the progress of the work.[53]

Field Marshal Jodl testified during the Nuremberg trials that at the time of the Czech crisis in 1938 the West Wall was still 'little better than a building site.' A year later, the situation had hardly improved. A vivid description of the state of the Western defences at the outbreak of war was given by Consul Smallbones in his final despatch. The reference to Hitler's rage is chilling. There had been much talk in Frankfurt recently about the weakness of the Siegfried Line: the cement work had been hastily done; tanks were able to knock the defences down; Hitler had, after a personal inspection, ordered some of the engineers in charge to be executed; Todt, the builder of the motor roads who had built the Western fortifications, was in disgrace; the ventilation in the deep trenches was so bad that the soldiers had to come out to have their meals; some of the dugouts were below the level of the Rhine when in flood and had to be abandoned because they were full of water.[54] General Halder declared after the war that the French could have walked into Germany. The efforts of the clandestinely organised German workers had effectively spiked Hitler's guns. It was, however, labour in vain. The West Wall was not needed to keep the enemy out. They never tried to get in.

But it was not only the physical defences which were unreliable. In February, 1939 the Foreign Office received a report from Christie of the deterioration of morale in the German Army. In a long conversation a German source had detailed many instances of mutinous behaviour, particularly among reservists. The worst instances occurred among units from South Germany and Austria. Soldiers spoke openly of their unwillingness to go to war for Hitler. Acts of insubordination were so widespread that officers avoided reporting them because of the impossibility of singling out the guilty individuals. Indeed many of them, reservists themselves, shared the attitude of the troops. In one South German reserve battalion on the Western Front, the men openly declared that if war broke out they would let the French through the Siegfried Line. The narrator's cousin heard the battalion commander respond that, after making an armistice with the French, 'we will shoot every Nazi boss we can find.' The situation was so serious that the Commander-in-Chief, Brauchitsch, had ordered that the constant cases of mutiny and insubordination must be brought to an end by more severe methods. In forwarding this report to the Foreign Secretary, Vansittart hoped that these factors 'which are of the utmost value to us' should not be ignored: 'There are far too many people in this country, including many in high places' who were inclined to see only British difficulties 'and to overlook completely the fundamental weakness of the German position which is a very great one.'[55]

As Himmler had promised, there were mass arrests of thousands in every large city at the end of August and the beginning of September, 1939. During the war, news of arrests and executions reached the outside world mostly through Sweden. Social Democrat refugees abroad who knew many of the victims personally or by name, monitored reports when possible from the German press. Increasingly long terms of penal servitude became the rule. The radio criminal – one who listened to foreign broadcasts and disseminated the information received – was liable to a sentence of ten years, according to some of the cases reported in the press. There was a particularly vicious law relating to these sentences. Time served in prison during the war did not 'count' so the duration of the war was to be automatically added to the length of the original sentence.

Severe penalties were also inflicted on Germans who failed to observe the strictest reserve towards foreign prisoners and deportees put to work in the fields and factories of the Reich. The newspapers reported lists of convictions for rendering small services to relieve the human misery, such as gifts of cigarettes or food or clothing; mending a watch; forwarding a letter; drinking beer out of the same bottle. A taxi driver was imprisoned because he drove some Poles to church; the owner of an estate because he had given some first aid to some French prisoners; his daughter because she had spoken French to them and given them tea. A farmer was arrested and his farm impounded because he had allowed a Polish labourer to take his meals with the family. Another farmer suffered because a Polish labourer could be seen in a group photograph which had been taken of the family. There appears, however, to have been more to this policy of persecution than normal Nazi brutality. In 1943, Allen Dulles, the OSS chief in Berne who had close contacts with the Opposition inside Germany, informed Washington that relations between German and foreign workers were reported to be generally good. There was an impression that at some opportune moment they could make common cause. This dangerous solidarity had evidently been perceived by the authorities, and efforts were made in workplaces to keep them separated from each other.[56] It must have been a revelation to many of those deported to Germany as forced labour to find themselves among a people also living under the Nazi yoke but without the long-term hope and comradeship of those suffering under *foreign* domination. No doubt before the war, in their own countries, they too had believed in Goebbels' filmed phalanxes demonstrating strength, joy and unity.

Shortly before the fall of France – in June 1940 – a British consul in the United States passed to the Foreign Office a letter from an undisclosed source which had come into his hands. He knew only that it was written by 'an intelligent and educated German.' This was the reality behind the newsreels:

> Who knows the man in Germany whose life has become one deadly dangerous game of hide and seek? Who only in the night, only behind closed doors, whispers with the one or the other of his friends? Who is aware that his children may never know that he is anti, perhaps even his wife may not know too much. Who has burnt his favourite books, who has lost his best friends by emigration. Who sees how his children are educated, become young brutes. . . . Perhaps at this time he has to fight and to die for what he hates most in the world. . . . He is the most isolated, the most forgotten man in Europe. He on whom the reconstruction of Germany depends, is not known. . . . When one day as we all hope, the French and English armies will enter Berlin, to whom will they turn?[57]

One 'traitor' was executed on average every fortnight during the first two years of the war, the majority on a charge of 'espionage in the service of a foreign power', which meant having maintained contact with refugees abroad. Often the reason given was: 'Shot for offering resistance to arrest', which eliminated the need for any sort of judicial proceedings. In a letter from Sweden in 1943 to his friend Lionel Curtis in London, Helmuth von Moltke wrote of 'nineteen guillotines working at considerable speed without most people even knowing this fact, and practically nobody knows how many are beheaded per day. . . . Nobody knows the exact number of concentration camps and their inhabitants'. He himself, who had access to much unpublicised information, could not discover more exact figures.[58] A United States Survey published at the end of the war recorded that by 1944 approximately one in every 1,200 adults was arrested by the Gestapo for political or religious offences.[59]

Count von Moltke, who himself died at the hands of Hitler's executioners, wrote poignantly of the ultimate tragedy of the unknown soldier who fell on Himmler's 'internal battlefield':

> The worst is that this death is ignominious. . . . The relatives hush it up, not because there is anything to hide but because they would suffer the same fate at the hands of the Gestapo if they dared tell people what has happened. In the other countries suppressed by Hitler's tyranny even the ordinary criminal has a chance of being classified as a martyr. With us it is different: even the martyr is certain to be classed as an ordinary criminal. . . .[60]

For some, there might just be the brief memorial for a day of a poster on a Berlin hoarding: 'Condemned to death for high treason by the People's Court of Justice, X was executed this morning.'

What cannot be computed is the number of lives which were saved through the covert but effective fraternal spirit of opposition throughout the country with which people supported each other where they could. Although Nazi *apparatchiks*, whose only work was to watch other workers, were installed everywhere, even in the Civil Service much was achieved, even under their noses. The US Survey referred to above described the system. Quietly working within the confines of the machine there were elements opposing National Socialism. As far as the police were concerned, it was clear that the detective force contained substantial numbers of the old supporters of the Republic who had mainly belonged to the Social Democratic Party.

Such men might go as far as to arrange escapes for intended victims of the Gestapo by entering their names in the missing persons files, after having warned them of impending arrest. It was known to 'insiders' that there were quite active cells of this nature in government agencies, such as the Ministry of the Interior, the Ministry of Justice, the Ministry of Labour and certain courts and prosecutors' offices, not to mention local government services. Such persons could, and sometimes did, effectively sabotage Nazi law enforcement.[61]

Helmuth von Moltke, as an expert adviser on international law to the army, moved in influential circles and travelled widely. In a letter to Lionel Curtis he described how such opposition was functioning. Their achievement, he said, was to throw sand into the machine:

> The extent to which that has been done is very considerable especially in the higher bureaucracy. There is seldom a week when I do not notice something that must have been done in order to prevent a command from being executed or at least from becoming fully effective. . . .

But they were doing more than just obstruct policy:

> The Opposition is saving individual lives . . . and this is done in all walks of life. People who have been officially executed still live; others have been given sufficient warning to escape in time. This is especially so in occupied countries. . . . People will perhaps come to realise that many thousands of lives have been saved by the intervention of some Germans.[62]

Sebastian Haffner wrote of the 'strangely numerous rifts' in the 'terrifying power machine': warnings of imminent arrest; countless smuggling routes through and out of the country for news, money and men. Haffner and Moltke were telling the same story, before the war and during it, of 'a secret Germany, a shadow Germany, intangible but omnipresent.'[63] In 1939, Haffner wrote hopefully of the 'unparalleled luck' for Britain and France of the existence of the mass of 'disloyal' Germans, who could be counted in millions though unorganised, dispirited and often in despair:

> The most natural means of shortening the war and at the same time finding a solid foundation and a reliable partner for the future peace, consists today, as yesterday, in winning over and mobilising those

Germans who have the same enemy as France and England – namely, their present rulers. . . .
And their ruling political passion exactly coincides with the aim of the civilised powers; which is the overthrow and chastisement of Hitler and the Nazis at almost any price.[64]

It is remarkable that in the concentration on the struggle against Nazism those members of the 'other Germany' could look towards larger horizons. At a propaganda meeting at the Foreign Office in 1941, Eden declared that he had 'no confidence in the ability to make decent Europeans of Germans.'[65] (In years to come, others were to find the same difficulty with Eden himself.) But the former German Ambassador to Italy, Hassell, who was executed as a member of the conspiracy in 1944, declared that, for the Opposition, Europe represented neither a battlefield nor a power-base but rather a fatherland, of which a sane and strong Germany would be an indispensable part.[66]

The German Opposition was alone among resistance movements in Europe in looking ahead to the sort of world which would exist after the war. Count Helmuth von Moltke had set up the 'Kreisau Circle', a group of leading citizens drawn from the whole spectrum of political, social and religious opinion in Germany. They were the 'think tank' of the Opposition. They came together secretly at the Moltke estate at Kreisau in Silesia, to engage upon intensive discussions. In the course of these, long-established differences were resolved, strongly-held positions surrendered, and consensus arrived at for the future of Germany. Defeat was considered inevitable: to some it was even desirable as a form of expiation. Draft constitutions for the new Germany were hammered out. When liberation came the Opposition would be ready, with a government and the structure of a democratic state. But the Kreisau circle did not limit its thinking to a new political start for Germany; they were also concerned with the wider context of the Europe in which this new state would exist.

Their vision was prophetic. Europe must be resurrected in a new spirit of co-operation. They looked to a confederation, a community of nations based on rejection of nationalism, even of sovereignty. There should be a common economic policy leading to economic union. Free trade, the abolition of customs barriers and the free movement of labour would help to eliminate unemployment – a continuous element of discontent in all countries. There should be

European courts of arbitration and a governing council drawn from the member states. A European army (for the control of Europe) should be established under central leadership in which the German Army could participate. In the wider field they looked for an international forum for the whole world for the settlement of disputes, and an international currency bank.

Both before and during the war the ideas which were evolving in Opposition circles were communicated to the British by Carl Goerdeler, Adam von Trott, Helmuth von Moltke and others who had contacts they could use. However, the subsequent history of attitudes to Europe in the post-war years would seem to suggest that the British would hardly have looked with favour on these supranational concepts. And to encourage and support the Opposition would be to foster the eventual creation of a new Germany founded upon such principles.

Virtually all the members of the Kreisau Circle died on the scaffold. 'We are to be hanged,' Moltke wrote to his wife from prison, 'for thinking together.'[67]

Too late, Hitler having failed him, Chamberlain turned towards the German people and saw what Churchill had seen in 1938 – a people gripped by the neck by a tyranny bent on war. In a broadcast to Germany on 4 September 1939 he told them:

> In this war we are not fighting against you, the German people, for whom we have no bitter feelings, but against a tyrannous and forsworn régime which has betrayed not only its own people but the whole of Western Civilisation and all that you and we hold dear.[68]

It was the intention of the Government, declared the Foreign Secretary, Lord Halifax, to lay emphasis on the fact that 'this was Hitler's war'.[69] Such expressions of solidarity came too late and rang hollow. In all the years up to 1939 there had been no active opposition to Hitler in Western Europe. In those years, wrote the exile Sebastian Haffner, 'Germans experienced a physical and spiritual sense of being utterly forsaken and lost, such as no one can realise who has not felt it.'[70]

— III —

'Warnings – though Given – Were not Always Followed'

When the pre-war records are opened on the origins of the war, it will be found that the intelligence given was accurate and ample, the opinions sound, and the warnings – though given – were by no means always followed.

Lord Hankey
Former Secretary to the Cabinet

The French say: 'C'est prodigieux ce que les Anglais ignorent'. I shall content myself with saying instead that what the English do not know is far less prodigious than what they do not want to know.

Lord Vansittart
Former Head of the Foreign Office

I N November, 1944, as the Allies pushed forward towards the frontiers of the Reich, the Foreign Office received a call from 10 Downing Street. Could they recommend some reading matter on Germany for the Prime Minister? 'The PM was aware that he did not know much about Germany and was casting about in his mind for scraps of information to work on.'[1] It is arguable whether this breath-taking request was addressed to the right quarter.

When Professor Woodward, the official Foreign Office historian and member of the wartime Political Intelligence Department, was writing *The History of British Foreign Policy* in 1950, he drafted a criticism of the Foreign Office organisation which he wished to include. The Foreign Office, he complained, had lacked an Intelligence Section. No member of any Political Department was specially assigned the task of keeping himself informed about the political, social, economic and cultural conditions of that country for which his particular Department was responsible. 'Consequently,' wrote the Professor, 'the standards of knowledge of the Foreign Office were not comparable with those of the foreign department of a great newspaper.'[2] This was a formidable indictment, particularly by one who was in every respect the Foreign Office's man. It was, however, entirely justified. In the case of Central Department, the lack of such a post was crucial at a time when, in Germany, every aspect of human activity had been taken over by the State. If, from the earliest years of Hitler's emergence on the political scene, the information flowing – pouring – into the Foreign Office about the Nazi State had been collated and analysed, the existence of an anti-Nazi Opposition would have been a recognised factor. Properly assessed, its leaders 'vetted', its unique potential realised, it could have been given the strategic diplomatic support on the international scene which was essential to its success.

As late as November, 1940, a member of Churchill's own staff urged upon him the fact that 'you do not get put up to you the fullest possible intelligence about the enemy, his internal conditions, difficulties and probable courses of action.'[3]

Military intelligence, too, suffered from the effects of under-funding and lack of organisation between the wars. But the Chiefs of Staff felt that any drastic reorganisation should not be attempted 'at the moment when we are fighting for our lives.' The response of the Deputy Prime Minister, Attlee, was swift and to the point. It was precisely because we were fighting for our lives 'that we ought to do now, late though it is, what should have been done years ago.'[4]

It would indeed have astonished Attlee to know that members of the German Army were attempting to supply the British with the intelligence which their own services were failing to deliver. There were members of the anti-Nazi Opposition in the highest posts in the army. They had access to advance information of Hitler's moves (insofar as anyone could be completely sure of what Hitler would do next). By alerting the enemy they did not betray any military secrets: like Weizsäcker they would do nothing which would endanger the lives of German soldiers. Their aim was to give advance warning of aggressive acts so that preventive measures could be taken by the victims. So long as battle was not actually joined, time might be gained for the pursuit of possible peace measures and, most desirable of all, the overthrow of Hitler and the régime.

In October, 1939, General Reichenau, regarded as one of Hitler's more compliant generals, was appalled when the Führer announced to his Service Chiefs his intention to launch an attack through Belgium and the Netherlands. Reichenau considered such a move 'absolutely criminal' and with an independence of spirit which surprised many of his colleagues, he actually remonstrated directly with the Führer himself, not surprisingly without success. The only hope of averting the attack on the neutrals would be to alert the British and through them the Dutch so that visible counter-invasion preparations in those countries could be mounted (the general even suggested some himself). This would demonstrate to the German High Command that the vital element of surprise had been lost. The abandonment of the attack would defer the opening of Hitler's Western offensive and allow time, in the words of the Opposition general, Halder, to press more realistic military views and support any possibility for peace. Reichenau approached the Opposition network in the person of Carl Goerdeler, whom he knew had links with London. Goerdeler duly launched the message on its way. A contact in Hamburg alerted a businessman, Hans Robinson, in Copenhagen who had fled there from Germany after the pogrom in November, 1938. When an emissary arrived from Berlin with Reichenau's message, Robinson telephoned another refugee and Opposition contact in Stockholm, Dr Walter Jacobsen, who was on friendly terms with the British press attaché (an MI6 officer). Jacobsen was told that he must get someone from London to go to Copenhagen, as 'the British cause was much endangered'. Within hours Robinson received a telephone call, which was followed by a meeting with a mysterious Englishman which took place, at Robinson's suggestion, in the strong-room of his bank. The next day they met again and the Englishman confirmed that the message had been transmitted and that it had in fact also been received from another source. (After the war Robinson learned that it had been duplicated via Switzerland. Goerdeler was obviously taking no chances.)[5] In the event, Hitler cancelled the attack after receiving adverse reports on the weather and the state of rail transport. It was the first of no less than 28 cancellations of his attack in the West between the autumn of 1939 and the spring of 1940. Hitler's vacillations undermined the credibility of Opposition attempts to keep the Low Countries forewarned. The officer concerned in this early warning system was Colonel Oster, second-in-command to Admiral Canaris of the Abwehr, the counter-intelligence service which provided so much support to the activities of the Opposition.

Oster himself was an outstanding figure in the underground fight against Hitler, whose executioners ended his life in 1944. The Netherlands Military Attaché in Berlin, Colonel Sas, was an old and trusted friend of many years. Every time Hitler fixed a date for the attack on the Low Countries, Oster alerted Sas who then briefed his superiors; but the constant changes of plan by the German warlord not unnaturally damaged Sas's reputation as a source of reliable intelligence.[6] Nevertheless he persisted. No-one in Germany could ever tell whether an announcement by the Supreme Commander was a false alarm. His final desperate message was sent only hours before the German Army crossed the Dutch border – to find bridges over the Meuse still unblown.

In March 1940, Hitler, turning away from the West, launched a new adventure to the North: the invasion of Norway and Denmark. The General Staff did not conceal their opposition to what they declared to be a 'lunatic venture'. In the event, the OKH had little to do with the enterprise, which was masterminded by the OKW, Hitler's own staff as Supreme Commander of all the Services. The Opposition perceived that Hitler's plan could be aborted by a British display of naval strength if the British Fleet moved purposefully eastwards as the German invasion was launched. The expected failure of the expedition – Hitler's own brainchild – would damage his prestige both at home and abroad and advance the possibility of successfully overthrowing him. But the British naval movement would have to be made at the right psychological moment and timely intelligence was essential. As soon as the Opposition were sure of the date – 9 April – it was Oster's task to pass the crucial intelligence to the British through his contact in neutral Holland, his friend Colonel Sas. Sas hastened to pass the information by ciphered telegram to The Hague for transmission to British Intelligence. The message never reached Britain.[7]

The root of the tragic failure of this heroic attempt to undo Hitler's plans lay in a bumbling adventure by the British Secret Service. Even at the time the Second World War broke out, a romantic and chauvinistic aura with hints of outposts of Empire still hung about the Service, much fostered between the wars by such writers as John Buchan and E. Phillips Oppenheim. A Cambridge don wrote a serious memorandum to the Foreign Office Political Warfare Department claiming that 'there was no limit to the credulity of the Germans about the insidious power of the British Secret Service.' For instance, it had long been believed that the death and funeral of T. E. Lawrence were merely cover for his real movements on some secret mission:

> The Germans expect that kind of thing from us and it would probably be child's play to start the rumour today that Lawrence was still alive and suitably disguised, travelling about Germany – even perhaps, sitting in at Nazi councils. . . .[8]

There were Buchan-style freebooters such as Claude Dansey running their own show within the service. But authority for the disastrous 'Venlo affair' came from the very top. The historian Wheeler-Bennett was to claim that the British could be 'exonerated from all but perhaps a little impetuosity and naïveté' (terms hardly exonerating when applied to the government and the Secret Service).[9] The British, having set their faces against talking to the German Opposition when there was a chance of eliminating Hitler and circumventing the war, now embarked upon what was to be a calamitous charade. A German agent, established for some years in Holland, had succeeded in gaining the confidence of the British Secret Service. He persuaded them that he was in close contact with Opposition elements in the highest circles of the Wehrmacht. The Secret Service, under the supervision of the Foreign Office, activated two agents in the Hague to meet representatives of these circles in neutral Holland. Sigismund Payne Best had been in intelligence in the First World War and had been running a business in Holland since 1916. Major R. H. Stevens, newly arrived in the country, had spent most of his regular army service in India. Best himself expressed some reservations but was overruled. Dutch Intelligence assigned an officer to the operation to ensure that arrangements went smoothly and four meetings took place in October and November, 1939. The interest on the British side was to seek a basis for peace acceptable to themselves and to those in Germany who might come to power after overthrowing Hitler and his régime. Chamberlain and Halifax personally approved the questions and answers drafted by the Foreign Office. But the 'Opposition' officers were in fact Gestapo agents. According to evidence after the war by Captain Schellenberg who masterminded the operation, the aim on the German side was to gather information on the work and methods of British intelligence in Holland, particularly with regard to activity directed against Luftwaffe bases in the West. The Gestapo agents were aware that Best and Stevens were acting under supervision from the highest quarters. An 'Opposition' officer was present on one occasion when Stevens was informed by telephone that the head of the Secret Service, Admiral Sinclair, and the Foreign Secretary, Lord Halifax, approved the course of the negotiations. Schellenberg was ostensibly reporting back to Opposition leaders in Germany and obtaining their response to British proposals. When the British asked to see a high-ranking officer, Schellenberg roped in an old friend, a member of the Army

Medical Corps, who could 'presentably' act the part. Radio equipment and secret codes were exchanged to ensure safe and speedy communication.

The affair came to a sudden end when, at a meeting at Venlo on the Dutch-German border, the Gestapo unmasked themselves. The British agents were swiftly abducted across the frontier (the Dutch officer was shot). But Schellenberg himself had been taken by surprise by the turn of events. On 8th November he had been telephoned by Himmler, with whom he had had no previous contact. He was told that the two British would be apprehended by a special military unit at the meeting the following day. Then came the explanation. There had been an attempt on Hitler's life in a Munich beer cellar. The British agents were to be taken alive, said Himmler, to provide evidence that the attack had been the work of the British government. Their photographs duly appeared in the German press, together with those of the former and current heads of the Secret Service – Sinclair and Menzies. Best and Stevens spent the remainder of the war in a German prison. The Venlo affair provided Hitler with another advantage. He was able to cite Dutch complicity with British Intelligence as a breach of neutrality and thereby to 'justify' his attack on the Netherlands in May, 1940.[10]

For the Opposition itself, alas, the ill-starred British adventure was to have serious and long-lasting consequences. In putting forward to the British Government the proposals which the Opposition had consistently stood by, and then revealing themselves as the Gestapo, the pseudo-generals had ensured that the real Opposition would henceforward be suspected of being Nazi agents. At least the doubt had been planted: nobody would ever be quite sure. The Venlo affair would undermine the credibility of any approaches which the Opposition might make to foreign governments.

A Parliamentary Commission of Inquiry was held in the Netherlands after the war, but, extraordinarily, neither Payne Best nor Stevens gave evidence. Van Kleffens, who had been Prime Minister of the government-in-exile in London during the war, was requested by the Commission to call them as witnesses but he 'thought it might cause difficulties'. General Fabius testified that the Prime Minister at the time, De Geer, had given orders in writing that no further contacts were to be had with the agents of foreign powers.[11] This order effectively closed off the possibility of Colonel Oster's message to his friend Colonel Sas in Holland. And it is almost certainly the reason why the message from Germany giving the date of Hitler's invasion of Norway was never passed on to the British. The chain had been broken. Deprived of the assistance of the Abwehr, the British were left with their own intelligence services. The assault on Norway took them, of course, completely by surprise.[12]

It was through a German general that an account of a dramatic event came into the possession of the Foreign Office. On 22 August 1939, the very day on which Ribbentrop was travelling to Moscow to sign the Nazi-Soviet Pact, Hitler called the heads of his fighting forces to his retreat in Obersalzburg to hear the plans which he was now free to implement. His excitement with the success of his Russian ploy inflamed his rhetoric. He announced not only the imminence of the attack on Poland but the 'provocation' which would be staged to launch it and the barbarism with which the campaign would be conducted. The decision to invade Poland, the Führer told his audience, had been taken in the spring. The Four Year Plan had failed, a long war was impossible – 'we are at the end of our strength if we do not achieve victory. . . . I have given the command and I shall shoot anyone who utters a word of criticism'. The aim of war was not territory but the extermination of the opponent. 'Our strength lies in our quickness and our brutality.' Genghis Khan had light-heartedly sent millions of women and children to their deaths and history only saw him as a statesman. 'I have put my death's-head formations in place with the command relentlessly and without compassion to put to death women and children of Polish origin.' Hitler's only fear was that 'Chamberlain or some other pig of a fellow' would come up with some proposals at the last moment. He would be kicked downstairs and Hitler would personally trample upon him before the eyes of the photographers. Munich had shown Chamberlain and Daladier to be poor worms who would be too cowardly to attack. As for Russia: 'Stalin and I are the only ones who visualise the future. So in a few weeks hence I shall stretch out my hand to Stalin at the common German-Russian frontier and with him undertake to re-distribute the world.' Hitler told his generals: 'Ribbentrop has orders to make every offer and to accept every demand.' And why not – in due course the fate of Russia was to be exactly the same as that of Poland. 'Then there will be the dawn of German rule of the earth.' Hitler concluded on a rousing note:

Be hard, be without mercy, act more quickly and brutally than the others. The citizens of Western Europe must tremble with horror.

An addition at the end of this surreptitious report recorded the fact that Goering had jumped up on a table applauding enthusiastically and had endorsed his leader's address in 'bloodthirsty' terms.[13]

Admiral Canaris, Head of the Abwehr, was present at the conference and – although note-taking was forbidden – managed to make a record of Hitler's speech. The following day he read salient passages to some of his horrified fellow-conspirators. A copy was added to the cache of incriminating Nazi documents which the Opposition was assembling for future revelation to the nation when Hitler was overthrown. But it was agreed that some impression of the speech must be made known at once to the Western Powers and indeed the world, as proof both of Hitler's declared aggressive intentions and his demonic personality.[14] Other senior officers had also taken notes, including General Halder, who had masterminded the frustrated *putsch* of September, 1938. General Beck, the leading figure of the Opposition, was provided with a copy. He had not been present at the conference, having been dismissed as Chief of Staff for opposing the attack on Czechoslovakia. Beck passed it to Herman Maass, a Socialist whose task was to keep contact with the military Opposition. Maass took it to the American journalist Louis Lochner, head of the Berlin Bureau of the Associated Press, who was a close confidant of Hitler's opponents. He in turn took it to the American Embassy. There the Chargé d'Affaires refused to accept it, saying that it was 'dynamite' (this was just at the time when President Roosevelt was appealing to Hitler to consider a peaceful solution to the crisis). Lochner then pressed on to the British Embassy where he handed the paper to the Chargé d'Affaires there, Sir George Ogilvie Forbes. Forbes wrote across the top of the document: 'Communicated to Counsellor, Berlin, by a reputable journalist, August 25th, 1939' and sent it by bag to London with an accompanying memorandum:

The Ambassador has seen the enclosed which was communicated to me by Lochner of the Associated Press of America. His informant is a staff officer who received it from one of the Generals present, who is alleged to have been horrified at what he heard and to have hoped for the curbing of a maniac.

If the Americans considered the document 'dynamite', the British certainly did not. The imminent assault on Poland; the planned duplicity of the 'provocation' in Silesia and the ghastly fate in store for the Polish people, made no impression in Whitehall. Sir Alexander Cadogan made a laconic note: 'I mentioned it at lunch. Sir Nevile Henderson [in London for the Cabinet Meeting on the 25th] had a copy. I am not sure whether he showed it to the Prime Minister or the Secretary of State or not'. Cadogan was evidently not sufficiently interested to enquire. Furthermore the transmission of the document through a succession of 'Opposition' and American hands would not have recommended it to the consideration of the Foreign Office.[15]

Yet the report of Hitler's address to his generals at the Berghof on 22 August 1939 was declared at Nuremberg to be one of the four key documents proving conspiracy to wage aggressive war and crimes against humanity. The Prosecution were alerted to the fact of the Berghof Conference by the document which had come into the possession of the British Foreign Office at the time. This was described by the Prosecution as having 'come into our possession through the medium of an American newspaperman and purported to be the original minutes of this meeting at Obersalzburg. It was transmitted to this newspaperman by some other person.' The precise circumstances, and the date, of its receipt in 1939 were not stated. The document (795-PS) was not produced in Court, explained the Prosecution, because they had no proof of the actual delivery to the intermediary by the person who took the notes. (This of course could easily have been ascertained from Louis Lochner. Secrecy was no longer necessary: Maass was executed in 1944 in the aftermath of the July Plot.) 'The document merely served to alert our Prosecution to see if it could find something better,' claimed the Prosecution. It then proceeded to submit two further, similar documents (798-PS and 1014-PS) which they claimed to have turned up in captured OKW files in Flensburg. The President of the Tribunal asked whether there was any indication of where the speech took place. Counsel admitted that this only existed on the original (British) document, which was not being offered in evidence. However, he brushed this difficulty aside, saying that it was the time that was important not the place. The President raised no objection.[16]

Although the investigators were unable to supply the defence with details of the files in which the second two documents had been discovered, or the name of any officer mentioned therein, they were admitted as evidence as they were *captured* documents. The British version was withdrawn as being of 'doubtful origin'.[17] It was of course the only document whose origin was not only undoubted but was recorded in the files of the Foreign Office of one of the Allied powers. Testimony that it had been received as it were hot from the conference would have been powerful and unassailable evidence that such an event had taken place. But this would have meant disclosing its history and the fact that it had been in the hands of the Foreign Office a week before the invasion of Poland. It was not a story which the British Government cared to lay before the world. The Tribunal was happy to accept the unauthenticated version in its stead. The original document still exists in the Foreign Office files. It bears signs of haste in the translation and typing which suggest a journalist in a hurry.[18] (In *The Nemesis of Power*, Wheeler-Bennett wrongly states that this document was a copy of official minutes taken by Hitler's adjutant, Colonel Schmundt. No such minutes were ever taken.)[19]

Among all those who read – or at least saw – that document in August, 1939: the Head of the Foreign Office, the Adviser on German Affairs, the British Ambassador, the Chargé d'Affaires at the Embassy and, almost certainly, the Foreign Secretary, there was no-one able to perceive that it contained an item of intelligence which could have been turned against Hitler at the eleventh hour. Hitler had told his generals that the date for the attack on Poland was 26th August. The report was in British hands on the 25th.

Hitler was deeply concerned to present Germany as sinned against and not sinning. His naked aggression had to be covered up, not just in the world's eyes but also before his own people. He was repeatedly told in 1938 by his generals that the people did not want war and at the time of the Czech crisis had been able to see this for himself. He had to have the nation behind him if he were to prosecute a successful war and maintain his own prestige.

At a conference with his generals in summer 1938, the Führer had stipulated that a 'pre-requisite' for invasion was a manufactured incident 'through which Germany has been unbearably provoked and in the face of which Germany can justify military action. . . ."[20] A year later, as the document in British hands revealed, the Führer had told his generals that he had arranged the 'provocation' which would 'justify' the invasion of Poland. The plan was an assault on the radio station in the German border town of Gleiwitz in Upper Silesia. The SS were to do the shooting and condemned criminals from concentration camps (supplied by the Gestapo) would be left dead on the field, *in Polish uniforms*.[21] If the Western press had splashed all over its front pages on 26th August the revelation of the planned Silesian masquerade, it is arguable that events would have been paralysed. Hitler himself had told Ciano, the Duce's Foreign Minister (as the British knew), that 1st September was the ultimate possible date for launching an attack in Eastern Europe. It would have been physically impossible to 'manufacture', in time, a new 'provocation'.

To have deduced and seized upon this psychological advantage which had come into their hands did not enter Foreign Office thinking. The Adviser on German Affairs, Kirkpatrick, merely confined himself to underlining what he called 'characteristic passages' – the more lurid of Hitler's declamations.[22]

After the war Samuel Hoare (Viscount Templewood), a member of Chamberlain's Inner Cabinet, dared to assert in his memoirs:

> Very little military intelligence slipped through to us from the German side. Now, as a result of the publication of German secret papers, we know that Hitler was constantly planning acts of aggression.[23]

The perspicacious Sir Horace Rumbold had early realised the danger of a lack of authentic information from inside the Third Reich reaching the outside world. In 1933, after Hitler had been Chancellor for only three months, the Ambassador had warned: 'Germany's neighbours have reason to be vigilant. . . . I foresee that as time elapses it will be increasingly difficult to ascertain what is actually taking place in this country and to gauge the real intentions of the German government.'[24] One man who passionately shared this concern was Sir Robert Vansittart. Any hope which the former Head of the Foreign Office might have entertained that a change of Foreign Secretary might end his total exile from the field of policy-making was not fulfilled when Halifax succeeded Eden. But in one area Sir Robert was free to pursue his activities – probably because his masters were not interested in them. As Head of the Office he had also been Head of the Secret Service. As the Nazi menace became more and more palpable so Vansittart became more concerned about the failure of official sources to provide authentic information which would contradict the picture of Nazi Germany put out by Goebbels. It was impossible to build a sound foreign policy on deficient intelligence. Impatient of – and alarmed by – this intelligence vacuum, he had set about filling it himself.

On 8 December 1937, as he was on the point of being axed as Permanent Under-Secretary, a rather Gothic tale about Vansittart's role appeared in the Italian newspaper *Il Popolo* under the title: '*The Secret Master of the Foreign Office*'. The writer claimed that, although the public assumed that the foreign policy of Britain was directed by the Foreign Secretary, the elegant Captain Eden, all the chancelleries of the world knew otherwise. Eden was just a figurehead and spokesman for 'the most mysterious man in Europe who, together with the Duce and Hitler, is said to exercise the greatest influence on European politics'. This influence, it appeared, was rooted in the intelligence service which for 20 years he had been directing – from behind the scenes – on delicate missions, or more correctly espionage, in the various continents. He was 'the only member of the government' [sic] who could see the numerous dossiers of secret information sent from every part of the world. 'The Prime Minister and Mr Eden,' concluded the article, 'have to content themselves with such information as Sir Vansittart sees fit to supply.' This somewhat Machiavellian portrait of Vansittart did have some authentic touches: the overshadowing of Eden which was eventually to contribute to his downfall; and the network of private intelligence sources which he controlled. However, the writer was mistaken in believing that the Head of the Foreign Office kept his masters short of information. On the contrary, he was continually pressing it upon them. But there are none so deaf as those who will not hear. Sir Horace Rumbold's despatches from Berlin were first-class but neither they nor those of his successor, Sir Eric Phipps, were receiving the attention they merited. And with the arrival of Sir Nevile Henderson at the Embassy, even that reliable source dried up. The Berlin Embassy was now, minuted Vansittart, 'so close to the régime that it has not its ear close enough to the ground to pick up the informed murmurings of the malcontents. Yet there are plenty in high places, if they can be tapped. . . .'[25] One of those in high places with whom Vansittart had established a valuable relationship while still Head of the Foreign Office was Dr Carl Goerdeler. A former mayor of Leipzig, who had resigned as a public gesture against Nazi anti-Semitism which had demanded the removal of the statue of Mendelssohn from a public place, he was also ex-Price Commissioner of the Reich, and still had access to many important figures in the sphere of finance, industry and economics. His status enabled him to travel widely abroad, where he was able to make contact with leading personalities. Above all, he was the leading figure on the civilian side of the anti-Hitler Opposition. Vansittart described him to Eden, the Foreign Secretary, as 'impressive, wise and weighty.'

A coincidence of events in the summer of 1937 demonstrates the greater weight given in the Foreign Office to the views of an 'insider' of Central Department after a single visit to Germany, as against the urgent advice of this highly-placed German economic expert and known opponent of the Nazi régime. In July Mr Gladwyn Jebb attended an International Congress of Chambers of Commerce in Berlin. On his return, he wrote up his impression for the Department. He had, he said, talked to 'Embassy staff, consuls, Reichsbank officials, Jewish bankers, journalists, diplomats, businessmen and quite unknown persons in provincial pubs. . . . I believe I have enough background against which to form impressions which may not be entirely misleading'. With regard to Hitler himself, Jebb's conclusion was that 'the best to be hoped for is that the side which wins the next *Bludbad* should immure him in Berchtesgaden as a living Buddha. Or is there a faint hope that he may get absorbed in his plans for re-building Berlin and Munich, producing the Volkswagen, etc.' Jebb then offered his advice on the best course of future policy:

> I believe and hope that we shall adopt no very definite attitude, but deal with each individual crisis as it arises in the hope of finding the middle way. . . . The right way to deal with the Germans, it seems to me, is to keep them guessing and treat them well, especially Goering. . . .

This effusion was received in the Office with acclaim, not least for its style. Strang, Head of the Department, minuted: 'An admirable piece of work. Mr Jebb has contributed something to our knowledge, much to our entertainment, and I think his conclusion is wise.'[26] In that same month of July, Goerdeler had called upon Vansittart, who submitted a lengthy account to Eden of what he had learned from his German visitor. Goerdeler had imparted much detailed valuable information about the serious difficulties of the German war economy – problems which could affect the issue of peace or war. Vansittart reported that Goerdeler had also offered some direct and heartfelt advice to the British:

> He said he wished to impress on any his words might reach, with the greatest earnestness, that the worst disservice we in this country could do to Germany and to ourselves was to base our treatment of her on illusory hopes and false premises. . . . The most helpful thing you can do, (he said), 'is to get at the true facts, so far as ever you can; base your dealings with Germany and your policy on a clear realisation of them; let that policy be firm and clear; and above all, let the world and Germany see that you know the truth by stating it as best you can'.[27]

Here were two reports on Germany in total contradiction. On the one hand was the recommendation of the Foreign Office 'amateur' to adopt no very definite attitude, keep Germany guessing and be nice to Goering. On the other was the advice of the German to have a firm, clear policy on the facts, and to let the world know about it. The Department recommended that Jebb's report should be sent to the Prime Minister: Goerdeler's advice did not get further than the Foreign Secretary, who suppressed it.

Vansittart did have one opportunity of doing some intelligence work on his own account inside Germany. He spent a fortnight in Berlin at the time of the Olympic Games in 1936. His wife was deputising for her sister, Lady Phipps, the Ambassador's wife, who was indisposed. Vansittart managed to meet most of the Nazi leaders. But he also managed to talk secretly to some of those in high places who opposed the régime. According to Lady Vansittart, these meetings took place in the Embassy bathroom – the only place which her husband felt was sufficiently secure.[28]

In the face of the inadequacies of official sources, therefore, Vansittart at an early stage set about establishing his own lines of communication on the grounds that forewarned was forearmed. In his autobiography he wrote of the 'brave men' in Germany, who knew that he at least realised the danger, and who felt that 'if they fed me with sufficient evidence I might have influence enough to arouse our Government and so to stop it. Of course they were wrong, but we tried.'[29] Lady Vansittart remembered clandestine visitors at Denham

Place, their country house: comings and goings of 'men in raincoats' about whose identity she never enquired.[30] But Vansittart's most important 'agent' was without a doubt Group Captain Malcolm Christie. He had been educated in Germany, had graduated as an engineer there before the First World War and had served in the RFC and the RAF between 1914 and 1930. He had been Air Attaché at the Embassy in Washington from 1922–1926 and at the Embassy in Berlin from 1927–1930, when he had retired through ill-health. What Christie had observed during his years of service in Berlin had convinced him, even at that early date, of the impending danger to other countries of the advent of Hitler. Like Ambassador Rumbold, he saw the Nazi threat extending beyond the borders of Germany and its own enslaved people. When he retired, therefore, he decided to put his intimate knowledge of Germany to good use by monitoring the course of events as the Nazi régime established itself. He had unique qualifications for his self-imposed task. He was independent. He had private means: 'The government has had my services for the last six years and I have never taken a penny for it,' he wrote to Vansittart in 1938.[31] He was self-motivated, driven by his anxiety to keep Britain alert to the march of events which he, like Ambassador Rumbold under whom he had served, foresaw with such accuracy. He spent over half of each year travelling in Germany, Austria, Czechoslovakia and other European countries where through his engineering interests he had many contacts. Most of his sources were friends or personal acquaintances of many years' standing, from school and university days. Some had become Nazis. Many occupied high positions in industry, labour, finance, public service, the Foreign Office and the upper reaches of the Services.

In a memorandum to the Foreign Secretary Vansittart listed some of the well-known names of heavy industry with whom Christie had close contact: Krupps, Thyssens, Voglers, Potts, Kirdorfs.[32] All Christie's friends talked to him without reserve, though many of the anti-Nazis knew to what use he would put their information. As Vansittart wrote of the Opposition: 'They would never have worked for a foreign intelligence but they hoped to serve Europe by revealing the German conspiracy.'[33]

How valuable Christie was as a source of intelligence had already been established as early as 1932. A Foreign Office minute records: 'Group Capt. Christie has exceptional opportunities for gauging certain elements of German opinion. He is in close touch with Wilhelm-strasse, Reichswehr and Nazi circles. He has just returned from Germany where he has seen Goering and other Nazi leaders.'[34] In the same year, the Foreign Office gave him a glowing reference when supporting him as a candidate for the Presidency of the Governing Commission of the Saar. Group Captain Christie had 'unrivalled knowledge' of political and economic conditions in Germany: 'From time to time he has provided Central Department privately with reports about the trend of events in Central and South-Eastern Europe which have proved most useful in supplementing our knowledge from official sources.'[35] By 1934 Christie was reporting directly to the Head of the Foreign Office, having found in Vansittart someone who saw eye to eye with him on the Nazi menace and on whose discretion as to his sources he could abso-lutely rely. Christie's most outstanding source was Goering, whom he had known since 1931 when he was a member of the Reichstag, and with whom he had built up a close acquaintance over the years. The General would invite Christie to his house for long conversations. These could last two or three hours, during which Goering would unburden himself not only of his worries about the Reich and its economic problems, but also of attitudes towards Britain and the trend of foreign policy. The substance of these talks was duly reported to Vansittart. It was a penetration of the inner counsels of the Nazi Party beyond the wildest dreams of any secret service agent.

Christie sent the Foreign Office a formidable amount of intelli-gence. He could report not only upon what was happening inside Germany; but also upon what was going to happen. Yet such price-less intelligence was largely ignored or discounted, almost certainly because it came through Vansittart. The latter recounted in his memoirs the subterfuge he was obliged to adopt to force urgent and vital information to the attention of the Government. One of Christie's most important sources was a friend in the German Air Ministry, from whom he was able to obtain the German Air Esti-mates and particulars of aircraft construction during pre-war years. Sir Robert, realising that the information would not be given proper consideration, because he himself was, as he said, 'tarred as an alarm-ist', arranged with his old friend Maurice Hankey, Secretary of the Cabinet and of the Committee of Imperial Defence, that *he* should pass the figures privately to the Air Ministry. But Vansittart refused absolutely to indicate the identity of the German informant 'in justice to a courageous man. . . . Informants died slow and horrible deaths if detected.'[36] On a memorandum by Vansittart, relaying information from one of Christie's informants, Cresswell of Central Department minuted: 'Sir Robert Vansittart's correspondent is evidently violently anti-Nazi and with such people the wish, and frequently the fear, is apt to be father to the thought.'[37] 'Such people' had little hope of penetrating the closed minds inside the Foreign Office.

Christie's efforts were reinforced at the beginning of the critical year of 1938 by the addition to Vansittart's 'team' of Professor Philip Conwell-Evans. He too had access to one of the men at the top in Nazi Germany – Ribbentrop. During a spell of teaching at Königsberg University, about a year and a half before Hitler came to power, Conwell-Evans had formed strong links with Germany and had become an ardent advocate of Anglo-German friendship. After his return to Britain he became honorary secretary of the newly-formed Anglo-German Fellowship, set up by Ribbentrop in 1934 to replace the existing Anglo-German Association. The latter had been formed to cultivate relations between the two countries at the time of the Weimar Republic and counted many distinguished figures among its members (most of whom did not transfer their membership to the new organisation).

Conwell-Evans' work for Anglo-German friendship brought him into close and amicable association with Ribbentrop. The importance of this association to Ribbentrop himself is indicated by a surviving handwritten note to Hitler. He told the Führer that on the occasion of a recent visit by Conwell-Evans, he had invoked his assistance as a go-between in an attempt to persuade Ramsay MacDonald to visit Berlin – 'MacDonald is our most important ally in the Cabinet'. He had also urged his British friend to press Germany's case for rearmament both on sea and in the air. Conwell-Evans did in fact discuss Ribbentrop's proposals with Ramsay MacDonald, who, Ribbentrop told Hitler, had been 'very interested.'[38] But the professor was not in any sense Ribbentrop's 'agent' (as another Englishman, E. W. Tennant, was described in the same memorandum). At the time he genuinely believed in the cause of Anglo-German friendship, the sincerity of Ribbentrop and the good intentions of the Führer. When Ribbentrop took over the London Embassy in 1936 he found Conwell-Evans more than ever useful as a confidential adviser. The Ambassador was rather short of British friends. However, Ribbentrop had brought with him as First Secretary Erich Kordt, a friend of Conwell-Evans from his German days. Kordt, a key figure in the Opposition inside the Foreign Office, soon opened his friend's eyes to the realities of the Nazi régime. With the ardour of a convert – and perhaps with a sense of personal betrayal – Conwell-Evans became a dedicated foe of Nazi Germany and put his high diplomatic contacts in the Reich at the service of the Foreign Office through Vansittart. When Ribbentrop returned to Germany to take up his post as Foreign Minister he took Erich Kordt back with him. But Erich's brother Theo replaced him in the Embassy in London and the close friendship was sustained in private. Above all, Conwell-Evans remained *persona grata* with the unsuspecting Ribbentrop to whom he always had access whenever he visited Berlin. Because of his work for the Nazi-sponsored Anglo-German Fellowship he was able to travel there without exciting unwelcome attention. Even Hitler took a benevolent interest in him and invited him to receptions at the Chancellery when foreign visitors were being entertained. Meetings with friends at the Foreign Ministry were open and sociable, although in fact most of them were members of the Opposition. They, like Christie's friends, were anxious that he should take information back to London which would leave the Government there under no misapprehension about Hitler's policies. Conwell-Evans went even further than gathering intelligence. He made a practical contribution to the underground battle against Hitler by making his flat in Cornwall Gardens, Kensington, available as a 'safe house' where Opposition diplomats visiting London could pass information and warnings to members of the British Foreign Office. Another, more public, rendezvous for discreet exchanges was the Travellers' Club of which both Christie and Conwell-Evans were members.

How intimate Conwell-Evans' connection with Ribbentrop was is indicated in a report he made to Vansittart in February, 1939 on return from a visit to Berlin. He had lunched with the Foreign Minister in his private room at the Ministry. Ribbentrop 'had ranted most of the time, raising his voice at certain moments to an embarrassing degree.' When therefore Conwell-Evans brought back information about Hitler's plans for Czechoslovakia there was every reason to take it seriously:

From first-hand knowledge I can state that the German Chancellor has decided to complete the plan of last September which was frustrated by the intervention of Mr Chamberlain, namely the complete incorporation within the Reich of Bohemia and part of Moravia. He will apply the familiar method of creating unrest by stirring up factitious claims for self-determination, this time on the part of the Slovaks. The Czechs will naturally resist this attempt at a second partition of their country. Hitler will then be furnished with a pretext to intervene by military force and will end by wiping out Czechoslovakia as an independent State.[39]

A despatch from Christie, almost at the same time, virtually repeated what Conwell-Evans had said. This confirmation was based on a letter he had received 'from a very reliable source in touch with the German Staff.'[40] Time was to prove both reports absolutely accurate.

The reaction of Cadogan, now Head of the Foreign Office, to this high-level intelligence was to complain that 'Our sources of information have lately become so prolific (and blood-curdling) that I am beginning to regard them all with a degree of suspicion.'[41] His attitude had not changed some three weeks later when the head of MI5 'came to raise my hair with tales of Germany going into Czechoslovakia in the next 48 hours. . . . This can wait.'[42] On the eve of the German entry into Prague, by which time he was receiving 'all sorts of reports' of the imminence of the event, he summed up the whole affair: 'Question is one of saving our faces. This can be done with least loss of prestige after the event, by registering disgust.'[43] Vansittart, he noted, 'was in a neurotic state.' No wonder! In the House of Commons on 13th April, Churchill expressed his astonishment that the Government could have been so taken by surprise. 'The whole time-table was laid down. The whole programme was known beforehand.'[44] Sir John Simon, Chancellor of the Exchequer and a member of Chamberlain's Inner Cabinet, tried to cover up for the Government with a suggestion of much beavering away at conflicting intelligence reports:

What had to be remembered is that we do not get one set of information saying that one thing is likely to happen, but we get a whole series of messages stating all sorts of alternative developments, which have to be sifted out. After the facts are known it is easy to assume that the course of events was equally clear and certain beforehand.[45]

This ready equivocation about careful 'sifting' of intelligence is disproved by many a dismissive Foreign Office minute.

Some weeks after Munich, Vansittart sent a despairing memorandum to the Foreign Secretary accompanying a collection of reports 'derived from various first-class sources in Germany.' They were in fact almost all based on Christie's and Conwell-Evans' material. Vansittart pleaded for their consideration by the Cabinet. These sources had proved so invariably correct, particularly during the recent crisis, he pointed out to the Foreign Secretary, that he wished that their substance was known to some at least of his colleagues 'for I feel that there is still a great amount of very dangerous delusion as to the real projects of the ruling gang.'[46] The proven accuracy of the information from Vansittart's informants during the Czech crisis had indeed brought about a change of heart in Halifax towards secret reports from Germany. When in January the following year, Vansittart passed Halifax a considerable body of material from his two informants, the Foreign Secretary presented it at a meeting of the Foreign Policy Committee at which the Prime Minister was in the chair. He drew the attention of his colleagues to the fact that these reports were from the same sources whose information in the previous summer and autumn 'had so unhappily proved, on the whole, accurate and correct. In these circumstances he did not think that it would be right to neglect this information and the warnings embodied in it.'[47] But this cut no ice with the Prime Minister. The disdain with which Chamberlain dismissed the Christie-Conwell-Evans early warning system can be discerned in a speech he made to the House of Commons shortly after that meeting of the Foreign Policy Committee. 'Perhaps it would not be a bad thing,' he told the House, on 22 February 1939, 'if we ourselves were to show a little more confidence and not allow ourselves to believe any tale that comes to us about the aggressive intentions of others.'

That Christie and Conwell-Evans were bitterly aware of the way in which their warnings went unheeded is implicit in the title of the book on which they collaborated: *None So Blind*. The book had a curious history. After the outbreak of war, Conwell-Evans discovered that Christie was beginning to destroy his papers. He restrained him, feeling that they contained matters of considerable historical interest. With Christie's permission he edited a selection of the reports into a book, relating them to the passage of events of the period. He also included some of the material with which he himself had provided the Foreign Office. Both Christie and Conwell-Evans had complete confidence in Vansittart. Certainly it can be proved that Vansittart played his part to the hilt. He was scrupulous in not attributing to Christie by name reports which were printed for Cabinet circulation but their authorship can be authenticated in many cases by comparing these with the text of *None So Blind*. Although some were edited by Vansittart himself into digests, many match word for word. But far more of the reports can be read in the book than have survived in the Foreign Office files. These, too, are only a selection but it is sufficient to indicate the extraordinary quality of the intelligence which Christie was passing to Whitehall.

Conwell-Evans completed the book in 1941 but both men agreed that, as the Foreword states, 'it would not be helpful to raise during the war issues that might be contentious.' In 1947 *None So Blind* was printed privately in a limited edition of 100 copies. Christie drew up a distribution list which included senior British, Canadian and American universities; certain major libraries and historical institutions; a selection of leading British newspapers, and personal friends.[48] But *None So Blind* did not see the light of day until twenty-five years later, in the early 1970s, when both its authors were dead. Somebody, somewhere, must have embargoed the book. And yet Christie, as a former diplomat, would have been well aware of avoiding contravention of the Official Secrets Act. The material in the book was their own. They had not been paid by the Crown to collect it but had done so voluntarily for patriotic reasons. They had quoted no official documents. They made no reference to Foreign Office activities and attitudes, of which they knew nothing. Their criticism of the failure to follow-up their intelligence was not based on any inside knowledge but was deduced from the march of events.

One can see that the publication of such a book would have filled the Foreign Office with horror. Not only did it relate the specific warnings which were given of such events as the reoccupation of the Rhineland; the Austrian *Anschluss*; the Sudeten crisis; the rape of Czechoslovakia; the Nazi-Soviet Pact and the form of the attack on Poland. In addition there were tables of intelligence on German air strength in 1935 and 1937. Together with general political and economic reports there was the material arising out of the personal relationship with Goering and Ribbentrop. And the Foreword did state that before 1934 Christie had sent his reports to 'friends in the

Foreign Office' and from that date onwards direct to Vansittart, 'a friend on whose discreet silence he could entirely rely, and one whose brilliant and unconventional mind was quickly responsive and sympathetic. . . .' And yet the book was not written in any spirit as an *exposé* or an attack on the Prime Ministers and Foreign Secretaries who had held office during the period from 1930–1939. It was intended as a contribution to contemporary history, provided at Christie's own expense and destined for institutions of learning or serious periodicals. These numbered less than half of the distribution list. Because the book is not easily accessible, Christie's unique contribution to British intelligence is accorded only the briefest mention by writers who have probably not read it, or have not made the connection between what appears in it and relevant documents in Foreign Office files. In view of the attempts, as will be seen, inside the Foreign Office to re-write the history of the period for public consumption, interference with the publication of *None So Blind* would not be surprising. That there was some kind of delaying action is indicated by the fact that as late as 1965 Christie (who was in poor health and evidently expected to pre-decease his friend and collaborator) made an arrangement whereby a sum of money should be paid from his estate to Conwell-Evans (or in default to a relative of his) to defray the cost of distributing the book. It was obviously taken for granted that this would one day happen. In the event, Conwell-Evans died first – in 1968 – and Christie three years later. The lady who inherited the task of distributing the book according to Christie's wishes, and who knew nothing about its contents, recalls that she had considerable trouble getting the bank which was acting as executor to release the copies. Christie bequeathed his papers to his housekeeper of thirty years and they eventually passed to the archives of Churchill College, Cambridge. What is available there does not, alas, reflect the 'voluminous files' to which Conwell-Evans refers in his Foreword to *None So Blind*. Nor do the files of the Foreign Office, to which Christie was submitting reports at times of crisis as frequently as twice a week. Probably this was due to Vansittart protecting his sources and also to the fact that much material was officially destroyed when German invasion appeared a likely and imminent possibility in 1940.

Christie and Conwell-Evans both had close friendships within the German Foreign Office and much of the information they conveyed came from those sources. But there was also first-hand information available to London from that quarter. The line of communication between Weizsäcker, the Head of the German Foreign Office; Erich Kordt, Head of Ribbentrop's Secretariat, and Theo Kordt, Counsellor at the German Embassy in London, has already been described. Through this channel information flowed directly from the source of Nazi foreign-policy making to the British Foreign Office. They saw Vansittart as their strongest and most influential ally. Theo Kordt soon established a relationship of mutual confidence with the British diplomat and they met frequently, their first meeting in 1938 being at the instigation of Vansittart himself.[49] These encounters (authorised by Halifax, according to Vansittart and Kordt after the war) sometimes took place at Vansittart's house in Park Lane; sometimes in Kordt's residence at 7 Cadogan Place; sometimes at the Travellers' Club; even occasionally at the home of R. A. Butler, Minister of State at the Foreign Office, in whom Kordt had misplaced confidence as a 'man of peace'.[50] He did not seem to be aware that Butler's way to peace was through appeasement. But at times of crisis the rendezvous was Conwell-Evans' flat at 31 Cornwall Gardens in Kensington. Even Sir Horace Wilson, Chamberlain's closest confidant and adviser, was a visitor. Lady Vansittart, who sometimes accompanied her husband – probably to suggest a social call – remembers descending from the taxi and making the last part of the journey on foot, with many feints and diversions. Vansittart felt that he was being shadowed, although she did not know by whom.[51] (Chamberlain is reputed to have had him under surveillance because of his close association with Churchill.) Theo Kordt too has left a note of his own similar subterfuges. He never used his own car, dismissed his taxi before arriving at his destination and made sure that as far as possible meetings always took place after dark. He was well aware of the spies which the Gestapo and Ribbentrop had placed in London.[52] The Kordts' confidential secretary, Hilde Waldo, whom they had extricated from Nazi Germany and whose entry into Britain had been facilitated by Vansittart, helped to organise some of these meetings, though she was never allowed to attend. She still remembers the urgent comings and goings in Kensington.[53] The family connection ensured that contact between Berlin and London was unlikely to excite the interest of the Gestapo, although the brothers maintained a code for telephone calls, whether private or official. Sometimes 'couriers' were used. Reinhard Spitzy, a young Austrian in Ribbentrop's office who was won over to the cause by Erich Kordt, was engaged to an English girl, the daughter of a general. The British Ambassador had himself arranged a diplomatic visa for him so that he might visit her from time to time without bureaucratic complications. Erich Kordt took advantage of these circumstances to send high-level intelligence to his brother of what was being planned by their hierarchy – information which would not have come to the Embassy in the ordinary course of diplomatic business. Spitzy would memorise the information and when in London would meet Theo openly in a restaurant where he could pass the information to him. Even after the projected marriage to a foreigner had obliged Spitzy to resign from the Foreign Office and go into business he still managed the occasional mission for his friend Kordt.[54]

The courier who was least likely to fall under suspicion was the Kordts' young cousin, Susanne Simonis, who was completely in their confidence. She would memorise lengthy and detailed messages from Erich, then travel to London on family visits. Looking, as she later told an American friend, as ostentatiously German as possible and bearing baskets of 'goodies' from home, her visits were totally unremarkable. It was she who, in September 1938, brought the critical message which was transmitted by Theo Kordt to Lord Halifax at a secret meeting, which it was hoped would achieve the final solution of Hitler and the Nazi régime. An account of how the Kordts used their unique relationship with Vansittart will be given later.

It is difficult to know how much of the material pouring into the Foreign Office in the inter-war years was actually seen by the Cabinet. It certainly presented a picture of life inside the Third Reich which it would have been difficult to ignore. At least some evidence exists which reveals that it was sometimes withheld. In June, 1937 Eden's friend, the ex-diplomat Nigel Law, wrote to him on his return from a business visit to Germany. He had heard in Berlin that friendly overtures towards Germany by England were in the wind. This, he was informed both by Englishmen in Berlin and by patriotic Germans who did not like Nazism, would be a most disastrous mistake.

A member of Central Department minuted:

An earlier letter from Mr Law was shown to certain members of the Cabinet. It may be held desirable to do the same with this one and draw attention to the fact that the view expressed by Mr Law is shared by Englishmen in Berlin and by patriotic anti-Nazi Germans.

Vansittart concurred: these were the views held by Goerdeler and nearly all moderate Germans. 'I think it is very important that the Cabinet should have *this* passage at least,' he wrote. But by now Chamberlain had succeeded Baldwin as Prime Minister and Eden was less anxious to press such unappeasing recommendations upon his new chief. He minuted without enthusiasm: 'Let us circulate this letter, a little edited, for Foreign Affairs Committee.' But almost immediately he had second thoughts and the Department was informed without explanation that: 'The Secretary of State has on reconsideration decided *not* to circulate this to the Foreign Policy Committee.'[55]

A month later Eden was to withhold from the Cabinet material of infinitely greater importance than Law's unwelcome advice. It came, through the anti-Nazi Opposition, from the very heart of the war establishment in the Third Reich.

All the main enterprises in Germany not directly taken over by the State were now so dependent upon it that the slightest disturbance of confidence could – indeed must – cause the collapse of the whole German economy, as Schacht warned. The memory of the great inflation of the 1920s made any suggestion of lack of confidence in the State and the collapse of the economy a particular nightmare. At the end of 1938, Goerdeler relayed to the British Foreign Office the contents of a critical speech made by the Minister of State Dr Brinckmann to a hundred industrialists in Cologne. All the money secured through the annexation of Austria was entirely spent. The luxury and senseless expenditures in high State and Party circles were most offensive. The raw material position and the foreign trade balance had brought Germany to the verge of catastrophe. The State budget must be reduced by 6,000 million marks immediately. There must be similar cuts in the budget of the Party and new high taxation must be introduced immediately. If these measures were not implemented, Germany faced economic collapse within the next few months.[56] His audience must have shuddered at the possibility of another financial catastrophe. No doubt many of those present had been early supporters of Hitler, whom they had thought would be their puppet, and were realising too late their ghastly mistake. But most industrialists, in Schacht's opinion, were too terrified to act; and it was the view of the head of the Gestapo that 'as long as these capitalists have one mark left to lose, they will obey orders.'[57]

One articulate exception was Thyssen, the Ruhr steel magnate. In 1938 he resigned from the Prussian State Council in protest against the persecution of the Jews. He spoke in the Reichstag against the coming war and in December, 1939 left Germany for Switzerland. Thyssen offered to pass on to the British his intimate knowledge of the current state of the régime and of German industry if they would send a specialist out to see him. It was an offer, surely, to be seized with alacrity. But not by the Foreign Office. Information from Germans was never welcome. Orme Sargent minuted:

> I am inclined to distrust the facts and figures of émigrés, even when they are men of such standing and knowledge as is Thyssen. All the same, it might be worth sending an emissary to interview Thyssen.[58]

But a couple of months were allowed to pass before they did so.

The constant rejection of inside information from Germany and the preference given to that from domestic intelligence agencies was a dangerous tendency, particularly when there was conflict between the two. A clear example of this can be cited in connection with the critical subject of the state of the German railway system. In January, 1939, Vansittart received a report from Goerdeler which described the 'terrible breakdown' of the railway system which had taken place during Christmas and New Year; experts had claimed the situation was worse than in 1918. The railway companies claimed that during the last three years they had been left with no money for maintenance. All the money was taken by the Party for free transportation of members; for the building of motor roads, and for compulsory contributions to endless Party organisations.[59] A report by Conwell-Evans at about the same time corroborated this grave deterioration of the railways which he described as a striking example of the defects of totalitarian planning. Such was the breakdown of the system that it 'finds itself short of 3,000 locomotives and 30,000 coaches. Goods from Hamburg to Vienna have to go via Trieste and make use of the Italian railways.' Cadogan, Head of the Foreign

Office, minuted: 'I think it will be found that his information regarding the railway does not tally very closely with the very detailed information given us by the Industrial Intelligence Section.'[60] One's curiosity is aroused. What could the British intelligence report contain that so conflicted with the information from Germany? Indeed, the state of the German railways was so often commented upon by informants that the Industrial Intelligence report *must* have been inaccurate. But Cadogan did not recommend referring the matter back so that these conflicting reports could be tested against each other and the 'very detailed information' analysed. Certainly there is evidence here of the crying need for that central point where all intelligence would be screened and collated. Had such a post existed, its occupant might have remembered that in June, 1938 Christie had reported that Hitler had decreed that the Army should make good the defects in transport which were so clearly revealed in the invasion of Austria: the rotten condition of locomotives, rolling stock, sidings and railroads. There was also a serious lack of heavy lorries. These defects, ordered Hitler, had to be made good by 1 October 1938.[61] (This was the date Hitler had secretly announced to his generals for the invasion of Czechoslovakia.) The fact that six months later they had not been made good, in spite of Hitler's personal order, and that the transport system had deteriorated even further, should surely have made even Central Department think. How could a country go to war which could not efficiently transport its armies to its own frontiers?

The Industrial Intelligence Centre which had supplied the dubious information about the German railway system was a new creation. It had been set up when it became plain that there was a connection – and a pressing one – between economics and war. The Director, Desmond Morton, wrote: 'The real trouble is that Modern War Economics is a new subject – particularly to us English. We have somehow got to train up a new brand of State official to deal with it. . . .' But this new Service 'must spring from civilian parents. We want the belligerent rabbit, not the crocodile, the lion and the eagle in plain clothes!' Rivalry with the three Services was there from the beginning (and the Navy might not have cared to be described as a crocodile). It was the usual pattern of internal non-cooperation in British intelligence.

In January, 1938, the Military Attaché in Berlin, Colonel Mason-MacFarlane, wrote to the War Office about the paramount importance of getting the clearest possible picture of the state of the German war industries. The time could not be far off, he felt, when Hitler would feel strong enough to risk having his bluff called. Did we know from year to year exactly what state of preparedness had been reached by the Germans regarding munition production, provision of reserves, etc? Clearly not. 'We are not in a position to say at any moment that Germany's bluff is callable,' claimed Mason-MacFarlane. It was a point which was extremely well taken, even though a little late in the day. The Colonel told the War Office that he had discussed the matter with the Head of Chancery and the Finance Officer at the Embassy and they were all agreed that a full-time officer should be appointed with the sole responsibility of gathering such intelligence.

The War Office promptly took up the matter with the Industrial Intelligence Centre where Desmond Morton immediately saw the proposal as an implied reproach and an encroachment on his territory. A meeting was held between Burrows of the War Office, Morton of the IIC and Mallet of the Foreign Office, with the Department of Overseas Trade holding a watching brief. Intelligence priority was subordinated to departmental prestige. Morton, while admitting that 'our greatest need at the moment is information on *stocks* of foodstuffs, raw materials and munitions' (and he only wished the SIS were more help), did not feel that a Service Officer was capable of gathering this information. The study of the war economy was primarily a civilian task. The Foreign Office had a cost-effective attitude towards intelligence gathering. Mallet's contribution to the discussion was to find 'serious administrative difficulties' in the appointment of an officer of any ilk, 'since after his training and term of service in Germany, he would be wasted in appointments elsewhere.' In place of the high intelligence so urgently required (the lack of which the Foreign Office found merely 'disquieting') an arrangement was made which seemed mainly designed just to keep everyone quiet. It was agreed that another source of information had not been adequately tapped: German technical publications. The IIC should therefore take in a selection and study them. However, it was reckoned that the Germans produced 250 of these every week, apart from monthlies and annuals. The present IIC staff could only cope with about a dozen per week and extra staff could not be applied for until it had been established that these publications were sufficiently valuable to warrant this. The Embassy should therefore take out a three months' subscription for a selection of these and forward them to IIC. Titles should correspond roughly to such British titles as *Copper World, Aluminium Exchange, Nickel Bulletin, Tin, Scrap World*. It took no less than three whole months to arrive at this preposterous conclusion. How many more months of magazine scanning would have to elapse before Britain would be able to say, in Mason-MacFarlane's words, that Hitler's bluff was 'callable'? The letter by which Sir Orme Sargent conveyed the decision to the Embassy was dated two weeks after German troops had marched into Austria.[62] Not even Hitler could inject a sense of urgency into the Civil Service.

What lifts the affair of the proposed *'Wehrwirtschaft'* officer in Berlin from the merely ludicrous to the truly appalling is that six months *before* Mason-MacFarlane had raised the matter, a document had reached the Foreign Office from secret sources. It contained the very information – what the IIC described as 'the greatest secrets in the country' – which the British so lacked: how far was Hitler's aggressiveness actually backed by military capacity? Once again the anti-Nazi Opposition in Germany was to plug the gaps in British intelligence. It is indeed an extraordinary story.

Mention has already been made of the suppression by Eden of a memorandum by Vansittart, written on 6 July 1937, which had transmitted an impassioned plea by Goerdeler for British firmness against Hitler's aggressive policies. But the main burden of Vansittart's memorandum was to pass on to the Foreign Secretary a lengthy report he had recently received 'from a source invariably reliable' concerning the state of German heavy industry and its relation to military strength. The report had been prepared by the *Association of Heavy Industries in the Rhineland and Westphalia*, a title popularly abbreviated in Germany to *Langnamverein* (the Long-name Association). Vansittart had already confirmed the report's authenticity from other secret sources, but the arrival of Goerdeler in England in July had given him the opportunity of discovering the full history of the document. He was thus able to provide Eden with both contents and context. It had originated as a result of a conversation between Goerdeler himself and General von Fritsch, Commander-in-Chief of the Army. The latter distrusted Goering's over-optimistic claims about the Four Year Plan and consulted Goerdeler, who undertook to produce a true appreciation of the situation 'in a form easily comprehensible to the General.' Goerdeler as former

Price Controller had friends in the right places. He enlisted the help of the head of the *Vereinigte Stahlwerke* who approved of a report being compiled with the use of the staff and files of the *Langnamverein*. This was in due course handed to Fritsch. The Intelligence Department of the Reich's War Ministry considered the memorandum to be an accurate statement and it had been used by the Commander-in-Chief in discussions with Goering.[63] It may well be that Goerdeler himself had a hand in the report, including as it does a detailed presentation of the finances of the Reich and their attendant problems. It was this information with which he had been primed that almost certainly led General von Fritsch to oppose Hitler's war policies at the fateful conference the following November which was to lead to his downfall and to much else besides, as will be seen later.

Vansittart's 'abbreviated form' of the report in itself covers half-a-dozen long and closely printed pages. It is a catalogue of deficiencies, maladministration, an unbalanced budget, precarious currency and the unproductive investment of capital, material reserves and labour. To return to normality, equilibrium would have to be reached in both commercial and political spheres. In the first place it would be necessary for a political decision to be taken internally. The State should be established on a constitutional basis in which justice was administered; and Germany's political rights would have to be woven into some international agreement and peace system.[64]

The report is notable not only for its contents but for the light it throws on another dimension of German life – opposition. A considerable number of hands must have been at work on its preparation, from leading industrialists to researchers, typists and printers (it is 30 pages long). To have been associated in any way with a document so critical as to be subversive was to take a fearful chance. And by whatever means the material had reached the outside world – through Christie to London, and through German Socialists to those in exile in Prague and Vienna – those involved put their lives at risk in ensuring its transmission. It was high treason to pass information of any kind abroad. The penalty for those who 'obstructed the work of national regeneration', as this was called, was death.

In a further appendix to his Memorandum Vansittart attached an extract, dealing with the position of raw materials, from a Secret Report on the state of German industry and of the armament industry in particular. This report, dated 1st June, was the work of General Thomas, Chief of the Economic Section of the War Ministry. The crucial sentence was: 'The most necessary demands of the Combatant Forces cannot at present be fully met.'[65] Yet in a statement to the Foreign Office by Morton of the IIC, written a few months later, it was claimed:

> Sufficient raw materials have always been forthcoming to meet all the demands of the current programme for armament manufacture, the latter never yet having been suspended or seriously checked through a shortage of raw materials.

R. A. Butler, the Minister, minuted: 'Most instructive. I hope that papers of this quality will always be marked to me.'[66]

Vansittart did not reveal how he came by General Thomas' report, referring to 'an invariably reliable' source, and he emphasised 'the need for treating this paper as a matter of the utmost secrecy in the interests both of the authors and recipients of the memorandum.' The book *None So Blind* supplies the information. Conwell-Evans writes: 'Christie's information included authentic copies of valuable confidential reports destined only for members of the German Government and the General Staff; these dealt with the progress of the Four Year Plan and were issued by Colonel Thomas. . . .'[67]

Vansittart's own Memorandum to Eden was a lengthy appraisal (which he described as 'a brief explanation') of the development of Nazi Germany as a 'Total Military State'. This was largely based on Christie's material and was intended to serve as background to the German documents. Vansittart drew attention to evidence of dissatisfaction with the régime: 'the greed, ostentation, racketeering and corruption . . . right up and down the political ladder'; the 'recurrent distrust between German and German under the present régime'; low wages and endless deductions for Party funds; Gestapo supervision and the curtailment of personal freedom. 'None of these factors must be exaggerated,' he wrote, 'but it may be generally said that enthusiasm for the National Socialist régime and for Hitler himself has inwardly diminished. . . . All these circumstances, taken with the growing distrust of the Four Year Plan, are slowly leading towards a crisis in the economic and foreign policies of the Reich. . . .' There was much in Vansittart's paper to be digested and the advice which he offered in conclusion was a clear statement of anti-appeasement policy and obviously intended for Cabinet consideration:

In such a welter of ambitions and fears, the circumstances urged by the Army and Herr Goerdeler, and described in the memoranda of the *Langnamverein* and of Oberst Thomas, supply a brake which may be of great importance; and while we may be unable to do anything to strengthen this brake, we ought to be careful to do nothing to weaken it.[68]

Vansittart's memorandum and its appendices had been printed, which indicates that they were intended for Cabinet circulation. But the copy in the files is simply marked 'Enter Green' (the Secret Index). Across the copy of the memorandum surviving in his private papers, Vansittart has written, in his usual bold hand, 'Suppressed by Eden'.[69] It is not known how and when Vansittart learned of the Foreign Secretary's action but 'suppressed' is a strong word and there seems no doubt that he knew what had happened to it. Ian Colvin, author of *Vansittart in Office* and a leading newspaper correspondent in Germany during the 1930s, raised the question of the fate of the *Langnamverein* memorandum in an interview with Eden after the war. The former Foreign Secretary maintained that he had no recollection of the affair. Yet it was Colvin's opinion that if the Cabinet had been able to study the material there might have been a change in attitude towards rearmament: 'Here was a paper on which the fatal course of appeasement might have been arrested.'[70] It is incomprehensible how such outstanding intelligence material from inside Germany could have been suppressed. Certainly Vansittart had offended in the usual ways: the length of his own memorandum, the anti-appeasement stance and the demonstrable superiority of his own private sources. Nevertheless, he was the Head of the Foreign Office and was entitled to expect that his advice would at least be heard. It is difficult to see on what grounds Eden could have withheld Vansittart's communication. He knew where the duty of the Foreign Office lay: 'We should bear in mind the need for keeping the Cabinet informed of our appreciation of the German situation,' he once minuted on some reports from Goerdeler which had *not* come through Vansittart. Could personal antipathy have been allowed to override the demands of office? Or was he anxious not to appear to be advancing arguments against the policy of appeasement of the new Prime Minister?

On 8 July 1937, two days after Vansittart had submitted his memorandum, Eden personally handed a letter to Chamberlain (probably deliberately by-passing the Head of the Office). 'In the course of my work this evening,' he told the Prime Minister, 'I have been looking through a number of reports on the situation in Germany.' These had been received from the Chief Economic Adviser, Leith-Ross, from the Consul-General in Munich, and from the Secret Service. They had also included, said Eden, 'an interview with a Dr Goerdeler, a former high official in Germany who is a friend of Neurath's and of Goering. . . .' This points directly to Vansittart's memorandum in which he had included biographical details of Goerdeler, who was not at that time well-known in the Foreign Office. But Eden makes no mention of Vansittart, nor of the secret information on the German war economy. Nor does his letter indicate that his evening's labours had uncovered anything really pressing. Though varying in emphasis, wrote the Foreign Secretary, all the accounts seemed to indicate a very considerable deterioration of the German internal position; that the Nazi leaders were very conscious of this and consequently very uneasy. 'I am considering whether we have enough material to prepare a paper on the situation for the Cabinet.'[71]

The *Langnamverein* Report did not however die with the Foreign Secretary. It may never have reached the Cabinet and received the serious consideration it warranted, but it was certainly kept in play. Even before it had come into Vansittart's hands in the summer of 1937, a copy had been received by the Embassy in Berlin but had been dismissed by the Financial Adviser as a forgery, which perhaps accounts for the Military Attaché Mason-MacFarlane's apparent ignorance of its existence in January, 1938. In the middle of July a copy was sent to Central Department at the Foreign Office by the British Minister in Vienna who had received it from his American colleague, Messersmith. 'The Report is of considerable interest,' wrote the Minister, 'especially in view of its origin.' Messersmith's version of this tallied exactly with the account which Vansittart had received from Goerdeler.[72] In spite of all this verification (even the British Secret Service considered it genuine) the Financial Adviser in Berlin, Pinsent, persisted in his opinion that it was a forgery. The Treasury asked him for a second opinion. He reiterated his opinion that it was the work of a journalist with extensive but superficial knowledge and not that of industrialists with specialised knowledge. As to whom it was written for, this could hardly have been the General Staff whose own experts, assisted if necessary by other government departments, 'would make pretty short work of a memorandum which, clever as it is in some ways, is at the same time superficial, vague and confused.'[73] The answer to these objections was, of course, that it was not meant for the eyes of experts and 'other government departments' but for the secret scrutiny of General von Fritsch and it had been prepared, as Goerdeler told Vansittart, in a form easily comprehensible to him and his fellow officers.

In December the Treasury approached Pinsent again, on behalf of the Industrial Intelligence Centre, where the report had now turned up. (By this time it had become 'a paper submitted to Hitler by a group of financiers and industrialists'!) Pinsent stood by his guns but admitted that the Foreign Office did not altogether share his opinion. In his letter he inadvertently highlighted one of the major obstacles to the efficient exchange of intelligence between Berlin and London – the British Ambassador. In support of his rejection of the report Pinsent wrote: 'The Ambassador's comment is that, until we know more of the worth of the evidence from secret sources, we are not inclined to modify our original view.'[74] But the British Ambassador, as has been shown, was considered an unsafe conduit for secret information by those in Germany who wished to pass it. Conwell-Evans had first-hand evidence of the attitude of the sort of men who would almost certainly have been members of the *Langnamverein*. At a dinner in Berlin of the Anglo-German Fellowship he noted the presence of 'the moderates – mainly representative of the great industries of Germany.' He also observed how the British Ambassador was given a wide berth: 'Even at the dinner I noted that the industrial leaders who had anything to say avoided him, as they felt it would be dangerous to communicate anything to him as they did to me. . . .'[75]

Perhaps in order to avoid taking sides against the Embassy, the Foreign Office did not come down firmly on the side of Vansittart's authentication but merely returned an 'opinions differ' reply to the Treasury's enquiry about the *Langnamverein* Report. Presumably on receipt of this 'don't know' vote, the Treasury pursued the matter no further. This unique collection of intelligence on the German war economy appears to have been passing around Whitehall from May to December without coming officially to rest anywhere. The subject of the *Langnamverein* Report disappears from the file on 30 December 1937 without having made an impact on anyone except Vansittart. Two weeks later the Military Attaché, Mason-Macfarlane, made his urgent request for the appointment of the expert '*Wehrwirtschaft*' officer.

The *Langnamverein* Report had been prepared in the summer of 1937. Two years later some improvement in the war economy might have been expected. But in the summer of 1939 Christie sent Vansittart the gist of an important conversation he had had with an old friend in Germany whom he described as 'an experienced industrialist.' The importance of the conversation lay in the identity of Christie's friend. Beginning with the statement that 'the economic position of the Reich is definitely more unfavourable than is usually believed in foreign countries', Christie's friend ranged over the whole field of the German economy. He stressed the crucial shortage of raw materials which held up production and the increased bank debts. The quality of Germany's own raw materials was deteriorating. Coal and coke contained increasing impurities. Germany was desperate for foreign currency to pay for imports of raw material. They were just managing to keep going because of low prices abroad. But any increase in prices or in the hold-up in supplies must throw whole branches of the huge armament industry into idleness. If there was an interruption of only a few weeks in the supply of mercury, for instance, the bulk of the electrical industries would be brought to a standstill. Germany was bartering with Brazil for timber. Roumania might be a future supplier but first new railways had to be built in the mountains of Transylvania and it was proving difficult to raise capital for this enterprise. Oil was a great problem. The previous year millions of marks, in dollars, had been paid to the United States for oil. Home-made synthetic oils were not too satisfactory. Their use on the German State Railways the previous winter had caused damage to engines and rolling stock because they could not stand up to very low temperatures.

The speaker had a specific reason for giving Christie this detailed and adverse report on the economy. He had a request to make. He wanted Britain to use its own economic strength against Germany's weakness in the cause of peace and the future of Europe. It was a powerful appeal: 'The chance of preventing war or of removing the Hitler régime at the lowest cost of blood and destruction appears to me to lie solely in applying an economic squeeze. . . . Your powerful front, with the assistance of the United States, has the fate of Hitler, the Nazi system and of Europe in its hands.'[76]

In introducing his source to Vansittart, Christie had described him as an old friend, an experienced industrialist, and not a friend of the Nazi Party. He had commenced his career as a diplomat. What relevance did this last fact have to a discussion of the parlous state of the German economy? None – but it is a very pointed indicator to the speaker's identity. Astonishingly, the man who fits this description of a diplomat turned industrialist is none other than Gustav Krupp von Bohlen. He started his career as a member of the Foreign Ministry and served in Washington, Peking and the Vatican, but after marrying Bertha Krupp he gradually took over the family business. He had certainly opposed the rising Nazi movement in the 1920s: in fact the day before Hindenburg appointed Hitler Chancellor, he warned him against doing so. But he was present at the meeting with Thyssen and certain other major figures in industry organised by Goering, at which an appeal had been made for election funds for the Nazis. Thyssen spoke in 1939 of how he 'perceived with growing anxiety, and then horror, the mistake I made in 1932 when I financed the NSDAP. . . .' It seems that Gustav Krupp too had become aware of the nature of the genie which they had let out of the bottle. Perhaps this contributed to the stroke which, after war broke out, removed him from active control of Krupp, which passed to his son.

It is astonishing to find the head of the best-known and largest armaments firm in the world – three months before war broke out – talking about 'the chance of preventing war' and of 'removing the Hitler régime' and appealing to Britain, the obvious enemy, to achieve this. It is noteworthy that Christie, the dedicated opponent and monitor of the evils of Nazism, should refer to him more than once in his paper as his friend. This extraordinary exchange demonstrates how well-established were Christie's friendships in key areas of German life and how totally he was trusted: not only to keep confidences but to transmit crucial information to the British Government so that they would be under no dangerous illusions.

The authors of the *Langnamverein* report had stated that nothing could be achieved until equilibrium was restored in Germany. But equilibrium had been lost for ever. This was a country which had gone mad at the top. Within a few months of Hitler taking power, Sir Horace Rumbold had summed up in one of his despatches: 'I have the impression that the persons directing the policy of the Hitler Government are not normal.'[77] Sir William Strang was to write of his Foreign Office colleagues that their whole upbringing conspired against understanding that such people could exist and that the Nazi state was a lunatic state. But there were those in Germany, too, whose upbringing was at odds with the world in which they now lived but who had no doubts about its lunatic nature. For ordinary professional men, trying to reconcile their anxiety for the financial stability of their country with inane directives from above, the strain could be overwhelming. In 1939, Conwell-Evans reported the tragic case of Dr Brinckmann, Vice-President of the Reichsbank:

> Owing to the impossible tasks imposed upon him since the resignation of Dr Schacht – tasks which he regarded as utterly disastrous – he has lost his reason, and his madness broke out at a lunch which he gave to some Americans at the Reichsbank, when he invited them into the great reception room and danced and played the violin in their presence.
> He afterwards led them to the Library where he proceeded to appoint one of the young assistant librarians as chief of the institution and asked her to reorganise the bank, in the grand manner. He took a cheque-book and said, in the best style of the Chancellor, that he would let her have as much money as she wanted for the purpose.[78]

(The incident is also recorded in von Hassell's Diary.) Distressing as this scene must have been to Brinckmann's American guests, they could not have been aware that what they were witnessing was not merely a personal breakdown but the expression of a malaise which was affecting all those with responsibility who were endeavouring to pursue their normal avocations in the service of their country. They no longer had a sure footing in the manic world in which they now had to live. All the bastions of the old, respectable Germany were falling. Conwell-Evans summed up the situation in a report to Vansittart on his return from a visit to Germany early in 1939. He had seen the ominous symptoms of the gradual capture of the Foreign Office by Himmler's SS, together with the manning by these guards of other great positions in industry and commerce: 'In other words, the forces that can exercise a brake on further adventure, the last hindrances to a policy of brutal conquest in the future, are being removed.'[79]

Two years earlier, in submitting the *Langnamverein* and Thomas reports to Eden, Vansittart had referred to the existence of this very 'brake' and hoped that 'we would be careful to do nothing to weaken it.' The juggernaut was now gathering speed and Conwell-Evans' plea on behalf of those still inside who tried to halt its progress was a heartfelt one:

> It is of no use to shut our eyes to realities nor to turn a deaf ear to the pleadings and warnings of those representatives still in office of the real Germany, among whom I have so many friends of long standing, and who are now, by asserting their convictions as to the unwisdom of the policy pursued in their country, facing great personal danger. . . .[80]

In June, 1944 when the assault on Hitler's Fortress Europe had just begun, Miss Irene Ward rose in the House of Commons to express the hope that after the war there would be full disclosure of how it all began:

> We must know whether, when the reports coming into the Foreign Office from all these various sources were put forward in the form of memoranda to the Foreign Secretary of the day, he put a wrong political interpretation on them. I cannot believe that it was so, but something must have happened.[81]

— IV —

Dialogues with the Deaf

It is at the request of those people in Germany – still in office, though helpless – that we are asked now to be adamant and unyielding in our attitude towards the present régime of tyranny and oppression.

M. G. Christie
Secret Report to the
Foreign Office, 1938

I am inclined to be rather wary of unsolicited advice from Germany.

Sir Alexander Cadogan
Head of the Foreign Office

Discussion between the German resistance and the Allies remained till the end a *dialogue de sourds*.

Visser 't Hooft

I N the opening months of the critical year of 1938 the pieces on the diplomatic chessboards of Britain and Germany began to be moved in significant directions. On 1st January, Sir Robert Vansittart, Permanent Head of the Foreign Office, took up (or was shunted into) the formerly unknown post of Chief Diplomatic Adviser to the Government: a post which had never existed before and never would again. The arch-enemy of appeasement was removed from any participation in, or influence on, foreign policy-making. The most powerful personality in the Foreign Office had been booted upstairs to the concerted relief of Downing Street, the Cabinet and Whitehall. Vansittart was succeeded by Sir Alexander Cadogan, not a man to rock Chamberlain's boat. On 20th February the Foreign Secretary, Anthony Eden, resigned on the issue of Anglo-Italian policy and was replaced by the complaisant Lord Halifax. The new Foreign Secretary had a new opposite number in Germany. On 4th February the German Ambassador in London, Ribbentrop, achieved his greatest desire: he became Minister of Foreign Affairs and the willing tool of Hitler's aggressive policies. The following day Erich Kordt was appointed Head of the new Minister's Secretariat and left his post at the London Embassy to return to the Wilhelmstrasse. By 17th February he had organised the transfer of his brother Theo from the Athens Embassy to replace him in London. A few weeks later Weizsäcker became State Secretary – Permanent Head of the Foreign Ministry and opposite number to Cadogan. The Opposition was in place.

1938 was the year when the world went to the brink of peace. The possibility of the removal of Hitler and the Nazi régime was offered by the German Opposition. But vital support from abroad was needed in the form of firm diplomatic moves by the Western democracies which would undermine Hitler's position both at home and abroad and create the circumstances in which Hitler's opponents could make their move. Everything depended on leadership by Britain and it was Britain that failed at every moment of opportunity throughout that fateful year.

In March, 1936 Hitler had challenged the Versailles Powers' resolution: he sent his troops into the Rhineland to re-occupy the demilitarised zone established by the Treaty. The Army Commander-in-Chief, von Fritsch, was certain that France would mobilise. The General Staff and the German Ambassador in London, von Hoesch, sent urgent warnings to Hitler. Hitler was indeed risking his entire political life and the existence of the Nazi Party. Christie, who had learned the exact details of the invasion from his anti-Nazi sources, telephoned the information to Vansittart from the Continent just before midnight the day before.[1] Some weeks later he learned just how big a personal risk Hitler had taken. General von Fritsch had issued a secret order on 7th March: if the French Army should cross the frontier, the German troops were to withdraw immediately. Not a shot was to be fired. To avoid any untoward incident only blank ammunition was issued to the troops.[2] Hitler could never have survived having exposed the country to such international humiliation. But the gambler kept his nerve and won. Christie, who had taken it for granted that his warning would be acted upon, was appalled at the failure of the Treaty Powers to crush Hitler at so little cost. 'We are committing suicide,' he wrote to Vansittart. 'Hitler and Goering are now convinced that power politics are safe and easy and that Britain and France will not march to the support of Austria or Czechoslovakia.'

On 5 November 1937 Hitler summoned to the Chancellery the War Minister, Blomberg; the Commanders-in-Chief of the Army, the Navy and the Air Force – Fritsch, Raeder and Goering – and the Foreign Minister, Baron von Neurath. The only other person present was his Wehrmacht aide, Colonel Hossbach, whose notes of the proceedings were to survive to become one of the key documents at the Nuremberg trials. The entire theme of Hitler's address was war. The Führer believed personally, recorded Hossbach, that in all probability England and perhaps also France had already silently written off Czechoslovakia. Although those present had hardly been summoned to debate Hitler's pronouncements, nevertheless the two generals and the diplomat made bold to demur at a foreign policy based on such an assumption. But a way suddenly opened for Hitler by which he could not only rid himself of those who dared to raise objections to his plans but also secure for himself a position where he would at least be out of reach of dissident voices. It began with a wedding and developed into an affair of Byzantine proportions. When it was all over, three of the five present at the November 5th Conference were out of office; Hitler had assumed a position of total and unassailable power, and the opposition to him had taken coherent shape.

On 12th January, Field Marshal Blomberg, a widower, remarried. Hitler and Goering were witnesses at his wedding. There had been much talk of the bride's lowly social origins but after a week of rumours in the capital something infinitely worse broke the surface. Not only did the young lady have a 'past', she actually had a police record as a prostitute. In fact, Goering, in whom the infatuated War Minister had confided, had deliberately eased his path towards matrimony with an eye on the post of War Minister which he himself coveted, and which Blomberg would assuredly be forced to relinquish when the story came out. Goering deliberately allowed the unwitting Hitler to be compromised by being a participant in the dubious nuptials. When, in due course, he 'sorrowfully' revealed the facts to him, the Führer was enraged by his personal humiliation. On 25th January, Blomberg was dismissed.

With Blomberg out of the way, the road seemed clear for Goering. But the natural successor to the post of War Minister was the Commander-in-Chief, General von Fritsch. Hitler might decide that he was obliged to appoint him. Goering had anticipated such a possibility, however, and everything was well prepared. The Blomberg affair had involved the manipulation by Goering of an already existing situation; the Fritsch affair was a deliberate criminal conspiracy. There were powerful forces against Fritsch. He was known to have opposed Hitler's foreign policy: his plan to use force against Austria and to intervene in Spain. He had also consistently blocked Himmler's attempts to extend the power of the SS into the Army. Now Goering, Himmler and Heydrich moved in on Fritsch. On the day Blomberg was dismissed Goering put before Hitler evidence accusing von Fritsch of homosexual behaviour in a public place. A suborned gaolbird was actually introduced into Hitler's office in the Chancellery to confront the Commander-in-Chief. Appalled by the attack, Fritsch resigned, but his fellow officers demanded a proper investigation of the affair. Suddenly, what had been the cynical pursuit of personal ambition by Goering brought the whole régime into deadly peril. It also gave Hitler the chance to make a move which was a milestone on the road to war. With Blomberg married and done for and Fritsch dismissed (though not convicted), Hitler seized the moment of disarray in the High Command to take action which would put his policies beyond the reach of internal opposition. In a move which left everybody standing, he issued a decree on 4th February by which the War Ministry was abolished. In its place there was to be a High Command of the Armed Forces (OKW) to which all three ser-vices would be subordinated and of which the Führer himself would be the head. His deputy would be the subservient Keitel. Hitler was now truly a War Lord. It was announced that Blomberg and Fritsch had resigned for health reasons and that Fritsch had been replaced by Brauschitsch. Sixteen senior generals were retired and forty-four others whose loyalty to the régime was in doubt were transferred. There were plenty of younger officers waiting in the wings who would serve the new Supreme Commander in their stead.

Having therefore fashioned his weapons, as it were, Hitler turned his attention to that other pillar of the state which he knew stood between him and his plans: the Foreign Ministry. Von Neurath was replaced by Hitler's lackey, Ribbentrop. Three senior ambassadors were simultaneously recalled: from Rome, Tokyo and Vienna. Ambassador von Hassell, who had opposed the Pact of Steel with Mussolini, returned to Germany to become one of the most impor-tant members of the Opposition.

With internal obstacles now eliminated, the Führer from his new position of power moved swiftly ahead with his plans for Austria. On 12th February he peremptorily summoned the Austrian Chan-cellor to a meeting at Berchtesgaden. As Vansittart minuted: 'Now we have the new lot of generals tied up in the antechamber to intimi-date Schuschnigg into accepting the Diktat. Fritsch would never have been found there.'[3]

But even in this exalted moment, the Blomberg-Fritsch affair began to cast a threatening shadow over the régime. In their machina-tions against Frau von Blomberg and General von Fritsch, the Party chiefs Goering and Himmler and the Gestapo had been involved in some pretty dirty work which now, unfortunately for them, was being unmasked by some particularly dedicated investigators. The preliminary enquiry into the Fritsch affair was under way, conducted by Judge Sack and Dohnanyi of the Ministry of Justice, both dedicated opponents of Hitler. They had the co-operation of two other secret Oppositionists: Nebe, Head of the Criminal Police, and Helldorf, Chief of Police in Berlin. It was a rare opportunity to investigate – openly and with authority – the misdeeds of the Gestapo. Gisevius, another leading member of the Opposition and lawyer at the Ministry of the Interior, also followed up the investigation, together with Admiral Canaris' deputy, Colonel Oster of the Abwehr. By persistent and meticulous investigation, these lawyers and policemen, linked by hatred of the régime and its system of secret police, uncovered a deliberate false accusation based on the case of a retired officer of humbler rank, with a very similar name, who had been blackmailed for years. But the Gestapo had not been clever enough in constructing their case. Gisevius, relating the story in the witness stand at Nuremberg and later in his book, *To The Bitter End*, described the plot which they uncovered as being of astounding proportions.[4] It included Goering's behind-the-scenes manipulations of Blomberg's misalliance, as well as the sordid construction by Himmler and Heydrich of the case against General von Fritsch. With so many Party leaders involved in these matters Hitler's opponents saw a heaven-sent opportunity of toppling the whole régime. The evidence – of criminal conspiracy, forgery, blackmail and death threats – was so damning that the Chief of Staff, General Beck, begged the new Commander-in-Chief, Brauchitsch, to confront Hitler with it. But the latter, always loath to bear bad news to Hitler, declared that the trial should be allowed to go ahead first, acquitting Fritsch and exposing the Nazi criminality. He would move after that. The danger to the Führer and the Party was acute, as the leading Nazis were well aware. Coupled with the inside story of the Blomberg affair and Goerings's machinations, the attack on Fritsch would have been perceived as an attack by the SS on the Army. The exposure of a criminal conspiracy of such a nature by leading Party members and, by implication, the Führer himself, against one of the most respected figures in public life would have created a national crisis which the régime would almost certainly not have survived. In view of Fritsch's rank, Goering himself had been appointed by Hitler as President of the Military Court. Although he dragged his feet in the matter, the Court was at last convened for 11th March. After a couple of hours of deliberation the sitting was suspended in dramatic circumstances. Fate, it would appear, had intervened.

On 9th March Schuschnigg had declared that he would hold a

plebiscite of the Austrian people on his own terms on the question of independence. Hitler, seeing his prey slipping away from him, fell into one of his nervous crises and in the hours which followed Schuschnigg's announcement marching orders were given and cancelled, rages were fallen into, panic rose and fell. Such was the danger in which the Party stood in the Fritsch affair that Goering himself seized control of events, fearful lest the opportunity of such a vital diversion should be missed. The new Field Marshal took the initiative and issued an ultimatum demanding the resignation of Schuschnigg in favour of the Nazi Seyss-Inquart and giving the signal for the unleashing of Austrian Nazis throughout the country. Hitler was later to acknowledge with admiration and gratitude Goering's 'icecold' command of the situation and the swiftness of his action. When Goering, Raeder and von Brauchitsch were summoned to the Chancellery from the Military Court it was to prepare the entry of German troops into Austria the following morning. Certainly there is evidence of the precipitateness of the decision to invade Austria on that particular date. Ribbentrop, the new Foreign Minister, was away in London, taking formal leave of the British government on relinquishing his post as Ambassador. He was actually lunching with the Prime Minister when the news was given to him. Hitler was forced to call on the recently deposed Minister, Neurath, temporarily to resume his Foreign Office functions in order to handle the diplomatic consequences which would inevitably ensue. Neurath recalled the circumstances in his evidence at Nuremberg.[5] Hitler had telephoned him at home late in the afternoon and asked him to come and see him. In the anteroom at the Chancellery he found the German Ambassador in Vienna, Papen; the Commander-in-Chief Brauchitsch, and other leading personalities. Goering was with Hitler. The Führer informed Neurath that the *Anschluss* was a fact and that German troops would cross the frontier during that night. Neurath was then asked what the Foreign Office should do in the absence of the Foreign Minister in London. This confirmed to Neurath that the invasion had not been planned in advance because Hitler himself had sent Ribbentrop to England only a few days earlier.

Reported reaction to the events of the night of 11th March does give some credence to the idea that Hitler's sudden move may have been linked with Fritsch's trial and the trouble in which the régime found itself. Schuschnigg's announcement of his intention to hold a plebiscite does not seem to have aroused expectations of imminent action, although the issue of the *Anschluss* was obviously a live one at the time. The British Consul in Frankfurt contributed his observations to the Foreign Office:

> During the decisive days in March I happened to meet socially an exceptionally large number of members of the Party both here and at Stuttgart, and several senior Army officers, and I am definitely under the impression that the course of events took them by surprise.[6]

Meanwhile, a summary of events to date, supplied by Goerdeler, was transmitted to R. A. Butler, Minister of State, at the Foreign Office, by Professor Reinhold Schairer, Goerdeler's confidant in England, who was also acquainted with Butler. In this communication the nature of the charge against Fritsch was defined, together with the fact that the evidence against him had been based on documents forged by Himmler and the Gestapo. If such criminal activity against a distinguished officer (in which Goering was also involved) should emerge at the Court of Honour, Hitler faced the real danger of being overthrown. This was so acute that Hitler had been forced to bring forward the invasion of Austria before the trial could take place. It had been postponed, but only for a short time. This entirely accurate summary was passed to Central Department, where it received short shrift. Mallet minuted: 'This is the first I have heard of a trial of Fritsch (presumably for complicity in an alleged monarchist plot).' With regard to the rest of the information in the memorandum he pronounced: 'All this sounds rather far-fetched. . . . We have no evidence to support the suggestion that the Army are finding Hitler intolerable.' Upon receipt of this negative and uninformed judgment, the Minister expressed himself 'obliged for the *éclaircissement*.'[7]

When Fritsch's trial was reconvened on 17th March the political landscape had changed. Hitler had had another political success in the Austrian *Anschluss*: the Party leaders no longer felt threatened. The trial was over in two days. Goering was briskly magnanimous to the calumniated General. The wretched creature who had obediently provided the false evidence was 'miraculously' – as Fritsch thought – found and had recanted. Fritsch had his day in court but was out of his depth and did not fight back. The evidence assembled by the members of the Opposition with which the accusers were to be accused was not produced. The former Commander-in-Chief did not understand the world of perfidious intrigue in which he found himself. He was of course acquitted but not reinstated. Hitler had already given his job away on 4th February.

Although Fritsch's conduct at the trial had failed to force the revelations of criminal conspiracy into the open, there was still the back-up plan that upon Fritsch's exoneration Brauschitsch should confront Hitler with the evidence of the plot. Alas, a sudden and unexpected obstacle arose. Goerdeler, whose enthusiasm often outran his discretion, had while in London talked too freely in British banking circles of a forthcoming purgation of the Third Reich. An example of this was the statement, duly reported to the Foreign Office, which he made to the British Commissioner of International Chambers of Commerce:

> Goerdeler said if Schuschnigg had postponed plebiscite for a fortnight, an internal revolt would have been staged in Germany by the Army and Nazi government swept away. Hitler had precipitated his action in Austria in order to dispose of the internal danger. The army was still ready to act given a suitable opportunity.[8]

No doubt convinced that Brauchitsch would be fulfilling his promise to confront Hitler after the trial, Goerdeler was rash enough to drop Brauchitsch's name in the hearing of his British contacts. This news filtered back to the Commander-in-Chief in Germany who was now running scared: his only consideration was to affirm his loyalty to the Führer by telling him the story and protesting his innocence. Hitler apparently suggested that he should take legal proceedings.

The history of the affair has been testified to by some of those involved.[9] It is interesting as a commentary on the extraordinary difficulties of communication in those days and of the way in which members of the Opposition could be dealing with each other without being aware of it. A German visitor to London, William Roloff, was dining in a public restaurant with an Austrian banker, a member of the firm of Lazard Brothers, called Erwin Schueller. The latter, who was resident in London and was awaiting naturalisation, had many friends in the Opposition movement. During dinner he had disclosed what Goerdeler had said when he had visited the Bank. To Roloff's alarm, Schueller mentioned both Goerdeler and Brauchitsch loudly enough to be overheard by other diners. On his return to Germany the following day, Roloff sought out a kindred spirit, Count Gerd Schwerin, an army officer. Could a warning be sent to Opposition circles in Berlin? It was essential to suppress any indication that the Army might be willing to take action against the régime. Schwerin used his own contacts to get a message to Berlin. But matters took an unexpected turn. Roloff and Schwerin were summoned to an interrogation at an hotel in Hanover by two members of the State Justice Department, at which Roloff was informed that Brauchitsch had instituted a libel action against him, evidently on the advice of Hitler. Absolute secrecy was imposed by the law officers: the two friends were positively forbidden to discuss the matter even between themselves. Roloff gained the impression during the interview that the lawyers were actually interested in protecting Goerdeler. It was decided that the matter could be resolved by Roloff travelling to London accompanied by a lawyer, Eduard Waetjen (who later during the war was to be one of the close contacts of Allen Dulles of the OSS in Switzerland). There they would secure from Lazards a letter to the effect that the whole thing had been a misunderstanding. Permission had to be obtained for the journey from Woermann at the Foreign Office. There too Roloff had the feeling that Goerdeler was being protected. The senior member of Lazards, Mr Brand, who had indiscreetly confided in Schueller, produced the necessary letter attesting that Goerdeler had never said such things. Roloff was told that the matter was now closed, though he was given nothing in writing. A short time later he was able to give the whole story to those pillars of the Opposition – Oster and Gisevius. Roloff had reason to believe that Gisevius prevented the affair reaching the Gestapo: in the course of the twenty-one interrogations which he was to undergo at their hands after the July Plot in 1944 the matter was never raised. Evidently it was not on his 'file'.

The unfortunate repercussions of Goerdeler's visit to London resulted in the defection of Brauchitsch from his promise to confront Hitler. It was a bitter blow to the Opposition who thought they had victory over the régime within their grasp. The Blomberg-Fritsch crisis had created for the first time the possibility that the régime and its leader could be toppled by legal process. The Opposition had provided the ammunition but the new Commander-in-Chief had failed to take aim and fire. Infirmity of purpose among the generals was to bedevil the efforts of the conspirators to the end.

There was a further dimension to Goerdeler's ill-starred visit to London that Spring of 1938. On his way to England he had stopped in Brussels where he had visited an old friend, Daniel Heineman, an

American engineer and financier with international connections at a high level. Quite by chance, Goerdeler arrived at Heineman's office while Brüning was there. Goerdeler recounted the details of the Fritsch affair. He was in his usual optimistic mood and felt that something could be accomplished as a result of it, if the British Cabinet could be persuaded. The ex-Chancellor replied that he had never, since 1934, succeeded in influencing anyone in the governments of Baldwin or Chamberlain. The one possibility seemed to be to bring Goerdeler into touch with Churchill, who would undoubtedly come to the forefront in a year or two. Brüning himself had had a discussion with Churchill some weeks earlier at the latter's home in London. He had pressed upon Churchill the necessity for the British Government to work out a clearly defined plan which, conveyed to reliable people in the German Army, might lead to their attempting a *coup d'état*. But they must know what to expect once the despots had been overthrown. Churchill had seemed impressed and had spoken of removing the gangsters and of making the European situation secure. Brüning told Goerdeler to contact him in England and he would try to arrange something. But Brüning urged Goerdeler to be careful. He was not happy that he and his family should be escorted by British secret service agents (detailed by Vansittart) who would be recognised by the Gestapo who, he warned, travelled regularly on the Channel boats observing the passengers.[10] The events which followed in England, of which Brüning left an account, give a rare glimpse of the problems which members of the Opposition faced when making important contacts abroad.

In due course the two Germans came together in London. Goerdeler told Brüning that he had already spoken to Chamberlain, Halifax, Vansittart and others and (as usual) he took an optimistic view of their attitudes. Brüning went ahead with setting up the meeting with Churchill. The meeting was arranged for Sunday, 3rd April and was to take place at Old Surrey Hall, East Grinstead, home of Brüning's friends Ian and Mona Anderson. Brüning instructed Goerdeler that a car bearing trade number plates would be waiting outside his hotel at 9 a.m. The Andersons' son would be at the wheel. But when Brüning himself arrived at Old Surrey Hall on the Saturday afternoon, things had taken a mysterious turn. An unknown caller had telephoned Mrs Anderson to say that Goerdeler could not join them for lunch the following day, when Churchill would be there. She was suspicious about the call and Brüning made her contact Goerdeler's hotel at once. But as soon as Goerdeler answered and the operator announced her name, he hung up and she could not be re-connected. The mystery remained until the following day when, half-an-hour before Churchill was due to arrive, Dr Reinhold Schairer telephoned to say that the reason Goerdeler could not come was because he had been warned that Anderson was in the Secret Service. On Brüning demanding further information, he declared that the warning had come from Vansittart. He had also had a note from another member of the Foreign Office to whom he had mentioned the meeting. Goerdeler, he said, would like to meet Churchill but not in the company of Brüning. Brüning managed to contact Frau Goerdeler at the hotel and she confirmed that her husband had indeed received the warning. Brüning explained the circumstances to Churchill as best he could and hinted that perhaps the warning had come from one of the latter's personal opponents: for instant, Goerdeler had mentioned that he had seen Halifax. But Churchill replied that Halifax had in fact urged him to talk to Goerdeler and had been very pleased to learn that they were to meet.

Brüning had a talk with Churchill before he left after lunch. He told him that in the course of the changes brought about in the Army as a result of the Fritsch affair, many of the generals who were set against 'warlike' adventures had been pushed into the background. The former Chancellor advised that in order to avoid war in the long run, the British Government would have to decide what concession could be made to resolve Germany's legitimate border claims. They should then let their maximum offer be known to certain influential commanders (whose names he could supply) and tell them that this was their last chance. If they did not then overthrow Hitler, matters would have to take their course. Churchill, however, doubted that the Chamberlain Government could come to a firm resolve, which would demand a certain amount of imagination and psychological insight into the German Army and the anti-Nazis.

Goerdeler called on Brüning the following day. He said he had had to rely on the advice of Schairer, who was close to the Foreign Office and the Secret Service. He wanted to discuss an alternative meeting but Brüning was too put out to pursue the matter.[11] Curiously, it turned out later that there was in fact a spy in the Anderson household. A woman on the staff was in the pay of the Gestapo.[12]

Out of their failure to bring Hitler and his Party to justice during the February crisis had come a new dimension for the Opposition.

Key figures on the military and civilian sides had co-operated well during the Fritsch affair. The men who had worked together to undo Hitler through the courts were to be for the most part the same men who in July, 1944 so nearly finished him by assassination. Now in the spring of 1938, elements hostile to the régime began to come together for the first time as some sort of coherent entity. Circles of like-minded people, already brought into existence by a common hatred of Nazism, began to link up in a way which extreme caution had hitherto made impossible. Political and confessional differences were submerged in a common purpose. Time was pressing. The Opposition raised its sights. The aim was nothing less than the total elimination of the Nazi régime and the re-establishment of a law-abiding state worthy of respect both at home and abroad and a threat to no-one. From this time onwards the two leaders of the Opposition – one on the military side, the other on the civilian – were Beck and Goerdeler. Beck, in retirement, was the guiding spirit and arbiter of all action. Goerdeler, with his boundless energy, was considered the driving force or 'motor' of the movement.

Colonel-General Ludwig Beck, Chief of Staff of the Army until his resignation in the face of the projected aggression against Czecho-slovakia in 1938, was the very antithesis of the epithet 'militarist', automatically applied by the British to all German officers. In many ways more philosopher and historian than typical military man, Beck was held in the highest esteem both in the Army and by the nation as a whole. His character and reputation were unimpeachable. His opposition to Hitler was based, in the first instance, not on military differences but on moral principles. Every aspect of Nazi activity outraged him. Furthermore, he rejected the use of the Army, which he had shaped for the defence of the realm, as an instrument of criminal aggression against other countries. Evidence of Beck's 'unhawkish' attitude is to be found in a report for which the notes still exist among Christie's papers. Beck had paid a visit to France in May, 1937 and Christie passed on to Vansittart the gist of what Beck had told his German friends in Paris. Vansittart incorporated some of this information into the memorandum on the Heavy Industries Report which Eden suppressed. Beck revealed that the Party radicals – Goebbels, Goering, Himmler, Heydrich, Ley, Rosenberg – kept urging Hitler that a success in the international field was necessary to counter internal discontent. 'We military men are opposed to any such adventure,' Beck had said, 'but we can no longer guarantee against it.' Since the re-occupation of the Rhineland, their influence with Hitler was much weaker. The General Staff had wanted to keep absolutely clear of the war in Spain but had only managed to prevent direct intervention. Himmler and the Party had drawn up a plan, with Hitler's consent but without the knowledge of the War Ministry, to march into Austria with SS troops and occupy the country. Fortunately von Papen, the Minister in Vienna, and General Muff had found out and had joined with the General Staff in persuading Hitler to withdraw his approval. But it must be realised, continued Beck, that the Party radicals were pressing Hitler for some heroic gesture. With regard to a visit he had made to the French Army, Beck told his friends: 'I came as a gentleman to talk with gentlemen in order to try to improve our relations.' He had not broached the subject of limitations of armaments 'because I knew the Nazi government would most certainly break any such agreement. Nor would Goering and Raeder keep to it. . . :'

> As to the Army's attitude, General von Fritsch and others of us could vouch for that, but to what purpose, when we know that Himmler and the Party leaders would get round it by persuading Hitler to form and equip several new divisions of SS troops. The Führer would never include his SS troops in any limitation of armaments pact. . . .[13]

Something of the stress under which Beck lived can be glimpsed in an account by the British Military Attaché of a dinner party at the General's house at which the other guests were all German officers. The Attaché was amazed and somewhat nervous to hear the Chief of Staff strongly criticise the Party in terms of profound distrust and disapproval. He spoke openly of the evil accruing from the economic policy and from the treatment of religion. 'He gives the impression of a tired old man,' noted the British officer, 'but when the talk turned to other subjects he became bright and vital.'[14] When Beck's confrontations with the Führer forced his retirement, he continued in private life to be the acknowledged head and focal point of authority in the conspiracy against Hitler. He emerged to take his part in the plans for the assassination attempt of 20 July 1944. He was waiting at the Bendlerstrasse on that day, ready to take his place in the new government which was to assume office as soon as the news of the success of the attempt was received. In the aftermath of its failure he was allowed to take his own life rather than face execution.

Goerdeler, Beck's civil counterpart, was a very different man in personality though not in principles. The inexhaustible energy and optimism which he brought to the cause, his uncompromising attitude and the sheer moral force of his convictions attracted to him men of all shades of political opinion. It was his frequent cry that the situation would be transformed if only – just for twenty-four hours – the truth should be spoken in Germany. But Goerdeler was not merely a moral force; he was an expert administrator and economist. He had been Reich Commissioner from 1934–1935 and had kept useful contacts even among Nazis. Yet he resigned from his post as Lord Mayor of Leipzig when Party activists removed the statue of Mendelssohn from the town square. Thereafter, a kindred spirit, Robert Bosch, a leading Stuttgart industrialist, engaged him as adviser, providing him with cover – and funds – to travel extensively throughout Europe and the United States. Goerdeler used these opportunities both to sound out foreign opinion and in turn to press upon statesmen in other countries, and influential circles, the danger which the Nazi régime posed for themselves and for world peace. Goerdeler was well known in financial and business circles in Britain and to the Chief Economic Adviser to the Government, Sir Frederick Leith-Ross. In 1936 he was introduced to Sir Robert Vansittart, Head of the Foreign Office, in whom he found a ready audience for the high-level, inside information which he was able to impart about the true state of the Third Reich. Over the next few critical years he had many talks with Vansittart either in his room in the Foreign Office or his country home, Denham Place. But these confidences were always intended for the purpose of buttressing Goerdeler's undeviating thesis: that a firm diplomatic stance against Hitler would bring about his downfall and that of the régime. In the composition of the provisional government which the Opposition intended would bridge the period between the removal of Hitler and democratic elections, Beck was nominated Head of State and Goerdeler Chancellor.

Those oppositionists in key positions in government administration who had early recognised the dangers of the régime had hitherto envisaged being able to bring strong enough pressure to bear within the machinery of the State to force Hitler into different paths. Schacht had flattered himself he could do so. But after his experience of the Fritsch affair he had learned that Hitler could not be out-manoeuvred. Weizsäcker at the Foreign Ministry had hoped that enlightened diplomatic moves abroad could force Hitler's policies into peaceful channels and chasten his aggression. But the elevation of the malign Ribbentrop to the post of Foreign Minister had blocked any prospect of a responsible foreign policy and the appointment of an inexperienced dilettante to the Ministry of Economics could only hasten catastrophe in that area. The Army too had believed that their staunchly upright Commander-in-Chief Fritsch would have put a brake on Hitler's dangerous foreign adventuring. But now he had been replaced by a figurehead and the autonomy of the Army had been destroyed.

The removal of Hitler was not yet considered by the Opposition to be essentially a question of assassination. Goerdeler in particular felt that the new state should not be founded on political murder; and many shared his view even throughout the war. He set great store on the importance of Hitler being produced in person at the bar of the nation. Only thus could he be thoroughly and publicly disgraced. Dead, he might become a martyr figure. Some of the younger spirits took a more pragmatic view. There was the danger he might somehow elude justice. Mad dogs had to be put down. In any case, the march of events would probably decide the outcome.

As yet unaware that his garrulity at the dinner table in London had already sabotaged the efforts to bring Brauchitsch to heel after Fritsch's trial, Goerdeler, as he later told Brüning, had called upon Vansittart. It is unlikely that he would have been less forthcoming with the Diplomatic Adviser in private than he had been with his City friends in public. There can be no doubt that he gave Vansittart a full account of the recent events in Berlin. Vansittart's report of the interview which he sent to Halifax has not survived but there is at least some indication of what passed between them in a letter which Halifax sent to Chamberlain condensing to a few lines what was no doubt a lengthy memorandum: 'Van had a long interview yesterday with the usual highly-placed and patriotic German.' The moderate elements in the Army and elsewhere were struggling to reassert themselves, reported Goerdeler. The one thing which would help them and check further 'dangerous adventures' would be a very clear declaration by the British about Czechoslovakia. Halifax told Chamberlain that he was passing the information to him 'because Van begged me to do so' but he himself did not feel that this was important enough 'to deflect us from any conclusions that we may reach on the main issues.'[15]

★

With Hitler's swift assumption of total control of the armed forces in the midst of the Blomberg-Fritsch convolutions, and with the successful annexation of Austria, the Second World War, as far as the German opposition was concerned, had now begun. The next item on Hitler's agenda was Czechoslovakia and it seemed inconceivable that the other major powers would stand by and see it swallowed up into the Reich. Nevertheless, the very inevitability of the situation could, with proper co-operation and synchronis-ation between Hitler's enemies at home and abroad, be used not only to prevent war breaking out, but to eliminate any further prospect of war being generated by the evil genius of the Third Reich.

At his secret conference on 5 November 1937 during which Blom-berg, Fritsch and Neurath had so fatally expressed their dissension, Hitler had stated his belief that Britain, and perhaps also France, had already silently written off Czechoslovakia and that they had got used to the idea that one day this question would be cleared up by Germany. On 21 May 1938 a sudden crisis blew up which seemed as if it might prove Hitler wrong. On 20th May the Czech government conveyed both to the German Minister in Prague and to London their unease at what they described as the concentration of Ger-man troops near their borders. Captured German documents sub-sequently proved after the war that there was in fact no sinister German intent at the time and indeed British diplomats carrying out investigations reported no evidence of a strike on the Austrian model. The Military Attaché in Prague, Colonel Stronge, rather suspected that the Czechs were taking advantage of some post-*Anschluss* German troop movements as an excuse to test and demonstrate the efficiency of their mobilisation organisation. If so, it passed the test. Partial mobilisation was ordered overnight. By the morning every post along the frontier, bunker and fortifications, was ready to open fire. In fact, a possible clue to the German military activity can be found in General Halder's statement during interrogation by Allied Intelligence officers after the war to the effect that divisions were marched up and down opposite the Czech frontiers to convey a greater impression of strength than actually existed. (This statement does not appear in the transcripts of the interrogations. It was given to the author by Lord Kaldor, who was one of the officers who carried out the initial interrogation of the former German Chief of Staff.) Certainly the Western Powers were ready to believe that

Hitler was about to strike again. The British and French ambassadors were instructed to make representations in Berlin, warning of the danger to peace of any such aggressive move. The French, supported by the Russians, reaffirmed their commitment under treaty to Czechoslovakia. German denials of any aggressive intent were loudly hailed by the Western press as a diplomatic defeat for Hitler, who was assumed to have pulled in his horns. The effect of all this on the Führer's prestige both at home and abroad drove him wild. The international rebuff which Hitler had received damaged his prestige even in his private world. Hitler's state of mind and the atmosphere at his Court are vividly portrayed in a memorandum from Christie to the Foreign Office.[16] Christie had his information from 'a member of Hitler's immediate entourage', obviously Captain Fritz Wiedemann. Wiedemann had been Hitler's commanding officer in the First World War and had been called out of retirement by Hitler in his early days to be his adjutant. With the passage of time he became more and more alienated by the moral degradation of his old comrade. Although he would not raise a hand against him, he gravitated towards those who opposed him. The picture which Wiedemann painted of Hitler's inner sanctum is positively mediaeval in its terrors and tensions:

> He is therefore primarily moved by a wild desire for revenge and reacts to his loss of prestige among his closest collaborators by brutal outbursts, and by long sphinxlike silences. . . . His colleagues live in the fear that if they dare to contradict him they may, owing to his highly irritable condition and bitter fury, pay the penalty with their lives. Persons such as Goering, Himmler and Goebbels are kept guessing as to what the Führer really wants them to do and this results in the various curious, uncoordinated activities by which one or other of them hopes to gain the favour of the much feared tyrant. . . .

Goebbels for instance, as Gauleiter of Berlin, had recently ordered a rounding up and ill-treatment of Jews simply because Hitler had happened to mention in conversation with someone that it appeared to him that the Jews were apparently flourishing again.

> Everything indicates a timid groping in an endeavour to guess the real will of this uncanny Führer and to smooth him down before he unloads his fury in any particular direction. . . .[17]

But Hitler was to unload his fury in a very particular direction indeed. He had been inflamed by having been forced to appear to retreat in the face of international disapproval when in fact he was keeping to his own timetable for the criminal action of which he had been prematurely accused. Now he would not wait. (Weizsäcker once told Theo Kordt that 'uncontrollable resentment' played a decisive part when Hitler was making decisions.) On 28th May he called his Wehrmacht generals together and thundered: 'It is my unshakeable will that Czechoslovakia shall be wiped off the map.'[18] The Directive for 'Operation Green' had previously stated that it was *not* Hitler's intention to smash Czechoslovakia in the near future. This was now amended to the contrary: 'It is my unalterable decision to smash Czechoslovakia by military action in the near future.' Plans must be put in hand and the execution of the Operation must be guaranteed by 1st October at the latest.[19] Even the faithful Jodl was forced to contrast in his diary the intuition of the Führer which demanded the attack on Czechoslovakia that year, and the opinion of the Army that the Western Powers would intervene – 'and we are not yet equal to them.' Nevertheless, a further amendment to the Directive in the following month, June, indicated that Hitler's intuition was not entirely beyond the reach of outside influences and that the concerted diplomatic move by the four Powers on 21st May had at least given him pause:

> I will only take action if I am firmly convinced that France, and with it, England, will not attack (as in the case of the occupation of the demilitarised zone and the annexation of Austria).[20]

It was in order to convince Hitler precisely to the contrary that the Opposition were imploring Britain to make a firm declaration of its intention to oppose further aggression. The world looked to Britain, not to France, for leadership. The Czech Director of Artillery told Colonel Stronge:

> You English possess a powerful weapon to a degree which no other country enjoys and that is, your national prestige. That prestige . . . derives its real strength from your high moral standards in public life and policy. A single departure from those standards would mean moral suicide for you and disaster for the rest of the world.[21]

On Hitler's command on 30th May that military preparations must now begin, Beck promptly produced a report for the Commander-in-Chief Brauchitsch, based entirely on military arguments, which stated that the Supreme Commander must be told that his directive 'Operation Green' could not be implemented. Beck was right, but Hitler was more right. What never entered into Beck's assessment was the factor that the Western Powers would deliver Czechoslovakia to Hitler without a struggle. On 18 March 1938 Cadogan had written in his diary: 'Foreign Policy Committee unanimous that Czechoslovakia is not worth the bones of a single Grenadier. And they're quite right too!'

One of the more curious features of 1938 was that both German and British military chiefs were urging upon their respective heads of government their inability to engage upon a successful war. The one army which was both ready, willing and able – that of Czechoslovakia – was prevented from doing so. It is extraordinary that the claim is still often made today that in 1938, France was weak, Britain was weaker, and Czechoslovakia was *hors du concours*.

The failure of other countries to perceive the disparity between the façade of German strength and its reality had enabled Hitler to achieve his diplomatic successes throughout the 1930s and it continued to do so with spectacular success in 1938. While Austria was settling down to its first week as the 'Ostmark' of Greater Germany, the British Cabinet was meeting to unburden itself of any involvement in the fate of Czechoslovakia. At the request of the Prime Minister, the Chiefs of Staff had produced in March a report *On The Military Implications Of German Aggression Against Czechoslovakia*. They produced a 'worst case' assessment of the situation:

> We conclude that no pressure that we and our possible allies can bring to bear, either by sea, on land or in the air, could prevent Germany from invading and overrunning Bohemia and from inflicting a decisive defeat on the Czechoslovakian Army. . . .[22]

The report by the Chiefs of Staff was exactly what Chamberlain wanted to hear. It buttressed his policy of appeasement and he used it to put down any dissenting voice among his colleagues. It was, said the Prime Minister with some relish, a melancholy document which no government could afford to overlook.

But what makes the Chiefs of Staff Report an even more melancholy document in fact than Chamberlain found it to be is the evidence which existed against it. A week *before* the Chiefs of Staff reported to the Cabinet, Major General Spears presented a report on his return from a visit to Czechoslovakia where he had reviewed the situation and talked to President Beneš:

> Morale of the army first class. Czechs can mobilise a million trained men. Supplies of all kinds sufficient to resist for 5 months. French staff have assured them will attack Germany if Germany attacks Czechoslovakia. Morale of the whole nation so staunch and people so calm that it must be seen to be believed.

Beneš was persuaded that the only possible chance of maintaining peace was for Britain to declare that she would support France if the latter went to the aid of Czechoslovakia. Such a declaration, thought the President, would rally the countries of South-Eastern Europe 'in a way we in England do not perhaps realise. . . .'[23] These impressions were certainly borne out by the professional reports of the Military Attaché at the Embassy in Prague. Long after the war Brigadier Stronge, who served in Czechoslovakia from November, 1936 until December, 1938, still felt sufficiently deeply about the events of that time to compose for the record a lengthy *Personal Memorandum*[24] to show 'the faulty judgment which was made at the time concerning the potential of the Czech Army to offer effective and highly damaging resistance to the invading Wehrmacht' which he considered most historians either underrated or ignored. In none of the histories he had read, wrote the Brigadier, had this subject received the attention due to its relevance in an issue of peace or war.

In June, 1938 Stronge had attended a conference of Military Attachés at the War Office. The gist of the intelligence the Attaché provided was that the more he saw of the troops, the General Staff and the whole military ensemble in Czechoslovakia, the more convinced he became that here was a force capable of defending its frontiers and willing to do so. There was in Czechoslovakia an army of one million well-trained and well-equipped men. The balance of strategic advantage lay almost entirely on their side; they would benefit from the difficult terrain, and from operating on interior lines with detailed knowledge of the country. They would also gain from short lines of communication to supply depôts and arsenals and from the support of a loyal and steadfast population. There was a strong protective screen of fortifications against penetration; even where these were not yet completed, on the pre-*Anschluss* Austrian border, a German attack would be a lengthy and hazardous operation and the Wehrmacht would certainly have to stand and do battle. Most importantly, morale was high: inspired both by their own efficiency, faith in their leadership and by the cause they would be defending – their existence as a sovereign nation.

Why did the 'melancholy' report of the Chiefs of Staff, submitted *after* Stronge's evidence to the War Office Conference and to individual Ministers, go unchallenged in Cabinet? The answer is surely that what the Cabinet heard from the COS was what they wanted to hear. In fact, it is not too much to say that intelligence which was to their – or at least to Chamberlain's – taste was virtually commissioned. This can be clearly demonstrated from the Notes of Informal Meetings of Ministers when the crisis was at its height. The Military Attaché was summoned, with the CIGS, to give his judgment. But it was not the man on the spot in Prague who was called upon, but the Attaché in *Berlin*, who had just returned from a 'short tour' of Czechoslovakia. He performed admirably. Morale in the country was poor, he reported, and much of the material preparations were not complete. Frontier guards appeared scared stiff. The Czechs were very ill-prepared on the Southern frontier. His French colleague in Berlin was also doubtful of the value of Czech resistance. The Attaché concluded by saying that he thought it very rash to base any policy on assumption that the Czechs would fight like tigers.[25]

Stronge's reaction at the time is recalled in his *Personal Memorandum*. Twice during the crisis period, he wrote, the Berlin Attaché, Colonel Mason-MacFarlane, had come through Prague:

> After both of his visits, Colonel MacFarlane sent in adverse views to the War Office. I did not then see the first report, which was highly inaccurate in other respects also, but on seeing the second I took steps at once to contradict his opinions. . . . It is unfortunate that his views on Czech army morale would seem to have been accepted in Whitehall rather than mine, as a factor affecting official policy.

The German Army commanders shared the opinion that the Czech Army, unaided, could put up a stiff resistance. They were not confident of their own ability to pierce the Czech fortifications speedily (a judgment confirmed when in due course they were able to inspect the fortifications at close quarters). They would certainly not have agreed with the insouciant assessment of the Czech Army's position given by the editor of *The Times*, Geoffrey Dawson:

> A row of fortresses in the hills cannot mean much more than the chance of holding up an invasion for a few days. It is a case of being killed on Friday instead of on Tuesday![26]

Keitel's evidence at Nuremberg set the record straight. The German Army, he said, were very glad not to have been called upon to break through the fortifications: 'From a purely military point of view we were not strong enough.'[27] This was also the opinion of Field Marshal von Manstein who testified: 'There is no doubt whatever that if Czechoslovakia had defended herself, we should have been held up by her fortifications for we did not have the means to break through.'[28]

There was also the problem Germany always faced of war on two fronts. An attack on Czechoslovakia would leave Germany's Western frontier manned by only six or seven divisions – all that could be spared. The Chief of the French General Staff, Gamelin, declared in London that he could mobilise 100 divisions, sixty of which would face Germany. In spite of this overwhelming superiority he could only talk of defensive operations. (So weak was the West wall that, as a German general said after the war, 'the French could have walked into Germany.')

Even the Foreign Office, for some reason, contributed to the military disinformation. Creswell of Central Department asserted a few months before the crisis that the Czechs 'have only 24 regular divisions while Germany can put 70 divisions into the field practically within a few days, and will be able to mobilise at least 120 divisions in a far shorter time than it will take the Czechs to get going. . . .'[29] (The Adviser on Germany, Kirkpatrick, was later to record that 'Hitler told us at Godesberg he could mobilise 90-odd divisions.' There was no reason, he added, to suppose that this was incorrect.)[30]

How wide of the mark all this was can be seen from the statements made by the former Chief of Staff, General Halder, in his sessions with Allied Intelligence officers after his liberation from Gestapo custody in 1945. The Germans had 22 divisions on the Eastern front against the Czechs' 35, and five or six in the West. Even at the outbreak of the war with Poland, although the military strength had improved, transport, signals and supply were not ready, according to Halder, and had to be improvised by making use of civilian staff from the Reichbahn, the Reichpost and industry. 'All through the war, we had to live on improvisations.' And in the Polish campaign, declared the former Chief of Staff, he did not have a single soldier in reserve.[31]

General Beck refused to accept – as Fritsch and Brauchitsch had refused to do in November, 1937 – Hitler's basic strategy: that Britain and France would not fight. He considered the French army to be the best in Europe; that the support of Czechoslovakia would be a point of honour with France and that Britain would stand behind her. Beck also knew that though Germany could eventually overcome Czechoslovakia, in the process the Wehrmacht and the Luftwaffe would suffer a mauling which would affect their capacity to face an escalating international conflict. It was against this background of Czech strength and German weakness that the Opposition were urging the Western Powers to challenge Hitler's aggressive plans.

It had been Beck's hope, in the several memorandums he produced in the early summer of 1938, to prove by military arguments that Operation Green was an unacceptable risk. In a final memorandum of 16th July, Beck rehearsed all the arguments against military action while emphasising the dangers of a general European – or even world – war. He also stressed the fact that the German people themselves did not want war and this mood in the country would be dangerous for the morale of the fighting forces. He concluded with the statement that the Supreme Commander, Hitler, must be induced to halt the preparations for war: 'Extraordinary times demand extraordinary measures.' Beck was not alone in his thinking. The Naval Chief of Staff, Vice-Admiral Gruse, shared the opinion that the responsibility for events rested with the leadership, and that the leadership should be made to realise the extent of its responsibility in pursuing a course of action which threatened the very existence of the country.

Although as Chief of Staff Beck rightly advanced his objections on military grounds, the mainspring of his opposition to Hitler's policy was moral principle. He now bent his efforts to arousing the consciences of his fellow officers. On 29th July Beck told Brauchitsch that it was now a matter of urgency to decide upon the moment when the Commander-in-Chief should approach the Führer. He himself had drafted the words which should be used:

The Commander in Chief of the Army, together with his most senior commanding generals, regret that they cannot assume responsibility for the conduct of a war of this nature without carrying a share of the guilt for it in the face of the people and of history. Should the Führer, therefore, insist on the prosecution of this war, they hereby resign from their posts.[32]

This, pronounced Beck, was nothing less than their duty. Beck had never regarded the military oath as an impediment. Blind obedience to one man was the invention of the Führer himself when he imposed the oath of allegiance – not to the country, but to his person. The Prussian code of military law stipulated that criminal orders were not to be obeyed and that soldiers acting otherwise were liable to punishment. Military obedience should not go beyond the point at which knowledge, conscience and responsibility forbade the execution of an order. On 4th August, Brauchitsch called a conference of all commanders at which virtual unanimity was reached with regard to Beck's assessment of the situation. However, Brauchitsch – as he had done in the Fritsch affair – failed to follow through. The speech calling for collective protest which Beck had drafted for him was not delivered. He did however submit Beck's memorandum, which had been the subject of the conference, to Hitler. The Führer's reply, through the Commander-in-Chief, was that he did not accept political dispositions from others: he alone knew what had to be done.

Faced with Hitler's inflexibility and Brauchitsch's vacillations, Beck realised that he could achieve nothing further. But he would not remain in a position in which he would bear any responsibility for what was to happen. On 15th August Hitler reiterated to his generals his intention to attack Czechoslovakia. On 18th August the Chief of Staff asked to be relieved of his post. Hitler agreed, but craftily requested that for policy reasons it should not be made public for the time being. Beck allowed himself to be prevailed upon to keep quiet. Like Fritsch, he failed to go out with a bang. He was finally retired from the Army by Hitler after the Czech crisis, on 31st October. Other members of the Opposition regretted his resignation, particularly Weizsäcker and the Kordt brothers who felt that Beck had 'played his cards too soon.' The weight which his position carried and his personal prestige would have been more value to the Opposition's struggle than a principled withdrawal. Nevertheless, in his retirement Beck became the focal point of the opposition for military and civilian alike. No move was made without being referred to him and his high moral courage remained an inspiration.

Beck's successor, though not quite matching the personal standing of his former Chief, was an excellent staff officer and a dedicated anti-Nazi. The British Military Attaché, Mason-MacFarlane, had him rather differently within his sights. He told the Foreign Office: 'The new Chief of the General Staff, General Halder, is heart and soul a Party man and a convinced and almost fanatical National Socialist. He is disliked and mistrusted by most of the officers of the War Ministry. . . .'[33] This was well up to the standard of Military Intelligence. But a former editor of *The Times*, Wickham Steed, who frequently passed information to the Foreign Office from contacts in Germany, gave Halifax a rather different picture. Addressing an audience of general officers and staff officers at the *Wahrakademie*, Halder had declared that although it was not the business of soldiers to discuss political aspects of the situation (it was July, 1939) he knew well that many German officers disliked both the present political system in Germany and the ideas which it expressed.[34] In fact, Halder had been chosen by Beck to succeed him because he shared Beck's principles with regard to the morality of Hitler's policy and because he was prepared to oppose him by force.

It is clear that already, before his resignation, Beck had begun to think the unthinkable. He foresaw that a 'strike' by the generals would almost certainly result in some upheaval, though he hoped this could be confined to the capital. There would at last be the resolution between the Army and the SS which the Fritsch affair had deferred. With the disarming of the Party's military arm, and with the Wehrmacht no longer obeying him, Hitler would no longer be able to play the rôle of dictator. Beck's thinking had now advanced to the positive contemplation of a *coup d'état*. General Witzleben, commander of Berlin District, and General von Stülpnagel of the General Staff began to discuss plans with the Chief of Police Helldorf, who had worked on Fritsch's defence and was a reliable anti-Nazi. Whatever the circumstances in which Hitler might be deposed, the non-military conspirators in the Foreign Office and in legal circles considered it vitally important – as indeed did the Army itself – that the false idea should never be allowed to take hold that the Führer had been the victim simply of a *putsch* by self-seeking Army officers. Obviously the assault must be executed by the Army:

Hitler was well guarded. But it had to be shown that the deed was carried out in association with responsible and highly-placed people in civilian life reflecting many sections of society. The leaders knew that they had support among large numbers of the population who were in no position to voice it. They therefore felt that they were acting on their behalf and not against the wishes of the nation as a whole. Their most urgent task was to mobilise the diplomatic forces abroad which would push Hitler into a dilemma from which there would be no escape. The report which Wiedemann had made to Christie about the effect on Hitler of the diplomatic action against him on 21st May contained the significant passage:

> It is the agreed opinion of various highly placed observers that any forthcoming political setbacks to the Nazi system or to the Führer himself, would have the greatest influence and would accelerate the crisis which, since May 21st, would no longer appear to be avoidable.[35]

Here was vital confirmation from the heart of the régime of the damage to Hitler and the Party of 'political setbacks' and the effectiveness of concerted diplomatic action abroad. More than that, there was the clear indication that a swift follow-up on the same lines should be made while Hitler was still badly shaken both in his national prestige and in his personal following. How could this intimate despatch, revealing as it did the effectiveness of the British move already made, have been ignored? Was it the usual internal politicking in the Foreign Office which overrode intelligence considerations where Vansittart was involved? The report had provided valuable support to his oft-repeated advice that a resolute diplomatic stance would deter Hitler. Sir Nevile Henderson, however, took a completely opposite view and one which was more to the liking of the Chamberlain Government. The Ambassador claimed that Hitler was seeking a peaceful solution to the Sudeten question and hostile attitudes might provoke him to extremism. Such gestures of deterrence as that of 21st May ought not to be repeated. The Prime Minister was of the same mind.

Chamberlain saw a way in which Hitler could be placated and the Sudeten question resolved. He would send to Czechoslovakia a 'mediator' between the Czechs and the Sudetens, ostensibly quite independent of the British Government. The chosen mediator was

Lord Runciman, former President of the Board of Trade and a ship-owner – which made the more apt his claim that he felt as if he was adrift in the Atlantic in a dinghy. The Prime Minister told the House of Commons on 26th July that the appointment had been made in response to an appeal by the Czechoslovak Government. This was untrue; it had been imposed upon them.

Vansittart, however, was not deceived and redoubled his efforts to stiffen the British Government. While General Beck in Berlin was conducting his war of words against Hitler's projected aggression, the Chief Diplomatic Adviser in London was fighting the same battle. In August – a couple of weeks before Beck resigned in despair – Vansittart submitted a Memorandum to the Foreign Secretary to which he annexed a selection of intelligence reports from his own sources which he had received over a considerable period of time. These reports called for 'the gravest and most urgent attention', and his sources were 'first hand and first-rate: they all occupy positions of importance and responsibility [in Germany].' All their information was borne out by Christie's own investigations. These reports, Vansittart claimed, all showed in detail and in contour the pattern of the Nazi designs. Germany intended to realise her ambitions by force if she could not get the whole of what she wanted – which was everything – by other means. Hitler was now ready to make his next move: the Germans were going to invade Czechoslovakia. 'Only the strongest and clearest action on our part can prevent the catastrophe. . . .' The memorandum, which was dated 7th August, offered the suggestion that an emergency Cabinet Meeting should be called, letting it be known that the subject under discussion was Czechoslovakia. An alternative suggestion was to indicate the likelihood of Parliament being summoned. Vansittart saw in the current situation a resemblance to July, 1914. It was widely held, he said, that catastrophe then could have been avoided by British diplomatic action. Had our attitude been made absolutely clear in July, 1914 Germany would not have gone to war. Sir Robert hoped that disaster would not again emerge from silence: 'If we leave Berlin under any further illusion where we shall stand in a European war, there will be a European war.'[36]

It was the straightest possible talking, but the last thing the Government wanted from its Chief Diplomatic Adviser was advice. Vansittart had ranged against him the Prime Minister, the Foreign Secretary, the Chiefs of Staff, his successor as Head of the Foreign

Office, and His Majesty's representative in Berlin. It was against this unbreachable wall that the German Opposition, all unwitting, was about to launch itself.

On 17 August 1938 an emissary of the Opposition arrived in London. Ewald von Kleist-Schmenzin, a landowner from Pomerania, a Conservative and a Monarchist, had already been imprisoned several times because of his unconcealed opposition to the régime. Under the auspices of Canaris and at the instigation of Beck, he travelled to London with the intention of seeing a very limited number of key figures upon whom he could impress the message that Britain should declare loudly and unequivocally its intention to resist any further aggression on Hitler's part. And he sought the assurance that it was indeed Britain's intention to challenge Hitler. Colonel Oster had told him before he left for London: 'Bring me certain proof that England will fight if Czechoslovakia is attacked and I will make an end of this régime.' Ian Colvin, European Correspondent of the *News Chronicle*, who was well acquainted with the oppositional elements in Germany, put Kleist in touch with Lord Lloyd, Chairman of the British Council, former government minister and a leading figure in the Conservative Party, who had the ear of the Prime Minister and the Foreign Secretary. Shortly after the Anschluss, Colvin had had a conversation with Kleist which he duly reported to Sir George Ogilvie-Forbes, Chargé d'Affaires at the Embassy. If England were to say no, if only through diplomatic channels, Kleist had told him, the Czechoslovakian 'adventure' must be put off. Hitler feared 'like the plague' that England would caution him, for he would have to give way: 'Let them know in England that the General Staff needs a sheet anchor. The British Government alone can throw it to them by a firmly spoken word.' Lord Lloyd had received advance notice of Kleist's visit to London from Colvin, who wrote that it had been organised by Canaris' Abwehr.[37]

Kleist's first call was on Vansittart, who reported their conversation to the Prime Minister. The German had spoken with the utmost frankness and gravity. War was no longer a matter of extreme danger but of complete certainty – unless the British stopped it. Hitler was encouraged by Ribbentrop who continued to assure him that Britain and France would do nothing. All the generals were against war. They needed help from outside the Reich in the form of a powerful statement from a leading British statesman which would reach the Germans, emphasising the horrors of the inevitable catastrophe which must ensue. Hitler must be made to realise that Britain and France would intervene if he should use force. Vansittart recorded that Kleist 'talked a good deal' about the line of policy of those he represented, which the Diplomatic Adviser found 'essentially reasonable', but he did not think it necessary 'to burden this paper with them.' No doubt Kleist had put before the British diplomat the nature of the new state with which it was intended to replace the Third Reich of the Nazis. Vansittart however was mainly concerned to emphasise the German visitor's plea for outside assistance in the form of a diplomatic challenge to Hitler, to which 'he adhered very firmly and persistently.' This demand was, wrote Vansittart, 'the same as that which I have been reporting to you as being the desire and the almost open request of a number of other German moderates who have been in communication with me during these past weeks.' Kleist stressed that he was risking his life to warn that Britain was 'in the presence of the certainty' of war. There was no hope as long as Hitler was at the head of affairs but if war could be avoided 'it would be the prelude to the end of the régime and a renascence of a Germany with whom the world could deal'; but 'they alone could do nothing without assistance from outside.'[38] On the evening of the same day Kleist met Lord Lloyd, who reported to Lord Halifax that he had had a visit 'by a German of considerable importance who came over here to warn me as to the gravity of the situation.' His visitor had confirmed what he himself had written to Halifax a fortnight earlier (after receipt of Colvin's letter) that 'Hitler has taken his decision to move on Czechoslovakia between the middle and end of September . . . and that unless England and France react, the thing will happen.' His 'German friend' had told him, continued Lord Lloyd:

Today the German Army was united and unanimously hostile to Hitler. The general feeling of anxiety and dislike of the Nazi régime was definitely in the ascendant in Germany. . . . If England and France today made a firm stand over Czechoslovakia they would strengthen, he claims in a degree far greater than appears to be understood here, a general opposition to Hitler and his policy. Much more he told me, and told me impressively – and I feel that I should at least tell it to you. I cannot do more – or less.[39]

Because of the danger of his mission, Kleist wished his contacts to be kept to a minimum but there was one more important person still to see – Winston Churchill, by whom he was received the following morning at Chartwell. Churchill recorded an account of their meeting which he passed to the Foreign Office. Again Kleist stressed the imminence of an attack on Czechoslovakia. The diplomatic action taken by Britain and France on 21st May was regarded by Hitler as a personal rebuff 'whose recurrence he must avoid and whose memory he must obliterate.' Kleist urged that some gesture from abroad was needed 'to crystallise the widespread and indeed universal anti-war sentiment in Germany.' Everything must be done to encourage the generals. In the event of the generals insisting on peace, there would be a new system of government within forty-eight hours. Churchill wrote Kleist a letter of encouragement for his friends in Germany. Knowing that the Government would never make any such declaration against Hitler as that for which the Opposition hoped, he himself intimated that if Germany attacked Czechoslovakia, the spectacle of 'bloody fighting' would have its effect on the whole British Empire. Well enough informed to be aware that Germany could only sustain a short war, Churchill stressed that it was not the first few months which should be considered 'but where we shall all be at the end of the third or fourth year.' Continuing in the same strain, he was in fact saying all the things which Kleist had begged Vansittart that some leading British statesman should state publicly. Churchill added that he was authorised by the Foreign Secretary to confirm that the Prime Minister's statement in the House of Commons on 24th March still defined the position of the Government in relation to Czechoslovakia. Without making any definite commitment, Chamberlain had spoken of the 'bounds of probability' and the 'inexorable pressure of facts' on countries closely allied which could bring about ultimate involvement in the event of war between two governments. Churchill concluded by looking forward to 'the true reunion of our countries on the basis of the greatness and the freedom of both.'[40]

While Kleist was closeted with Churchill on the morning of 19th August, the Prime Minister was digesting Vansittart's report on his own meeting with him the previous day. No German opponent of Hitler was a friend of Chamberlain. He wrote to Halifax from Chequers in his own hand:

> I take it that Kleist is violently anti-Hitler and is extremely anxious to stir up his friends in Germany to make an attempt at its overthrow. He reminds me of the Jacobites at the Court of France in King William's time and I think we must discount a good deal of what he said.

Only by a double negative was Chamberlain able to produce a positive thought. Although rejecting any sort of public declaration, 'nevertheless,' he went on, 'I confess to some feeling of uneasiness and I don't feel sure that we ought not to do something.'[41] His idea of a 'warning gesture' was to summon the British Ambassador to London in ten days' time and for him to let it be known in Berlin that 'he had been sent for to consult about the serious position in connection with Czechoslovakia.'

Vansittart's report was also passed to Central Department for their consideration. There is a curious reference in the minutes to Kleist speaking 'on behalf of the leader of the German Army', a fact which does not appear anywhere else. However, mention is made of the existence of an intelligence report containing what information could be found concerning Kleist. Mallet, Sargent and Cresswell fumbled around the Kleist message, the delivery of which had been a matter of life and death to himself and his fellow-conspirators. Indeed the latter aspect was briskly dismissed: 'There is always something suspicious about "anti-Nazis" coming to this country in fear of their lives, especially if they get away with it.' If, however, it was true that Hitler was intent on war, it was felt that there was only one way to stop him. Far from standing up to Hitler, the Foreign Office plumped for standing up to the Czechs. The only possible course to pursue was to get Lord Runciman 'to produce recommendations containing all that the Sudetens could reasonably desire.' There would have to be very strong pressure on the Czechs, 'amounting to a statement that we would leave them to their fate if they do not accept the Runciman proposals.' Mallet agreed with Cresswell's views and was all for strong pressure on the Czechs. He opposed a repeat of the 21st May tactic. It might weaken the prestige of the régime, 'but it would be rash, I think, to imagine that we should bring the régime down.' So much for the urging of Weidemann to Christie, from Hitler's inner circle.

This then was the result in Whitehall of Kleist's visit 'with a rope round his neck.' Not a ringing declaration of *ne plus ultra* to Hitler, but a stampede to pressure the Czechs into surrendering everything to save the British and the French. The letter which Churchill had written for Kleist went by diplomatic bag to the Embassy in Berlin, whence it was collected and delivered to him by Fabian von Schlabrendorff. Kleist passed a copy to Canaris, Head of the Abwehr and staunch opponent of Hitler. Proof, according to Schlabrendorff, of a stiffening attitude in Britain.[42] Its contents were included in a German Foreign Office memorandum (discovered among captured documents after the war) entitled 'Opinion at present available to us on the attitude of the different powers in the event of war breaking out over Czechoslovakia.' The material was identified as 'Extract from a letter of Winston Churchill to a German confidant.'[43] The original, found in Kleist's desk after the July, 1944 plot, brought him to the gallows.

Even as Foreign Office vapourings were being exchanged in London, a despatch was on its way from Berlin enclosing a report by the Military Attaché on the effect which the looming Czech crisis was having in Germany, based on information from his German contacts:

> German General Staff staggered by the fact that it is being taken so quietly abroad. Normal life of the country is directly disorganised. Spirit of people generally, and most of those called up, is bad, and there is everywhere terror at the prospect of a catastrophe. . . . If by firm action abroad, Hitler is forced at the eleventh hour to renounce his intentions, he will be unable to survive the blow.[44]

The German Staff would have been even more staggered had they known that throughout the fraught month of August, 1938, the Head of the British Foreign Office was absent on holiday. On 31st July, Sir Alexander Cadogan had departed for Le Touquet where he divided his time between the casino and the golf course, following the crisis in the newspapers. On 24th August an agitated Private Secretary, Gladwyn Jebb, urged his immediate return. The following day Cadogan telephoned the Office and offered to do so but had no reply. On the 26th Jebb telephoned again but Cadogan replied rather testily that he must know whether or not his presence was in fact required. Four days later he recorded in his diary:

> *Daily Mail* this morning full of Van and all the conferences he attended, with a photo of his grinning mug. Evidently a crisis was going on and I ought to have been back. Well, I gave them a chance to recall me. But I can't stay on here after this week. Played after tea

on the Old Course. Very well, too. Best score I think I have ever done here.[45]

Cadogan finally arrived back in London on 2nd September, where he found it was 'obviously touch and go – but not gone yet.'

The reports which Christie was sending in to Vansittart reflected from a different angle the information received from the General Staff. Vansittart passed them on to the Foreign Secretary:

> The following information has been obtained by Colonel Christie from various important members of German heavy industry in close touch with such firms as Krupps, Thyssens, Voglers, Potts, Kirdorfs, etc. All these sources have been personally known to Colonel Christie since his childhood. . . .

Opinion was unanimous that Hitler intended to invade Czechoslovakia and that a 'bold determined attitude or action by France and Great Britain might still prevent this war, as public sentiment in the Reich is very much opposed to it.'[46] In another report Christie quoted 'a very old friend and the head of a world-wide industrial concern in Germany' who had telephoned him from Belgium. The Nazi Party, he said, were in full cry. He was convinced that unless France and Great Britain made it clear to Berlin as soon as possible that they would oppose by force an attack on Czechoslovakia, the German Army would be sent into Prague in the autumn. 'The Party leaders are at the moment quite sure that Great Britain will not move beyond verbal protests.'[47] Vansittart's other valuable source, Conwell-Evans, was able to confirm the warnings Christie was receiving. He visited Berlin on 24th August with the intention of staying two weeks, but was positively hustled home again by his oppositionist friends in the German Foreign Office to try and convince the British authorities of Hitler's decision to attack. He arrived in London on 29th August and immediately saw Sir Horace Wilson, impressing upon him the message he had been given and its source: 'if Hitler knows beforehand that France and Great Britain will fight, and if we mobilise the Fleet in the North Sea, he will even now hesitate. . . .' He gave the same information to Vansittart and a day or so later gave the Foreign Secretary some impressions of the atmosphere in Berlin: 'I said that the Nazis were quite unable to understand any warnings couched in the usual Parliamentary language of ministers; clear words must be accompanied by action. I thought the Fleet should be mobilised as soon as possible.'[48]

Conwell-Evans was aware that Sir Nevile Henderson was also in London on 29th August. This was the ambassadorial summons Chamberlain had decided upon in the wake of Kleist's visit. Conwell-Evans felt that his own information would usefully support what he imagined would be a similar report on the part of the Ambassador. He was gravely mistaken. At 11 a.m. on 30th August there was a Meeting of Ministers, presided over by the Prime Minister, at which Henderson was present to give his views. The minutes reveal how the tide was running against adopting any diplomatic stance which would deter Hitler. They also reveal clearly the British attitude towards the German Opposition, as expressed by the Foreign Secretary:

> Many moderate Germans are pressing us to go even further than the Prime Minister's speech of 24th March and that if we do so the Nazi régime would crack. He received these messages with reserve. He did not believe the internal régime of one country was destroyed as a result of action taken by some other countries.

His policy, he declared, was to keep the Germans guessing. If this policy failed, continued Halifax, the Government would be told that if only they had had the courage of their convictions they could have stopped the trouble. Such criticisms left him unmoved. The Ambassador reassured the meeting: 'It was noticeable that all statements to the effect that Herr Hitler had made up his mind to use force came from enemies of the régime, who would be unlikely to know the facts.' His Excellency thus demonstrated his unawareness that these enemies of the régime occupied some of the key positions in the country, outside the Nazi Party, and were indeed extremely well placed to know the facts. Only an uneasy Duff Cooper proposed an admonitory gesture – the mobilisation of the Fleet and its despatch to Scapa Flow.[49]

The most important development at this time however was discussed not at the Meeting of Ministers but at a much more select affair which had taken place the previous day. Only Chamberlain, Horace Wilson and Henderson were present. Chamberlain confided in Henderson an idea, which he had conjured up entirely by himself without consultation with Cabinet colleagues or Foreign Office advisers. The Sudeten crisis could, he felt, be sorted out on a man-to-man basis between himself and the Führer and he proposed to do just that by going to see him. He and Wilson had decided on a code name for the adventure – 'Plan Z' – and Chamberlain himself was designated 'Mr X'.[50] Not a word of this was disclosed at the Meeting of Ministers the following day.

When Henderson returned to Berlin, he went to call on Weizsäcker at his office. The State Secretary, aware that Henderson's visit to London had been for the specific purpose of discussing the Czecho-slovak problem, waited to receive a stern warning for presentation to the German Government. As Conwell-Evans was to learn later from his friends in the Wilhelmstrasse, Weizsäcker was staggered to be told by the British Ambassador that he had informed the Cabinet that Hitler had not decided upon war, although others were urging him to do so; that Hitler did not belong to the 'War Party' – he had spent four years in the trenches and knew what war was.[51] Dining that night with Henderson at the Embassy, the State Secretary tried to make some impact on his host. Echoing exactly Vansittart's own reminder to the British Foreign Secretary, Weizsäcker remarked that war in 1914 might have been avoided if Great Britain had spoken out in time. Henderson replied, according to his report to the Foreign Office, that he personally regarded it as undesirable to use language which might damage Herr Hitler's prestige and provoke his resent-ment. While agreeing that public threats might be a danger, the German diplomat pressed the point: 'At the same time, [Weizsäcker] asked whether it might not be possible for me to have a personal talk with Herr Hitler at Nuremberg?'[52] (the Party Rally at Nurem-berg the following week at which Henderson would be a guest.) Alas, the subsequent history of the warning at Nuremberg was to be the most dismal chapter in Henderson's disastrous ambassadorship.

The month of August 1938 ended with one notable contribution to the debate from outside the Government. On the 31st, Churchill wrote to the Foreign Secretary suggesting a Joint Note from Britain, France and Russia to Hitler, which should also be shown formally to President Roosevelt. The President should then address Hitler to the effect that it seemed inevitable that a world war must follow an invasion of Czechoslovakia. 'It seems to me,' wrote Churchill, 'that this process would give the best chance to the peaceful elements in German circles to make a stand.' He also suggested certain Fleet movements 'which would make a great stir in the naval ports, the effect of which could only be beneficial as a deterrent and a timely

precaution if the worst happened. . . . It is clear that speed is vital.'
Churchill added a note in his own hand: 'Perhaps you may care to
show this to the Prime Minister if you think it worthwhile.'[53] It is
significant that Churchill should have linked these proposals directly
with the Opposition element inside Germany. It was a clear recognition and acknowledgment that the British could actually assist that
element by taking certain steps. No doubt he had Kleist's recent visit
in mind. But Churchill was also close to Vansittart and must have
been kept well-informed of approaches from Germany and
the constant pressure for a sign from Britain. Unlike the men at the
Foreign Office – 'the Germans always [sic] want us to make their
revolutions for them' (Cadogan); 'It is the interest of the moderates
to make our flesh creep in the hope that we may be able to assist
them' (Roberts) – Churchill actually saw that co-operation with
Hitler's opponents was a partnership from which all would benefit.
How seriously Churchill held to this opinion can be seen in his
broadcast to the United States after Munich and in his speech in
Brussels in 1945.

'Extraordinary times,' General Beck had declared, 'demand extraordinary measures.' As the crisis month of September began, with
Hitler hell-bent on his aggressive policies, the Opposition began
actively to make its preparations. As soon as the Führer gave the
order which would drag the unwilling nation into war, he would be
seized. If on the other hand he was forced by the long-hoped-for
challenge from the Western Powers to recoil and abandon his plans,
the myth of his invincibility both at home and abroad would be
destroyed. He and his régime would be swept away, forcibly if
necessary. With the Leader dead, or behind bars awaiting the judicial
exposure of his criminal régime, the warring Party factions would
disintegrate. Whichever course events should take, Hitler would be
exposed as having wantonly hazarded the security of the nation and
the peace of Europe, if not of the world. This was not a matter
merely of removing a dictator but of taking over the State itself.
The possibility of civil unrest and the danger of resistance by the
formidable SS had to be faced. This was to be no cloak-and-dagger
affair. It was a meticulously planned military operation. Action had
to be swift and decisive. Troop movements were plotted: a Panzer
division was to be moved to Berlin and put under the orders of the

Commander of the Berlin Garrison, General Witzleben. Plans were made to neutralise SS formations in other districts. Gisevius worked out plans for the police: the police chiefs Helldorf and Schulenburg in Berlin were to participate in the action. Oster maintained contact between Beck's successor, General Halder, and Weizsäcker at the Foreign Office. As Halder would be giving the signal for the *coup*, it was essential that he should be kept informed of any international moves. Schacht was also consulted on the political side and as a Reich Minister was able to exert influence on various generals. In order to widen the scope of participation, an assault force of thirty young officers, students and workers was assembled. While the Panzers surrounded the Chancellery, they were to rush the building. Erich Kordt, whose position close to Ribbentrop gave him privileged access to the building, would ensure that the great double doors were open. Although the senior generals and civilians envisaged the arrest and subsequent trial of Hitler, for which they had long been assembling the evidence, the younger men, with Oster's approval, looked for a swifter resolution. Hitler, like so many of his victims, would probably be 'shot resisting arrest.' Besides the Chancellery itself, other key points such as SS and Gestapo headquarters would be seized. The radio station, too, would be taken over. Everything was planned. Gisevius and General Brockdorff, driven round Berlin by a woman member of the Opposition group in the guise of tourists, visited key points and plotted locations on the map and noted the force which would be required to seize them.[54] Nothing was to be left to chance. Action was keyed to the moment when Hitler would give the order to march into Czechoslovakia. Halder, as Chief of Staff, would personally receive the order. This would be the signal for the launching of the *coup*. Meanwhile, Weizsäcker and his colleagues had already launched a secret offensive in London in a series of moves unprecedented in normal diplomatic usage.

On the day before Conwell-Evans left for Berlin on 24th August, a meeting had been arranged in his flat in Cornwall Gardens between Theo Kordt from the German Embassy and Sir Horace Wilson. According to Kordt's record of the occasion, he told Sir Horace that opposition to Hitler's and Ribbentrop's policies existed and was growing. It was the conviction of the Opposition that Hitler was heading for war and it was hoped to circumvent his evil intentions by secret but totally frank co-operation with British statesmen to whom the preservation of peace was just as much a question of honour and conscience as it was to themselves.[55] Kordt reported this conversation to Weiszäcker officially but in such a form that, should the letter fall into the wrong hands (a sharp watch was kept on the courier service) the real truth would not be perceived. Kordt's introductory words that he had met Wilson 'at the house of Mr Conwell-Evans' (the secret rendezvous) would have alerted his Chief that this was a communication which should not be taken at its face value. Officially, Conwell-Evans was a friend of Ribbentrop. When Kordt wrote that he had 'specially pointed out to Sir Horace how necessary it was that the British Government should now speak and act clearly', the State Secretary would have understood what statement had been requested of the British Government. As they parted, Sir Horace assured the German diplomat that he would discuss the situation with the Prime Minister and perhaps a decisive step by Great Britain would result. 'I told him,' wrote Kordt, 'that things were moving towards a decision one way or the other. If Great Britain wanted to help in achieving a reasonable solution of the Czechoslovak question . . . she must act quickly.'[56] The Opposition well knew that Ribbentrop was insisting to Hitler that Britain and France would never intervene by force, thus inciting him to pursue his aggression. No-one from the Foreign Office could gain the Führer's ear to contradict the Foreign Minister. In his despatches from the London Embassy, therefore, Theo Kordt would impute to the British rather more hawkish attitudes than actually existed. For instance, writing on 1st September, he reported that the British Government was unable to imagine that the Führer would pursue a policy which in all probability was bound to lead to a world war; however, it was on the alert, had established contact with the Dominions and was in constant touch with the French Government. No final decision had as yet been taken. However, Britain would be prepared when the decisive moment came. Kordt declared that it was his personal opinion that France would consider it irreconcilable with her honour to leave Czechoslovakia in the lurch. At the British Foreign Office visitors (non-German) were openly given to understand that Britain would not yield this time (as with the Italians in 1935) and had to make up its mind to confront the Germans with a categorical 'stop' in conjunction with its allies, 'if need be by force of arms.' There was, continued Kordt, a growing mood of grim determination, reminiscent of the mood prior to the outbreak of World War One. The idea prevailing among 'the masses' was that if

Chamberlain could not achieve a compromise with Germany, 'there is no other way but to go to war.' Kordt later recorded that 'I was more than once instructed by Ribbentrop in a threatening tone that I was to report only facts, but was to avoid drawing any conclusions from them.'[57]

Meanwhile, Theo's brother Erich, the head of Ribbentrop's Secretariat, and Weizsäcker shared an increasing anxiety that time was running out without the British having made any definite move. It was decided that a direct approach must be made to the British Government. It was impossible that such a message should be confided either to the post or the telephone. It was decided to send the Kordts' cousin, Susy Simonis, who occasionally acted as courier between the brothers, to London. As it was too risky for her to carry a written document, she committed the whole communication to memory. Erich drove her to the station and on the way they stopped at Weizsäcker's home to clear the message finally with his Chief.[58] When Susy arrived in London she spent the evening with Theo, transmitting the message. The following day, the German diplomat had another meeting with Sir Horace Wilson, this time in the latter's office in Downing Street. Kordt was later to record that at this second meeting he had given Wilson exact details of Hitler's resolve to go to war over the Sudeten question and his confidence that he would not have to face intervention from Britain and France.[59] Wilson in fact seems to have been impressed by what Kordt told him. Not only did he feel that it was important enough for the ears of the Foreign Secretary; he went further. He asked the diplomat to draft a letter containing all the points which the Opposition group wanted to be made clear to Hitler and to the German people. (Kordt did indeed draft such a letter but the matter was not pursued.)[60] Wilson reported the fact of this visit to Cadogan who noted in his diary that Kordt (whom he referred to as 'Herr X') had staked his life in putting conscience before duty.[61]

Wilson arranged a clandestine visit to Halifax. Kordt was to arrive at Downing Street on 7th September, in the evening. 'I was asked to come to Number Ten through the garden entrance,' he related in the account of the occasion which he gave at Weizsäcker's trial in 1947; he gave no details of his arrival or of what he thought of this dramatic precaution. Elsewhere he referred to his constant awareness of the all-seeing eyes of the Gestapo spies at the Embassy. For his own safety he would perhaps have been better arriving openly at the front door. Nevertheless, Sir Horace Wilson's touch of cloak-and-dagger no doubt raised Kordt's hopes that this was to be a momentous encounter with the British Foreign Secretary.

Kordt began with Beck's phrase – that extraordinary times demanded extraordinary measures. He came, he said, not as German Chargé d'Affaires but as the representative of political and military circles in Berlin who wanted at all costs to prevent war. His message had been carefully considered and warranted the attention of the British Government. Hitler was planning to attack Czechoslovakia, confident that he would be allowed a 'localised' war by Czechoslovakia's allies, who would not support her. Kordt declared that those on whose behalf he spoke were conscious of the parallel with 1914 and the failure of Sir Edward Grey to declare clearly Great Britain's intention to support France. Had this been done, at the right time, it would have moderated the Imperial Government's attitude. If France intended to stand by her treaty with Czechoslovakia and if, as Mr Chamberlain had stated, the British Empire could not then stand aside, this should be made quite clear. Such a declaration should be sufficiently firm and unequivocal for the German people to understand that Hitler's aggression would make war inevitable. Kordt then gave a clear sign of the Opposition's plans. If Hitler persisted in his bellicose policy, 'I am in a position to assure you that the political and military circles I am speaking for will "take arms against a sea of troubles, and by opposing end them".' If the statement for which they asked was issued, 'the Army leaders are prepared to act against Hitler's policy. A diplomatic defeat would be followed by a serious political setback in Germany and would practically mean the downfall of the régime.' Kordt concluded by saying that it was not easy for him to speak to the British Foreign Secretary in this manner, but that German patriots 'did not see any other way out of the dilemma than by close co-operation with the British Government to prevent the greatest crime that had ever been committed in human history.'[62]

It was a uniquely tragic moment. The responsible, honourable and peaceable elements in German society were beseeching the British to join hands with them in achieving the greatest boon which could be conferred on Europe and the world. They were not asking Britain to take any risks. They themselves had consistently stressed Germany's military and economic weakness and no doubt they assumed that British intelligence was well aware of Czech strength. It must have seemed to those Germans that their request was unassailable: something the British could not and would not refuse. If only Churchill had stood in Chamberlain's place the right words would have been said. He had offered them himself to Chamberlain and Halifax: 'We should tell Germany that if she set foot in Czechoslovakia we should at once be at war with her.'[63] Halifax assured Kordt that he would inform the Prime Minister and his Cabinet colleagues and that the matter would be dealt with in a very careful and confidential way.[64] As Kordt slipped out again through the garden of Number Ten into the darkness of the Horse Guards, he took with him the impression that at last the unequivocal statement the Opposition had hoped for would be forthcoming.

The sheer desperation which reigned in the German Foreign Office as the Opposition tried to galvanise the British into action is dramatically illustrated by the step which Weizsäcker himself took in the first week of September. In Danzig, the Swiss High Commissioner, Carl Burckhardt, Weizsäcker's close friend, received a visit from an art historian from Berlin. After casting an eye around the office with what Burckhardt later described as 'that well-known glance which at that time the French called "le regard Europe Centrale",' he whispered that Weizsäcker wanted to see him urgently. Burckhardt, who was about to travel to Geneva, broke his journey in Berlin. Weizsäcker came straight to the point. As Burckhardt noted it, his message was:

> Something must be done. We are on the very brink. The British must send somebody as quickly as possible so that one can talk, but not a personality too high in rank. No Prime Minister; none of these all-too-polite Englishmen of the old school. If Chamberlain comes, these louts will triumph and proclaim that some Englishman has taken his cue and come to heel . . . they should send an energetic military man who, if necessary, can shout and hit the table with a riding crop; a marshal with many decorations and scars, a man without too much consideration. . . .
> I earnestly entreat you to go to Switzerland as quickly as you can and to contact London. Unless negotiations are conducted we risk his bombing Prague and invading Bohemia.[65]

Impressed by his friend's urgency, Burckhardt drove 900 kilometres without stopping to the British Legation in Berne, where he roused the British Minister, Sir George Warner, who was in bed with gout. A telegram was sent to Lord Halifax stressing that the information

1. State Secretary
Ernst von Weizsäcker

2. Erich Kordt

3. Theodor Kordt

4. Ambassador Ulrich von Hassell

5. Carl Goerdeler

6. General Ludwig Beck

7. Admiral Wilhelm Canaris

8. Colonel Hans Oster

9. General Franz Halder
and General Walter von Brauchitsch

10. Carl Burckhardt

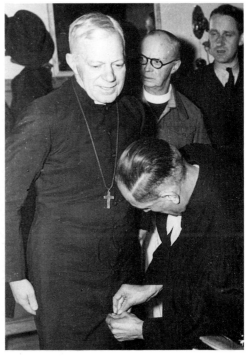

11. Dr. W. A. Visser 't Hooft

12. Pastor Niemöller assists Bishop Bell
at a service in Berlin, 1946

13. Cadogan and Weizsäcker, Geneva, 1933

14. Sir Robert Vansittart and Sir Alexander Cadogan, successive heads of the Foreign Office

15. Ambassador Ribbentrop, newly-appointed Foreign Minister,
entertains Sir Robert and Lady Vansittart

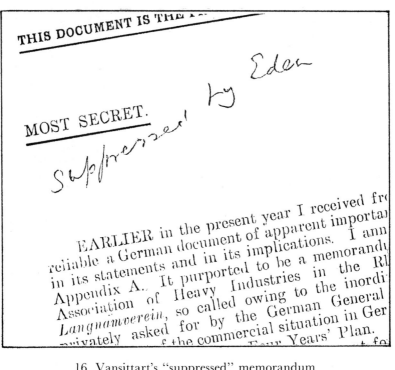

THIS DOCUMENT IS THE

Eden

MOST SECRET.

Suppressed by

EARLIER in the present year I received fr
reliable a German document of apparent importa
in its statements and in its implications. I ann
Appendix A. It purported to be a memorandu
Association of Heavy Industries in the Rl
Langnamverein, so called owing to the inordi
privately asked for by the German General
of the commercial situation in Ger
Four Years' Plan.

16. Vansittart's "suppressed" memorandum
on the German war economy

17. Foreign Secretary
Anthony Eden at the time
of his resignation in 1938

18. Erich Kordt (second
row, wearing glasses) in
Ribbentrop's entourage

19. Sir Nevile Henderson,
Ambassador to the Third
Reich, and Lord Halifax,
Foreign Secretary

20. Sir Nevile Henderson with Hitler
and his personal interpreter, Paul Otto Schmidt

21. Sir Nevile Henderson with Field-Marshal Goering
at the Nuremberg Rally, September, 1938

came from a highly placed personage; that Hitler was definitely going to attack Czechoslovakia, and that General Beck had resigned as he refused to be party to an attack on a friendly state. The personage in Berlin, who was in despair, saw as the only hope of peace a letter from the Prime Minister through an intermediary, referring to his desire for a peaceful settlement but emphasising that if Czechoslovakia were attacked, England would support her with all forces at her command.[66] This telegram hardly reflected the tone of Weizsäcker's message. However, the following morning Burckhardt spoke on the telephone to the Minister of State, R. A. Butler, when he 'emphatically presented Weizsäcker's view.'

On his arrival in Geneva, perhaps still uneasy about whether his message had made sufficient impact in London, Burckhardt sought out and confided in a British League of Nations colleague, Skrine Stevenson. Weizsäcker, he said, had told him that Ribbentrop and Himmler were inflaming Hitler's extravagant ideas. No-one who could give any sensible advice was allowed near him. The State Secretary felt that the only hope was a letter from the British Prime Minister to the Führer, to be put into his hands by a personal messenger. This should state unequivocally that if Germany attacked Czechoslovakia, Britain would respond totally with force in support of France. The messenger whom Weizsäcker had in mind was General Ironside, a man of powerful physique who was credited with an ability to speak fluent German. To come face to face with such a personage, who could shout him down in his own language without the protection of an interpreter, would, Weizsäcker believed, bring Hitler to his senses. Stevenson was obviously impressed by Burckhardt's statement, and it may be that the latter expressed some uneasiness about Sir George Warner's telegram to London. An incoming telephone call from Oliver Harvey, Private Secretary to Lord Halifax, gave him an opportunity to raise the matter and he asked whether that telegram 'had been given really serious consideration.' Harvey replied that 'it had been taken into consideration with other elements in the situation.' Stevenson said he gathered that the Berne telegram was short and that he feared a great deal of background would have necessarily been omitted. Would further details be of interest? Harvey said they would – 'Hence this letter,' wrote Stevenson to Strang, Head of Central Department, 'which in view of its interest and urgency I am sending by special messenger tonight. For you will agree that it is quite unprecedented that a very high official of the proved loyalty of Burckhardt's interlocutor should take a step of this kind.'[67] Extraordinary times, extraordinary measures.

A curious thing about Weizsäcker's message was the insistence that the Prime Minister should not visit Hitler. 'If Chamberlain comes, these louts will triumph. . . .' Such a possibility was still at that time Chamberlain's own cherished secret which he had shared with no-one but Horace Wilson and – on 29th August – with Henderson. It was not an eventuality which would have been envisaged by anyone, least of all a German. It was 8th September before Chamberlain took Halifax, Sir John Simon and Cadogan into his confidence and another two days before he extended this confidence to the other member of his inner Cabinet, Sir Samuel Hoare. 'Plan Z' was not revealed to the Cabinet until 14th September. And yet Weizsäcker was fiercely advising against it on 5th September. The – no doubt unwitting – mole must have been Henderson himself, who had entertained the State Secretary to dinner at the Embassy on 2nd September immediately on his return from London. So soon after having learned of Plan Z, the Ambassador's head must have been full of it and, as Vansittart said on another occasion, 'his indiscretion was notorious.' It is easy to imagine that he babbled a hint of what was in the Prime Minister's mind.

While Weizsäcker in Berlin was charging his friend Burckhardt with his urgent message for London, in Whitehall Halifax, Horace Wilson, Orme Sargent and Cadogan (at last disengaged from Le Touquet) were meeting to discuss the current state of affairs. High on the agenda was the British Ambassador's forthcoming visit to the Party Congress at Nuremberg and what opportunity, if any, should be sought to convey to Hitler the British attitude towards the Sudeten crisis. Wilson, the only non-member of the Foreign Office present, took it upon himself to convey the results of their discussion in writing, first to the Chancellor of the Exchequer Sir John Simon (of the 'Inner Cabinet') and secondly, after an unsatisfactory telephone call the same night, the 4th September, to the Prime Minister, in Scotland for the shooting. Referring in his letter to Simon to 'many representations from people who claim knowledge of German opinion', Wilson spoke not of plain declarations but of 'the right sort of hint.' He also introduced quite a new angle on the idea of concerted action by Britain and France in response to an attack on Czechoslovakia: '. . . it must be understood by Hitler that no British Government could stand by and see France defeated if, as a result of events,

France should get into hostilities with Germany.' This was an implication that Britain would wait and see how the battle went before
joining in. It also seemed to take almost for granted that France
would be defeated. The Foreign Office, Wilson told Simon, felt
there were great objections to public statements because these would
put Hitler in the position of being publicly asked to change his plan
(which, of course, was precisely what the Opposition were hoping
for). It was recognised, however, that any message to Hitler which
Henderson might have the opportunity of delivering personally
would lack something in importance if it were put forward as the
Ambassador's private opinion. Also 'there is always the risk that
Hitler . . . may be irritated at almost anything that Henderson may
say with any point to it, however carefully the point may be concealed.' It was the thought of Hitler's 'irritation' which seems to have
dominated Foreign Office thinking.[68] Wilson said very much the
same in his letter to Chamberlain, again referring to France as going
it alone: '. . . if in the end France were involved and in danger, we
should have to come to her aid.'[69]

Halifax meanwhile wrote to Chamberlain on the same date on the
subject of 'what Henderson should say to Hitler in the event of
his having an interview with him at Nuremberg.' Halifax was at his
most vague in advising the Prime Minister: 'At one moment I was
rather disposed to feel there was a case for consideration whether
Henderson should not mix into his general and less definite observations something more precise . . .' about Britain being forced to
support France if the latter herself engaged in hostilities with Germany: 'I feel doubtful, as would perhaps you, about the wisdom of
enunciating so definite a statement of the British position even if this
were only done on the basis of a personal opinion by the Ambassador, in advance of any clearly proved necessity. . . .'[70] Chamberlain's reply was altogether more bracing. He had been able to keep
in touch with Horace Wilson through the telephone, he wrote, and
he was glad they had all arrived at the same conclusion. He would
only add that Henderson might say something about the effect on
Anglo–German relations of any violent action by Hitler at a moment
when British opinion was unanimous that violence was unnecessary.
'I feel that that is an argument that might appeal to him without
touching his very sensitive *amour propre*.'

Chamberlain ended on a note which illustrates exactly the contrast
between the failure on the British side to come to grips with the

reality of the crisis and the frantic anxiety on the part of Hitler's opponents in Germany, even then organising the *putsch* for the success of which they relied so much on moral support abroad. Chamberlain wrote:

> If in spite of all [Hitler] should march or show that he intended to march, a very serious situation would arise and it might be necessary then to call ministers together to consider it. But I have a notion that it won't come to that. . . . I hope all goes well with you and that you are not unduly worried.[71]

'The Impossible had Happened . . . our Revolt was Done For'

I was able to inform [the Foreign Secretary] in the very early days of August of the whole German plan, which worked out to the actual day. He knows, too, where that information came from. Why did we not take our courage in our hands?

Lord Lloyd
Munich Debate, House of Lords

WHEN Weizsäcker had sent Burckhardt to Berne to urge the British to deliver a stern warning to Hitler, he had impressed upon him to make clear the necessity of such a communication being delivered before the end of the Party Congress at Nuremberg. And it was at Nuremberg that the drama was to continue, with Sir Nevile Henderson as the chief actor on the British side.

On the day he left Berlin for Nuremberg, Henderson wrote two letters to Halifax – one, official; the other personal and handwritten. Both reveal the mental disarray in which he approached the critical days ahead. In the first letter he moaned to his Chief:

> I am constantly reminding myself of the importance of not getting wrong the psychology of this strange man, but when all is said and done one is all the time groping like a blind man trying to find his way across a bog, with everybody shouting from the banks different information as to where the next quagmire is![1]

The second letter struck an almost hysterical note:

> I do wish it might be possible to get at any rate *The Times*, Camrose, Beaverbrook Press etc. to write up Hitler as the apostle of peace. It will be terribly shortsighted if this is not done. . . .
> Give Hitler as much credit as possible. The last word is his. We make a great mistake when our Press persists in abusing him. Let it abuse his evil advisers but give him a chance of being a good boy. . . .[2]

As all the good hotels in Nuremberg had been commandeered by the Party, the diplomats were accommodated in a sleeper train in a siding at the North Station. Apart from the discomfort, the

Ambassador was unable to use a cypher. Furthermore, having omitted to take any writing materials with him, the agitated communications with London in which he was subsequently involved had to be made on the blank end-papers of detective novels which he had brought with him. The Ambassador was assigned a 'minder', SS-Unterstürmführer Baumann, whose account of the Nuremberg days provides an interesting counterpoint to the Ambassador's own.[3] Henderson as usual talked too much and his indiscretions were duly reported by Baumann to his superiors. The SS officer's day-to-day record reveals Henderson as having a rather more agreeable time socially than he revealed to London. It also sheds light on some of the diplomatic hassle to which Henderson was subjected.

The Ambassador arrived in Nuremberg on 7 September 1938 by the night train from Berlin. He was almost immediately carted off to a review of the Labour Service, which he declared to be the best thing in the National-Socialist programme. (Fabian von Schlabrendorff remembered Henderson telling him that the way in which the German Labour Service handled their spades had struck him as being especially impressive.) In the afternoon he attended the Führer's tea party at the Deutscher Hof Hotel, but according to Baumann, 'the opportunity for a private conversation does not seem to have come his way.' In the evening, noted the conscientious SS officer, the Ambassador received a visit from Sir Roger Chase, Head of the Press section of the British Embassy.

Early the following morning he had another visitor: Philip Conwell-Evans. Conwell-Evans was attending the Congress as an official guest and Erich Kordt had arranged for him to be quartered, like himself, in the Grand Hotel. They managed to talk together privately each morning before the business of the day began.[4] Kordt told him of the alarm and consternation among his colleagues in the Foreign Ministry at the fact that, although Halifax had been informed secretly of Hitler's intentions, Henderson had made no move to convey any message of warning to the German Government since his arrival in Nuremberg. The diplomats begged Conwell-Evans to see the Ambassador and impress upon him the realities of the situation. Baumann, who recognised Conwell-Evans as a leading member of the Anglo-German Fellowship, recorded that he and Henderson talked for an hour and a half, walking up and down between the railway tracks. In his book, Conwell-Evans confirmed that it took an hour and a half to convince Henderson that Hitler had made the decision to invade Czechoslovakia. Nevertheless, the Ambassador doggedly insisted that the solution was to bring pressure to bear on the Czechs to give way, rather than to address stern admonitions to the Germans. It must have been a traumatic encounter for Conwell-Evans.[5] Baumann noted that when he gave the latter a lift back into town from the railway siding, 'I had the impression that he was striving to conceal a great shock from me.'

Meanwhile, Erich Kordt received news from his cousin Susy Simonis, now returned from her mission to London, of his brother's interviews with Wilson and Halifax at 10 Downing Street. But after 48 hours had elapsed without any sign of a statement from Britain, Kordt begged Conwell-Evans to return to London and try to see the Prime Minister. Conwell-Evans hastened to London arriving on Sunday morning, 11th September. He saw Lord Halifax the same afternoon and gave him the gist 'of what I had been told by my German Foreign Office friends.' Hitler, convinced that France and England would not intervene by force, would attack Czechoslovakia on a date between the 20th and 29th September. Hitler was against a plebiscite, which would interfere with his plans to annex Bohemia and Moravia. The German diplomats favoured a warning letter from the British Prime Minister, accompanied by mobilisation of the Fleet. They were also considering the expedient of a letter from Mussolini. They had had several indications from Rome that in the event of a conflict the Duce would not come in. The Chief of the Italian General Staff had caused such a message to be conveyed to the Germans at Nuremberg. During the course of their talk, Halifax asked whether Sir Nevile Henderson confirmed the information which Conwell-Evans was relaying from the German Opposition. 'I doubt,' replied Conwell-Evans, 'whether the Ambassador fully appreciates the position. I spent an hour and a half trying to convince him that Hitler had himself personally decided on war with Czechoslovakia.'[6]

Conwell-Evans might have reeled a little further from shock had he been able to observe how Britain's Ambassador passed the rest of the day following his own early morning call. First, Baumann took Henderson up to Nuremberg castle to see the newest Hitler Youth Hostel. During the drive the Ambassador appeared 'unusually serious' and confided in his SS friend that he had had 'extremely grave news' the previous evening (presumably from Sir Roger Chase). Various communications received by the British Government pointed to the fact that the Germans intended to settle the Czechoslovak question by military force, without waiting for the results of Runciman's mediation. France would then be obliged to march: Britain could not put any contrary pressure on France since 'each nation was the guardian of its own honour.' The Ambassador was extremely apprehensive – for Hitler. A false step might have unpredictable consequences: 'If the Führer decided in favour of military intervention, he would risk his whole mighty work of reconstruction.' Baumann loyally assured him that the Führer would never make a wrong decision, but that conditions for the Sudeten Germans were intolerable. 'Sir Nevile Henderson replied that he personally had no sympathy at all with the Czechs, and moreover considered the placing of Sudeten Germans under Czech domination to be a grave mistake. He expressed his aversion to the Czechs in very strong terms.' However, the visit to the Hitler Youth Hostel induced a more cheerful mood. The Ambassador declared that he would prefer to stay there on his next private visit rather than in a hotel. He did, however, demur at the presence on each bed of a copy of *Der Stürmer*, which he did not regard as suitable reading matter for the young. They then adjourned to the Bratwurstherzle, as Sir Nevile had expressed a desire to eat sausages in a real old Nuremberg restaurant.

In the afternoon Goering's car arrived to convey the Ambassador to the 'Pfeifferrhutte' outside Munich for a private meeting. After coffee on the terrace, they strolled up and down together for an hour or so in conversation. The alert SS man observed that they halted from time to time, when the Field Marshal appeared to be at pains to talk Sir Nevile round to his point of view. Sir Nevile's version, as reported to the Foreign Office, was that he had spoken 'with brutal frankness' to Goering and that the conversation was 'pretty hostile on both sides.'[7] (The social aspects of the afternoon were not included in Henderson's report.) Goering's most significant statement was his insistence that Germany would not be the aggressor. Although the air force was ready to move at an hour's notice it would not do so unless the Czech Government went to extreme lengths of provocation.[8] Goering was of course fully aware of Hitler's plan to stage a provocation to which German military action would merely be reaction. The obvious inference he wished his guest to draw was that in such a case France would not or could not – or need not – regard Czechoslovakia as having been the victim of aggression.

Certainly any hostility soon evaporated. Goering swept Henderson away in a fast car to Burg Neuhaus, where he had spent much of his boyhood. More coffee on the terrace and cordial conversation followed. According to Baumann, Goering expressed his pleasure at having received congratulations from Lord Halifax on the birth of his daughter. The Field Marshal jovially suggested that Sir Nevile should join him in a letter to Lord Halifax proposing that Britain should disclaim any interest in Czechoslovakia if the four best stags in Germany were placed at the disposal of the Foreign Secretary's gun. Henderson replied that personally he would be glad to do so but unfortunately the decision did not rest with him. Baumann records that 'an open postcard with a view of Burg Neuhaus, written by Sir Nevile Henderson and signed by him and the Field Marshal, was sent to Lord Halifax. It was addressed to the Foreign Office.' Alas, the assiduous Baumann does not reveal the message ('Wish you were here'?) nor is there any record at the British end of its receipt in Whitehall though it must have been read by many interested eyes on its way to the Foreign Secretary's desk. Finally, the Field Marshal pointed out to Sir Nevile alterations to the castle, which would be completed before next year's Party Congress. He hoped that the Ambassador would then be his guest (according to Baumann) 'in essentially more carefree circumstances since Czechoslovakia would then no longer exist.'

The following morning Henderson visited Ribbentrop and then Weizsäcker. He found Ribbentrop less unreasonable than he had expected. The State Secretary, on the other hand, 'was very uneasy and worried, and one noteworthy fact at Nuremberg was the extreme uneasiness of all the Ministry of Foreign Affairs officials.' It obviously did not occur to him that he himself could have been a major cause of this unease.

Meanwhile, events had been moving in London. On his return from Scotland, Chamberlain had had a meeting with Halifax, Sir John Simon (the Chancellor of the Exchequer) and Sir Horace Wilson on 9th September, at which the question was considered, as Halifax later informed the Cabinet, 'whether in the light of the information which continued to be received from responsible official sources in Germany as to Germany's intentions, it was necessary to deliver a further and final warning to Germany.'[9] The description 'responsible official sources' was used to indicate the Opposition inside the German Foreign Office and Vansittart was later to object fiercely to its use on paper as being dangerously revealing. It can be deduced from Halifax's words that he was referring both to his own meeting with

Theo Kordt in Downing Street and to Weizsäcker's desperate expedient through Burckhardt. Alas, Halifax's tentative proposal received short shrift. Cadogan, who was present, noted later in his diary: 'PM doesn't think warning message much good. Thinks he should go himself. I agree.'[10]

On 10th September, the First Secretary at the Embassy, Harrison, arrived in Nuremberg by the night train from Berlin. What he brought with him was the nearest thing to a warning to Hitler which London had felt able to concoct. It was not the personal letter from Chamberlain to Hitler for which the Opposition had asked: any personal approach Chamberlain was reserving for his planned visit. It was a message formally addressed to the Minister for Foreign Affairs, Ribbentrop. The British Government, the message stated, were so greatly disturbed by the seriousness of the consequences of any other than a peaceful solution that they were impelled to approach the German Government for their co-operation. If instead there was recourse to force, the Czechoslovak Government would ask for assistance, and the British Government were convinced the French would consider themselves bound to discharge their Treaty obligations. Great Britain could not stand aside from any general conflict. His Majesty's Government felt it their duty to express plainly their view of the momentous issues at stake and they strongly urged the German Government to join them in using every effort 'to avert a tragic and avoidable disaster.'[11]

Although the moment called for something simpler and more forceful, couched in less diplomatic language, and addressed directly to Hitler himself, nevertheless the very formality of the statement and its delivery would make it impossible to ignore. To Henderson it appeared the reddest of rags:

> If the worst comes HMG can truly say that the instructions they are now sending will have already been communicated by me to Ribbentrop and Goering and to Neurath and to others. Everybody here knows that I've been running round here like a lunatic myself. . . . The messenger has just come for this so I must stop.[12]

In his telephone report to London that evening the Ambassador reiterated that he had already spoken to everybody who counted 'on the lines of your instructions. . . . My conviction is that in the unbalanced state of mind in which I think [Hitler] is, any solemn warning, which he will regard as repetition of 21st May however worded, will drive him to the very action which we seek to prevent.'[13] And which of course the Opposition sought to achieve. The whole point of a stern warning, which the British seemed unable to grasp, was to flush Hitler out into the open and leave him with no hiding-place.

When Henderson called on State Secretary Weizsäcker in his private room at the Grand Hotel after attending the Youth Rally at the stadium, he received 'an enquiry' from him, as he reported to London that evening. The Ambassador had replied 'that I have instructions of a kind but I have been told not to carry them out unless circumstances alter, and that, while greatly disturbed by the danger inherent in the situation, His Majesty's Government remain convinced for the moment of the sincerity of the Chancellor's declared desire to achieve a pacific solution.'[14] Meanwhile, Baumann, who was waiting outside in the corridor, was approached by the Under-Secretary of State, Woermann, who enquired whether Henderson had finally delivered the letter which he had been carrying on him for a long time.

Henderson's objections were quickly accepted in London. The Prime Minister, after all, had been against the warning from the start. At 4.30 p.m. that afternoon a meeting was held at 10 Downing Street. It was, as usual, the Prime Minister's inner cabinet: Halifax, Simon and Hoare, with Horace Wilson, Cadogan and – for once – Vansittart, as advisers. The decision was taken to withdraw Henderson's instructions.[15] A handwritten note by Halifax the following day notes that Eden had called at the Foreign Office and had been informed about Henderson's refusal to deliver the warning at Nuremberg and the Cabinet's withdrawal of instructions: 'AE thought we could not have done otherwise.'[16] Halifax's Private Secretary Oliver Harvey entered a different version in his diary: 'AE said he saw the point of not sending the warning in view of Nevile Henderson's advice but he mistrusted the man's judgment.'[17] In a statement to the Press, Chamberlain, rather wide of the mark, claimed that Henderson had met all the 'principal leaders of Germany except Hitler' at Nuremberg and 'from the full reports he has given to us of these conversations we have every reason to feel confident that our views have been conveyed fully to the proper quarters.'[18] A few days later Harvey noted:

Van is extremely agitated over failure of HMG to give Hitler a final warning and maintains that all moderate opinion in Germany was wanting us to do this so as to give them something to enable them to stop Hitler with. Conwell-Evans who was at Nuremberg has come back with passionate pleas from moderate German leaders begging HMG to take some step to stop their mad Chancellor![19]

The Times printed an account of a tea party Hitler had given during the celebrations. Although the British Ambassador had not been able to talk to him, the Führer had a 'friendly conversation with some of his English guests of honour – Lord Stamp, Lord Brocket, Lord McGovern, Lord Clive and Lord and Lady Hollenden.' Professor Conwell-Evans' name is also included in the list of lords and ladies, which is evidence of how well-placed he was in Nazi circles.[20] Conwell-Evans must have found his English fellow-guests hard to take.

On this same day, 12th September, Chamberlain held a Cabinet Meeting, though not all members were present, and set out the affair of Henderson and the non-delivery of the Nuremberg warning. All the Ambassador's arguments were rehearsed, but not everyone was convinced. Lord Lloyd was worried that 'we had not made our attitude quite plain.' Halifax was obliged to confess that in fact 'we had no precise record of what Henderson had said.' In conclusion, Halifax admitted that he and the Prime Minister had seen Churchill the previous day: 'He proposed that we should tell Germany that if she set foot in Czechoslovakia we should declare war on her.'[21]

Meanwhile, relieved of the awful possibility of having to upset Hitler (which had much to do with his arguments against the warning), Henderson was able to relax and enjoy the final days of the Nuremberg Congress. The march past of the SA and the SS lasted from 11.30 a.m. to 4.30 p.m.. The Diplomatic Corps were allowed to leave after an hour but after lunching with the Belgian Ambassador Henderson slipped back again to the parade with his SS friend. They found the diplomatic stand now occupied by Austrian girls in national costume who had been sent to Nuremberg for the first time. Henderson happily signed autographs – 150 by Baumann's calculation – on cards already adorned with the signature of Dr Goebbels. The Ambassador also bestowed his signature on uniformed members of the Sudeten-German formations. As in the previous year, he spent the evening at supper with Himmler in the SS camp, where he had the pleasure of meeting Unity Mitford. The following night Henderson returned to Berlin after a final engagement: dinner with officials of the German Foreign Office '*sans* Ribbentrop.' Henderson reported to London that 'some of them talked a lot of treason.' Weizsäcker came early to have a talk: 'He was blackly pessimistic. . . . I asked him if anything could convince Hitler of the reality of our warnings. Weizsäcker's only answer was that nothing must be omitted. . . .' 'I shall not,' wrote Henderson when it was all over, 'forget Nuremberg, 1938 in a hurry!'[22]

Whilst the Opposition in the Foreign Ministry were talking treason and anxiously looking for a sign from the British Ambassador at the Nuremberg Congress, Goerdeler was furthering the anti-Nazi cause through his own channels. Early in August, unable to get permission to travel to Britain, he had asked one of his close British contacts, Robert Stopford, to come to Germany to meet him. Stopford, who disclaimed after the war that he had ever been a member of the Secret Service, nevertheless had an intimate association with the Foreign Office and, as he later wrote to Wheeler-Bennett, went with Goerdeler at least once to 'discuss the generals' position with Van.'[23] At the time of Goerdeler's request he had just been appointed to the Runciman Mission and it was agreed with Vansittart that it would be better if he kept clear of such contacts for the time being. An alternative messenger had to be found.

On a business visit to England the previous year (when he had paid his first call on Vansittart) Goerdeler had formed a warm friendship with a Mr A. P. Young, the managing director of the Thomson-Houston engineering works in Rugby. Even as early as 1937 Goerdeler was openly advocating in British business circles the necessity of dealing firmly with Hitler. Subsequent meetings had cemented their friendship and Young had been infected with Goerdeler's enthusiasm and with admiration for his idealism. It was now arranged that Young, a business man of some standing with good connections abroad although without any experience of diplomacy or the world of secret intelligence, should act as the go-between for Goerdeler with the British Foreign Office, via Vansittart. At their first meeting in Germany, on 6 August 1938, Goerdeler stressed Hitler's intention to go to war against Czechoslovakia; the generals and the people were against war and discontent was growing in the Party itself. Internal revolution was anticipated. At the top of Young's lengthy report Vansittart wrote in his own hand:

> This is a message from a very highly-placed German – well-known to me personally – who urgently asked that he should be given the chance of oral communication. A messenger was accordingly selected, went out and brought this back to me.[24]

A month later Young was summoned again, this time to Zurich, where he met Goerdeler on 11th September. The British Government still held the key to the situation but time was running out, declared Goerdeler. The leading generals and Schacht had expressed to Hitler their opposition to aggression against Czechoslovakia. Hitler believed he could create a situation which would give him the territory he wanted without a war. It was possible that Henlein, the Sudeten leader, or even Lord Runciman, might be murdered in circumstances which would implicate the Czech Government. (This was precisely the possibility which Goering had hinted to Henderson three days previously at his mountain retreat.) To prove the dastardly lengths to which the Nazi leaders could go, Goerdeler told Young the whole story of the Fritsch affair.

The main thrust of Goerdeler's message was that a dictator must move steadily from one spectacular success to another. This was now the moment when, for the sake of humanity and the world, Hitler's series of successes must be broken finally 'through appropriate action by the three great democracies.' The effect on Hitler himself might easily be physical and mental collapse. Goerdeler recommended as a major step the sudden and dramatic summoning of Parliament and a firm and open pronouncement by the Prime Minister to Germany and the world. He should say that any act of violence on the part of Germany in Czechoslovakia, whatever the alleged reason, would be met with force. The French and British peoples would join together to fight with all their might, with the confident hope that the people of the United States would assist them for the cause of Justice, Law and Decency. Young wrote out a report of his meeting with Goerdeler during the return journey to London, where he arrived at 4 p.m. on 12th September. He went straight to the Foreign Office and handed the document to Vansittart personally.

Having gone through the motions of agreeing to a message of

warning to Hitler – a plan he now happily abandoned – Chamberlain was free to finalise his other plans. Before informing the Cabinet, he first had to address himself to the King. On the 13th September he put his case in a letter to Balmoral:

> Reports are daily received in great numbers not only from official sources but from all manner of individuals who claim to have special and unchallengeable sources of information. Many of these (and of such authority as to make it impossible to dismiss them as unworthy of attention) declare positively that Herr Hitler has made up his mind to attack Czechoslovakia and then to proceed further East. . . . On the other hand, Your Majesty's representative in Berlin has steadily maintained that Herr Hitler has not yet made up his mind to violence. . . .
> With these contradictory views before us, Your Majesty's Ministers have acted on the basis of the latter and more optimistic forecast. . . .

The Prime Minister then explained his plan to visit Hitler: 'I should hope to persuade him that he had an unequalled opportunity of raising his own prestige. . . .'[25]

Chamberlain departed from Heston aerodrome on 15th September for Munich ('It would seem that the spectacular effect on public opinion everywhere of making the journey *by air* is likely to be considerable.') Among those standing on the tarmac as the Prime Minister winged on his way was Theo Kordt, the German Chargé d'Affaires. It was only a week since he had made his impassioned plea at 10 Downing Street. Now the Foreign Secretary approached him. 'We were not able to be as frank with you as you were with us,' said Halifax. 'At the time in question, we were already considering a personal initiative of Chamberlain.'[26]

In Berlin meanwhile, the preparations for the *putsch* of which Kordt had spoken were in hand. The members of the raiding party which was to spearhead the assault on the Chancellery and the seizure of Hitler had been provided with weapons by the Abwehr and were already being accommodated in various apartments throughout the city. An armoured division in Thuringia under the command of General Hoepner was ready to move if the SS division in Munich should attempt to intervene. Proclamations to the nation had been drawn up. Whether Hitler went forward or jumped back, the conspirators were ready for him.

Hitler's speech with which he closed the Party Congress was a vicious attack on Czechoslovakia and its President. He harped on the 'humiliation' of 21st May, for which he blamed Beneš. The Czechs were an unreconcilable enemy. But the world should note that the Sudeten Germans were neither deserted nor defenceless. The speech was a signal for an uprising in the Sudetenland with the loss of life. A few days earlier, Halder, with Brauchitsch and Keitel, had been present at an all-night conference with Hitler in Nuremberg in which he had announced that the attack on Czechoslovakia would be preceded by an uprising by the Sudeten Germans. Events were evidently going according to plan. There was no doubt about Hitler's intentions.

On the 13th September Halder went to Witzleben's office to finalise the arrangements for the *putsch*. A complication had arisen because Hitler had not returned to Berlin after the Nuremberg Rally but had gone to Berchtesgaden. While the two generals were together news came – almost certainly from Erich Kordt – that the British Ambassador had informed Foreign Minister Ribbentrop that Prime Minister Chamberlain had proposed a visit to the Führer to seek a peaceful solution to the Sudeten problem and that Hitler had agreed. The meeting would take place in two days' time. The news was an absolute bombshell for the Opposition leaders. It threw them into utter confusion. Not only was Hitler to be spared the challenge to his policies by the other Great Powers in the public arena of diplomacy; the British Prime Minister had come in person to try to accommodate him by personal negotiation. In other words, Britain had backed down. It was impossible to launch a *putsch* against Hitler when he was talking peace with the British premier. Moreover, the event was proving Hitler right and the generals wrong: the British and the French would not fight.[27]

On the 15th September Chamberlain arrived in Munich and was driven to Berchtesgaden. Sir Horace Wilson, of course, went too. But Chamberlain took no interpreter with him. The record of his *tête-à-tête* with Hitler was made by Hitler's personal interpreter Schmidt who, as already mentioned, was a close collaborator with the Opposition through Erich Kordt in the Foreign Minister's office. Ribbentrop was excluded from the meeting at Henderson's request, which enraged him so much that he refused to allow Chamberlain to have a copy of Schmidt's record. The Prime Minister had to trust to his memory in reporting subsequently to his colleagues in the Cabinet. The meeting lasted from 5.20 p.m. to 8.15 p.m. Chamberlain had no idea it would last so long. No doubt he envisioned something more brisk and business-like in line with his own methods. There were no signs of insanity in Hitler, he had found, but many of excitement. Nevertheless, 'it was impossible not to be impressed with the power of the man.' The three-hour discussion between the two men was in fact distilled in one critical question and answer. Hitler asked whether Britain would agree to the cession of the Sudetenland to Germany. According to his own report, Chamberlain replied that he would have to discuss the point with his colleagues and with the French.[28] Schmidt's report recorded him as saying that 'he could state personally that he recognised the principle of the detachment of the Sudeten area' and that he would be seeking Government approval of his personal attitude.[29]

Throughout all the conversation with Chamberlain, Schmidt kept Erich Kordt informed by telephone and he in turn reported to Oster at the Abwehr. After Chamberlain's Berchtesgaden visit Schmidt let Kordt know in a prearranged code that Hitler had by no means abandoned his war plans. He intended to present the Western Powers with particularly humiliating conditions which would constitute a diplomatic defeat for them, and if the Czechs should refuse to accept such conditions, Hitler would go to war, now more than ever convinced that there was no danger of British and French intervention.[30] The conspiracy, which had been frozen by Chamberlain's visit, came to life again. Oster told Kordt to remain in Berlin at his post in the Foreign Minister's office and to keep the various groups informed of new developments. Since there might be a need for quick action it was essential to keep in direct contact with the group in police headquarters and with Witzleben who was coordinating the Führer's movements. The police vice-president and the General's liaison officer would be in touch several times daily. Above all, begged Oster, 'Do everything you can to lure the bird back into the cage in Berlin.' Erich risked a telephone call to his brother in London, using the code for the probable outbreak of war: 'The house sale will be continued.' Theo was so taken aback that his brother had to repeat the message three times before he properly grasped it.[31]

Chamberlain returned to London on the 16th and made his report to the Cabinet on the following day. Advocating the ceding of the Sudetenland, he said that he believed that Hitler's objectives were strictly limited. One had to make up one's mind whether this was the end of Hitler's aim or only the beginning. One could only exercise one's own judgment. His own view was that Hitler was telling the truth. By the end of the afternoon of the 18th, Cadogan was drafting a 'message to Beneš telling him to surrender.'

When Chamberlain arrived on 22nd September ready to concede everything asked for at Berchtesgaden, the Führer took the wind completely out of his sails by declaring that this was no longer enough. He now demanded military occupation of the Sudetenland by 1st October. Evacuation should begin on 26th September and be completed by the 28th. Chamberlain, outraged and abashed, replied that he could only submit these demands to the Czechs, who he was sure would reject them. He returned to London. It looked as if Hitler might yet achieve his desire to 'smash Czechoslovakia' by military means. He rattled his phantom sabre at the departing Chamberlain, saying that it was manifestly impossible for the German Government to wait indefinitely with 90 or 100 divisions under arms.[32]

The French, suddenly, seemed to be made of sterner stuff. Daladier got his Cabinet to reject the Godesberg demands. The Maginot Line was manned and fourteen divisions were mobilised. At a meeting in London he maintained a firm attitude and brought in General Gamelin who spoke optimistically of the military prospects. It was decided that Chamberlain should send a letter to Hitler confirming that the Czechs would not accept the Godesberg demands and asking him to negotiate directly with the Czechs on the basis of the Anglo-French proposals already accepted in principle by the Czechs (though under duress from their Allies). The letter was to be taken to Hitler by, of all people, the ultimate civil servant, Sir Horace Wilson. However, on his arrival at the Chancellery in Berlin, accompanied by Henderson and Kirkpatrick from the Embassy, he found himself exposed to one of Hitler's pyrotechnic displays of rage. He would have the Sudetenland by the 1st October by whatever means. He would 'smash the Czechs.' In fact, it was Nuremberg all over again. The civil servant was too terrified to throw more fuel on the flames.

But the British were not the sole authors of the ultimatum and Wilson had to stay on the hook, though Chamberlain tried to make things easier for him: 'We do not consider it possible for you to leave without delivering special message in view of what we said to the French. But message should be given more in sorrow than in anger. . . .' Wilson was therefore obliged to return to the lion's den the following day at noon. The amended message was at last delivered. It was merely interpreted by Hitler as a declaration that

France and Britain were ready to attack Germany, which was, he said brusquely, a matter of complete indifference to him. He was prepared for any eventuality. There was much reiteration of his determination to 'smash the Czechs.' Wilson finally took leave of the Führer, having promised to 'try to make the Czechs see sense.'[33]

On his return to London Sir Horace gave an account of his interviews with Hitler at an Informal Meeting of Ministers. It might have been some comfort to Sir Horace had he known that in the city from which he had so thankfully departed a few hours earlier, Hitler had run into some unexpected trouble.

After Wilson's departure, the Führer had issued a most secret order that all units should move forward from their training areas towards the Czech frontier and be ready to launch Operation Green when the order was given at noon on 28th September. By the end of the afternoon he was ready to play the Supreme War Lord who would lead his people into battle. Arrangements had been made for a motorised division to parade past the Chancellery where Hitler would be waiting on the balcony to take the salute. As the troops themselves were aware, it was a propaganda exercise. In fact, Jodl identified it as such in his diary at the time:

Der Führer hat für den Abend einen Propagandamarsch motorisierten Truppen durch das Regierungviertel für 27 Abends angeordnet.[34]

The route of the parade also took it past the British Embassy – an exercise in intimidation, as Erich Kordt testified.[35] What happened that evening, Kordt heard from Walter Hewel, Hitler's liaison officer with the Foreign Ministry. The march-past had been arranged to coincide with the time when the maximum number of people would be on the streets, leaving their places of work. It was to be a stirring occasion. But Hitler was in for a rude shock. The Berliners believed the troops to be actually departing for the front and they greeted the parade in icy silence. There were no cheers for the army nor salutes for the Führer. The American correspondent William Shirer who had gone expecting to see a tremendous demonstration, described it as 'the most striking demonstration against war I've ever seen.'[36] The Foreign Office Press officer, Ridsdale, was told by one of his German contacts that the parade 'was like a procession of ghosts – a terrifying experience.'[37] Hitler, furious and appalled, withdrew from the balcony and ordered the light to be turned off in the room. After watching unseen for a few minutes he snarled: 'With people like this, I cannot go to war!' General Beck had warned him that the people did not want war and that their attitude would be dangerous to the morale of the fighting forces. Now the Führer could see it with his own eyes. What Hitler also saw was the nadir of his own popularity. He had received a public rebuff from his own people in the heart of the capital. The news of it would spread throughout the country and abroad, as indeed it did. Hitler was now in the dilemma for which the Opposition had striven. He could not march against Czechoslovakia if this was the national mood. If he did not carry out his threats, he would be seen to have retreated not just before the British and French, who had still not made their position clear, but also in the face of the refusal of the Czechs to be intimidated. Everything seemed to be going wrong at once. The French attitude seemed to be hardening. Italy was proving a broken reed. The Czechs were mobilising. No doubt the march-past at the Chancellery was to have been to some degree a morale-booster to the Führer himself. But Hitler was not beaten yet. There was one man who might extricate him from his difficulties – the British Prime Minister.

Before the night was much older Hitler dictated a letter to Chamberlain. Schmidt, who was summoned to put it into English, sensed that Hitler was drawing back from the abyss. The tone was certainly more conciliatory than his recent utterances. (Weizsäcker had a hand in the drafting.) He rejected the Czech contention that the Godesberg demands would rob their country 'of every guarantee for its national existence'; nor was German military occupation of the Sudeten areas anything but a security measure to secure 'the quick and smooth achievement of the final settlement.' The government in Prague was deliberately distorting the proposal for military occupation in order to mobilise the forces in other countries, particularly in England and France 'to achieve the possibility of a general warlike conflagration.' He left it to Chamberlain's judgment whether, 'in view of these facts you should continue your effort . . . to bring the government in Prague to reason at the very last hour.'[38] Hitler telegraphed his letter to London at 10.30 p.m. While he had been in the throes of composition, Chamberlain had been broadcasting to the British nation about this quarrel 'in a faraway country between people of whom we know nothing.' It would not be possible, he said, to involve the whole British Empire simply on account of a small nation confronted by a big and powerful one, however much we might sympathise. 'If we have to fight it must be on larger issues than that. . . .'

On the afternoon of 27th September, Chamberlain was holding a Meeting of Ministers – that is to say, not a full Cabinet. At 3.15 p.m. the First Lord of the Admiralty, Duff Cooper, telephoned 10 Downing Street and asked to see the Prime Minister. He was told by the Private Secretary that the Prime Minister was 'in conference with other Ministers.' Duff Cooper thereupon dictated a message to be taken in to him: 'In my opinion, we ought to mobilise immediately. I can see no justification for delay.'

The First Sea Lord, Admiral Backhouse, returned to the Admiralty in due course, bringing back with him the message which Duff Cooper had sent in to the Prime Minister. On it Chamberlain had written: 'Take the necessary steps tonight. N.C.'. The Prime Minister had told the Cabinet that he would announce the mobilisation of the Fleet in his broadcast to the nation at 8 p.m.; in the meantime, he did not wish this decision to be made known. When, inexplicably, Chamberlain omitted any reference to the Fleet from his broadcast, Duff Cooper chose to assume he had written authority and went ahead with mobilisation, but withholding the bulletin from the BBC. At the 9.30 p.m. Cabinet Meeting he asked the Prime Minister whether he now had any objection to a public announcement. He had not. The communiqué was issued to the news agencies at 11.28 p.m. Release to the Dominions and foreign countries was cleared and the issue was completed at 11.45 p.m.[39] In view of the repercussions in Berlin during the next few hours, the Prime Minister's radio silence seems particularly regrettable.

Although Duff Cooper had long advocated the importance, from both the strategic and the psychological point of view, of the mobilisation of the Fleet, he could never have guessed the effect the news would have at the heart of the Nazi war machine in Berlin. How right the Opposition had been in their repeated requests to the British for naval demonstrations as a sure way of intimidating Hitler. At 8 p.m. on 27th September, while Chamberlain was preparing to broadcast to the nation, Goebbels summoned all newspaper editors to the Ministry of Propaganda. He announced the details of the ultimatum which was to be presented to Czechoslovakia when the time limit set by Hitler for the acceptance of his Godesberg terms – 2 p.m. the next day – should expire. Suddenly, at midnight, the news of the mobilisation of the British Fleet was picked up from the news agency wires. By 1 a.m., Goebbels was issuing a denial of the ultimatum story which he had given the editors. By 4 a.m. the Press was being further instructed to explain that in fact no such ultimatum had ever been conceived.[40] An entry in Hassell's diary confirms that: 'It was rashly denied that there had been an ultimatum and a threat of mobilisation. . . .'[41] What happened between Goebbels' issue of the retraction at 1 a.m. and the extraordinary about-face contained in the statement that 'no such ultimatum had ever been conceived' can only be guessed at but it must have been a stormy few hours.

The effect of the mobilisation of the British Fleet was considerably greater than is ever accorded to it in the history books, where it is usually passed over as just another of the events of the crisis. The following details appear in the Foreign Office files under the heading: 'Message to Col. Christie from a German friend.'

> From the moment of the British mobilisation Hitler and Co. began their retreat. However much they may now bluff, they are prepared to give way. Public opinion against Hitler and the Nazis has increased extraordinarily in Germany during the past few days. . . . Hitler's speech at the Sportspalast did him much harm. I beg of you to hold fast today on all counts. . . .

A note on the file records:

> The above was confirmed at 9.00 a.m. this morning by a well-known German industrialist who had just got back from Germany: 'Do not give way and give Hitler a victory after having undermined him so effectively during the past 48 hours.'[42]

Conwell-Evans related in his book that the information which Christie had passed to the Foreign Office about the Press retraction was received by him from a reliable friend who was a member of the German Press. Conwell-Evans also wrote that after the crisis he was informed by 'a member of the German Foreign Office' (presumably his friend Erich Kordt) that 'the mobilisation of the British Fleet was one of the decisive factors which prevented the attack on Czechoslovakia, the other being the demonstration at the march past the Chancellery the day before.'[43] Hitler's former adjutant, Captain Fritz Wiedemann, told American intelligence after the war that 'Hitler gave in at the very last moment' after a conversation with Goering and Neurath, who must have been roused from their beds.

Goering told Wiedemann that Hitler had said: 'I think that the English Fleet might shoot after all'; he had never believed they would really go to war.[44] The former British Ambassador to Berlin, Sir Horace Rumbold, discussed the matter with former German Chancellor Brüning, now lecturing at Harvard, who maintained close contacts in Germany. The two men had collaborated closely in the pre-Hitler years. Hitler got cold feet at the last moment, Brüning told Sir Horace, 'as the result of what his generals had told him and of the mobilisation of the British Fleet.' As regards British policy, Brüning said that he regretted that the British Fleet had not been mobilised much earlier.[45]

The timing of the news from the press agencies of the mobilisation of the British Fleet, within an hour of the receipt of Hitler's letter in London, must have seemed to the Führer that this was Chamberlain's answer. But in fact, the reply which was to be delivered by the Ambassador the following morning, was anything but warlike. Chamberlain was certain that Hitler could 'get all essentials without war, and without delay,' he wrote. He himself was ready to go to Berlin and discuss the arrangements for the Sudeten transfer with the Führer and Czech representatives, and those of France and Italy if desired. 'I feel convinced we can reach agreement in a week. . . .'[46]

The German conspirators, still holding on in spite of the devastating blow to their plans for a *putsch* delivered by the arrival of Chamberlain in Germany, had begun to feel that they were going to have a second chance. Had not Wilson told Hitler at his interview (Schmidt had been present) that if France became involved in war with Germany Britain would support her? That day they made the decision to act on the 29th, when the orders for mobilisation were to be given at noon for action on the 30th. On the morning of the 28th Erich Kordt gave Oster the text of Hitler's letter to Chamberlain of the previous night. Gisevius took it to Witzleben. Witzleben passed it to Halder. Gisevius recorded that the latter was moved to tears of rage by the Führer's behaviour. Where Chamberlain had chosen to see in Hitler's letter an opportunity for further talks and the possibility of negotiation, the Opposition saw only a rejection of Chamberlain's attempts at mediation through the visit of Wilson, and a stubborn insistence on the Godesberg terms. It was unequivocal proof that Hitler was absolutely bent on war. Halder took the copy of Hitler's letter to Brauchitsch, the Commander-in-Chief.[47] But the Opposition were completely unaware that during the night Hitler, faced with seemingly determined resistance abroad, had – as they had always predicted he would – backed down. Nor did they know that Chamberlain had already launched a rescue attempt for Hitler. At the Chancellery that morning both the French and the British Ambassadors were trying to get in to see Hitler. Sir Nevile Henderson wanted to deliver the encouraging reply which Chamberlain had transmitted during the night. Parallel to these *démarches*, the conspirators were pursuing their own plan. The Deputy Head of the Police, Schulenberg, brought the news to Erich Kordt in his office in the Wilhelmstrasse that the Commander-in-Chief, Brauchitsch, had been convinced by Hitler's letter and was ready to join the *putsch*. In an agony of apprehension that the plot might even yet be discovered, Kordt begged that action should take place that very day and not, as arranged, on the morrow. He repeated his own undertaking to go to the Chancellery and ensure that the doors were opened for the entry of the assault force.[48] But before Schulenberg could report back to Kordt, events took another, and wholly unforeseen, dramatic turn.

The telephone rang in the office of Ribbentrop. Kordt took the call. Ciano, the Italian Foreign Minister, wished to speak to his German opposite number. Kordt had the impression that the Duce was at Ciano's elbow as he spoke. Kordt replied that the Minister was not in his office (he was in fact in the Chancellery). Shortly afterwards, a breathless Attolico arrived at the Foreign Office; the Ambassador had had a personal call from Mussolini. Chamberlain's instructions to Lord Perth in Rome had been carried out first thing that morning and Mussolini had seized upon the suggestion that he should act as mediator with Hitler. The message was to be delivered at once. 'Hurry!' Mussolini had adjured him. The Duce was neither willing nor able to get involved in international conflagrations. Attolico arrived, still breathless, at the Chancellery, announcing his message almost before he was within earshot of the Führer.[49] The way of escape had opened. 'At the request of my great friend and ally, Signor Mussolini,' Hitler told Henderson, at last admitted to the presence, 'I have postponed mobilising my troops for 24 hours.' Henderson was still with the Führer when Attolico returned with the news that Mussolini was ready to attend a conference.[50] A few minutes before the expiry of the 2 p.m. ultimatum, Germany was issuing invitations for the following day, in Munich. The Soviet Union and Czechoslovakia were not to be among the participants.

Meanwhile the 'postponement' of mobilisation remained in force. This suggestion of Hitler reining in his overwhelming forces would create a most favourable atmosphere for him in which to face the other powers.

Halder and Witzleben were together in Halder's office finalising the details of the troop movements for the *putsch*. Witzleben was now ready to receive from the Chief of Staff the order to go into action. At this critical moment came the news of Mussolini's intervention, the twenty-four-hour postponement of mobilisation and Hitler's agreement, on the recommendation of the Duce, to accept Chamberlain's proposal for an international conference.[51] Erich Kordt telephoned the news at once to his brother. It was a very different call from the one he had looked forward to making that day. 'It is by far the "second-best" solution which they have reached where you are,' he commented bitterly to Theo in England.[52] After the war, three of the conspirators described the traumatic effect of this news. Halder told a member of the American prosecuting team at Nuremberg: 'I therefore took back the order of execution because, owing to this fact, the entire basis for the action had been taken away. . . . We were firmly convinced we would be successful. But now came Mr Chamberlain and with one stroke the danger of war was averted. . . . The critical hour for force was avoided.' If Chamberlain had not come to Munich, the General was asked, would the plan have been executed and Hitler deposed? 'I can only say the plan would have been executed,' replied Halder.[53]

The announcement of the four-power conference at Munich miraculously lifted Hitler off the horns of his dilemma. The retreat which he had privately begun in the small hours of the 28th would have been a mortal blow to his prestige: it was now deflected by Chamberlain. It was the other side who were asking for talks. Nor would he be forced to try and save face by a disastrous attack on Czechoslovakia. His restraint would demonstrate that he was truly a man of peace who would not refuse to enter into international discussion although (of course) possessing the power to crush opposing force from whatever quarter.

But the secret information which had been received in the Foreign Office at the time about the immediate and palpable effect on Hitler of the news of the mobilisation of the Fleet provided the British with a powerful weapon to take with them into the council chamber at

Munich. On the eve of the conference Goerdeler had telephoned from Switzerland and his message is recorded in Foreign Office files:

> Don't give way another foot. Hitler is in a most uncomfortable position. See that you keep the responsibility for any use of force on his shoulders. . . . The *Stimmung* against Hitler and his Nazi henchmen has risen very remarkably during the past few days. . . .

Goerdeler had further 'pressed us not to confine this settlement merely to the Sudeten question, but to demand a conference on collective guarantees and limitation of armaments. That would please the German people.' Questioned about broadcasting, Goerdeler had advised "carrying on at full blast" with information about British and French mobilisation and the intention to meet force with force.[54] This advice echoed that given by Christie's friend in his message: 'Luxembourg and Strasburg have done splendid broadcasting work, but the British wireless must emphasise firmly the British mobilisation.'[55] With the pressure being thus kept up, and with the priceless intelligence from Germany of Hitler's overnight collapse, the Allies were in a position to outface him openly on the international stage of the Four-Power Conference. Hitler, unaware that his weakness had been exposed, would have found such escalating firmness confusing and intimidating. But the inestimable advantage which the intelligence from Germany had given the Allies was thrown away by Britain.

On 29th September a telegram was drafted to be sent – rather late in the day – to the British delegation in Munich by the Foreign Secretary. The original draft, in which one detects the hand of Vansittart, read:

> Information has reached me from moderate circles in Germany that the firm attitude taken by HM Government during the last few days has become known to wide circles in Germany by means of broadcasts in Germany from this country and from Luxemberg and Strasburg and have [sic] been largely responsible for the fact that Hitler has now adopted a more reasonable attitude.
> I feel it is most important that there should be now no weakening in our attitude, the more so as I understand that moderate circles in Germany have been greatly heartened and strengthened by the success of our policy.

Several hands fell upon this draft, including those of Mallet, Cadogan and the Foreign Secretary himself. Mallet added the phrase 'especially the mobilisation of the Fleet' after the statement about the recent firm attitude shown by the Government. Cadogan struck out the phrase about Hitler having 'adopted a more reasonable attitude' and replaced it with the less important one of 'had considerable effect on German public opinion,' thereby eliminating any reference to Hitler at all. Most lamentably, Halifax completed the emasculation of the message by crossing through the whole of the second sentence. The sentence which he penned in its stead managed in its hesitancy, ambivalence and blandness, to torpedo the whole efficacy of the message: 'This may, if true, assist you in negotiations.'[56] Although Christie's message, to which reference is clearly made (in fact it is the preceding paper on the file), was received on the 28th, the telegram to Munich was not despatched until 9.30 p.m. the following day, by which time all was over bar the shouting. In the words of Maisky, recalling thirty years later the rejection of his own country's positive efforts during the crisis, 'The British and French premiers turned into a club wielded by Hitler.'[57]

As the participants of the conference converged on Munich, one gesture was made towards the Czechs to alleviate to some extent their fate. Weizsäcker and Erich Kordt, together with Neurath and (strangely enough) Goering, hastily prepared basic terms for agreement which reflected the Berchtesgaden rather than the escalated Godesberg demands of Hitler. Goering submitted the draft to Hitler who gave it merely a quick glance and agreed it. Erich passed it to Schmidt who translated it into French. Forthwith Weizsäcker handed it to Ambassador Attolico who rushed to meet Mussolini at the frontier. Mussolini was pleased that he would be able to arrive at the conference with a proposal ready. When the conference opened he produced the document as his own suggestion greatly to the surprise of Ribbentrop and others.[58] In his report of the conference, Sir Horace Wilson recalled that: 'The German proposals for evacuation and occupation surprised us by their moderation and by the degree of latitude which they left to the international commission.'[59] But these efforts were in the end negated when Hitler's High Command took over and railroaded the proceedings. Strategic and economic factors replaced ethnic ones, while the British and French ambassadors on the International Commission looked the other way. Only the Italian, Attolico, took the side of the Czechs.

Chamberlain's supporters claimed – and still do – that the Munich Agreement allowed an unready Britain time to accelerate rearmament. But this was not how Chamberlain saw it, as Cabinet Minutes show: 'A good deal of false emphasis had been placed on rearmament. . . . The Prime Minister hoped that it might be possible to take active steps and to follow up the Munich Agreement by other measures. . . . Our foreign policy was one of appeasement.'[60] But no British rearmament programme, however vigorously embarked upon, could have matched in production what Germany acquired when in due course Hitler completed his unfinished business with Czechoslovakia, the following spring after Munich. 'You have no idea,' Hitler told Carl Burckhardt, 'how much war material we found in Czechoslovakia. It was astounding. We could hardly believe our eyes. And everything in splendid order. . . .' Hitler particularly admired how well the books had been kept.[61] Germany had also of course acquired the goose that laid these golden eggs: the renowned Czech arms industry.

For Sir Nevile Henderson, the tragedy of Czechoslovakia was reduced to a personal trauma. In a handwritten letter to Lord Halifax after the Munich Conference he declared:

> To me personally all this affair has been intensely disagreeable and painful. I want to wash the taste out of my mouth and I would rejoice from the bottom of my heart if you could remove me to some other sphere. I never want to work with Germans again. . . . In my blackest pessimism I tried to console myself with two thoughts (a) that war would rid Germany of Hitler and (b) that it would remove me from Berlin.

The Foreign Office itself seemed to have been able to put the whole affair behind it by the end of the year. In December a letter was received from the *New York Times* asking for a photograph of the title page and preamble of the Agreement and of the signatures at the end. The Foreign Office found itself chapfallen. 'The Munich Agreement (re Czechoslovakia),' minuted Central Department (evidently feeling the necessity to identify it) 'presents an awkward problem':

> We have never had it! We believe that there is only one signed copy and that is in the German FO. We have just asked for a certified copy but that will not meet their need for facsimile signatures, even when we get it.[62]

According to the British editor of the captured German Foreign Office documents after the war, both a British and a German version were signed. The Germans at least could remember where they had put theirs!

While Chamberlain faced critics at home, to the German people he was a saviour. Unaware that, but for the rashly over-confident English statesman, their salvation might have been permanent, they saw him as the man who had saved the peace. The fact that peace had been placed in hazard by the Führer had not been lost upon them: the public rebuff in the Wilhelmstrasse at the height of the crisis had shown that clearly. The reports of the British consuls give a most vivid picture of the attitude of the ordinary German citizens as the crisis unfolded. The Consul-General in Hamburg wrote of the air of unreality which was abroad in the city, the chief cause of which was undoubtedly the absence of any desire for war. 'The man, and still more so the woman, in the street' had been speaking openly against 'the National-Socialist attempt to drag the country into war. There has never been such widespread disaffection in Hamburg since the National-Socialists came into power.' There was no rush, wrote the Consul, to buy German newspapers but English newspapers immediately sold out in the early hours of the morning. Disapproval of Nazi policy, lack of faith in the press, coupled with the knowledge of their inability to influence events in any way, induced in the mass of the people a kind of fatalism. 'The part played by the Prime Minister in preserving peace is gratefully recognised on all sides, from high and low, acquaintances and strangers alike.' Two poorly-dressed Germans had come in the early morning to the Consulate bringing an expensive bouquet of flowers.[63] The Consul in Munich declared that 'Bavaria was against war *as* war and not merely an unpopular war of doubtful outcome.' Most noticeably, under the stress of anxiety, caution had been abandoned and the Party was freely criticised, Hitler himself being declared a madman. People now had a better idea of how things stood. They realised how unreliable their own press and radio was and how truth was suppressed.[64] In the Northern port of Bremen, the Consul reported in almost identical terms and confirmed that people were now looking to Britain for news. The presence of the British and French premiers in Germany, it was said, was like a window letting in the light.[65]

One report is particularly moving because of its origin – Dresden. It is worth quoting at some length:

There was and still is a very strong and widespread resentment against the leadership which had resulted in such a crisis. Although people got hourly more and more pessimistic as to the possibility of a peaceful solution, I found no single German who did not ardently desire it. They all recognised, however, that they were helpless. . . .

A mass meeting held at Dresden was attended by large crowds who gave very little support to the expected endorsement of the Führer's policy and who left in large numbers before the singing of the National Anthem.

People are certainly profoundly thankful at being saved from war, but see no cause for thanking anyone but Mr Chamberlain. If, as one must hope, the Central Government is prepared to be impressed by strong popular feeling, the weight of Saxon opinion could not fail to be an influence for peace, friendliness and political unadventurousness.[66]

The consensus between three cities so disparate geographically and culturally – the Northern Protestant seaport of Hamburg; Munich, in the old Catholic kingdom of Bavaria in the agricultural south; and Dresden away to the east on the borders of Czechoslovakia – is in itself remarkable. It caught no discerning eye in the Foreign Office.

In the Debate in the House of Lords, the Foreign Secretary defended the Government position:

Nothing has been more persistently pressed upon me during the last two or three anxious months than this: If only Great Britain would say clearly and unmistakably for all to hear that she would resist any unprovoked aggression on Czechoslovakia, no such unprovoked aggression would be made. We never felt able to use that language.

He was answered by Lord Lloyd:

I was able to inform him [Halifax] in the very early days of August of the whole German plan which worked out to the actual day. He knows too where that information came from, and there was counsel from that source that to save the situation there should be an immediate declaration.

We had an assurance from an authority which has proved right in every other aspect that if that declaration had been made before mobilisation, things would almost certainly have been saved. . . . Why did we not take our courage in our hands?[67]

The voice of the German Opposition thus faintly penetrated the walls of Westminster.

The tragedy of the aborted *putsch* of 1938 is that it was the moment of maximum opportunity with minimum risk of failure. The favourable circumstances which existed could never be re-created nor the *dramatis personae* re-assembled. Although the Opposition never gave up hope of achieving their end, the outbreak of war called for a different kind of action in overwhelmingly different conditions. But by that autumn, the German people had already come to realise that the man on whom so many of them in the early days had pinned their hopes to lead them out of the traumas in the aftermath of the Great War – the ignominy of defeat; the political turbulence; the devastating inflation; the crushing unemployment – was actually leading them backwards into disaster again. One foreign commentator described the German people as having had no rest since 1914. Deliverance from the evil genius they had conjured up would have been an enormous relief. The immediate assumption of the rôle of government by known and distinguished citizens of all political persuasions, instead of by a gang of upstart adventurers, would have assured that there would be no descent into political chaos. In his memoirs Schacht wrote that this first attempt at a *coup d'état* was the only one which could have brought a real turning point in Germany's fate. The intervention of foreign statesmen was something that could not possibly have been taken into account.[68] Gisevius used more dramatic language in his account:

> The sensational report crashed down upon our heads. The impossible had happened. Chamberlain and Daladier were flying to Munich. Our revolt was done for. . . .
> A few days later, Schacht, Oster and I sat around Witzleben's fireplace and tossed our lovely plans and projects into the fire. We spent the rest of the evening meditating, not on Hitler's triumph, but on the calamity that had befallen Europe.[69]

— VI —

Voices from Germany

There is no time to lose. . . . I wish I could convey the terrible certainty with which my German informants spoke of the plans that are laid.

T. P. Conwell-Evans
Secret Report to the
Foreign Office

Unless it is fully comprehended that after the success of Munich these gangsters are determined to behave as 'beasts' – then terrible happenings will have to be faced by us all.

Carl Goerdeler
Message to the
Foreign Office

FOR the conspirators of the Opposition the immediate effect of the Munich Agreement was felt in the dispersal of key military figures through the postings and re-groupings following in the wake of the diplomatic events. The critical construction of the *putsch* inevitably came apart. From now on attempts to get rid of Hitler would have to take a different form, mostly in the far more difficult circumstances of war. It was the civilian members of the conspiracy, particularly those in the diplomatic sphere, who had to pick up the torch.

The leading figures in the German Foreign Office, who had been the cutting edge of the conspiracy in the approaches abroad, revealed their own nervous reaction. Erich Kordt recorded in a private memoir written in January, 1946, how he had been overcome by a feeling of despair. The conspiracy had been carried on under the eyes of the constantly suspicious Ribbentrop. At any moment the Gestapo might have learned about it by mere chance. At the time, wrote Kordt, 'I was never without a cocked gun. With Ribbentrop one was dealing with a criminal person. Everyone who ever had anything to do with him will corroborate my statement that Ribbentrop is a high-grade psychopath, whose presence can be borne only with great nervous strain and considerable expenditure of energy.'[1] After the pogrom at the beginning of November, 1938, Kordt provoked an argument with Ribbentrop on the subject of the administration of the Foreign Office, which his Chief was packing with inferior Nazi personnel. Kordt asked to resign but permission was refused. The following day he reported sick and departed on unofficial leave. He planned a long sea-voyage to South America, ostensibly for his health, although after the strains of the previous months this cannot have been far from the truth. He chose to sail from Southampton, in order to confer with his brother in England. On 19th December the two brothers met Vansittart and Conwell-Evans in the latter's flat. According to Theo, the main subject under discussion was the idea which the two brothers were considering, that of resigning from the Reich civil service. Vansittart and Conwell-Evans pleaded with them not to withdraw as all contact with Hitler's opponents in Germany would then be endangered.[2] During this visit, Vansittart undertook, at Erich Kordt's request, to issue visas to Britain for certain Germans who because of their origins were in danger in Germany. This included his personal confidential secretary, Miss Hilde Waldo.[3] As regards the future, Erich asked for time to think things over until he returned from South America. State Secretary Weizsäcker had had his own confrontation with Foreign Minister von Ribbentrop (news of which actually reached Whitehall) and had retired on leave.

Through his friend Dr Schairer, Goerdeler sent a message to the Foreign Office in which he summed up the effects of the Munich Agreement on Hitler's opponents. The Führer was now satisfied that he could in the future create a situation in which the British and French would give way at the eleventh hour: 'The moderates continually stress that any slight yielding, even on the smallest point, banishes the hope of internal resistance to his régime, and at the same time increases the inner desperation of the masses. . . .'[4] Goerdeler's fear that the Munich Agreement might have set a dangerous precedent for future diplomatic activity was shared by others of the anti-Nazi Opposition. This was forcefully set out in a letter which Vansittart received from 'a German friend in close touch with the Officer Corps' and which he 'warmly recommended to the Foreign Secretary.' He also begged him to bring it to the notice of the Prime Minister. Vansittart's correspondent described the difficulty which the Munich Agreement presented for those in the Army who opposed Hitler. Britain and France continued to justify their actions. It could therefore be assumed that they would do the same again in 1939. This made opposition to Hitler's gambling policy impossible. 'No senior officer feels that he can criticise Hitler's foreign policy because he can no longer prove that he is steering a dangerous course. . . .' The British Prime Minister could nevertheless activate the internal opposition in Germany to an extent that would make conditions very threatening to Hitler if he would exhibit more clearly a greater display of energy towards the blackmailing and bluffing tactics of the Axis powers. 'Please do not take offence when I tell you that you English are wrong in stating the "peace was saved at Munich". It was Hitler and his régime who were saved. . . .'[5]

During his interrogation in 1946 General Halder confirmed that even in the circles of Hitler's opponents – the senior officers' corps – Hitler's achievement had made an enormous impression. 'I do not know,' he said, 'if a non-military man can understand what it means to have the Czechoslovak Army eliminated by the stroke of a pen, and Czechoslovakia, stripped of all her fortifications, standing as naked as a new-born child.'[6]

Nothing could have been more contrary to the hopes of Opposition circles in Germany than the ideas which were being put forward in the *Review of Foreign Policy and Policy Outline for the Coming Year*, prepared by the Foreign Office at the end of 1938.[7] Far from repeating the performance of Munich, the Western Powers would surrender to Hitler's demands before he even made them:

> If Germany was still to harbour the intention of acquiring further territory at the expense of her neighbours or of other European states . . . there might be some advantage in promoting further territorial changes in Germany's favour in good time, in order that the international atmosphere may not be further disturbed by the existence of unsolved territorial problems. . . .

It was felt unlikely that a crisis in German-Polish relations would arise in the near future, but 'it might be in our interest' to persuade France to terminate her treaty with Poland so that a situation like that of Czechoslovakia would not arise.

Cadogan, Head of the Foreign Office, contributed to this policy-making: 'Munich, like many other promising initiatives, is likely to remain without effect if we let the opportunity pass and not follow it up,' he wrote in his draft paper. We should tell the Germans we were anxious to join in devising a general settlement, 'even if it involves scrapping what is left of the Versailles Treaty (including colonies).' The best method of approach might be a visit to Britain by Field Marshal Goering, 'if it is thought that feeling here would not lead to embarrassing demonstrations.' Plans for disarmament and limitation of armaments could be discussed and agreed. The French would also be pressed to denounce the Franco-Soviet Pact. The 'real if unavowed' intention of this rupture would be to indicate to the Germans that if Germany required further expansion 'she could always seek it in the Ukraine.' If Germany 'organised' the equivalent of colonies in Eastern Europe she would no longer have a case for making demands in Africa – although a token colony for prestige purposes need not be excluded. Orme Sargent felt that a refusal to settle Germany's colonial claims would be 'in direct conflict with the policy of appeasement by means of seeking an understanding with Germany.' The answer might be that such an understanding would represent another success for the extremists in the Nazi Party and therefore ought not to be worked for. 'But in that case what becomes of the policy of appeasement? Are we to abandon it . . . ?' Cadogan replied: '*We* are not to abandon the policy of "appeasement". We have done our best for it. . . .'[8]

While these deliberations were proceeding, Ashton-Gwatkin, Economic Counsellor to the Foreign Office, who had had friendly connections with Goerdeler since 1937, invited Mr A. P. Young to visit him 'on a special matter.' In view of the subsequent confusion in Central Department, it is worth quoting Young's own description of the meeting. He called on Ashton-Gwatkin at the Foreign Office towards the end of November:

> He wanted me to visit Dr Goerdeler secretly, and obtain from him the conditions which Germany would desire for close collaboration with Britain, in a possible post-Hitler era, with Goerdeler functioning as Chancellor.[9]

On 3rd December, Ashton-Gwatkin reported to Central Department that Young had left for Switzerland that day to see Goerdeler and ascertain (*inter alia*) 'his political programme (which he will be asked to draw up for us to see).'[10]

On 4th December Young met Goerdeler in a Zurich hotel, where they spent the afternoon and evening together. This time Young was to take back to London a document from the hand of Goerdeler himself, in addition to the digest of their conversation which he himself normally made after such visits. A typewriter was borrowed from the hotel manager and Young watched Goerdeler typing out his ideas with one finger, fortified by coffee and sandwiches. According to Young, Goerdeler worked at his task from mid-afternoon until late in the evening. It obviously took him many hours to reduce to a succinct document of ten paragraphs the fundamental principles for which he had been asked. Young delivered the document, entitled

Heads of Agreement between Great Britain and Germany, together with his own report, to Ashton-Gwatkin on the 6th December.[11] Ashton-Gwatkin submitted Goerdeler's memorandum (after translating it) with a recommendation: 'Nothing in this programme appears to me to be inadmissible by us; there is much in it that would bring us immense advantage.' He hoped that a favourable reply would be sent to Dr Goerdeler.

Goerdeler had opened with a plea for the abolition of the Polish Corridor as a source of continuing disturbance to the justified feelings and interests of the German people. Poland's access to the sea could be assured in another way. Germany should receive colonial territory to be administered according to the principles of international law. (This in fact reflected the terms proposed to Hitler by the British Government in March.) Germany should also receive an interest-free loan of 4–6 milliards of gold marks to be amortised at the rate of 2%. This would assure Germany's currency in the international market and make it possible to remove foreign exchange controls. Return to the free exchange system would force Germany to balance her budget. Thus one of the main centres of contagion in the world would be removed. Further rearmament was to be stopped at once and the aim should be to decrease armaments. If there was danger from other powers – e.g. Italy or Japan – Britain, France and Germany should jointly agree on any necessary increase in armaments. Germany aimed at no hegemony in South Eastern Europe where trade should remain open for all nations. Germany would guarantee the *status quo* in the Mediterranean and withdraw from involvement in Spain, except to support an early peaceful settlement. England, France and Germany should immediately establish a new League of Nations to which all states would be invited. It would have no compulsory powers but work through the force of ideas and reason – to deliberate, mediate and act as arbitrator at the common wish of all concerned. The time was ripe in Europe for co-operation to abolish wars. Economic self-government ought, under the supervision of the State, to provide for respect for labour, for capital, for initiative and achievement and for social justice.[12]

The reception of Goerdeler's document by the Foreign Office was extraordinary. Every point he made was forcibly rejected even though it matched the recommendations embodied in their own *Outline of Policy*. This is easily apparent when the two documents are considered side by side. The Foreign Office paper suggested telling the Germans that 'we were anxious to join in an attempt to devise a general settlement, even if it involves scrapping what is left of the Versailles Treaty.' But Goerdeler's reference to the Polish Corridor was met with: 'This is not the time to make concessions to Germany.' It had been recommended that an attempt should be made to initiate a discussion with Germany of economic and financial problems. A similar proposal by Goerdeler was dismissed with: 'Germany has brought her financial and economic troubles upon herself;' any claim to financial assistance should be met with 'a categorical negative.' Disarmament was next on the list. Did Germany require her vast armaments to secure the remedy of grievances, the Foreign Office had wondered. 'If a plan for limitation of armaments could be agreed, we on our side would do everything we could to remedy just grievances.' Goerdeler's insistence that further rearmament would be stopped at once, which was attached to no remedy of grievances, was dismissed as intending to avoid other Powers producing more modern weapons than those already stockpiled by Germany. The *Outline of Policy*, 'on the assumption that some effort was to be made to satisfy Germany's claim for colonies,' had proposed a new colonial régime in a given area of Africa to which all Powers involved should contribute territory. But Goerdeler's proposal for colonial territory administered under international law was also dismissed with a 'categorical negative.' Finally, we should end up 'helping them to realise their ambitions as to a Four-Power Pact.' But the policy paper had recommended: 'The Four-Power idea should be kept alive and given a trial.'

It was essential for the Opposition to include revision of the Treaty of Versailles in its programme in order to consolidate the widest support on the military side for a coup. The Opposition felt also that the new government should have something to offer the nation; after all, Hitler had managed *unlawfully* to breach the Treaty with international impunity. This would, furthermore, take the wind out of the sails of the more aggressive revisionists and nationalists. Certainly there was support in many quarters in Britain for revision. Churchill himself declared: 'That insane Treaty has brought about the most hideous rule of the Nazis which is darkening the world.'[13] Cadogan admitted that if support of Versailles 'really was our policy, we ought to have reacted against the occupation of the Rhineland, when we could have done so effectively. We did not, and the policy is now out of date.' And only a few months later the British Government was telling the Poles not to be intransigent over bargaining. As for the colonial question, as far back as May, 1937 Cadogan had noted rather cynically in his diary that it had been agreed that there should be partial restoration of colonies to Germany; that someone else should do it and that 'some of us can find a lot of desert wholly covered with stones that we could throw into the pot.'[14]

Why did the British reject so emphatically the proposals made by Goerdeler when a few weeks earlier they had been embodying such ideas in their own forward policy papers? As opposition to the message was not logical, the only conclusion must be that they rejected the medium. The German Opposition was a thorn in the side and a pain in the neck; worse, they had been right before Munich. Now Goerdeler was harassing them again. A report by A. P. Young, summarising Goerdeler's conversation during their meeting in Zurich, had accompanied the Goerdeler memorandum. As usual Goerdeler was full of advice which no doubt irritated the British diplomats profoundly: for instance, the projected visit of Chamberlain and Halifax to Rome should not go ahead: it would be taken as a sign of weakness by both dictators:

> Firm action with Mussolini at this juncture would also prove a severe jolt for Hitler. It would pave the way for that firm British policy in dealing with the Hitler régime which X. [Goerdeler] had consistently advocated. Unless British policy is quickly orientated in this direction; unless there is full recognition in high quarters that the Nazi régime is composed of gangsters; unless it is fully comprehended that after the success of Munich these gangsters are determined to behave as 'beasts' – then terrible happenings will have to be faced by us all.[15]

Linking Young's report to the Goerdeler memorandum, Sargent chose to see Goerdeler as asking the British to refuse Hitler, but to 'give everything Hitler is asking for to any future German Government which overthrows him;' not because such a future government would be more friendly disposed towards Britain, but because, wrote Sargent, from the internal point of view it would socially and politically be a conservative government under the control of the Army. 'But what reason have we to suppose that from the international point of view we and Europe would be better off with such a government?'[16] This was a deliberate misinterpretation. The Foreign Office knew, primarily through Goerdeler and the Kordts, that the anti-Nazi Opposition heartily wished to be friends with Britain, and that the new government would be very broadly based politically (as had been the September *putsch*). Above all, it would emphatically not be an army régime (Sargent talked about a military dictatorship). The Army had a specific role: to carry out the attack on the régime, which it must have been obvious even to the Foreign Office had to be executed by armed men given the military forces on the side of the régime; and to control any civil disorder which might follow. Cadogan added his own minute to Sargent's: 'I fail to detect any positive indication that Dr Goerdeler or his associates can do anything effective for the overthrow of the present régime.' Halifax merely added his initials. What shape such 'positive indication' of a conspiracy to carry out a *putsch* could possibly have taken it is difficult to see.

The Foreign Office accused Goerdeler of making demands, but that was Hitler's game: the Opposition did not make demands. They expounded the policies, both internal and external, of the post-Hitler government which they would establish. Goerdeler's memorandum dealt only with questions which would involve co-operation with Britain, *which is what he had been asked for*. It did not include those policies, which appear in every Opposition statement which survives, which reflected the intention to right wrongs caused by Nazi aggression which only Germany was in a position to do. Internally, these included the abolition of measures against the Jews and restitution of their losses sustained through persecution. Externally, the Opposition were pledged to the restoration of the independence of Austria. They would not have agreed with the statement in the British Foreign Office policy paper that 'Austria and Czechoslovakia are gone.'

While his colleagues were minuting their dismissal of Goerdeler's document, Ashton-Gwatkin, who favoured it, was having a conversation with Goerdeler's confidant in London, Dr Reinhold Schairer. Perhaps in the hope of pressurising the British Government to respond positively to the proposals, Schairer asserted that 'a favourable reply from England' would be followed by a military seizure of power in Germany.[17] That this was not an element in Goerdeler's proposals was already established by the message which A. P. Young brought back from Zurich. Goerdeler had asked that it should be made known to him verbally by the British Consul in Leipzig 'whether HM Government would accept his programme as a basis of their future relations with Germany.' *If the answer was favourable* he would contact military, industrial and religious leaders with a view to organising a body of opinion sufficiently strong *to swing German policy in the direction indicated.*[18] No mention here of armed revolt. But nobody in the Department queried Schairer's assertion and the Government naturally recoiled from any suggestion that Britain might, in Cadogan's words, 'identify ourselves with those who may be plotting revolution in Germany.' Cadogan did go so far, however, as to envisage sending a message through Young to the effect that while the form of government in Germany was an internal question in which Britain could not intervene, 'we should be ready to co-operate with and assist any German government of whom we could be assured that they desired to live at peace with their neighbours and work for better conditions in Europe.'[19] This enlightened attitude was very much at variance with his comments the previous day, nor did it survive a meeting with the Head of the Secret Service: 'He is very sceptical. I think I am too, but don't like to ignore it altogether. . . . I went at 7.0 to see the PM. He would have none of it: and I think he's right. These people must do their own job.'[20] Ashton-Gwatkin did not give up, and Halifax conceded that he should try to work out a reply to Goerdeler, to be submitted to the Prime Minister and himself. But meanwhile Vansittart saw Schairer and told him that it was not practical politics for an authoritative message to be sent to Goerdeler. 'I'm sure that is right,' minuted Lord Halifax.[21]

The reactions of Cadogan, Strang and Sargent towards Goerdeler followed their normal pattern. But for some mysterious reason Vansittart had undergone a complete change of heart. Goerdeler, whom he had once described as weighty and wise, of great intelligence and courage; whose opinions he had so often urged upon the Secretary of State, and with whom he had spent hours in private conversation, he now castigated in the harshest terms. He 'had for some time suspected' that Goerdeler was merely a stalking-horse for military expansion; there was very little difference between the German Army and the Nazi Party – 'the same sort of ambitions are sponsored by a different body of men.' Vansittart then, inexplicably, took a swipe at Ewald von Kleist: on his visit in August 'he had also made a point of demanding the Polish Corridor.' Yet there was no mention of this in the detailed report of their conversation which Vansittart made to the Prime Minister at the time. Vansittart continued:

I have long suspected that although Dr Goerdeler may from time to time be able to furnish interesting pieces of information on the internal situation in Germany, he is not only worthless but suspect as an intermediary for 'settlement'. . . . Do not trust Dr Goerdeler except as an occasional informant. He is quite untrustworthy and he is in with the wrong kind of person and mind because his own mind is wrong.[22]

It is impossible to discover what caused Vansittart's change of mind, but its violent tone seems to indicate some personal affront. There may be a clue in the sequence of the Young-Goerdeler reports. The first three of these – in August, September and October – were delivered into Vansittart's hands. Those of November and December were handed to Ashton-Gwatkin. Young noted in his book, that after Munich Vansittart's influence in the Foreign Office seemed to wane and that the Foreign Secretary had much closer dealings with Ashton-Gwatkin. Certainly Vansittart would have been aware that he had been by-passed. The fact that the Goerdeler memorandum had been both instigated by Ashton-Gwatkin and forwarded with his strong recommendations might have been enough for Vansittart to shoot it down in flames. Certainly he had a personal confrontation with Ashton-Gwatkin on the matter.[23]

If Goerdeler were indeed worthless, suspect and untrustworthy, then surely the information with which he provided the Foreign Office should have been considered tainted. In spite of Vansittart's character assassination, Roberts produced a paper entitled: *Possibility of a German Attack on the West* which was in fact a digest of all the reports which Young had brought back to London from Goerdeler between August 1938 and January 1939 (the 'X Documents'). Roberts identified their source: 'Dr Goerdeler [who] has for some time past provided us with much of our information about German policy':

Dr Goerdeler is extremely anti-Nazi and has, in fact, been working for the overthrow of the régime; but he has shown himself for the most part a respectable and reliable source of information. . . .
This source is extremely confidential and should on no account be compromised; nor should Dr Goerdeler's name even be mentioned, as he is a very well-known figure in Germany, where he is still enjoying a considerable measure of liberty. . . .

This paper was initialled by Halifax.[24]

Just before Roberts' paper was written, a long memorandum was received in Central Department headed: *Memorandum based on most trustworthy information received before January 15th, 1939*. Vansittart directed it to Orme Sargent, marking it: 'This comes from X again.'[25] A. P. Young gives the history of it in his book: 'This memorandum resulted from a meeting between Dr Carl Goerdeler and Dr Reinhold Schairer. The information was dictated to A. P. Young by Schairer at the Kenilworth Hotel. Young then submitted it to the Foreign Office.'[26] The paper covered a wide range of subjects (and has already been quoted from). Vansittart himself quoted from it *verbatim* in a brief annexe to a collection of reports which were presented by Halifax to the Foreign Policy Committee. And yet the memorandum had received a grudging welcome when it arrived in the Foreign Office. Sargent was brief and dismissive: 'It is a pity that Dr G. tries to curdle our blood by overstating his case.'

The fate which befell these various communications from Goerdeler at the hands of the Foreign Office in December 1938 and January 1939 lays bare the lack of any coherent policy in general towards the Opposition in Germany which might one day seize power. The Foreign Office reacted to each approach as it arose without placing it in context, often missing the mark and getting tangled up in conflicting minutes. It was essential that Britain should be aware in advance of the quality of the government which might take over the country. Its arrival in power was likely to be sudden and without warning. It was equally important on the German side to make exploratory advances to sound out British attitudes and to receive an assurance, it was hoped, that such a government would be well received on the international scene.

At the time of the Sudeten crisis, Halifax had undergone a conversion both with regard to Hitler himself and to the secret sources of information from Germany. On 14 November 1938 he called a meeting of the Foreign Policy Committee to discuss the subject of 'our relations with Germany in the light of recent developments.' With his usual deprecating attitude towards matters of urgent national concern Halifax told his colleagues that 'he did not wish to take up more time than was necessary' and he would therefore summarise as briefly as possible the reasons for the action he thought should be taken. The Secretary of State read to the Committee 'recent reports from highly confidential sources.' He confessed that he had always been disposed to discount information of this character but he had to point out that these reports were from the same sources which had proved so reliable the previous July and August.[27] (One of the reports can, in fact, be traced directly to Conwell-Evans and his contacts in the German Foreign Office, particularly Erich Kordt.) The Foreign Secretary informed the Committee that he had come to the conclusion that the German people did not wish to quarrel with us, but that it was by no means certain that this was true of the 'crazy persons' in control of the country. 'A resolute attitude on our part, backed by a display of strength, might discourage the extremists and encourage the moderates.'[28]

In January, 1939 Halifax summoned the Foreign Policy Committee to consider the subject of 'Possible German Intentions.' To this end he circulated to the Committee various documents consisting of secret reports. A prefatory Note warned that if any of the material leaked out the authors would be in grave danger of 'liquidation', and what was more important 'we shall be deprived of their information.' Section II of the paper consisted of a digest of information received; again the hands of Goerdeler, Christie and Conwell-Evans are discernible. Section III comprised two lengthy memoranda 'communicated to the FO.' These constituted a 'comprehensive account of German policy' which Vansittart had requested from Christie and Conwell-Evans in December, 1938. They contained significant references to the Czech crisis:

> The following information is derived *verbatim* from a high German official. On the 30th September before the Conference in Munich had commenced, Hitler had made all plans for a diplomatic-political-military withdrawal ('Rückzug').

Hitler had witnessed the reaction of the public to the parade past the Chancellery on 27th September. He had been shocked by the mobilisation of the British Fleet. He had thought (according to Christie's informant) that Chamberlain and Daladier might stiffen their terms at Munich as he on his part had done at Godesberg. Christie went on to make an explicit reference to the projected *putsch*, aborted by the British failure to stand up to Hitler:

> The German people, as distinct from the régime, are a factor on which the British Government must continue to rely, but more effectively than was done during the crisis of September. It was then felt that a firmer stand, while still effective in avoiding war, would have placed

Hitler in a position where he might have lost the confidence of the German people, and would have permitted action to be taken against him.

Enough had been written on all sides, continued Christie, about the existence of a large block in opposition to the Reich Government and its Nazi leaders. The Opposition would, however, be joined by the masses and would constitute a great danger to the Nazi Government should Hitler risk involving the country in war. The September crisis revealed to them that their Nazi leaders were not men of peace but the provokers of agitation and war. This public feeling was an asset for peace which could be gradually lost to us.[29]

During the early months of 1939, according to Conwell-Evans' book, Christie was sending reports to the Foreign Office as often as twice a week. The few which survived, either in the Foreign Office files or between the covers of Conwell-Evans' book, show Christie's information and conclusions to be completely at variance with those of Britain's official representative, the British Ambassador. 'We are back again in fact in 1938, when people like Professor Conwell-Evans, Colonel Christie and myself, who really knew what was going on in Germany, were in complete disagreement with Sir Nevile Henderson,' wrote Vansittart to the Foreign Secretary on 21st February. He had never read such dangerous rubbish as Henderson's latest telegram. 'In proof of the danger and the rubbish, I annexe herewith a report by Professor Conwell-Evans who has just returned from Germany.' The latter had authorised Vansittart to give to Halifax personally, but to no-one else, the names of his authorities. It was, wrote Vansittart, 'one of the most illuminating papers I have ever read.' The intelligence came straight from Germans in official positions.[30]

Much of the report by Conwell-Evans of February, 1939 has been cited in previous chapters: his description of the terror under which public servants functioned; the chaotic state of the economy; the desire among many leading figures in Germany for a firm stand by Britain; the undermining of the Army by the introduction into its ranks of the SS; Ribbentrop's infiltration of the Foreign Office by Party members. The image of Chamberlain fatuously waving his personal pact of eternal friendship between Britain and Germany after the Munich Conference contrasts starkly with Conwell-Evans' report:

We are asked not to be misled by Hitler's speech of January 30th. . . .
I was informed that he and also his Foreign Minister [Ribbentrop]
remain, as before, hostile to this country. . . .
From first-hand knowledge I can state that the German Chancellor
has decided to complete the plan of last September which was frustrated by the intervention of Mr Chamberlain.

The writer then defined the precise plan (which subsequent events
confirmed) by which Hitler would carry out his scheme for 'wiping
out Czechoslovakia as an independent state.' Hitler saw this projected
rape as 'inflicting the greatest possible humiliation on the Western
Democracies, particularly on the Prime Minister of England. . . .'

At the very time when Conwell-Evans was penning his lengthy
and sombre memorandum for the Foreign Office, Chamberlain was
writing to his sister – on 19th February –

With a thrush singing in the garden, the sun shining, and the rooks
beginning to discuss among themselves the prospects of the coming
nesting season, I feel as though spring were getting near. . . . All the
information I get seems to point in the direction of peace.[31]

So much for the cogitations of the Foreign Policy Committee a
month earlier.

How, in spite of the specific warnings which had reached them
from the Opposition, the British were taken by surprise by Hitler's
march into Prague has already been discussed. 'One can hardly
believe that with all their secret information His Majesty's Government could be so far adrift,' wrote Churchill.[32]

Christie reported to Vansittart the attitude in the German Army
towards the Prague invasion. If the British and French did nothing
and resumed friendly relations, the Army would conclude that
Britain was agreeing to, even desiring, German rule over Eastern
Europe, the Balkans, even Turkey. It was hoped that at last the West
might recognise that Roumanian oil and Hungarian wheat were all
that Hitler needed to make him stronger than they were. Once their
eyes were opened, this would result in a strong reaction: recall of
ambassadors, breaking of all personal contacts and strong, straight,
aggressive and severe language. 'Then we shall know, and Hitler
will know. It will be his first open failure.'[33]

But the West did not, as the Opposition Germans hoped, 'open
their eyes' and Hitler was left alone to wallow in his ill-gotten gains

in Czechoslovakia which fell into his hands in 'splendid order'. 'The inventories were much admired by our soldiers. . . .' In confiding this information to Burckhardt, Hitler also disclosed that the Germans had acquired the plans of the Czech General Staff. These were 'schoolboy efforts, precise, modest and narrow.' They were quite different from the Polish staff plans 'which we possess, and which leave the visions of Alexander and Napoleon a long way behind.'[34] Chamberlain would have done well to have been equally informed before he took his next momentous step.

Bitterly resentful of the situation in which Hitler's Czechoslovakian move had placed him – or in which he had placed himself – Chamberlain took what was intended to be a counter-move against Germany and a demonstrably firm stand against the dictator, under the mistaken impression that Hitler's inevitable aggression against Poland was rather more imminent than it was. Hitler had in fact been making moves towards Poland, but they had actually taken the form of conciliatory talks with Colonel Beck, the Polish Foreign Minister, about the Free City of Danzig and the Polish Corridor, two creations of the Treaty of Versailles which were now looked at askance even abroad as a continuing cause of tension. Hitler wanted Danzig to return to the Reich. He was also asking to build a motor road and railway link, which would be extra-territorial, across the Polish Corridor to link East Prussia with the rest of Germany. Hitler believed that these matters could be achieved by negotiation. He offered the Poles a 25-year extension of the 1934 Non-Aggression Pact and a formal guarantee of Poland's frontiers. When Beck refused, Hitler went so far as to improve his offer to a straightforward alliance. He also invited Poland to join the Anti-Comintern Pact. Beck again refused. But he was not only turning Germany down. On 21st March, the British and French asked Poland to join a Four-Power guarantee with Russia, of Rumania. But Beck would not have anything to do with any agreement which included Russia; and Russia would not join in the guarantee if Poland was a participant. Chamberlain was faced with a choice between Russia and Poland. 'I must confess to the most profound distrust of Russia,' he wrote. He chose Poland.

On the afternoon of 26 March 1939 Theo Kordt visited Vansittart at his house in Park Lane. His brother Erich had decided, in response to pressure from his friends in the Opposition, to return to his post with Ribbentrop after his voyage to South America and had been back in Berlin since February. Now Theo had information to impart to Sir Robert about the feelers which Hitler was putting out towards the Poles. These were not, at the moment, war-like. Vansittart, however, declared that the rape of Czechoslovakia had destroyed all confidence in the German Government and that consequently the British Government had decided to give Poland a guarantee. Kordt expressed his concern that such a move might encourage the Poles to reject even reasonable German offers. It was particularly risky just at that time, as one never knew with the Poles what situation might arise. Vansittart repeated his statement about the loss of confidence in the Nazi Government and added that it was time to take action against German expansion.[35]

Some of Kordt's concern was shared by the British Cabinet. Duff Cooper noted that never before in history had Britain left the decision of whether or not she should go to war in the hands of one of the smaller powers. The Foreign Secretary agreed. He 'thought it dangerous to allow ourselves to get into a position in which the issue of peace and war depended solely on the judgment of the Polish Government.'[36] In 1938 Chamberlain had advanced the objection that to back France because of her treaty with Czechoslovakia would mean French ministers could decide whether Britain went to war or not. Now he had placed that power at the disposal of the unstable triumvirate of 'Colonels' who governed Poland: Beck, Smigly-Rydz and Moscicki. This is how the Foreign Office described that government:

> The régime in Poland is truly remarkable. Despised and disliked by every decent Pole, supported by no political party and with continual dissension in its ranks, having at its head no-one with the slightest glimmering of political leadership, bungling opportunity after opportunity of making its peace with one section or other of the Opposition; it yet manages to maintain a complete stranglehold on the political life of the country![37]

Colonel Beck was an alcoholic with a shady past. In 1938 he had played the jackal during the Czech crisis and collaborated with Hitler in seizing the area of Teschen for Poland. This was hardly the man to whom to confide the fate of the British Empire. In putting the case for and against the Polish guarantee to the Cabinet, Halifax confessed in his gentlemanly way that 'his own judgment in the matter was perhaps somewhat influenced by the view which he took of the Polish Foreign Secretary.'[38]

On 31st March the Prime Minister announced to the House of Commons a guarantee to Poland which, had it been given to Czechoslovakia in September, 1938 could have changed the course of history:

> In the event of any action which clearly threatened Polish indepen-dence and which the Polish Government accordingly considered it vital to resist with their national forces, His Majesty's Government would feel themselves bound at once to lend the Polish Government all support in their power. . . .

The French Government had authorised the Prime Minister to state they 'stood in the same position in this matter.'[39] The 'temporary unilateral assurance' to Poland announced in the House was, within a week, upgraded to a pact of mutual assistance, to be evolved in due course into a permanent treaty. Having just reneged on their guarantee to Czechoslovakia, the British and French now offered assurances to Greece, Rumania and Turkey. No wonder the Ameri-can Ambassador in London described the British Government as 'punch-drunk'.

The opponents of Hitler with which the German Foreign Office was still largely staffed – in Wheeler-Bennett's slighting phrase: 'the pundits of "resistance" in the Wilhelmstrasse . . . von Weizsäcker and his clever young men' – viewed with some dismay the 'blank cheque' given to Poland and the approaches to other small states as giving Hitler a pretext to claim encirclement of Germany, a policy which would alarm the German people and make them feel threat-ened. It would also encourage Colonel Beck's swaggering belliger-ence and make him even more reluctant to consider any negotiated settlement with Germany. Hitler, as has been seen, was prepared, for his own purposes, to resolve the Danzig and Corridor problem with the Poles without armed conflict. A refusal by the Poles to consider terms could only have one result. Furthermore, this inju-dicious British move would provoke the Supreme War Lord to dangerous and unpredictable responses. Their apprehension was well-founded. In a rage after the British rebuff of 21 May 1938, Hitler had reached for 'Operation Green', the plans for military action against Czechoslovakia, and updated them to: 'Smash Czechoslovakia'. Now it was to be 'Operation White' and Poland's turn. Admiral Canaris witnessed the scene:

> With features distorted by fury, he had stormed up and down his room, pounded his fists on the marble table-top and spewed forth a series of savage imprecations. . . . 'I'll cook them a stew that they'll choke on. . . .'[40]

The apprehension of the German Army reported by Vansittart's source that Britain and France would succumb to another Munich was based not only on the self-justification of the Western Powers but also on the fear that they were not taking adequate steps to strengthen their position. It was this anxiety on the part of the Opposition which led to a series of visits to London during the last summer of peace. They had to find out what Britain intended to do and, if it was what they hoped, to advise the British on the most effective way in which this could be impressed on Hitler.

Oberstleutnant Graf Gerhard Helmut Detloff von Schwerin was in charge of the British and American sections of the Intelligence Department of the Ministry of War. He had established good and confidential relations with the British Assistant Military Attaché, Major Kenneth Strong (who was later to become Head of Intelligence at SHAEF and Eisenhower's right-hand man). On 26th January, Strong reported a visit from Schwerin. The German Staff officer had stressed that another crisis would certainly occur and hoped that Britain would speak as firmly to Germany as America had recently done. It was the only language Germany understood. If Britain was weak, no-one could foresee how things would end. Germany, he said, was ruled by 'a small clique of primitive beings' prepared to create a crisis. 'I asked him what Germany's aims were and he replied: "world domination".' The Foreign Office was not impressed and reacted in the normal confused, negative way towards an Opposition approach. Roberts minuted, rather obscurely: 'As usual the German Army trust to us to save them from the Nazi régime.' Orme Sargent wrote: 'Such an example as this of gross treasonable disloyalty by a senior army officer in a highly responsible position is very significant – or is the whole thing nothing but a Machiavellian lie – and if so with what object?' Cadogan: 'To test our nerves and try to find out how far Hitler can safely bluff.'[41]

Chamberlain's initial lukewarm response in the House of

Commons to the outrage of the rape of Czechoslovakia in March reinforced the ever-present doubts in the minds of the Opposition about the British commitment to inhibiting Hitler's continuing policy of aggression. It was essential to have some reliable information about the lie of the political land in Britain. Who better to make such an assessment than an intelligence officer and one whose credentials in the Opposition were well-established? Count Schwerin was the perfect answer. His post in the War Ministry made a visit to Britain to gather information quite acceptable to the authorities in Germany. His visit was also facilitated by Colonel Oster of the Abwehr, who knew the true reason for his spending six weeks' leave in Britain. His mission was two-fold: officially, he was to report to the General Staff about the mood in Britain: both public opinion and attitudes in official circles. Unofficially, he was to impress upon influential figures in London the urgent necessity of demonstrating clearly a firm determination to go to war if Germany attacked Poland. There was nothing clandestine about Schwerin's presence in London, where he arrived on 14th June. Indeed he had calling cards printed with his rank as a staff officer in the High Command, together with the address of the service flat in Hamilton Place where he was staying. The Secret Service reported his visitors and his telephone calls. (There was a call to the Chase Manhattan Bank; and to someone in MacFisheries whom the SIS believed to be a member of the British Union of Fascists.) One significant visitor was the German Ambassador, Dirksen, who obviously preferred to talk away from official premises. He must have avoided making any recorded appointment because he arrived at Hamilton Place to find Schwerin not at home. One can sense from this incident the presence of the secret service man hovering in the lobby. He duly reported that the Ambassador had left his card in an unsealed envelope and (he noted, darkly) Baron von Richthofen 'was later seen to remove the envelope and to place his own card inside it alongside that of the Ambassador.' No inference was drawn from the visit of another member of the Embassy that day – Counsellor von Selzam – who was one of the anti-Nazi members of the Foreign Office, married to an American and a confidant of Theo Kordt. He was also a close friend of Group-Captain Christie. The following day Schwerin was reported to have had a talk on the telephone with Mr Rykens of Unilever (a constant source of information to the Foreign Office from the Continent). He was also observed to have posted a letter to 'T. [sic] Conwell Evans'.

He was to have an interview at Barclays Bank Head office (an introduction had in fact been sent ahead by the manager of Barclays in Berlin). The agent further reported that the Colonel would be spending the weekend in Oxford.[42] Schwerin must have kept the SIS on its toes: he claimed after the war that he saw three or four people every day.

The Foreign Office noted that 'Major von Schwerin, head of the English section of the Intelligence Dept at the Ministry of War is at present in England on a scouting expedition and has seen a number of people, including Mr Butler.'[43] A member of the British Council wrote to say that he had had a conversation with Schwerin, and that the Colonel had lunched with 12 MPs and had had an interview with Marshal of the RAF Lord Trenchard. Germany, he had told them, listened to the BBC for news and no longer listened to Goebbels. But as long as Chamberlain was Prime Minister, Hitler believed that the British would follow the policy of appeasement. Schwerin himself was convinced that Britain would go to war for Poland but found it difficult, he said, to convince others. The German Government misinterpreted the moderate language of British politicians.[44] The last point was also taken by a friend of Lord Halifax, Lt Col Charles Grey, who was asked to entertain Schwerin for the day. He found the German officer 'absolutely straight' and 'a particularly pleasant and intelligent fellow.'[45]

In spite of his sponsorship by Strong in Berlin, the one place where Schwerin ran into trouble was the War Office. David Astor became involved in endeavouring to resolve the difficulties which he encountered. He was drawn into the matter through his friendship with Erwin Schueller, the member of Lazards Bank who has already been mentioned in the account of the problems caused by Goerdeler's London indiscretions in the spring of 1938, in which Schwerin and his friend Wilhelm Roloff had also been caught up. Now, a year later, the latter wrote to David Astor to ask if he would see Schwerin while he was in Britain. Adam von Trott was also in London at the time, so Astor was able to ask his advice, as a close friend whom he knew to be a member of the Opposition. Trott gave Schwerin a clean bill of health as an anti-Nazi of long standing (but asked that his own activities in London should not be mentioned to him). In due course, David Astor lunched Colonel Schwerin and found him forthright in his conversation. Hitler, he said, was convinced that he could venture further eastwards without precipitating a war. Those in the High Command who had contradicted him in 1938 had been proved wrong and were therefore no longer listened to. Only the British could convince Hitler that this time they were serious. How this should be done, Schwerin spelled out precisely. Astor approached the only senior officer he knew at the War Office – Robert Laycock (later to lead the Commandos during the war) – and he quickly arranged an interview with the brigadier in charge of German Intelligence, Hotblack. His only response to Astor's story was that Schwerin's visit to London was 'bloody cheek'.[46] This bluff soldierly attitude was hardly consonant with intelligence-gathering. Hotblack however did see Schwerin and reported that apparently Hitler had expressed no confidence in his senior general officers as being lacking in fighting spirit. The General Staff had very little contact with Hitler and had not the slightest idea what he was going to do next. Schwerin, he pronounced, though apparently disliking the 'Nationalist-Socialist Ministers' had a profound admiration for Herr Hitler himself! 'I would submit,' he concluded, 'that it is undesirable that very senior officers should meet this German.'[47] (A statement which very much reflects the Foreign Office attitude of rejecting intelligence because it came from *Germans*.)

Schwerin fared considerably better with the Navy. On 3rd July he had a meeting at the Admiralty with the Director of Naval Intelligence, Admiral Godfrey, and the Deputy Director of Plans, at which Jebb of the Foreign Office was also present. Jebb made a report of the occasion for the Office. Schwerin's line was that if the British really meant to fight Germany if she staged a *coup* at Danzig, they should not only *say* so in unmistakable terms but also *do* something rather spectacular. 'By this he seemed to mean anything from mobilising the Fleet to admitting Mr Churchill to the Government.' He was 'most insistent' on the necessity to impress upon Hitler the determination to go to war if necessary. Halifax saw the report and Vansittart minuted his agreement with Schwerin about mobilisation of the Fleet – he himself had advocated it last August and continued to do so.[48] When Schwerin did at last meet a senior officer of the Army, it was on Naval territory.

Whether Admiral Godfrey himself felt that the Director of Army Intelligence should meet Schwerin, or whether Schwerin had invoked his assistance, is not known but a few days later Godfrey gave a private dinner to which an invitation was extended to his opposite number Major-General Marshall-Cornwall, Director of

Military Intelligence. The only other guests were Count von Schwerin and the 'Second Parliamentary Whip to the Government'. The General sent a long report of the occasion, which had lasted four hours, to the Foreign Office. Schwerin, he said, had discussed the present situation fully and frankly. He reiterated what he had already told Admiral Godfrey. Military attachés, he said, were not allowed to send in reports on the political situations; and any reports indicating that things were not as Hitler conceived them to be are regarded as 'high treason' and earn the officer a black mark. The Colonel was extremely pessimistic about the European situation and felt now that war must result in the near future '*unless* we can convince Hitler that we mean business. . . . Hitler was the only person that had to be convinced, no one else counted.' He was pressed to suggest what could best be done to convince Hitler. Schwerin replied:

(a) Carry out a naval demonstration. When Germany announced she was going to send a cruiser to Danzig we should have replied by ordering a squadron.

(b) Take Churchill into the Cabinet. Churchill is the only Englishman Hitler is afraid of. He does not take the PM and Lord Halifax seriously, but he places Churchill in the same category as Roosevelt. The mere fact of giving him a leading ministerial post would convince Hitler that we really mean to stand up to him.

(c) Send our Air Striking Force over to France and station it there. This would produce an enormous effect on Germany.

Hitler, said Schwerin, took no account of words, only of deeds. Hitler was convinced that British foreign policy was thoroughly flabby. The fact that Britain had been floundering for three months in inconclusive negotiations with Russia only confirmed this opinion. The BBC broadcasts were excellent, continued Schwerin, and were recognised as the best and most reliable news service in Germany, but it was useless to broadcast propaganda. Germans were resistant to propaganda and switched off when Goebbels was speaking. Even Hitler was only listened to when making some specially important announcement.

The reaction by the British members of the company to Schwerin's urgent counsels was couched in the customary negative language of the Foreign Office and the Chiefs of Staff. Naval demonstrations were declared to be 'a particularly futile way of showing one's teeth.' Schwerin's hosts also made short work of his plea for Churchill to be taken into government, on the basis that 'Winston's entry into the Cabinet might make for discord rather than unity.' With regard to the Air Force, as all our petrol and bombs were stored ready on French aerodromes there was little point in sending over the machines: 'our bombers could fly over there in a couple of hours.' As for the necessity of bringing home to Hitler Britain's firmness of purpose: 'It would be difficult to draw the line between a firm attitude and a provocative threat.'[49] The tepid response by the Heads of Intelligence services may in fact have been directed less to the message than to the 'bloody cheek' (to quote Colonel Hotblack) of the medium.

It was the core of the British attitude to the German Opposition that disloyalty to the Nazi Government was high treason and those who took that stand were traitors, no matter how vile that government might be (a view in fact held by many – even non-Nazi – Germans). A copy of the General's report was also sent to R. A. Butler and the CIGS, Lord Gort. Gort sent a petulant letter to Cadogan complaining that Schwerin always told the same story – surely proof that he meant what he said and was trying to impress it on everyone he met. Gort was also unhappy because a newspaper happened to be running a campaign to bring Churchill into the Government, and that the RAF happened to have been flying to France and back: it would therefore look to the Germans as if we were gullible and susceptible to any outside influence.[50]

More important than Gort's views was the lack of response at the Admiralty to the pleas for naval demonstrations. To call these 'a particularly futile way of showing one's teeth' is inexplicable in view of the known dramatic effect of the mobilisation of the Fleet in September, 1938. Lord Trenchard wrote to Lord Halifax that a colleague who had had a talk with Schwerin had heard from him of the consternation in the German Embassy at the rumour going round of naval mobilisation. Apparently the Military Attachés had been particularly alarmed when the question was raised as to what Germany's attitude could possibly be if England decided to send warships to Danzig (as Schwerin had suggested at the Admiralty).[51] At the time of the Czech crisis the previous autumn the Naval Attaché at the German Embassy had called on the Director of Naval Intelligence at the news of certain movements concerning minesweepers and had declared himself to be 'greatly shaken' and 'overwhelmed'.[52] Every member of the German Opposition who ever made contact with the British pleaded for the Navy to be brought into play. Duff Cooper, the First Lord, would have been only too happy to oblige but those who had charge of foreign policy consistently rejected the idea as 'provocative'.

At the earlier meeting with Admiral Godfrey and Jebb, the former had emphasised British preparedness to fight. Schwerin, reported Jebb, declared that this statement coincided generally with what he had heard during the course of his visit. He had been profoundly impressed by the change in English public opinion and in the readiness of the nation, if necessary, to embark on war.[53] At the German Embassy, again according to Lord Trenchard's colleague, the Military Attachés had expressed very great surprise at the frankness with which Schwerin was reporting these impressions to the authorities in Germany. Certainly this was the message which he took back to the General Staff. His report, however, which was read by Keitel and Jodl, was not what they wanted to hear and somebody wrote in the margin 'enemy propaganda'. Schwerin himself was severely reprimanded because he was considered to have exceeded his official duties and disregarded the Führer's order which prohibited an officer travelling abroad from expressing any opinion which differed from the official one. He was dismissed from the General Staff and joined the fighting forces. Schwerin ended the war as a Panzer general. In 1944 he tried to prevent the useless defence of Aachen ordered by Hitler and endeavoured to put the citizens under the protection of the advancing American general. When the Gestapo arrived at his headquarters to arrest him, they were faced by machine guns mounted by his men, who threatened to shoot anyone who laid a finger on their commander. He survived the war to serve for a brief period as Military Adviser to Chancellor Adenauer.[54]

While Schwerin was able to carry the Opposition message into Britain under the guise of an official fact-finding operation, other emissaries had to be selected for their personal contacts in England. All such journeys were, when necessary, covered by Canaris, and Oster would take care of any problems with officialdom. One luminary of the Opposition, who was to pursue his rôle to his execution in 1944, was Adam von Trott. He had made many friends in England during his years as a Rhodes Scholar at Oxford from 1931–1934 through his great charm and considerable intellect. Some of the friends of his student days, such as Maurice Bowra and Richard Crossman, were eventually to let him down badly and seek to nullify his work for the resistance. Many of his Oxford friends expected him to repudiate his country simply because it had been taken over by Hitler's evil régime. Any right-thinking person, it was felt, would withdraw from all contact with Germany. Voluntarily to live under the system would be to endorse it. But to exile oneself from Germany unless actually in danger of death from the régime, was to stand aside from the fight merely to prove one's own integrity. The battle could not be fought from outside: the impotence of émigrés was to become all too obvious. The firing line was in Germany itself. Some of Adam's friends at least understood this. David Astor's loyalty was unswerving to the end.

It was because of his connections in spheres of influence in Britain arising out of his Oxford days that Adam von Trott seemed the ideal person to go there to promulgate certain policies which the opposition wished to see pursued. Since completing his law studies, Trott had made extensive visits to the United States and China, financed by Philip Kerr (later Lord Lothian), Secretary of the Rhodes Trust, and Sir Stafford Cripps. Cripps' son John had been at Balliol with Adam and he had become an intimate friend of the Cripps family. Trott produced a paper on 'Anglo-German Relations in the Far East' which was brought to London by Peter Fleming. Kerr thought it of sufficient interest and merit to pass it on to the Foreign Secretary. It was well received by the China experts in the Foreign Office.[55] Trott was not at this time a member of the German Foreign Office though he had found kindred spirits there who shared his desire to take active steps against the régime. But any 'sponsorship' of his enterprise in London by Weizsäcker was carefully avoided. Through a relative, Trott had become acquainted with Walter Hewel – like Captain Wiedemann an early friend of Hitler and more attached to his person than to his policies, though he did not oppose these. He was a member of Ribbentrop's personal staff and held the post of liaison officer both with the Chancellery and with the established Foreign Office of which Weizsäcker was head. Trott found that Hewel was genuinely alarmed at the prospect of war between Germany and Britain, a fear indeed not confined to the Opposition. It was therefore easy for Trott to obtain official permission to travel to England, under the aegis of Hewel and hence, officially, Weizsäcker, ostensibly to advance Hitler's policies there; but having, like Schwerin, a dual purpose. Also, again like Schwerin, he had to present a report at the end of his visit. Adam's Oxford friend, David

Astor, was his strongest card: through the Astor family he could hope for a chance to meet key political figures. Adam arranged a meeting with Hewel and his English friend. Over drinks in a Berlin hotel the latter was able to impress upon the Nazi liaison officer the opportunities which would await Trott in England.

These were indeed considerable for such a young man, unknown and a foreigner. Invited to a distinguished dinner party at the Astor home, Cliveden, Trott managed to have a long talk with Lord Halifax, the Foreign Secretary. He made a sufficiently good impression on his host for an interview to be arranged for him a day or two later with Chamberlain.

Adam was playing a complicated game. Two of his closest friends, David Astor and Peter Bielenberg, who were in contact with him at this time confirm the true motivation for the proposals which Adam put before the British Prime Minister. David Astor remembers his friend saying to him that 'he felt almost unkind in asking a very tired man, who felt that he had done his best, if he would now take part in a "foreign intrigue" of a kind that he had never imagined himself being asked to join.' The Opposition wanted at all costs to stave off Hitler's attack on Poland. They needed time to manoeuvre Hitler into a similar situation to that of September, 1938. It was absolutely essential that the Western Powers should make it clear that German aggression against Poland would mean war; and not, as Hitler himself hoped and had persuaded himself, a localised war between Germany and her victim. At the same time a political alternative should be put forward which it would be difficult for Hitler to refuse to consider. If Hitler could be bogged down in negotiations until the autumn it would be too late to launch his campaign and the longer it was deferred the better the chance for the Opposition to overthrow him altogether. The ploy was that it should be suggested to Hitler that if he restored political independence to Czechoslovakia, (though partially disarmed and economically linked to Germany) he could acquire Danzig and the Corridor by negotiation – another bloodless victory. Such a move would also restore Hitler's international prestige, lost by the march into Prague. This contrived diplomatic scenario, to make any impact, would need to be put forward by Britain. Although not intended as a practical proposition by Weizsäcker's Foreign Office, it might possibly have seemed not altogether fantastic to Chamberlain. He had been personally mortified by Hitler's rape of Czechoslovakia and had been forced by public opinion to reject him and his régime as being an unscrupulous breaker of promises. If the dictator could be persuaded to undo what he had done, it would boost Chamberlain's prestige too.

That the British mind was not closed on the question of Danzig has already been demonstrated by the extracts from the December, 1938 paper on future policy. A more recent indication of Foreign Office thinking appears in an entry of Cadogan's Diary of 20th April (Hitler's birthday!): 'Pole at 10.40. . . . I hinted to Pole that they mustn't be intransigent about Danzig now that we have guaranteed them.' In his 'official' report of his meeting with Chamberlain, Trott indicated that he had put it to the Prime Minister that, if Germany could prove that she respected the identity of other nations rather better than her own minorities were being respected, would Britain help to remove distrust by meeting Germany half-way in a generous and practical manner? Chamberlain had replied that he did not see how such proof could be possible, 'but that, if furnished, it would have to be taken very seriously in Britain, and would also restore to the British Cabinet a public platform for their policy towards Germany.' Chamberlain also told Trott that Tory rebels such as Churchill and Duff Cooper could be completely ignored and that his large Parliamentary majority ensured that he need not pay too much attention to his opponents.

On his return home Adam set to work to produce his official report. It was headed *Fact-finding visit to Britain June 1st–8th* and began: 'The task entrusted to me by Counsellor Hewel was that I should use my connections as a former Rhodes Scholar in England to make a survey of the attitude there towards Germany.' With the help of his friend in the Opposition Peter Bielenberg, a lawyer, he concocted a lengthy report of his meetings with Halifax and Chamberlain in the style of Nazi-speak which was obligatory in a document which was probably destined for Hitler's eyes. But he also managed to inject certain home truths from the British side through the device of setting them up and then knocking them down. He described how Chamberlain had declared 'very excitedly' that the British people were 'passionately stirred' and would fight if another independent nation were 'destroyed'. Adam reported himself as having countered by condemning the ostensible British policy of encirclement, which would have to be discontinued. It may well be that Adam had discussed with his friend Lothian the plan which had been devised to entice Hitler away from immediate war and that

Lothian had approved. But in his report Trott managed to put the idea across to Hitler, clearly enunciated, by actually attributing it to Lothian. He could hardly dare put words into the mouth of the Prime Minister or the Foreign Secretary, but Lothian was at least a solid establishment figure as well as being Ambassador-designate to the United States. In the course of the report, the author introduced the necessary salaams towards the Führer in the form of occasional fulsome references to Hitler's personal qualities and leadership.[56]

Although Weizsäcker officially recommended that the report should go to Hitler, it is unlikely that it actually did. Adam expected to be summoned to Hitler's presence and the Führer would surely have wanted first-hand information from someone who had so recently, so intimately and at such length, had talks with the political leaders in Britain. But he saw neither Hitler nor Ribbentrop. The latter, as the self-styled expert on Britain, would have greatly resented advice from a young man in no official position who obviously had better contacts in Britain than he himself had achieved there as Ambassador. Nor would he have wanted any information to reach Hitler which was contrary to his own emphatic assurance that Britain would not fight.

What Adam von Trott and Peter Bielenberg could not foresee as they carefully transposed Adam's report into Nazi-doublespeak was that it would eventually fall into the hands of the victorious Allies among the captured documents of the German Foreign Office. When a collection of these documents was published by the Allies in 1956, Trott's account of his visit to London in June, 1939 was seized upon by the British press, and the headlines labelled him a spy.[57] There were those, particularly among his old Oxford friends, who were well aware of the dangerous activities Adam had been engaged upon during the war in the internal fight against Hitler. Only David Astor came out openly in defence of his reputation.[58] Although it was known that Trott had been executed after the failed July Plot of 1944 he was merely credited by British newspapers with having been a late convert to the Opposition against Hitler. Adam von Trott was not hanged as a first offender.

It is unfortunate for Adam von Trott's reputation that no known British account of the Chamberlain meeting exists. But this does not necessarily mean that one was never made. Chamberlain himself had made and initialled a lengthy record of an interview he had given the previous day – on 6th June – to the Swede Axel Wenner-Grenn, who had brought proposals from Goering for an understanding between Germany and Britain in the interests of peace.[59] (Chamberlain had not been responsive.) The Cabinet Office stated in 1950, in response to an enquiry from Foreign Office staff handling captured German diplomatic documents, that Mr Chamberlain had an interview on 7th June 1939 'with a man called Adam von Trott' but that 'there was no record of the talk.'[60] Alas, for many, Adam von Trott's memory remains tainted.

One Opposition emissary to London that summer was under no obligation to produce a report at the end of his visit – not an official one at least. He had an indisputable personal reason for travelling to London. Fabian von Schlabrendorff was the great-grandson of Baron Stockmar, Prince Albert's childhood mentor and confidential adviser to Queen Victoria. He had presented to King George VI, through the British Ambassador, some letters of Queen Victoria written to his kinsman. As a result, he had been invited to visit the archives at Windsor Castle and examine any material they contained about his great-grandfather. In pursuit of his other – secret – mission, Schlabrendorff first contacted Lord Lloyd with whom Kleist had talked at such length the year before. Lloyd was very scathing about Sir Nevile Henderson, whom he had known when they were both in Egypt. He was unable to give his visitor much hope of any solid declarations of intent being issued by the Government. Schlabrendorff had another message to give: the German negotiations in Moscow were heading for a successful conclusion. Lord Lloyd immediately passed this information to Halifax. The reply came back to Schlabrendorff that Soviet willingness to continue talks with the British indicated, in the opinion of competent experts in the Foreign Office, that an agreement between Hitler and Stalin was not to be feared.

Schlabrendorff also visited Churchill at Chartwell for a brisk and wide-ranging discussion. Churchill, who had had a visit from Goerdeler in May, showed great interest in the opposition to Hitler and his visitor told him of the scope and activities of anti-Nazi forces in Germany. Churchill asked whether there was any guarantee of a successful action by their group. But guarantee was too strong a word, given the difficulties of secretly working for the overthrow of a tyranny. Nevertheless, he felt that Churchill appreciated this and was only assuring himself of the sincerity of purpose.[61]

Schlabrendorff was so depressed by the negative results of his visit to England that when he was pressed by Oster to make another attempt about the middle of August he refused. It was too late, he felt, and all the chances to save the peace had been missed. He served in the Army during the war, where he was closely involved with the military Opposition and attempts which were made on Hitler's life. He escaped death after the Plot of July, 1944 by various miraculous chances and survived to pay another visit to Chartwell after the war.

June, 1939 was a busy month for the Opposition. Burckhardt, who had paid visits to Berlin, Warsaw and Danzig, met his British League of Nations colleague, Makins, in Basle, where he passed on from his friend, State Secretary von Weizsäcker, what was in effect a message for the British Government. The door to negotiation should be kept ajar – but only just. The best chance of peace was for England to maintain a solid front *'un silence menaçant'*. Otherwise Ribbentrop would continue to argue successfully that the British would not march. A minute by Kirkpatrick recalled that Weizsäcker had spoken in similar terms to Burckhardt at the time of the Czech crisis. Sargent commented that this at all events proved that the State Secretary was consistent in his advice. No attention was drawn to the fact that this advice had just as consistently been ignored. Kirkpatrick added a rider to the effect that if it was decided to circulate the report, Weizsäcker's name should be excised and he should be called 'a high German official'. (Without excising Burckhardt's name as well, this would hardly provide much cover for the State Secretary.) The report was duly initialled by Butler, Vansittart and Cadogan and discussed with Halifax, who instructed that a copy should be sent to the Prime Minister.[62] Chamberlain did not allow it to interfere with his secret plan to throw open to the Nazis the door which Weizsäcker had hoped would be kept barely ajar. Makins' French colleague, Arnal, who was also present at the meeting with Burckhardt, further reported that the High Commissioner had, at Weizsäcker's request, told Ribbentrop that there was no doubt that 'Britain and France would march.' He had not been able to convince the Foreign Minister.[63]

Weizsäcker seized every opportunity he could to undermine the effect of Ribbentrop's dangerous insistence to Hitler that the Western Powers would not oppose him. When he posted Herr von Bülow-Schwante to the newly-elevated ambassadorship in Brussels after Munich he had instructed him to 'throw sand into the machinery of the political adventurers' to maintain peace. In July, 1939 the Ambassador had a visit from an old friend, von Kühlmann, who had been Foreign Secretary in 1918. He was on his way back from England, where he had dined alone with Churchill at his club. They had discussed the political situation in detail and Churchill had said that he did not think the German Government were yet convinced of the fact that the Western Powers would intervene on behalf of Poland. Mindful of the State Secretary's instructions, the Ambassador embodied Churchill's statement in a 'sensationally-worded' telegram to Berlin marked to be transmitted 'to the Reichminister personally'.

It was to Ambassador Bülow-Schwante that the Italian Ambassador, Attolico, once confided the opinion that a statue should be erected to State Secretary von Weizsäcker in the Tiergarten![64]

— VII —

Milestones to Catastrophe

It is of no use to turn a deaf ear to the pleadings and warnings of those representatives – still in office – of the real Germany, who are now, by asserting their convictions as to the unwisdom of the policy pursued in their country, facing great personal danger.

T. P. Conwell-Evans
Secret Report to the Foreign Office

A WEEK after the announcement of the Polish Guarantee, the Easter holiday gave Erich Kordt an excuse to visit his brother in London. Since the Czech crisis, Theo Kordt had been having confidential meetings with Vansittart, sometimes at his own house at 7 Cadogan Place, sometimes at Vansittart's house in Park Lane, and more often at Conwell-Evans' flat in Kensington. According to Kordt, writing after the war, these encounters took place with the approval of Weizsäcker and Halifax. This is confirmed by a note Vansittart wrote to the Office after his retirement in which he referred to 'the talks I had with the Kordts with Halifax's authority.'[1] Indeed, the former Foreign Secretary acknowledged the fact in letters exchanged with Theo Kordt after the war. On Easter Saturday, Vansittart arrived at Theo's house, in sponge-bag trousers and black jacket, no doubt in keeping with the Bank Holiday weekend and to project the idea, should anyone be watching, of an informal visit. Mussolini had launched his invasion of Albania the previous day – Good Friday – and Erich Kordt was able to reveal that he had not informed Hitler beforehand of his intentions. There was no love lost between the dictators, he said. Nevertheless, Hitler was moving towards an alliance between Germany and Italy and Vansittart agreed with Kordt that Britain should make every effort to keep Mussolini away from Hitler. (The Pact of Steel was signed three weeks later.) Most significant of all Kordt's information was confirmation of a change of policy on the part of Hitler towards the Soviet Union.[2]

From the beginning of the year the air was alive with rumours. The Egyptian Ambassador remarked to the Foreign Secretary in February that when he was in Berlin recently he had frequently heard discussion of the possibility of Germany making a political arrangement with Russia; it had struck him as significant that Hitler's speech of the 20th February had contained none of the usual attacks.[3] The French Ambassador made the same point to Cadogan about Hitler's speech. 'It seems to me,' minuted Cadogan, 'that we shall have to watch carefully the development of any tendency towards a *rapprochement* between Germany and the Soviet Union.'[4] Yet with a direct line to the office of the German Foreign Minister, the British Foreign Office did not need to rely on speculation. In a speech on foreign policy on 10th March, Stalin had sent up smoke signals in which he had stressed the Soviet desire for peaceful and friendly relations with other countries, particularly those on its borders, and the improvement of trade relations. He accused the British and French of abandoning the policy of collective security and making concession after concession to the dictators. He charged that the two countries were looking to an attack by Germany on the Soviet Union from which, when both sides were exhausted, they themselves would benefit. The former US Ambassador to Moscow, Joseph E. Davies, became increasingly alarmed by the British negotiations with the Poles which appeared to exclude any rapport with Russia. Currently stationed in Brussels, he flew to England on 1st April and spent the weekend with Churchill. The latter agreed with the American's judgment that: 'It will be a disaster if the democracies do not use the strengths which exist here (i.e. in the USSR) against Hitlerite aggression.' Davies tried to prod his colleague in London, Joseph Kennedy, to warn Chamberlain but Kennedy did not share his anxiety. Kennedy's view was that Russia would have to come in on the side of Poland anyway, in her own interest, without any formal agreement with the Western Powers. Having failed to convince Kennedy, the American made no impact on Chamberlain. He wrote in his diary: 'Somehow or other, it seems impossible to make an impression on this London atmosphere.'[5] Curiously, these words were echoed by Weizsäcker at his trial by the Americans in 1946: 'According to my observations at that time, the official world in London was not ready to act as it should have been.' He continued, obviously with Churchill in mind: 'It may have been a little different in non-official, political circles.'[6] Weizsäcker and his lieutenants knew even better than Ambassador Davies how difficult it was to make any impression on the British. They had alerted them to Hitler's plans for the rape of Czechoslovakia: how it would be achieved and the probable date. Britain's surprise when the course of events followed these warnings testified to the extent to which they had been ignored or rejected. Only in retrospect were the German sources acknowledged to be 'accurate and reliable', in the words of the Foreign Secretary at the Cabinet committee of 19 January 1939.[7] This judgment in no way made the British more receptive to the advance warnings which now began to be received of further aggression by the Supreme War Lord.

Within a week of Erich Kordt's April visit to London, the Soviet Ambassador in Berlin paid his first call at the Wilhelmstrasse since his appointment a year earlier. He told State Secretary von Weizsäcker that the Soviet Union saw no reason why their two countries should not enjoy normal relations, and indeed why these relations might not get better and better. The previous day, 16th April, the Soviet Foreign Minister, Litvinoff, proposed to London a triple alliance of mutual assistance between Britain, France and the USSR. The approach was unwelcome. The Government allowed the proposal to lie on the table for the next three weeks (to the annoyance and dismay of Churchill). At last, on 16th May, Britain responded to the approach made by Litvinoff. Vansittart was chosen to present the British counter-proposals to the Soviet Ambassador, Maisky.

Right in the middle of these diplomatic exchanges, Vansittart sent Halifax an astonishing memorandum across the top of which he had written: 'This comes from the General Staff. It shows that there is no time to be lost in this Russian business.' It was marked SECRET. Vansittart reminded the Foreign Secretary that he had told him the previous day that Hitler was negotiating with Stalin through the offices of the Czech General Sirovy. The latter had taken over as President from Beneš and had had the task of broadcasting to the Czech nation the surrender 'under protest to the world.' 'The following confirmation comes to me today from an entirely reliable source,' wrote Vansittart.[8] This source was, in fact, Christie, as can be seen in the despatch printed in *None So Blind* which Vansittart repeats almost for word. However, in the book Sirovy is not named but described as a 'disgruntled Czech personage taking his revenge for Munich.' Hitler was striving for a reconciliation and a military alliance with Soviet Russia, Christie reported, and since the British negotiations with Russia, had been working intensively in that direction. The proposals delivered by the Germans to Moscow were (1) Poland to be divided between Russia and Germany: (2) Russia to take Bessarabia from Rumania with German aid; (3) Russia to dominate the Dardanelles and the Bosphorus with German aid:

(4) Germany undertakes to give Russia military support in an invasion of British India.

These various dispositions regarding the Eastern states were to become in due course the basis of the Secret Protocol to the Nazi-Soviet Pact. But Vansittart's urgent memorandum to Halifax was dismissed out of hand by Kirkpatrick, now translated from the Berlin Embassy to be adviser on German Affairs at the Foreign Office: 'This report seems unreliable for a variety of reasons which it would be otiose to set forth. I personally do not believe that Germany, so long as Hitler rules, will compound with Stalin.'[9]

But a note in Christie's papers records that the report of the 18th May came from 'Kn', his German source, and was 'handed to Halifax'. Halifax attended a working lunch at the house of the Under-Secretary of State, R. A. Butler, on 18th May, in Smith Square, the day after the second Maisky meeting and the day before the Russians rejected the British counter-offer. In addition to the Foreign Secretary, the guests were the German Ambassador, von Dirksen, and the Counsellor, Theo Kordt. Kordt described the occasion in evidence at von Weizsäcker's trial. He also reminded Butler, in a letter after the war, of what had passed between them on that occasion.

After the meal Butler took Kordt for a walk in St James's Park so that the Foreign Secretary and the Ambassador could continue their discussions in private. During the walk Butler told Kordt that the British were now entering upon negotiations with the Soviet Union as a last attempt to prevent a second world war. As Kordt remarked, he had previously been told that such a policy was not considered practical politics: 'Mr Butler had up to then maintained the point of view towards me that one could not kick out the devil by using another devil.' Kordt in turn revealed to Butler that Weizsäcker was the guiding spirit and protector of the anti-Nazi opposition inside the Foreign Office. He himself was due to fly to Berlin that very afternoon at Weizsäcker's request and would inform him of the new British diplomatic moves in Moscow.[10] In a letter to Butler in 1947 (the circumstances of which will be referred to later) Kordt emphasised this point. He reminded Butler that, at the time, he had stressed that it was of the greatest importance to inform the State Secretary, who was desperately fighting for the maintenance of peace against the evil intentions of Hitler and Ribbentrop. Why did Butler divulge information about the British negotiations with Russia to a member of the German Embassy? Either he accepted Kordt's statement about

Weizsäcker and believed he would make good use of the information in the cause of peace; or he did not, but saw an opportunity to pass some news to Berlin which might have a deterrent affect on Hitler. Certainly Butler never showed himself at any time to be well-disposed towards the Opposition.

At the beginning of June 1939, Theo Kordt was summoned to Berlin, officially to attend a Spanish Civil War Victory Parade. Kordt had his own ideas about the purpose of his visit. These were confided to an old and trusted friend, Pierre Milhaud, Deputy Chief of the French news agency Havas in London. It was through Milhaud that the Kordts directed their efforts to influence French policy. Because of the notorious indiscretion in Paris they could not use the methods of approach which they used with the British.[11] The Frenchman now confided in his friend Ridsdale of the Foreign Office Press Department, who in turn briefed Kirkpatrick. Kordt had good reason to fear that a definite move was under serious contemplation and that he had been called home to testify to the state of public and political opinion in Britain. 'I have marked this note SECRET because it so seriously implicates Dr Kordt. I hope to hear more from my informant [Milhaud] when Dr Kordt has returned.'[12] This memorandum was initialled by Halifax, Cadogan, Sargent and Vansittart. In due course Ridsdale received from Milhaud a digest of what Theo Kordt had learned in Berlin. As Milhaud would not have betrayed his friend's confidence, it can be taken for granted that the information was intended to reach the Foreign Office. Milhaud wrote that Kordt, who had been initially inclined to the view that an Anglo-Russian agreement might incite Hitler to some rash or desperate initiative, was now convinced that such an agreement would make for peace. Indeed, the failure to reach such an agreement would be extremely dangerous and would certainly encourage the Führer to believe that he could act with impunity. Hitler had recently consulted his generals about the chances of military success. Keitel was a yes-man and even Hitler did not totally rely on his judgment; but neither Brauschitsch nor Halder believed in the 'inevitability' of a German victory. 'All the leading military advisers consider that the chances of success with Russia on the side of the Western Powers would be extremely precarious – to say the least.'[13]

The actions of the Kordt brothers and their Chief, Weizsäcker, in the summer of 1939 in keeping the British *au fait* with Hitler's foreign plans and in advising how they might be thwarted, provoked an extraordinary exchange of minutes inside the Foreign Office. Sir Orme Sargent suggested that it might be useful to let the Ambassador in Berlin know that 'we are receiving this sort of information and advice from Germans in official positions.' Vansittart exploded:

> I disagree very strongly with your suggestion. It is the one thing that these people dread; they would consider it grossly unfair to them, and so it is. They would dry up at once at the very thought of such a betrayal of confidence. We have no right *whatever* to talk about Germans 'in official positions' to Sir Nevile Henderson. He could easily make guesses, of which one might hit the mark. And his indiscretion is notorious. This idea must be abandoned.

Sargent responded (unusually) by letter, not by office memorandum or minute:

> Am I to take it that your minute was written on the assumption that any information of this nature which may be given to Sir Nevile Henderson will not be kept secret, in other words that our Ambassador is not trustworthy?

Cadogan did not think so:

> Sir N. Henderson may be guilty at times of ordinary indiscretion, but I think we must trust him to keep to himself anything which we tell him to. Or else we ought to withdraw him at once.

Vansittart (who would have liked nothing better) refused to yield in defence of his sources:

> What I mean is that the people in question would not, and indeed do not, think him a safe repository in regard to their views and activities. And, if they feel that, is it quite fair to them to pass this particular kind of information to that particular destination with any indication that would point to them fairly clearly . . . ?
> They know that he is an indiscreet talker – there are plenty of examples – as do many other people – and they naturally prefer to reduce the risk of *life* to a minimum. Why speak of Germans in '*official*' positions? . . . It is the word 'official' that I object to.

He suggested a compromise: the use of an expression such as 'German sources that we respect.' Cadogan closed the exchange with a laconic 'All right.'[14] Vansittart's form of words did in fact become accepted usage but as no-one was seriously weighing up the information received from those 'official' sources, it was almost a matter simply of semantics. As Sir Nevile Henderson had said: 'It could be taken for granted that secret sources were anti-Nazi and were therefore unreliable.'[15] Having agreed the formula: 'German sources that we respect,' the Milhaud/Kordt memorandum was duly despatched to Henderson with an unemphatic covering note which hardly stressed the significance of its contents: 'You may be interested to see the enclosed copy of a memorandum which was given to a member of the News Department by one of his Press friends.'[16] And by the time it was sent, on 23rd June, Erich Kordt had already been to London and back again. Ribbentrop's chief assistant had arrived on the 15th June ostensibly to spend a week or so on holiday in Scotland.

Theo met his brother at Croydon airport and they spent the day together discussing the international situation and what, under Weizsäcker's instructions, Erich had come to London to do. The latter also saw his friend Milhaud who reported the following day to Ridsdale that Erich had told him that the Germans and Russians were now in contact as a result of a move by Ribbentrop and that 'the Germans feel a degree of encouragement at the reception given to their first approaches.'

> Herr K's conclusion [wrote Milhaud] is that if we want an agreement with Russia we had better be quick about it! His view, like that of his brother, is that an Anglo–Russian agreement would be a strong deterrent to war.[17]

This is the only record in the Foreign Office papers of Kordt's visit and his message. Only after the war, in his evidence at Weizsäcker's trial and in his book, is it possible to discover what passed at the meeting which took place at Conwell-Evans' flat in Cornwall Gardens.

Vansittart arrived in a taxi with a detective who took up a position on the other side of the road. This sentry-go by Special Branch can hardly have enhanced the would-be discreet encounter between the Chief Diplomatic Adviser and the German diplomats. Theo found Sir Robert, though as friendly as ever, considerably more nervous than on previous occasions and attributed this to overwork. (The

Kordt brothers were probably never aware of the sinecure which Vansittart's grand title concealed.) Erich began by saying that he was authorised to speak on behalf of the Opposition and what he had to say had been thoroughly discussed. They saw that the only chance of preserving peace was if the friends of peace in Britain and Germany worked together in close collaboration. He spoke of the grave concern of the Opposition at the British policy of guarantees – to Poland, Rumania, Greece and Turkey. Hitler could present these moves to the German people as an attempt at encirclement, always a sensitive matter in Germany. The Opposition had no doubts about Britain's peaceful intentions but feared that some action on the part of Polish radicals might give Hitler an excuse to attack. Vansittart assured the Kordts that the British Government exerted a calming influence on the Warsaw Government. Erich Kordt went on to say that there was considerable anxiety that the negotiations which Britain had initiated with the Russians had so far produced no result. Hitler had now made his own moves towards the Soviet Union and had not been rejected. He warned that Hitler would unscrupulously sacrifice the Baltic States, Finland and Poland in order to come to an agreement with Soviet Russia. (This absolutely confirmed the reports already quoted, which Vansittart had relayed to Halifax a few weeks earlier and whose consideration Kirkpatrick had dismissed as 'otiose'.) Relations with the USSR were a critical factor in Hitler's plans, said Kordt. If the British got to the Russians first, the Führer would not move. If, however, the British failed, Hitler would feel safe. Erich Kordt told Vansittart that he had this 'straight from the horse's mouth.' Hitler had recently said that if 'the Chamberlains' settled with Stalin he would do nothing and would convene a Party rally for peace in the autumn. If they did not, then he could 'smash Poland', assured that the Western Powers would not intervene and that when he marched he would not be attacked in the rear. (Kordt had spoken very forcefully and later recorded that not even Vansittart had been able to interrupt him.) Weizsäcker, he concluded, considered the situation extremely dangerous and that the British should be alerted.

When at last he could get a word in Vansittart assured the Kordts, in tones of 'total conviction', that they could put their minds at rest. This time the British would not be taken in by Hitler. They were not going to be caught napping: 'We are definitely concluding the agreement with the Soviet Union.' The Kordts believed him. It was, recorded Erich, a load off his mind. The reassuring information was reported to Weizsäcker, Canaris, Oster and Beck when he got back to Berlin.[18] Professionally, Vansittart was in no position to give such an assurance, being excluded from much inside knowledge of what was actually happening.

A week later, on 30th June, Halifax informed the Cabinet (as if the Kordt brothers did not exist) that it seemed that discussions of some kind were proceeding between the German and Soviet Governments but it was impossible to assess their real value. They were probably related to industrial matters.[19] The Head of Northern Department agreed that the utmost that was possible between the Germans and the Russians was a commercial agreement and a tacit understanding to leave each other alone for the time being.[20] Chamberlain himself could not bring himself to believe that a real alliance between Russia and Germany was possible. In his Cabinet statement, Halifax took his stand on comforting information from British Secret Service reports. It was not the voice from inside Ribbentrop's office which commanded attention in Whitehall. Where intelligence was concerned, British was best. But within a week of that Cabinet meeting Britain was in fact being forced to make a concession to the Russians. Basically, the talks in Moscow had been grounded by the British refusal to discuss military matters in advance of the signing of a political agreement, and by the Russian insistence that military and political conditions should be agreed simultaneously. On 23rd July, while still holding out on other points, the British agreed to negotiate a military convention, and on 1st August the departure of a Military Mission to Russia was announced.

On 3rd August Theo Kordt was in Berlin. The atmosphere in London, he reported, was one of moderate optimism. In political circles, it was believed that the military negotiations in Moscow would cause Hitler to pull back. In these circumstances, it would not cause remark if the Ambassador in London took leave of absence. But Weizsäcker told Kordt: the Ambassador 'according to the wishes of those in power' would not be returning to his post. This was to prevent the British Government entering on any political discussion with the German Embassy. In his absence, Theo Kordt would be in charge of the Embassy – for the third time, Weizsäcker pointed out, at a time of serious crisis. He should use this opportunity to the best advantage to pursue the cause of peace.

On his return to London from Berlin on 5th August, Theo Kordt immediately sought a meeting with Vansittart at the Kensington flat. He found the Chief Diplomatic Adviser as confident as he had been in June about the Anglo-Soviet negotiations. He asked Kordt to inform the German Opposition that any attack by Hitler on Poland would make war inevitable. That night Kordt communicated to Weizsäcker that he had heard from 'a most reliable source' that Strang's report on the Moscow talks was 'optimistic'.[21] The Kordts were in due course to be reproached by their friends in the Opposition for having taken Vansittart so readily at his word. After the war, Erich bitterly posed the question whether Vansittart was deliberately bluffing the Opposition, who risked their lives to convey their warnings and so many of whom were to fall into the hands of Hitler's executioners; and to what end? The most likely explanation of Vansittart's over-confidence was that, aware of the warnings which he himself had passed on to the Government, even he could not believe that the British could possibly miss this particular bus.

The possibility that Hitler might succeed with Stalin made it all the more imperative in the eyes of his opponents that his alliance with Mussolini should be destabilised. Weizsäcker and the Italian Ambassador, Attolico, had a close rapport, sharing the difficulties of striving for peace under their respective dictatorships. Their common aim was to keep their masters from inciting each other to aggressive adventures. If Britain could be persuaded to interpose herself between the two evil geniuses, Mussolini's basic reluctance to go to war would be reinforced and he could be manipulated to act as a brake on Hitler's headlong adventurousness. This was the message which the Kordts relayed to the British Government through Vansittart. Erich had given warning of the Pact of Steel when he came to London at Easter 1939. On his next visit at the beginning of June, Erich informed Vansittart that Mussolini had recently made it clear that he could not and would not contemplate a general war under present circumstances. The Duce had also made an emphatic reference to the consultative clause contained in the Pact of Steel. Kordt advised that Britain should maintain relations – even cordial relations – with Italy. She did act as a sort of brake on the Axis and could bring limited pressure to bear on Germany which isolation from the Western allies would make it difficult to effect.[22] The accuracy of Kordt's information is borne out by a long secret memorandum written by the Duce to the Führer on the 30th May which came to light in captured Foreign Office papers after the war.[23] It not only proves the reliability of Erich Kordt as a source but demonstrates the extraordinary access which he provided to the innermost circle of Nazi policy-making.

When Theo Kordt met Vansittart on his return from Berlin early in August, the rôle of Mussolini was raised yet again at Weizsäcker's urgent request. If Hitler were to succeed with Stalin, it was more than ever important to keep a wedge between him and the other dictator. Vansittart was full of confidence about the British negotiations – was not the British Odyssey already on the high seas? Nevertheless he agreed that the Embassy in Rome should sound out the Italian Government about bringing a pacific influence to bear on Hitler.[24]

Certainly Mussolini was under pressure from his Foreign Minister, Ciano, to distance himself from the German war-lord. On 25th July the Duce proposed to Hitler a forward-looking constructive peace policy and the settling of international differences by negotiation. His assurance that if Hitler felt war inevitable he would of course stand by his side, did not carry much conviction.[25] A proposed meeting between the two dictators was abandoned but it was arranged instead that Ciano should go to Germany for talks with his opposite number. On the day that the British Mission arrived in Moscow, Ciano arrived in Salzburg.

His visit began with a ten-hour conference with Ribbentrop on his estate. Ciano's assertion that a Polish conflict could not be localised and that the Western Powers would assuredly join in was rejected out of hand. The same line was followed during two meetings with Hitler. The unhappy Ciano replied that he hoped the Führer was right and went on to underline Italy's weaknesses, to Hitler's irritation.

Erich Kordt, who had been present in Salzburg during the meetings, contrived to have a talk with Ciano before he left Germany and was able to learn what had passed between the Führer and the Duce's Minister. Kordt would no doubt have offered an attentive and sympathetic ear to Ciano's anxieties. No doubt, also, Ciano would have been only too glad to ventilate his resentment to one of Ribbentrop's entourage. Kordt would have been able to measure not only the strength of the Italian diplomat's feelings, but what he intended to do about them. If the British were to let it be known in Rome in the strongest possible terms that Hitler would not be allowed a 'localised' Polish war and that Italy would certainly be involved in the ensuing general conflict, Kordt believed that this would vitally reinforce Ciano's efforts to abrogate the Pact of Steel. It was clear that he felt the Germans had already betrayed the spirit of the partnership. There was no time for a courier to London. Erich contacted his brother Theo through their own system of coded telephone conversations. A meeting was set up in Conwell-Evans' flat with Vansittart, who was given the gist of the Hitler-Ciano talks. Sir Robert seized upon the information that the Pact of Steel was under serious strain. Theo passed on his brother's advice that the strongest measures should be taken to inspire an unequivocal statement by Mussolini against war. Vansittart undertook to report immediately to Lord Halifax and to advise him that the Ambassador in Rome, Sir Percy Loraine, should be so instructed.[26]

The truth of Theo Kordt's own account of this meeting, which he gave after the war, is borne out by Foreign Office records. On 19th August Halifax sent a long letter to Chamberlain who was on holiday in Scotland. Earlier in the week, he wrote, Vansittart had given him 'a good deal of information which came from a reliable source which he disclosed to me and which I can disclose to you when I see you' regarding what had recently been passing between Berlin and Rome. Not only was Halifax able to relate what was in Mussolini's letter to Hitler which had preceded Ciano's visit, but also the fact that it was Hitler's irritation at the Duce's hesitant attitude which had sparked off the Salzburg meeting of the two Foreign Ministers. Halifax was able to summarise what had actually passed between Hitler and Ciano at their meeting, above all the assurance the former had given that the Polish difficulty would be localised and that the Western Powers would not join in. Ciano recorded in his diary that Hitler had told him the Polish question would have to be settled by the end of August. Vansittart had now received confirmation from his source (Kordt) that the actual dates involved were the 25th to the 28th August.[27]

Just how vulnerable the Führer was feeling during these critical days was dramatically revealed in a report which reached the Foreign Office of an interview which had taken place on 15th August between the High Commissioner Burckhardt and Hitler at the latter's instigation.[28] In conveying to the High Commissioner the Führer's invitation to visit him, Förster, the Gauleiter of Danzig, had confided to Burckhardt that Hitler would be glad to be able to talk to someone from England who could speak German well enough to be able to dispense with an interpreter. Förster then immediately retracted the statement, saying that he should not have made it. This had all the hallmarks of a calculated indiscretion.

The meeting took place at Hitler's eyrie in conditions of the greatest secrecy. Förster accompanied Burckhardt on the journey, which was accomplished in Hitler's private plane. Burckhardt found Hitler 'nervous, pathetic, almost shaken at times.' However, while Förster was present, he managed to range the gamut of the usual emotions while threatening to fall upon the Poles like lightning with all the powerful arms at his disposal. Burckhardt made a note of the moods through which he swung during his discourse: 'hysterical laughter'; 'screaming'; 'angry'; 'calm'. Förster was dismissed and Hitler led Burckhardt out into the garden, where they walked together. Hitler 'spoke nervously and in low tones.' If Britain and France were urging Poland towards war, he would prefer to accept it now rather than later, this year rather than next. But surely one should be able to find a reasonable way out? He wanted to live in peace with England. Burckhardt suggested that perhaps the Führer could talk directly to an Englishman. Hitler replied: 'Language is too big an obstacle. I realised it last year. I understand a little English, I stumble over a few words of French.' He had been too busy earning a living as a young man to have time to learn languages. 'An Englishman who could talk German? They tell me that General Ironside talks it fluently – the general who went to Warsaw. . . .' Burckhardt: 'Could I pass on such a wish?' Hitler: 'Yes. Could you not go yourself to London? If we want to avoid catastrophes the matter is rather urgent.' A mere ten days before the off, and Hitler appeared to be crumbling before Burckhardt's eyes. Burckhardt's vivid account, and its latent dramatic possibilities, were dismissed in the Foreign Office with a few dry words from Cadogan: 'Hitler apparently undecided, rather distracted, rather aged. . . .'[29]

It is odd to find Hitler himself embracing the 'Ironside' idea when it was a recurring theme among those who opposed him. It seems a theatrical, even trivial, concept. But when advanced by such a sober responsible diplomat as Weizsäcker, as it was so urgently in September 1938 when Burckhardt made his dash to Berne, it takes on a weightier significance. But whereas Hitler seemed to be seeking some rapport with his English visitor, Weizsäcker obviously had a different vision: General Ironside (whose name alone must have been worth something before he opened his mouth) towering over the corporal, medals flashing on his breast, telling him in no uncertain language – and that his own – just where his policies were leading.

Soon another couple were walking in a garden: Weizsäcker was entertaining the British Ambassador. In the safety of the open air the State Secretary was recommending that a British general (Ironside's name was mentioned) should be sent to Hitler to make it emphatically clear to him that any armed measures against Poland would bring about war with Britain in which Germany's chances would be most unfavourable.[30] On 18th August Henderson made such a recommendation to London. Halifax, in his letter to the absent Chamberlain in Scotland, recommended that a clear message 'defining our position' should be conveyed to Hitler. It was for consideration 'whether this should best be done through the agency of someone like Ironside who might speak verbally to Hitler, as suggested by Henderson.'[31]

But meanwhile, in Moscow, events were moving into top gear. 'Everything is going wrong here,' wrote Chamberlain on 13th August – from Scotland. 'We had heavy rain on Friday and I spent yesterday on the river but it was so dirty and full of loose weed that the fish would not look at a fly.'[32] The harassed Mission in Moscow could hardly have better described their own predicament. Negotiations had again become bogged down on the question of whether Poland would allow the passage of Soviet troops across their territory. The Russians demanded a categorical reply. French and British appeals to Colonel Beck not to wreck the negotiations were in vain. On 20th August the Poles formally rejected the Soviet request. Ribbentrop arrived in Moscow at noon on 23rd August. By the same evening both the non-aggression pact and the secret protocol had been agreed and signed, and the drinking had begun.

The Nazi-Soviet Pact came as a bombshell to the British. It is difficult to understand why. R. A. Butler, Minister of State at the Foreign Office, found himself with his back against the wall at Westminster: 'In the Commons last night everyone was asking me what "our intelligence" was up to.' His own reaction was one of sorrow rather than anger. He wrote rather plaintively to Cadogan:

> Should not our intelligence reports come more into the picture at an earlier stage? E.g. when the Foreign Policy Committee was considering sending the Mission to Russia, should not the meeting have started with an intelligence report?[33]

At Butler's request, Collier, Head of Northern Department, prepared a report which attempted to explain why they had got it so wrong. His summing up has a dilettante air to it:

> In general, we find ourselves, when attempting to assess the value of those secret reports, somewhat in the position of the Captain of the Forty Thieves when, having put a chalk mark on Ali Baba's door, he found that Morgiana had put similar marks on all the other doors in the street and had no indication to show which mark was the true one.[34]

In Cabinet, sour grapes were offered. The Foreign Secretary declared that the concluding of the German/Soviet Pact was perhaps not of very great importance, in itself, though the morale effect at the present time would be very great.[35]

The consummation of the Hitler-Stalin Pact had not deterred Weizsäcker from continuing to press for a direct personal contact with Hitler. What he was patently desperate for was that the British should seize the unique opportunity afforded by Ribbentrop's absence in Moscow to penetrate to the Führer himself, normally an impossibility. Then, in an eye-ball to eye-ball confrontation he would be forced to grasp the truth which Ribbentrop so persistently denied: that force would be met with force and that there would be no small war with Poland but a major European conflict.

During the Cabinet Meeting of the 22nd August – almost as if it had been stage-managed – Halifax received a message from the British Consul-General in Danzig. He had just received a visitor from Germany. Count Ulrich von Schwerin-Schwanenfeld had estates in the Corridor area and was able to travel there frequently without exciting remark. A dedicated member of the Opposition (he was to be executed in 1944) he often acted as a go-between for Weizsäcker and his friend Burckhardt, the High Commissioner. Now the State Secretary had sent the Count to Danzig with a message for the British. The opportunity should be seized of Ribbentrop's absence in Moscow on 23rd–24th to send a letter to Hitler by special emissary. Now, on the very eve of war, the British Cabinet was once again considering direct advice from the head of the German Foreign Office. But not for long. It was pointed out that any letter to Hitler would have to include suggestions for settling the dispute and it was obvious that any emissary should be capable of dealing with very delicate negotiations. Ironside would not be the right person. One detects perhaps a reluctance in a certain quarter to yield the position of personal peacemaker. Cabinet finally agreed that a letter should be sent to Hitler but left it to the Prime Minister and the Foreign Secretary to decide on the best method of sending it.[36]

Poor Henderson drew the short straw and had to fly down to Berchtesgaden from Berlin to face Hitler's wrath. ('Do you wonder that I regard Germany as a soul-scarifying job?') Chamberlain had given the Führer a stern warning against entertaining any idea that intervention by Britain on behalf of Poland was no longer something to be reckoned with: 'No greater mistake could be made.'[37] Nevertheless, the effect of Chamberlain's letter must have been slightly blunted by his concluding words in which he appealed to Hitler to seek a peaceful solution for the differences with Poland and promised British co-operation in such endeavours – not exactly Ironside material.

Already aware of the disaffection rapidly growing in Rome, Hitler had sent Mussolini a letter on the morning of the 26th August which was a sort of belated explanation for his silence about his negotiations with Russia: he had not, he said, expected things to go so far so fast. So, having put Mussolini on hold, Hitler now summoned the British Ambassador. The Führer was on his best behaviour, exuding calm, earnestness and sincerity. He told Henderson that he wanted to match his move towards Russia with one towards Britain. He proposed a guarantee of the existence of the British Empire and a promise to provide assistance towards that end wherever and whenever it should be required.[38]

But within a few hours Hitler learned that his bizarre offer to be the shield and buckler of the British Empire was irrelevant. The Anglo-Polish Treaty of Mutual Assistance had been signed that afternoon. On the heels of this news came at last Mussolini's reply to the Führer's letter. Italy would not march. In a localised conflict, economic and political assistance would be forthcoming; but if Poland's allies counter-attacked, the Duce wrote, 'it will be opportune for me not to take the *initiative* militarily' in view of the state of Italian war preparations 'of which we have repeatedly and in good time informed you, Führer, and Herr von Ribbentrop.' He reminded Hitler that they had always discussed war in terms of 1942, by which time he would have been ready.

In London Theo Kordt received instructions from Weizsäcker

which caused him to call at Vansittart's house on the evening of the 26th August. Relations between the Führer and the Duce were becoming critical and a further strain could to advantage be put on the Pact of Steel if the proposal which Hitler had just made to the British Government could be 'leaked' in Rome. This would prove to Mussolini how little Hitler had Italy's own interests at heart. There was the very real possibility that Mussolini might pull out of the Pact of Steel altogether. But time was pressing. Vansittart called for his car and drove to Lord Halifax's house while Lady Vansittart kept Kordt company. He returned after about an hour announcing that the necessary steps had been taken.[39] If it could be achieved, the disintegration of the Rome-Berlin Axis could not come at a better moment for the cause of peace. The night before, having suffered a right and a left from Britain and Italy, the Führer had cancelled the marching orders. Eight hours before the invasion of Poland was due to start, the Supreme Commander brought the German Army, already on the move towards the frontier, shuddering to a halt.

When on 25th August Hitler had countermanded the marching orders, General Halder, the Chief of Staff, had noted in his diary that Hitler was 'considerably shaken.' When, twenty-four hours later, the attack on Poland was reinstated by a telephone call to the Army High Command, Halder recorded that the Führer was 'very calm and clear.' It was the point of no return: 1st September was the ultimate date for launching an autumn campaign in Eastern Europe. Hitler had taken the plunge. It was the last of what Churchill called 'the milestones to catastrophe.'

At the Nuremberg trials, General Halder was asked why the Opposition did not, at the time of the Polish crisis, carry out the plot against Hitler which had been aborted in September, 1938. Halder replied that after Munich the conspiracy had been broken up and its members dispersed through normal military postings. General Witzleben, for instance, had been transferred to Kassel. The uncomprehending counsel demanded: 'Do you mean that the distance between Kassel and Berlin prevented another plot to overthrow Hitler and halt an aggressive war?' Halder replied that his question proved that he had no understanding of such a situation: 'these were matters of personal confidence.' Counsel: 'Yes or no?' Halder: 'That has nothing to do with distance.'[40] The total impossibility of ever re-establishing the delicately constructed network of trust between military, police and civilians in key positions which had made the conspiracy of 1938 so deserving of success made it necessary to contrive a different plan.

The Opposition chose for its leading spokesman at this time General Thomas, head of the key Department of War Economy (who had contributed to the Heavy Industries Report of 1937). Thomas could marshal the technical data to prove that a war against Poland must inevitably lead to a world war, a war which Germany could only lose. In conference with Goerdeler, Beck, Hassell, Schacht, Planck, Gisevius, Popitz and Oster, he agreed to produce a memorandum prognosticating a long war of attrition. A fortnight before the outbreak of war, he read this memorandum to General Keitel, who interrupted him to object that Hitler was not leading the country into a world war; he knew Britain and France would not fight and America would refuse to be involved. On the Sunday before the Polish invasion, Thomas returned to the attack with a further paper, to which Schacht contributed, contrasting in statistical terms the war potential of Germany and of other world powers. This time Keitel actually showed the paper to Hitler, who dismissed its argument on the grounds that there would be no world war now that he had got the Soviet Union on his side.[41] Having thus failed to prevail against Hitler's *idée fixe*, the conspirators devised a plan which did not rely upon military argument.

According to the Constitution (and it is surprising to be reminded that Germany under the Nazis still had one), war could not be declared without prior consultation with the Reich Cabinet. As a Minister, Schacht knew this had not taken place. Thomas, Schacht and Canaris would therefore present themselves at Army headquarters at Zossen (Schacht's ministerial status would assure them access) where they would confront Brauchitsch. The vacillating Commander-in-Chief would be requested to take immediate steps to defend the Constitution and to make troops available to the Minister for that purpose. It seemed an unlikely ploy in a dictatorship but it would give Brauchitsch a legality to shelter behind. At 4 p.m. on 25th August, Oster learned through his own secret sources that two hours earlier Hitler had ordered the directive for Case White (the attack on Poland) to be put in train. Within an hour, the three members of the Opposition were on their way to the Abwehr offices to collect Canaris and to carry out the plan to force the military leadership to outlaw the Führer's action. But before they had even reached the Abwehr Building, their plans had been overtaken by events. While Thomas went inside to pick up Canaris, the others waited in the car a discreet distance away. In a short time they were joined, not by Thomas and Canaris, but by Oster. He had some staggering news.[42] In London, the British and Polish Governments had ratified the guarantee of March, 1939 as a treaty of mutual assistance. Ribbentrop had always insisted that Britain was bluffing. Now Hitler, shaken, had cancelled the order, issued only hours previously, for the attack. Halder, Chief of Staff, noted in his war diary: 'Treaty between Poland and England ratified. No opening of hostilities. All troop movements to be stopped. . . .'[43] Oster had learned of this almost immediately and this was the news which he imparted to his fellow-conspirators as they cruised round the block in the car.

For Oster, the soldier, it seemed that all must now be over for Hitler. A Supreme War-lord who would change his mind on the issue of war and peace from one moment to the next; who, already having put his armies into motion, would halt the complex operation a bare three hours later – such a leader would surely forfeit the support even of those generals who were not of the Opposition. Canaris, with rare euphoria, declared that peace was assured for decades.

That night, Gisevius and Schacht dined together in quiet celebration and autographed the bill as a souvenir of the momentous day.[44]

The Opposition allowed itself to relax. Hitler had lost his nerve: he could never recover from the panicky cancellation of the marching orders. Further, if he was *not* going to fight it could only mean that he was going to make concessions to the Poles, who had the British behind them. It was the dual military and diplomatic setback the Opposition had always hoped for. Everyone knew that a campaign in Eastern Europe could not be launched later in the year than the beginning of September: Hitler himself had stipulated the first of the month. If, with only five days to go, negotiations were just being started, that dateline could not be met. The diplomatic action taken by Britain on the 25th had effectively stopped the German Army in its tracks. Hitler's demolition would be completed at the conference table. Everything seemed to be going right. But of the nature of those negotiations the Opposition were unfortunately quite unaware. Hitler had not given up yet.

The British Government were well aware that the decision of peace or war rested – indeed they had placed it – in Polish hands and they did not regard Foreign Minister Beck and his fellow-colonels as safe hands. Halifax, who had already experienced Beck's fatal stubbornness during the failed Anglo-Soviet negotiations, impressed upon the British Ambassador in Warsaw the importance from the point of view of world opinion of allowing the German Government no opportunity to pin the blame for any conflict on Poland.[45] Britain's situation was not lost on Hitler; Britain might yet be detached from Poland – might even be grateful for an escape route. On 28th August the British Government pressed Germany to settle its differences with Poland by direct negotiation, as the Poles had agreed to do. Hitler replied the following day, denying any designs on Poland's vital interests and independence and accepting the British proposals. He would draw up terms which, if possible, he would give the British sight of before the arrival of the Polish representative. But in the same breath, at the very end of his letter, the Führer made the impossible demand that the latter should arrive, with full power to sign, before midnight the following day, 30th August.

How these ostensibly reasonable and pacific terms were arrived at was recorded by Erich Kordt after the war. Experts from the Foreign Office were secluded in a hall in the Chancellery under the eye of the Führer, who posed seemingly factual questions about majorities and probabilities in the event of a plebiscite in the Corridor. The result of their deliberations were the sixteen points of the Polish proposals, which seemed sensible and moderate. But what was really going on in Hitler's mind is indicated by the fascinating description of how, every now and then, he 'withdrew to another part of the hall and emitted a roar like an angry beast of prey.'[46]

Late at night on the 30th, Sir Nevile Henderson presented himself at the Wilhelmstrasse with the British Government's reply. This stated that Hitler's demand for precipitate action was unreasonable and that time should be allowed for affairs to be conducted by normal diplomatic procedure. Henderson then asked for the proposals, sight of which Hitler had promised the British. Ribbentrop retorted that there was no point, since the midnight deadline had passed without the arrival of a Polish representative. Nevertheless, he proceeded to read them out, straight through without a pause. Even in English it would have been a great deal to take in and Henderson's German was not of the best. But he naturally assumed that the document, even if a dead letter, would be handed to him afterwards. Instead, however, Ribbentrop absolutely refused to hand it over: he had had his instructions from the Führer. Schmidt was astonished at this statement, so contrary to normal diplomatic practice. Even Ribbentrop, he noted, seemed somewhat out of countenance and repeated this statement as if to stress that he was under orders. Realising the importance of these (apparently) reasonable terms reaching the British Government, Schmidt now looked 'invitingly' at the British Ambassador, hoping and indeed expecting that he would ask for a translation. (Henderson always chose to use German although, in Schmidt's opinion, his command of the language was inadequate for delicate diplomacy.) It was Schmidt's intention to provide the translation at dictation speed to ensure that the Ambassador fully grasped it. But Henderson did not react to Schmidt's meaningful glance.[47] Perhaps his vanity forbade it.

Even though the Ambassador realised that the timing had been fixed to pressure the Poles, he had no reason to believe that the terms, which he had half-heard and partially grasped, were not genuine. Certainly they sounded reasonable, as Theo Kordt in London had already judged them to be. The American correspondent, Shirer, described how, when he heard them broadcast, he was 'deeply impressed by their reasonableness' and reported to that effect in a broadcast to the United States on the last night of peace.[48] In fact the proposals were no more than props in another of Hitler's 'politico-psychological' performances. Schmidt actually overheard the Führer say that this 'reasonable' offer to the Poles was his alibi so that the German people would believe that he had worked for peace up to the last moment and had been defeated by the intransigence of the Poles.[49] Hence the impossible timing; and hence all the orders that the document should not be allowed out of official hands.

On this same night, in Goering's camp, a parallel drama – or farce – was being played out. A Swedish businessman, Birger Dahlerus, a close friend of Goering, had since the summer been exerting himself in the cause of peace by making contact with British businessmen whom he had known since living in London. By the end of August he had established himself as a go-between for Goering with the British Government. Dahlerus was well-intentioned and his confidence in Goering, though misplaced, was genuine.

On the fateful 30th August, Dahlerus arrived late at night from London (where he had seen Chamberlain, Halifax, Cadogan and Horace Wilson) and joined Goering in his train at Luftwaffe headquarters. There he learned that the British Ambassador was to receive before midnight a note of the terms Hitler was to propose to Poland. Dahlerus asked permission to telephone the British Embassy to ascertain that the Note had indeed been received. Instead, he learned from the Chargé d'Affaires, Ogilvie Forbes, of Ribbentrop's rough usage of Sir Nevile Henderson, and that the document had not actually been delivered. Dahlerus immediately protested to Goering that this was no way to treat the Ambassador of the great British Empire if, as it was claimed, the German Government was seriously seeking peace. Goering seems to have taken the point. He produced to Dahlerus a copy of the Polish proposals and allowed his friend to telephone them to Forbes.[50]

The Opposition meanwhile had also put its shoulder to the wheel. Weizsäcker, frantic with anxiety as the last hours of peace ticked away, made an early telephone call to that other pillar of the Opposition, former Ambassador von Hassell. He begged him to come to his office. Quite out of touch with his chief, Ribbentrop, who did not conduct foreign affairs through the Ministry of Foreign Affairs, Weizsäcker saw the Polish proposals as a last hope of peace. The arrival – or even the promise of the arrival – of a Polish representative who could at least negotiate might yet save the situation. The danger was that the offer might be lost by default. Would Hassell, Weizsäcker asked, see his fellow-diplomat, Henderson, and beg him to press the British Government to press the Poles.

Hassell found the Ambassador at breakfast, having got to bed at 4 a.m. Henderson gave him an account of his stormy interview with Ribbentrop. He had already, he said, been in touch with London and with Lipski and would continue his efforts. He did not, however, divulge that the document denied him by Ribbentrop had reached him through Goering.[51] Hassell's account of the visit in his diary is corroborated by the record of Henderson's later telephone call to London in which he refers to Hassell as 'my German friend.'[52]

Within an hour of returning home Hassell was summoned by Weizsäcker once again. The British Ambassador had requested the text of the proposals in order to have something to show the Poles. (He could not of course admit that he had already acquired it.) But Weizsäcker, too, had been forbidden to let the document out of his custody. Now he made an extraordinary request of his friend. Would it be possible for him to convey details of its contents to Henderson, which would perhaps mean putting the document into his hands? 'The document,' recorded Hassell, 'lay before me on the table.'

Before he could reply to this hair-raising suggestion, the telephone rang. It was Ribbentrop. Almost as if he knew what was being discussed at that moment, he ordered that Henderson was not to be given the Polish proposals; that Weizsäcker was not to have any further dealings with the British Ambassador; and finally that Hitler had ordered all diplomatic advances to be rebuffed. There is a hint there that the State Secretary knew the proposals were never intended to be seen by the Poles. Was he already aware of Hitler's carefully orchestrated plan and did he make his perilous attempt to smuggle the proposals to the British in the desperate hope of sabotaging it?

That afternoon Goering entertained the British Ambassador and Chargé d'Affaires to tea.[53] What his guests did not know was that, long before the tea was mashed, Hitler had already issued his directive for the attack on Poland and his armies were on the march again. The Opposition were better informed. Oster, as usual, was first with the news. A telephone call had brought Gisevius racing to Abwehr headquarters. In a corridor he came face to face with Canaris. In a voice choked with tears the Admiral told Gisevius: 'This is the end of Germany.'

At 9 p.m. that night Theo Kordt arranged with Sir Robert Vansittart what was to be their final clandestine encounter in Cornwall Gardens. Kordt had received, shortly before 1 a.m. that morning, a telegram from the Foreign Office in Berlin:

For the Chargé d'Affaires personally. Until further instructions the following proposals are to be kept strictly secret and are not to be communicated to anyone else.

There then followed the details of the sixteen points. A similar cable had been despatched during the day to the embassies in Rome, Paris and Moscow, containing the same prohibitions.[54] Because of the exclusion of the Embassy from all diplomatic activity hitherto, and because the communication was addressed to him personally by Weizsäcker, Kordt put his own interpretation on this. When he studied the proposals he found them 'logical and reasonable, in contrast to the usual madnesses that we are used to reading.' He assumed that the signing of the Anglo-Polish Mutual Assistance Pact on the 25th had at last brought Hitler and Ribbentrop to their senses. Therefore, he surmised, they were now looking for a way out of the crisis without loss of face. Hence the proposals. It was obvious to him that

Weizsäcker would want the British to be aware of this as soon as possible, ahead of the official release. He would have to wait until after dark before he could meet Vansittart. When he made his way to Cornwall Gardens that night he took with him the cable he had received from Berlin.

Vansittart seized eagerly upon the document. He had heard something of Henderson's discomfiture at the Wilhelmstrasse during the night and had had some indication of what the German proposals might encompass. Now he could digest the full text. As he settled down to study the document, Kordt was summoned to the telephone. His wife was calling him from home. There had just been a special broadcast on the German radio. It had begun with a recapitulation of the exchange of notes between the German and British governments on the 28th and 29th August, and the request for the speedy arrival of a plenipotentiary from Warsaw in order to avoid a catastrophe. No such Polish representative had arrived. On the Polish side there had been merely empty subterfuges and meaningless declarations. In the circumstances the German Government could only regard their proposals as having been rejected. The speaker had then read out to the world the full text of the sixteen points of Hitler's 'generous offer'.

At first Kordt was stunned by his wife's news. Then, in a storm of indignation at Hitler's 'villainous trick' he returned to the room where Vansittart, in the company of Conwell-Evans, was still conning the German document. When Vansittart heard Kordt's news he leapt from his chair, crying out at Hitler's duplicity. Kordt himself felt that their world had fallen about their ears. All their efforts to prevent war had been in vain. Now Hitler would unleash it with all its awful consequences. In some excitement Vansittart declared that Britain would fight with all its strength to the bitter end. They would, 'like Samson in the Bible, tear down the columns of the palace and bury everything beneath it.' Kordt rejected this as the counsel of despair. On the contrary, they should keep in touch and work somehow even yet to bring hostilities to an early end. Recovering from his moment of rage, Vansittart agreed. It was essential to establish a system of communication through which the contact between Opposition and the British could be maintained. Kordt was aware that on the outbreak of war Weizsäcker intended to post him to a neutral capital, almost certainly Berne. There and then they made a plan. If Kordt wanted to make contact he would send a postcard, unsigned, either to Vansittart or to his secretary, Miss Dougherty, bearing a verse of Horace: '*Si fractus illabatur orbis pavidum.*' He would then make himself available, a fortnight later, at the place of postmark. Vansittart would then send Conwell-Evans to the place of rendezvous.[55]

The two diplomats took a last leave of one another. They were aware that war was now inevitable; they were not aware that it had already been launched hours before. Just after noon, Hitler had issued his directive for the dawn attack. An hour before Vansittart and Kordt had come together in Kensington, the 'provocation' – the attack on the Gleiwitz radio station – had already been carried out.

The Führer's proclamation to the Army of the opening of hostilities was broadcast at 5.40 a.m. on 1st September and the early editions of the papers appeared soon afterwards. The public lassitude which had marked the last days of peace in Germany – a 'grey apathy', Shirer called it – did not lift when Hitler's address to the Reichstag at 10 a.m. was broadcast to the nation. Gisevius drove through the streets to assess the public reaction to the Führer's address, which was publicly broadcast through loudspeakers. Most people were not listening; some small groups stood silently and then drifted away before the playing of the National Anthem.[56] Shirer, listening to the speech, noted an unwonted lack of enthusiasm among Hitler's audience. The Führer himself seemed 'strangely on the defensive.' Throughout his speech 'ran a curious strain, as though he were dazed at the fix he had got himself into and felt a little desperate about it.'[57]

On 1st September the British had warned Germany that unless aggressive action against Poland was suspended and the German Government 'was prepared to' withdraw its forces, the British Government would without hesitation fulfil its obligations to Poland.

At dawn on 3rd September, Henderson received the text of the ultimatum which he was to deliver. The British Government recalled that no reply had been received to their Note of 1st September calling for 'satisfactory assurances' that the aggression against Poland had been suspended and forces withdrawn. Noting that German attacks had been intensified since then, the British Government stated that if such assurances were not received by 11 a.m. Britain and Germany would be at war.[58]

Henderson had arrived at the Wilhelmstrasse at nine o'clock to find that Foreign Minister Ribbentrop chose to be 'not available' to the Ambassador, who was told to hand any communication to Dr Schmidt, the official interpreter. Henderson accordingly read the document to Schmidt, handed it to him and departed. Schmidt went along the Wilhelmstrasse to the Chancellery. The ante-room was crowded with officials and Cabinet members. All Schmidt would say in answer to their anxious enquiries was that 'there would be no second Munich.' Inside the Führer's office, Hitler was seated at his desk while Ribbentrop stood over by the window. 'I clearly saw,' Schmidt remembered later, 'that this development did not suit them at all.' Perhaps they had expected more temporising. When Schmidt had finished reading the translation of the ultimatum there was complete silence. What Ribbentrop had always insisted would never happen, had happened. After an interval which seemed to Schmidt like an age, Hitler turned towards his evil genius with a look of fury: 'What now?' he asked.[59]

The public lassitude which had been observed by Shirer, Hassell and Gisevius on the announcement of war with Poland did not lift when two days later the small local war exploded into a potential world war with the expiry of the Allied ultimatums. The departing British Ambassador had the impression that the German people were 'horror-struck at the whole idea of the war which was being thrust upon them. . . . The whole general atmosphere was one of utter gloom and depression.' On the Saturday afternoon before his delivery of the ultimatum the following morning, Henderson took a last walk down the Unter den Linden. There were few people about and those that were seemed 'completely apathetic.' When on Monday morning the Embassy was evacuated, a small but absolutely silent crowd watched the baggage being loaded on to military lorries. If they felt hatred or hostility, recorded the Ambassador, they showed no sign of it.[60] State Secretary Weizsäcker had occasion to pass up and down the Wilhelmstrasse past the British Embassy that day. He too saw no expressions of hatred or aggression from other passers-by: 'It was Hitler's and Ribbentrop's war against England, not the German people's war,' he wrote.[61] He had already lost a son at the front. When the Embassy staff and their baggage finally departed for Charlottenburg station the streets were still virtually empty. Henderson took a final look at Berlin: 'The whole effect was one of apathy and unhappiness, or bewilderment. . . . From the attitude of the German people no-one would have guessed that we had declared war on them, or could feel that they wanted to fight us.'

Ulrich von Hassell's observation was perhaps the sharpest. 'The feeling that war is really here,' he wrote in his diary, 'has not yet penetrated the public mind. They are for the most part apathetic and still look upon it as a sort of Party project.'[62] As, indeed, it was.

In London the German diplomats were also preparing to depart. Before he left, Theo Kordt received a moving letter of farewell from Christie which in itself gives the lie to Wheeler-Bennett's defamations, Namier's slurs and Vansittart's false testimony after the war. It was written from the Travellers' Club, the scene of so many meetings:

Dear Friend,
I hope you do not mind my addressing you thus, for friend you have been and are to your own great people, to us Britons, and to all who are struggling to restore the conceptions of honour and integrity amongst nations.

I am writing you these few lines to wish you a deeply felt 'Auf Wiedersehen'. If you must leave us soon, our's is the loss: if a miracle should keep you here, our's to rejoice. Thank you a thousand times for all your noble work: come what may, we shall regard you always as a great gentleman and a great Christian.

Believe me
Yours ever
M. Graham Christie[63]

— VIII —

Underground Channels

A process of question and answer through underground channels might give us an idea of what would be possible in the way of a new régime in Germany.

Minute by Sir Alexander Cadogan
24 January 1940.

The Opposition seem to be working in watertight compartments and we are going to get into a terrible muddle unless one clear, reliable channel is established.

Christie to the Foreign Office
19 February 1940.

THE failure before the war to establish a sound intelligence base with regard to the German Opposition, or to make any positive gesture towards its representatives, now left the British at a loss when faced with the bewildering possibilities which were opening up in all directions, and simultaneously, in the first static months of the war.

The Opposition were now playing in extra time. The final whistle had not blown on 3rd September. This was not peace, but it was equally not war. The Allies had declared war on Germany because Hitler would not abandon his attack on Poland. They had then made no military move against him. Hitler had achieved his conquest unmolested. The failure of the Allies to take to the field on behalf of Poland argued that an extension of the war was not likely to be initiated on their side. On the other hand, there could be no question surely of the Allies making 'peace' with the criminal dictator, Hitler. But did it have to be with Hitler? What if there was another government with which, in the oft-repeated Opposition phrase, 'one could negotiate'? Hitler's implacable intention to attack in the West against the concerted opposition both military and political of the Army, together with the situation created by the SS atrocities in Poland which were now becoming known, seemed to offer a renewed prospect of a *coup*.

The Opposition were faced with a number of imperatives. The Western offensive must be held off while they established communication with London and arrived at some form of agreement with the Government there. It was essential to be assured that the enemy would not take offensive measures to exploit a revolutionary situation in Germany. The prime duty of the Army was to defend the country. However unjust they felt the war to be, the professional soldiers, whose co-operation was essential for a *coup*, would not participate in the overthrow of the régime if this would leave the country exposed to the enemy. Further, there must be some assurance that Germany, liberated from Hitler and headed by a government 'with which one could negotiate', with all that implied of integrity in international affairs, would not be offered punitive terms of peace. If the German nation was to be offered terms which reflected Hitler's criminal aggression rather than the aspirations of a new and honourable government, that government would lose the public support which was vital for its establishment. As the order for the offensive in the West was to be the signal for a *coup*, it was essential to resolve these matters as soon as possible.

The Opposition had recovered swiftly from the psychological setback of its misjudgment of Hitler's momentary step back from the attack on Poland. During the last days of peace between Britain and Germany, Fabian von Schlabrendorff, who had been one of the emissaries to London a few months earlier, was given the task as a member of the Opposition of maintaining contact with British diplomats in order to exchange diplomatic and political information. On the day war between Germany and Britain began, he had some special news to impart to the British. An attempt on Hitler (the first but by no means the last of the war) was already being planned.

Its author was General Baron von Hammerstein, a former Commander-in-Chief, a resolute anti-Nazi and a man of formidable personal qualities. He had been called out of retirement to command an army on the Rhine, where German troops were protecting the Western Front against attack by the French, which it was assumed would come during the assault on Poland. Hammerstein's plan was to lure Hitler to the Western Front, ostensibly to boost the morale of the troops there while the Polish campaign was being waged in the East. Once there, far from Berlin and in the unfriendly Catholic Rhineland, he would be arrested by Hammerstein: if necessary by force. It was Schlabrendorff's task to alert the departing British to what was afoot. It was his own opinion that if anyone could carry out such an action, it was General Hammerstein. The British Embassy was already being vacated but Schlabrendorff managed to track down the Chargé d'Affaires, Sir George Ogilvie Forbes, at the Adlon Hotel. He got a nasty fright when, as he sat down to lunch with the British diplomat, two SS officers approached their table. Had they come to arrest him? But their only concern was an administrative matter in connection with the evacuation of British Embassy personnel.[1] The two 'enemies' finished their lunch in peace in the first few hours of the war. But alas, with the almost animal instinct for scenting personal danger which was to preserve him in future attempts, Hitler was to cancel his visit to the Rhineland. Shortly afterwards General Hammerstein was removed from his command and returned to the retired list.

The swift culmination of the Polish campaign combined with other factors seemed to suggest strongly to the Army leadership that the situation would now be resolved politically without further military action. Britain and France, although they had declared war on Germany, had not taken advantage of 'Germany's moment of greatest weakness' (i.e. exposure on two fronts), in September: they were hardly likely now to embark on a wider offensive. There had also been the astonishing affair of the entry of the Russians into Poland. Because of the intense secrecy of the agreement whereby the Soviet Union was to justify its move on the grounds of its own security with the collapse of Poland, the German Army chiefs were not to be informed in advance of the military arrangement. During the night of 16th–17th September, the German Military Attaché in Moscow telephoned General Warlimont, Chief of Operations Section at OKW, to tell him that Soviet formations were about to enter Eastern Poland. Completely baffled by this intelligence (as indeed was his informant), the General quickly contacted Keitel and Jodl. Their reaction to the news of the Russian move was the horrified question: 'Against whom?' There was a danger of bloody encounters between German and Soviet troops, marching towards each other across the remnants of the Polish forces. In fact, the German Army had already advanced 125 miles beyond the secret demarcation line and occupied an oil-bearing area which Stalin had earmarked for himself – as he pretty sharply pointed out to Ribbentrop on the telephone! This Soviet development seemed further proof that events were taking a political rather than military turn. In fact, all the directives issued to the troops being gradually withdrawn from Poland and transferred to the West were entirely of a defensive nature. There would be a build-up of men and material to match the enemy's forces confronting them. No plans were formulated for any further military action. The politicians would be taking over.[2]

But on the 27th September, as Warsaw was about to fall into the hands of the German Army, Hitler summoned the chiefs of the three services to a conference. Generals Keitel and Warlimont were in attendance. Hitler dropped his bombshell. He had decided 'to attack in the West as quickly as possible.' According to Warlimont, all the commanders, including even Goering, were 'clearly entirely taken aback.'[3] Although this was effectively a decision to embark on a second world war, no senior officer had been consulted, not even the Commander-in-Chief of the Army. There was widespread opposition among army commanders to the prospect of an offensive in which they expected to face the combined forces of Britain, France, Belgium and Holland. They could not foresee the violation of the neutrality of the Low Countries, or the collapse of France, or that the British would be virtually swept into the sea. Nor that all this would happen, not in the 'drear-nighted November' of Hitler's original intention but only, after many postponements, in the favourable days of spring. But it was not only the military objections, which were many, which caused concern. The nation was being put in peril, as indeed was the whole of Europe and possibly the world, by this wanton and iniquitous extension of hostilities. The efforts of so many senior generals to stand against Hitler's plans hardly fit the image of German 'militarism'.

The Opposition knew that it was hopeless to expect to talk Hitler out of his plans by military argument. But for many officers the alternative of a *coup* in war-time would be seen as a genuine stab in the back of the nation. Action which a substantial number of senior officers had been prepared to contemplate in peace-time, now took on the lineaments of treason and mutiny in the face of the enemy. But there was one unexpected development which drew many generals to the Opposition side: the atrocities in conquered Poland. Hitler had been as good as his word of 22nd August and the SS had taken control in the wake of the military advance. The result was something quite outside the normal military experience. The Army was appalled. The population of the country was being put to death in vast and systematic numbers: the leadership element – officers, clergy, intellectuals – and of course the Jews. An often quoted letter to his wife by Colonel Stieff, which has survived in the annals of the Opposition, expresses something of the feeling:

> The wildest fantasy of atrocity propaganda is feeble in comparison to what an organized murderer, robber and plunderer gang is doing there with the supposed tolerance of the highest quarters. I am ashamed to

be a German! This minority, which by murder, plunder and arson is besmirching the German name, will be the disaster of the German nation if we do not soon put a spoke in their wheel.[4]

(In 1944, by then a Major-General, Stieff went to the gallows for his implication in the 20th July Plot against Hitler.) Canaris filled a brief-case with evidence of the atrocities in the East and toured the military headquarters on the Western Front to stimulate reaction against the Führer. Brauchitsch himself protested to Supreme Head-quarters about excesses 'by persons not under the jurisdiction of the Army' and in due course to Hitler himself who (naturally) 'did not take any notice.'[5]

The history of the plans and activities of the military Opposition at this time is a complex one and must be read elsewhere. Beck in retirement was still the leading moral authority of the movement and the civilian element – Goerdeler, Hassell, the Kordts, Schacht, Gisevius – stood firmly behind the military. Everything was focussed on Hitler's decision to attack the Western Powers and thus launch a major European war. As Chief of Staff, Halder bore most of the burden. Behind him were the urgings of his Opposition colleagues and before him was the broken reed, the Commander-in-Chief, Brauchitsch. However much Halder primed his chief with data and arguments against the offensive, Brauchitsch simply went down before Hitler's maelstrom of words. On 10th October, in the face of all professional opposition, Hitler confirmed 12th November as the date for the attack to begin. The seven-day grace period conceded to the OKH meant that they would expect to receive the order to go ahead on 5th November. On 1st November, the Commander-in-Chief and the Chief of Staff departed for a tour of the headquarters of the units in the West in order to gather evidence from the Com-manders there of the difficulties which the offensive would present. Before leaving, Halder had indicated to the conspirators in his own headquarters and in the Abwehr that they should go ahead with contingency plans.[6] Brauchitsch was scheduled to have a meeting with Hitler on the morning of 5th November and Halder had high hopes that the facts which the Commander-in-Chief would put before him would cause the Führer to give way. But if he did not, the Opposition must be ready to take action.

The result of the Western tour had yielded much encourage-ment. Halder was able to note in his diary that the offensive was not believed by any High Command centre to have any prospect of success.[7] When he arrived back at Zossen, therefore, he knew that if Hitler resisted the arguments which Brauchitsch was to put before him in two days' time, action would have to be taken. Oster and Schacht were requested to reconstitute and revise the plans of September, 1938 and Oster was to confer with Halder's deputy, General von Stülpnagel, who had an armoured corps strategically located to dash to Berlin. Gisevius described the atmosphere as being as feverish as that at the time of Munich. He himself was shuttling back and forth between Army headquarters, police headquarters, the Ministry of the Interior; and between Beck, Goerdeler, Schacht, Helldorf, Nebe and others.[8]

On 5th November Brauchitsch, accompanied by Halder, presented himself at the Chancellery for his critical meeting with Hitler for which he had carefully rehearsed the previous day. Unfortunately, he went beyond the military data so carefully assembled and commented adversely on the fighting spirit and morale of the troops. These were not, he said, equal to those of 1914. Perhaps as a diversionary tactic and perhaps because he felt the Commander-in-Chief was impugning Nazi youth training and making adverse comparisons with the old Imperial days, the Führer seized upon the accusation in an explosion of rage. He shouted for Keitel to supply instantly chapter and verse of instances of insubordination, the names of the units and officers concerned and what death sentences had been passed. He then unleashed upon Brauchitsch a bitter tirade against the German Staff, of whose loyalty he was always unsure and who consistently obstructed his plans. He would, he declared, stamp out the 'spirit of Zossen'. Brauchitsch, always psychologically unnerved in Hitler's presence, collapsed under the torrent of insult. Hitler swept from the room. The interview had lasted a mere twenty minutes. Brauchitsch tottered out into the ante-room where Halder was waiting for him, his face ashen and twisted. On the way back to Zossen the Commander-in-Chief stammered out an account of the meeting stressing particularly Hitler's threat that he knew all about what was going on at Zossen and would crush it. For Halder this statement had a more terrifying dimension – Brauchitsch knew nothing yet about the impending *coup*. He could only think that Hitler had somehow got wind of it; perhaps the Gestapo were already there. As soon as he arrived back, to the horror of his fellow-conspirators, he ordered all evidence of conspiratorial activity to be destroyed. Files of evidence against the Party which had been carefully assembled in the Foreign Office; plans of the Chancellery and Government buildings; orders for the movements of armoured divisions to be used in the *coup*; proclamations, and various documents and memorandums prepared by the Opposition, went up in flames. Although he recovered his equilibrium when no SS personnel appeared, nevertheless Halder declared that the order for the offensive had now been given and there was nothing more to be done. As it happened, the order for the offensive, due to be issued at 1 p.m., had been all but overlooked in the aftermath of Brauchitsch's departure from the Chancellery, when Hitler continued on a top note his preposterous witch-hunt through the Army records. It was almost 1.30 p.m. when his aides recovered their senses and managed to catch Hitler just as he was getting into his car.[9]

Halder spoke again to Brauchitsch who affirmed that the offensive spelled disaster for Germany. The latter then made a declaration which summed up his whole attitude towards opposition: 'I myself shall do nothing, but I will not oppose anyone who does do something.'[10]

The military standstill after the conquest of Poland, which seemed to the outside world a time of total inactivity – the 'phony war', the 'Sitzkrieg' – was the Opposition's last chance to avert final catastrophe: the irreversible clash of arms between Nazi Germany and the Western Powers. The circles of resistance drew closer together. Weizsäcker appointed Hasso von Etzdorf, one of Erich Kordt's group and a cavalry officer in the reserve, as his representative with Army headquarters. He was to inform the State Secretary of any indication of an attack in the West; and he was to do all he could to promote the idea of a *coup* within the General Staff. He was to keep impressing upon Halder that the only way to peace was the removal of Hitler.[11] Oster had enlisted into the Abwehr a talented and experienced lawyer, Dohnanyi. He had been a prime mover in General von Fritsch's defence, at which time he had discovered the existence of conspiratorial groups and immediately associated himself with them. His new post was as head of an Office of Political Affairs, with the duty of reporting to Canaris political developments abroad. He had brought with him to the Abwehr records of Nazi criminality which he had collected during his service in the Ministry of Justice. Now he became the 'archivist' of the Abwehr, building up a dossier of material against the régime which was intended for use after the *coup*, either for the arraignment of the Führer and members of the Party, or in the event of his death, to reveal to the people the unassailable facts of the criminality of the régime. In the Foreign Office this work had already begun before the war, when Erich Kordt had assigned the task to his assistant, Georg Bruns.[12] Beck had insisted from the beginning on this assembling of documentary material, not only for its intrinsic value as evidence against the Nazis, but also to prove, when the Opposition government assumed power, that they had been working against Hitler even at the time when foreign powers were willing to do business with him. Another addition to Oster's staff had already been marked down by Canaris before the war. Josef Müller was a Bavarian lawyer, a long-standing opponent of Hitler and a devout Catholic with good contacts not only among the hierarchy in Germany but also in Rome. He was to be the spearhead of the most important connection between the Opposition and the British Government which was ever attempted.

The Opposition were faced with two urgent objectives: to secure from Britain a guarantee that no military advantage would be taken of any internal confusion while power was transferred in Germany from the régime to the new government; and to define what sort of peace Britain would be prepared to agree with the new government. As the situation would not be one of Germany making submission on the field of battle, peace terms offered would have to be such that, while sweeping away Hitler's territorial depredations, they would be acceptable to the Army leaders who must necessarily execute the *coup*. This was the message which had been conveyed by those who had come to London in the last few months of peace.

Weizsäcker was anxious to make reconnection quickly with the British after the disjunction of the declaration of war. Kordt took up his post in Berne on 11th September and almost at once carried out an arrangement he had made with Conwell-Evans before leaving London. This was that he would send the postcard with the Latin quotation as arranged with Vansittart. Fourteen days after the date of postmark Conwell-Evans should arrive in Berne and contact an old friend of Theo's – a Swiss – whom he had known since his service there in pre-war years. This friend would then tell Conwell-Evans where Kordt was staying. In implementing this plan Kordt selected a postcard of Interlaken, showing a small hotel, *Zum Weissen Kreuz*, which would indicate a place of rendezvous. However, after fourteen days there was no sign of Conwell-Evans in Berne. Frau

Kordt went twice to Interlaken to look for him, in vain. What had not been taken into consideration in Cornwall Gardens was the inevitable dislocation of the postal service under war-time conditions.

On 2nd October Kordt was summoned to Berlin by Weizsäcker for a special briefing. On 28th September, Ribbentrop and Molotov had signed the 'German-Soviet Boundary and Friendship Treaty' and Kordt was to be informed about the negotiations in Moscow. During his five-day visit he took part in a number of conferences with Weizsäcker, Oster and other members of their circle. There was general disappointment that contact with Britain had not yet been established.[13]

It was not until some twelve days after Kordt's return to Berne that word came from England. His postcard had evidently arrived in London too late for the rendezvous to be kept. A letter arrived from Conwell-Evans announcing his arrival on the 24th in Lausanne whence he would telephone Berne. The two friends must then have devised the arrangement which was followed the next day. (This letter survives among the defence documents of Weizsäcker's trial.)[14] Kordt presented himself at the station, allowed himself to be seen, and Conwell-Evans followed him home to his flat at 31 Junkergasse. The two men met three times: on the 25th, 27th and 29th October. Conwell-Evans said that he had been instructed by Vansittart to say that Chamberlain and Halifax considered it to be up to the Opposition to establish a German government with which negotiations could be carried on and which the British could trust. Kordt was able to tell Conwell-Evans the latest news from Berlin. Plans were afoot for a *coup* to be carried out as soon as the Western offensive was launched, which was expected in November. Conwell-Evans handed over a document which became the source of a serious misunderstanding on the part of the Opposition. On 12th October, Chamberlain had responded to Hitler's 'peace' offer of the 6th. Conwell-Evans had, with obvious haste, scribbled down certain extracts from that speech. Later, with a different pen and ink, he made a few alterations to the paper: 'A/c' became 'account'; 'cld' became 'could' and a few definite articles were added. But the critical amendment was from 'hMG' to 'HMG'. This was done by superimposing the capital H over the small one and thus almost obliterating both. The letters 'MG' could just pass as a form of 'N. C.' and this was Kordt's conclusion. He believed that he was receiving a personal message from Prime Minister Neville Chamberlain. But Conwell-

Evans had also added the date 'Oct. 12' at the top of the page, the date of Chamberlain's speech. The speech was fully reported in *The Times* but it is probable that Kordt had not yet seen it in print. Writing in 1946, Kordt referred to 'further elucidation' by Conwell-Evans. Perhaps this consisted of an emphasis on the points extracted from Chamberlain's speech and a suggestion that these were 'signals' that the British would be well-disposed towards a Germany under a different form of government: 'It is no part of our policy to exclude from the rightful place in Europe a Germany which will live in amity and confidence with other nations.' Just claims must be taken into account when the time came to draw up a new peace. The British had no vindictive purpose in embarking on war. 'I am certain,' the Prime Minister had declared, 'that all people of Europe including the people of Germany long for peace, a peace which will enable them to live their lives without fear. . . .'[15] Conwell-Evans obviously did not realise that there was any confusion arising out of his written notes and Kordt no doubt assumed, in view of the 'elucidation', that the introduction of the Prime Minister's initials into the text emphasised the personal nature of the message indicated by the selected extracts, and gave them particular weight. Certainly as seasoned diplomats, Theo and Erich Kordt would hardly have been so powerfully encouraged simply by the initials alone. Nevertheless they set great store by Conwell-Evans's paper, which was produced in court in Nuremberg and was later printed in facsimile in Erich Kordt's book: *Nicht aus den Akten.*

Curiously, an identical piece of paper in Conwell-Evans' handwriting, in which exactly the same sections of the Prime Minister's speech are transcribed, is to be found among Christie's papers. There are no abbreviations and the letters 'H. M. G.' are clearly printed. Across the top of the page is written, in different ink: 'Premier October 12 1939 H. of C. reply to Hitler at Reichstag.'[16] Can it be that Theo Kordt inadvertently received a rough draft of the original, on which Christie and Conwell-Evans collaborated?

There must have been some meat in Conwell-Evans' message from London. It was on the agenda of a lengthy conference held by the Abwehr conspirators on 14th November. Groscurth, who was present, recorded the fact in his diary.[17] Certainly the points from Chamberlain's speech, supported by Conwell-Evans's unrecorded 'elucidation', were evidently what the Opposition had been wanting to hear. Theo immediately conveyed the message to his brother by

Foreign Office courier, through a code which they had used before the war which involved references to family matters concerning property. Frau Kordt then travelled to Berlin to give the paper to Erich. Whatever verbal message she conveyed, Erich obviously felt that the personal note from Britain was a trump card which would remove the inhibitions of the General Staff. He took the paper to Oster, who immediately took him to Beck's house, a rare departure from normal practice. In his book Kordt records that he showed Beck the paper and added *what he had been told about the explanations given verbally by Conwell-Evans*. This certainly argues that some message came from England which was linked to the text of Chamberlain's speech. There must have been something more than the rather generalised benevolence of the statements which had been jotted down by Conwell-Evans. Beck warned his companions that negotiations should take place soon because if any breach of neutrality was committed, no-one would want to conclude a peace without retribution (as the paper had indicated) even with themselves, the Opposition. As they parted, Oster expressed the hope that, when the offensive began, as it was scheduled to do between the 12th and the 14th, the generals would not fall back again on their oath and plead their obligation to the living Hitler.[18] It was this reference to the 'living' Hitler, coupled with the message from England, which inspired Erich Kordt to take his decision to accelerate events personally.

One of the genuine problems, exacerbated by war-time conditions, had always been accessibility to Hitler's person. Kordt, alone among all the conspirators, did not share this problem. As Ribbentrop's *Chef de Cabinet* he had unrestricted access to the Chancellery at all times, and to Hitler's ante-room, into which the Führer would often emerge to greet a visitor or speed a guest. All he needed was a bomb and everything would be over. On 1st November, he went to Oster, who could call on the facilities of the counter-intelligence explosives laboratory. He should have his bomb, promised Oster, on the 11th, the day before the offensive would be launched. Kordt confided only in his close colleagues, Etzdorff and Keppel, and his cousin Susy Simonis. He prepared a statement of his intentions and those of his group, one copy for the American diplomat, Alexander Kirk, and one for a Swiss diplomat, Kappeler. He was also able to send a letter to his brother Theo by the latter's wife, who was just returning to Berne after delivering a message to the Opposition, as will be related later. Erich's letter was to be opened only after the *coup* which would follow his own sacrificial *attentat*. Theo should not obey any instruction to return to Germany unless it came to him direct from Weizsäcker, and included a certain code word.[19]

But a concatenation of events in the first days of November demonstrates how fatally events could impinge upon each other, generated by various activities – German or British, genuine or fake, Nazi or Opposition. On 8th November a bomb exploded in a Munich beer cellar where Hitler had been commemorating with his cronies the *putsch* of 1923. Whether the explosion was an independent action by a young Communist called Elser, or whether he was the 'fall guy' for something set up by the Gestapo to rally public enthusiasm for the Führer, has never been definitively established. Perhaps Hitler's famous instinct had made him shorten his speech, but the comfortable margin of twelve minutes suggests an organised incident. The following day the conversations between the British Secret Service and the Gestapo agents posing as 'dissident generals' culminated in the abduction of the British agents at Venlo. Shortly afterwards the Gestapo was able to report publicly that examination had proved that the bomb in the beer cellar had been the work of the murderous British Government who had at the same time been attempting to make subversive contact with a supposedly anti-Hitler element inside the Army.

Alas, when Kordt arrived at Oster's house on the 11th November, as arranged, it was to learn that there was no bomb for him. Since the recent incidents access to all explosives was rigorously controlled. Even Oster himself had not been able to obtain explosive material from his own sabotage laboratory. Whether or not the abduction on the 9th at Venlo had been timed by the Gestapo to follow immediately upon the explosion of the 8th at Munich, together these two events had succeeded in undoing Kordt's plan. In despair, Kordt declared that he would go ahead with a pistol but Oster dissuaded him. He could never hope to be alone with Hitler and to expose himself in an attempt which could only fail would endanger the whole cause.[20] Once again fate had intervened to protect Hitler. But perhaps fate is too indulgent a term to apply to the British blundering at Venlo. Erich Kordt's plan, by virtue of the total unexpectedness of such an assault inside Hitler's heavily-guarded inner sanctum, had stood every chance of succeeding.

The cancellation of the November offensive and the consequent standing down of the planned *coup* have already been described. Theo Kordt was summoned to Berlin by Weizsäcker and told to explain the situation to Conwell-Evans on his next visit, stressing that the intention for a *coup* remained. Conwell-Evans in due course relayed the message that the British were becoming impatient – the longer the delay the more dangerous the likelihood of total war.[21] Further meetings took place in December, January and February. On the British side the demand was made for the restoration of Polish independence immediately following a successful *coup*. This had always been in the forefront of Opposition aims. Nevertheless Beck warned, through Kordt, that it would be a question of timing. Any sudden withdrawal of German troops without a reciprocal withdrawal on the side of the Soviet Union might tempt the Russians to extend further westward across Poland. Conwell-Evans received these arguments 'with reserve.' Kordt did not succeed in persuading him that the instant restoration of Polish freedom might be 'easier said than done.'[22]

According to Theo Kordt, discussions took place in his apartment in Berne during the period of 13th–17th February. At about this time he also sent a long message to Vansittart. In a letter to Erich in July, 1947 he refers to this, when suggesting it as evidence for denazification, as 'the letter which I sent to Vansittart through Philip in March, 1940'. The copy in the Kordt Papers is marked 'March, 1940' but a year later at the Weizsäcker trial he gives the date as 16th February and Erich uses this date in his book, where he quotes a shortened form of the letter. Erich describes Conwell-Evans as having learnt it by heart but as will be seen later, Conwell-Evans did actually carry a letter to London on Theo Kordt's behalf. In the letter to Vansittart, Kordt recalled the talks they had had together before the war and their hopes for a new Germany and a future of mutual trust and co-operation to the benefit of the whole of Europe. Kordt still cherished these hopes. What he feared was a situation arising out of an extension of the conflict which would result in one side imposing a dictated peace upon the other. The situation on the Western Front now, with the two sides facing each other but not fighting, was the moment when negotiations could and should be started. 'My friends are trying with all their might,' he wrote, 'to produce a partner on the German side who could bring about the intended just peace by negotiation.' Kordt then referred to a 'pledge' by the British Prime Minister and Foreign Secretary that the state of uncertainty which would inevitably follow such a radical change [i.e. the overthrow of the régime] would not be used by England and France for military action: 'I know the men who have pledged their word, and Philip the bearer [of the pledge] as men of honour whose word I trust. With the agreement of Erich I have done all that is humanly possible to convince our friends of the absolute reliability of that pledge. . . .' Kordt then alluded to the changing date of the offensive – Hitler's 'uncertainty' – and hoped that the transfer of power could take place 'before the symbolical balance on the Western front is disturbed.' Even if Hitler violated the Low Countries, they should not lose contact with one another. Kordt reminded Vansittart of what he had said about Samson destroying the temple, when they had met for the last time on the eve of the war. 'I think too highly of British statesmanship and of the peace mission of the British Empire to believe its statesmen capable of the folly of Samson.' And he quoted once again the verse of Horace which was their password.[23] It was his last contact with Vansittart.

It had been arranged that Conwell-Evans should return to Berne on 12th April. He never came. On 9th April Hitler invaded Norway.

Although the agenda for the discussions in Berne must certainly have been laid down by Vansittart, it is to be wondered to what extent he was in touch with current trends in the Foreign Office, which hardly reflected his own thinking. With the German Army at the gates of Warsaw, in London minds were being turned towards the terms which the British would impose at the end of the war which, for them, had not yet begun. From some of the exchanges in Central Department it would seem as if an Opposition inside Germany had never existed and was now being invented in the Foreign Office. The Head of the Foreign Office News Department, Leeper, observed that after the last war 'we had to lay down the terms of peace without any preliminary contact with the Germans. Can we avoid it this time?'

> Can we get together, for example, on allied soil, Germans, Austrians, Czechs and Poles so that before the end of the war there may be an agreed programme?
> I fully admit the difficulties of doing this with the Germans because of the accusations that can be made against Germans that are in league

with the enemy, but if we can get the right Germans out of the country as the war goes on, we should gradually minimise this difficulty. . . .

Cadogan, who had consistently refused to countenance the real existing Opposition, actually accorded these aberrant ideas his support:

> I agree generally with Mr Leeper's diagnosis. . . . If we can establish relations with such a shadow Government all the better. . . . The difficulty is obvious. Suitable Germans have to be approached in wartime and got out of the country. I need not enlarge on the difficulties of this. Many of the Germans we would like to approach would probably refuse to desert to the enemy in war-time. . . .

His Deputy, Sargent, had also been thinking. His proposal was that, if Hitler should put forward an attractive peace offer, 'the Allies should not agree to an armistice but put Germany in quarantine while she produces a reliable government.' Leeper concluded his remarks with the resounding statement: 'My object is to break the Nazi power in Germany with the help of Germans and when the time comes to have something to put in its place.' But there had always been 'something to put in its place.'[24] It is noteworthy that discussions about a change of régime in Germany never once threw up the names of the leading members of the anti-Nazi Opposition or even referred to the latter's existence. Those who would have participated in a democratic régime with which they had replaced Hitler were known to the ruling establishment in Britain. But as F. K. Roberts minuted: they 'had no indication that they would be rather better in the long run than the present gang who rule Germany.' This was a totally unjustified statement. Cadogan seemed prepared to wait and see. As he told the French Ambassador, though he felt that as an immediate war aim the elimination of Hitler might be of the greatest importance, the sort of régime which might eventually emerge would be matter for later consideration. However, he could not help believing that the disappearance of Hitler 'would produce an immediate and possibly favourable change in the situation.'[25]

At last the British began to look towards Hitler's enemies within – the 'peace-loving and moderate forces' of which Churchill had spoken in 1938. There seemed to be no conception in the Foreign Office that an act which had had a solid chance of success in peacetime could be rendered almost insuperably difficult in war-time, for all sorts of perfectly obvious reasons. Cadogan declared that 'dissension in Germany would be worth a number of Army Corps.'[26] Indeed, as late at July, 1940 he was advising Halifax 'not to listen too much to Winston on the subject of "beating Germany". We must try every means of helping Germany to beat herself. . . .'[27] There is not a single blushing reference in the files to the efforts which the German Opposition had directed so vainly towards London in 1938 and 1939. Towards the end of 1939, in a private letter to Lord Lothian, Ambassador in Washington, Halifax admitted that many people were pressing for a definition of war aims and that if it could be done there might be advantage in it: 'more particularly if we could formulate objectives that would be acceptable to any "moderate" section in Germany that might have any chance of overthrowing the present régime.'[28] This was slamming the stable door with a vengeance. Halifax had had every opportunity to work with the 'moderates' (Foreign Office-speak for the anti-Nazis) before the war, as he was later to admit. On the eve of the Czech crisis – the moment of greatest opportunity – he had spurned the 'many moderate Germans' who, he had told fellow Ministers, were 'pressing us' for a firm stand which could cause 'the Nazi régime to crack.'[29] Suddenly, the German people, as distinct from their government, were 'in'. They had been castigated (and would be again) as an uncritical mass, solidly behind the Leader's every aggressive move and cheering him to the echo. Wasn't it there on film? Now they were being wooed, presumably in the hope that they would take to the streets in their thousands, throw themselves on to the barrels of Himmler's machine guns and expose their country to the enemy. In his broadcast to the German nation on 4th September, Chamberlain identified Hitler as the common enemy of both the British and German people. The Foreign Secretary took the same line in a letter to Bishop Carey two days later: '. . . It is a war, as you truly say, not against the German people but against those who have, as it seems to us, so cruelly misled and deceived them. And personally I should have no doubt at all, if only one could get rid of that régime, we ought to make as generous a peace as we could with the German people.'[30]

If only the sentiments expressed by Chamberlain and Halifax, quoted here, had been imparted to the Opposition before the war, or during the months of the 'twilight war', how might the course of history have been changed! Even Brauchitsch might have been galvanised into action. Nevertheless the Foreign Office was uneasy about distinctions being made, particularly in public, between the German leader and the German people, to the Führer's disadvantage. They found the Prime Minister's broadcast a little impetuous in this regard. It was decided that, although there was admittedly a good deal to be said for refusing to negotiate with Hitler:

> . . . it is somewhat dangerous to make such an assertion at this early stage, since we may later on find it convenient after all to negotiate with Hitler and our assertion may in that case be an embarrassment to us.[31]

With Hitler still in place, they were keeping an open mind as late as December, 1940. In advising on the Reply to a Parliamentary Question by a member asking for a public statement 'making it clear to the world that not in any circumstances can there ever be any negotiation with Hitler,' Central Department wrote: 'I do not think we can . . . commit ourselves to never undertaking negotiations in any circumstances with Herr Hitler. . . .'[32]

Meanwhile, as the efforts were being made to maintain the fragile connection with the British in Berne, Weizsäcker had seized upon the opportunity offered by a channel which had opened up in another, and supremely important, direction.

Adam von Trott, who had returned from the Far East in December, 1938 after an absence of over a year, had been proving himself a valuable and dedicated member of the Opposition. He was in close touch with Beck, Goerdeler, Schacht and other leaders and had joined the elements of resistance which numbered so many of his young colleagues at the Foreign Office. Trott had established something of a reputation in Far Eastern Affairs. He had important contacts in England. In June, 1939 he had been able to talk to the British Prime Minister and Foreign Secretary. Now a further international opportunity presented itself. He received an invitation to attend a conference of the Institute of Pacific Relations, to be held in Virginia in the autumn. State Secretary von Weizsäcker, realising the value to the Opposition of a visit by Trott to the United States, officially sponsored the acceptance of the invitation. In spite of the outbreak of the war the visit was allowed to go ahead, Weizsäcker stressing the importance of good contacts in America, whose neutrality was important to German foreign policy. Erich Kordt provided him with his passport.[33]

Trott arrived in America at the end of September. It is hardly surprising that his ability to travel there and the fact that he was representing Germany at an international conference should arouse suspicion in various quarters. Some émigrés were nervous of him. However, he had the support of the most distinguished of the expatriates, the former German Chancellor, Heinrich Brüning, who introduced Adam to George Messersmith, Assistant Secretary of State and expert on Central European affairs. Brüning later thanked the diplomat for seeing 'his young friend.' He wrote: 'He has seen much and no doubt will report his impressions to his friends. The plans which he and his friends have are good.' Messersmith replied that he found Trott honest, sensible and capable. He had given him the best information that he could and his own American observations should indeed be very useful for 'his friends' in Germany.[34]

With the collaboration of those Germans in his confidence, Adam drew up a memorandum, intended for the President. This set out the importance of a clear statement of Allied war aims which would reassure that widespread opposition which existed among all classes in Germany. These aims should be reasonable, rejecting dismemberment and looking forward to a Germany liberated from tyranny, integrated into a new European order of peace and justice. The psychological effect of such an announcement would contribute to the conditions for the successful overthrow of the régime. The United States would vitally assist by bringing its diplomatic weight to bear on Britain and France to define their stance. When, on 20th November, Adam delivered the memorandum to Messersmith he expressed anxiety lest there should be any premature agreement between Britain and Germany which would leave the régime, or something similar to it, in power. This would be a catastrophe both inside and outside Germany. There was, he claimed, a powerful group in Britain who desired some such compromise.[35] (This seems to indicate that the Opposition were aware of the Goering factor in British thinking.) Messersmith was impressed and recommended the memorandum to the attention of Sumner Welles, Under Secretary of State. A copy also went to Felix Frankfurter, judge of the Supreme Court, once a visiting professor at Oxford. But it was the Oxford connection which was to queer Adam's pitch. When he had visited England in the summer, after his return from China, Adam had confided to his friend Maurice Bowra, Warden of Wadham College, that he was actively associated with the Opposition inside Germany, particularly in the Foreign Office. He was deliberately vague, however, about the future policy of the Opposition should it succeed in achieving power. This left Bowra with the suspicion that Adam was, after all, playing a double game. Hearing from him of his impending visit to the United States, Bowra wrote ahead to warn certain influential friends against him.[36] One of those who received such a warning was Felix Frankfurter, a close friend of Roosevelt. Suspicion was fostered in State Department circles. Although he had had some success with leading journalists, it was the Presidential level which Adam was trying to reach. On top of everything else, the FBI put a tail on him and recorded his movements in a file headed: 'Adam von Trott. Subject: Espionage activities.' J. Edgar Hoover himself reported personally to the State Department.[37] In a letter to his friend David Astor on 26 December 1939, Adam referred to those in England who had misunderstood him as an 'appeaser' and had warned some Americans against him. Years later, when he learned of Adam's execution, Maurice Bowra was to feel the bitterest regrets for his lack of faith in his friend.

Trott's mission in the United States having been successfully undermined from England, he was forced to accept his failure to reach Roosevelt personally. In order to retrieve something from the disappointment, he prepared a simplified version of the memorandum which he had presented to Messersmith and the State Department. This he hoped to convey to Lord Halifax through the offices of a relative, Charles Bosanquet, who was returning to England. There is no record of its ultimate fate after it was handed to Ivone Kirkpatrick at the Foreign Office.[38]

But Trott's cause was to receive strong – even passionate – support in America from what seems today a most unlikely quarter, a British one. John Wheeler-Bennett was on the staff of the Government British Information Service in America, stationed in New York. He also acted in a confidential advisory capacity to the Ambassador, Lord Lothian. He had a wide acquaintance among German exiles in the United States. Chancellor Brüning, now a professor at Harvard University, was a close friend. Wheeler-Bennett, who had known Trott before the war and had met him both in England and Germany, warmly recommended him to Brüning. In the last days of December, 1939 a communication from the pen of this unlikely champion reached the Foreign Office in London. It was a ringing endorsement of the Opposition, a plea on behalf of the German people and a strong recommendation for positive action.

Wheeler-Bennett's communication was in two parts: a letter to Sir Robert Vansittart, dated 27th December, and a memorandum which accompanied it. The letter, which was a lengthy one, was couched in emphatic terms. The message was the same as that which Adam von Trott had addressed to the Americans. If a declaration of the terms which a 'new' Germany might look for from the Allies offered the prospect of generous treatment, it might bring about a rising in Germany by the oppositional elements in every class who hesitated to take action without such an assurance. Would it not be possible to give those elements with whom we *could* make peace an indication that there would be no political dismemberment of a Germany purged of Nazism? 'If we cannot say what we *are* going to do, we can at least say what we are *not* going to do,' wrote Wheeler-Bennett. The chief obstacle, of course, would be the French, 'who have definite plans for the partitionment of Germany.' Arguing that Britain's contribution to the war so far, both financially and in casualties, was greater than that of France, he continued: 'If Great Britain can afford to be magnanimous to a regenerated Germany, can we not legitimately bring pressure to bear on them?' The Allied statement which he visualised should be repeated continually in every kind of manner. It should also be 'conveyed directly to the leaders of the liberating elements within Germany. Channels exist for this.' Anticipating counter-action which would assuredly be taken by Goebbels' Ministry of Propaganda, Wheeler-Bennett discounted any pronouncements by Prime Minister Chamberlain 'partly because he is mistrusted abroad.' (The reference to Chamberlain was deleted and that section of the letter rewritten by Cadogan.) It was essential that there should be a statement by someone 'whom the German people could be reasonably expected to believe and trust.' He recommended Smuts. In addition to Smuts he further recommended endorsement of the good faith of the Allied statement by an outstanding German and suggested Brüning.

Wheeler-Bennett apologised for the length of his letter which he said was a measure of the importance he attached to the proposals. The matter was urgent as the war might be intensified in the Spring. He also felt it would have a good effect on public opinion in the United States 'which is becoming more and more confused as to the real issue of the struggle.'[39]

The memorandum, dated 28th December, which accompanied this letter, was drawn up in consultation with Trott. It is forceful and unambiguous. Wheeler-Bennett began by quoting from Chamberlain's broadcast to the German people at the beginning of the war and added some high-minded sentiments uttered by Halifax in a speech on 7th November about 'the quality of mercy in dealings between man and man, and in the great Society of civilised states.' The memorandum is worth quoting at some length:

> In a sense, then, the present struggle is a War for the Liberation of the German People and in the struggle the Democratic Powers have an ally within Germany itself in those high patriots of every class and calling who reflect the fundamental decency of the German People. These elements, more numerous and powerful than may be supposed, have a common aim with the Democratic Powers in destroying the Nazi régime and in restoring in Germany a Reign of Law (a *Rechtsstaat*). . . .
> It is therefore to the interests of the Democratic Powers that these elements within Germany should be strengthened and encouraged to the point where they themselves can take the initiative, and this point can only be reached when these liberating elements are themselves assured that the New Reich, which it is our common aim to achieve, will meet with just and generous treatment at the hands of the Democratic Powers. . . .

Although a full statement of peace terms would be inopportune, he wrote, and the world was aware that the Allies intended no vindictive or dictated peace, something more than this was required:

> . . . A more definite assurance is necessary before the elements within Germany antagonistic to the régime can feel themselves justified in taking the momentous and perilous step of rising against their national government. . . .

Wheeler-Bennett then outlined what the statement should contain: an assurance of no political dismemberment; collaboration with Germany in a new European Order in which negotiation would replace violence; the resumption of normal trade relations with financial support for the new German Government and greater economic collaboration in Europe; and active German participation in general disarmament. Delay in making clear Allied intentions towards a Germany purged of National-Socialism would, argued Wheeler-

Bennett, allow the lurid prophecies of the Ministry of Propaganda to extinguish the hopes of those elements of liberation and drive them – not to the support of Hitler – but inevitably to the ultimate defence of the Fatherland. Wheeler-Bennett concluded by saying that, because peace with any kind of Nazi government was unthinkable, 'for this very reason it is the more necessary to indicate to those elements within the Reich, with whom we *could* negotiate, our desire to conclude a peace of Statesmanship and justice, and thereby hasten the day when this will become possible.'

Appended to the memorandum was a statement of what would constitute the *Rechtsstaat*, the new state restored to the basis of law and order: abolition of the Reich and Prussian governments; abolition of single-party totalitarianism; free elections to a constituent assembly which would liquidate the Nazi Party in all spheres of national life.[40]

On 25th January, Halifax sent the papers to Chamberlain saying that he might care to see them and return them when they met the following day. Vansittart recommended caution in replying because 'whatever we say may go further.' A letter should be sent to the effect that they were 'thinking it over.' This letter was not in fact sent to Wheeler-Bennett until 12th February. Meanwhile, Cadogan had considered these communications in a long minute dated 24th January. Indications of a coming German attack presaged a 'peace offensive' backed by Roosevelt and the Vatican 'but the latest indications seem to show that they have not signed on yet.' But there might well be some proposal from Nazi Germany alone, couched in specious terms. This would certainly present a problem. Cadogan wished that, when the offer was turned down, 'we might have some terms which we could attach to our own refusal. . . . The real difficulty begins when we try to see whether we *can* define our minimum conditions in any way.'[41] Would it be any use, Cadogan wondered, to announce a readiness to participate in a Conference with another German government (without at the moment defining its complexion) on the basis of principles of settlement already indicated – righting of wrongs done to Austria, Czechoslovakia and Poland etc.

> . . . A process of question and answer through underground channels might give us an idea of what would be possible in the way of a new régime in Germany. But I hope it wouldn't lead us to another Venlo![42]

Cadogan's diary shows that he raised these points with Halifax on the same day but without either of them reaching a conclusion.[43]

The Wheeler-Bennett papers came back to Central Department from Downing Street on 22nd February. There was discussion of what to do next: 'I don't know whether the memorandum has been set by Mr Kirkpatrick or whether Sir A. Cadogan's minute is to be pursued.' The following day Kirkpatrick minuted, succinctly: 'This can go by.'[44]

By the end of the following year, Wheeler-Bennett had climbed on a different band-wagon. His close friend Eden had become Foreign Secretary. In the United States his patron (and Adam von Trott's friend), Lord Lothian, had died and Lord Halifax had gone to Washington to replace him. Churchill had decreed that any overtures of any kind from Germans should be treated with 'absolute silence.'[45] Over the next few years Wheeler-Bennett was to submit to the Foreign Office lengthy papers on Germany from the United States, where he evidently retained the misplaced confidence of the leading political émigrés, particularly Brüning with whom, as he had told the Foreign Office in December, 1939, he was on 'intimate terms of friendship.'

The reader of Wheeler-Bennett's *The Nemesis of Power* will not find any reference to the author's personal involvement in Trott's endeavours in America, or to his own fervent support of them. What Trott was actually attempting to do is dismissed in a couple of paragraphs, with a sting in the tail to the effect that Trott was 'uncompromisingly against the restoration of any of Hitler's territorial acquisitions.'[46]

In his book *Special Relationships: America in Peace and War* Wheeler-Bennett wrote of the twilight war period:

> At that time it was widely believed that many Germans, especially elements in the Army, were not fanatical in their support of Hitler and might, if encouraged, overthrow the Nazi régime. Few who had known Germany at any time during the Third Reich were of this persuasion. . . .

He refrained from admitting that he himself had been one of that few. Our author then goes on to call into contempt Chamberlain's broadcast of 4 September 1939 in which the Prime Minister distinguished between the German people, 'for whom we have no bitter feelings,' and 'the tyrannous and forsworn régime.' This is dismissed as primitive, clumsy and amateurish propaganda.[47] And yet it was this precise extract from the broadcast which he himself invoked, word for word, in presenting his Washington memorandum to the Foreign Secretary in December 1939. And thirty years afterwards, in direct contradiction to what he had written at the time, Wheeler-Bennett claimed that once hostilities had begun he '*had believed then*' that it was essential that Germany should be defeated in the field and compelled to surrender unconditionally – 'whatever government might be in control of *Reich* policies at the time.'[48]

Anthony Howard, the political commentator and biographer, described Wheeler-Bennett's abandonment of the German Opposition for the British Foreign Office establishment as 'one of the most nimble political somersaults the corridors of power can ever have seen.'[49]

Almost at the same time that Theo Kordt's line to the British was being finally severed and Wheeler-Bennett's plea on behalf of the Opposition was being allowed to 'go by' in the Foreign Office, an ill-starred attempt by a leader of the Opposition to establish fruitful contact with the British Government was also petering out. The German was Ulrich von Hassell, former Ambassador to Italy and a man of considerable stature both in German society and in the Opposition. Unfortunately, his British opposite number hardly measured up to him. J. J. Lonsdale Bryans was a peripatetic traveller whose background of Eton and Oxford seems to have afforded him contacts in establishment circles both at home and abroad of which he appears to have taken every personal advantage. In the book in which he recounts his self-imposed diplomatic activities – *Blind Victory* – he shows himself an inveterate name-dropper and he obviously managed to quarter himself on people of substance in various parts of the world. The probability is that he was that typically pre-war British character, the remittance man. His prolonged absences abroad and the fact that his only residence in England seems to have been Brooks's Club suggest the usual proviso in such cases – that he should stay out of England. Returning home in August, 1939 (after three months as the guest of the 'White Rajah' of Sarawak!), he happened to encounter Lord Halifax at the Dorchester Hotel, where the latter was staying at the beginning of the war.[50] With a certain natural effrontery he accosted his Lordship (whose father, he tells the reader, sat with his own father's uncle in the House of Lords). He detained the Foreign Secretary with an account of the anti-war feeling in Germany based on his own wide acquaintance there. Halifax managed to extricate himself and that would no doubt have been that. Bryans swiftly organised himself to Italy on behalf of a wealthy English friend with a valuable art collection there which required some attention.

In a bar in Rome, one day, he took up with two young men, an American and an Italian. The latter, Detalmo Pirzio-Biroli, had just returned from Germany where he had been staying with his fiancée's family. As the friendship ripened over several meetings, Bryans learned that his new friend's betrothed was the daughter of Ulrich von Hassell. Bryans obviously saw a chance of being busy. Having claimed that he was 'in personal touch with the British Foreign Secretary', he then received some remarkable confidences from his young friend, now graduated to the position of son-in-law. After dinner one night, Hassell had introduced Detalmo to a group of powerful anti-Nazis dedicated to the overthrow of the régime. It was of great importance for them to know how the British would regard an expurgated Germany under a non-Nazi government. Bryans persuaded Pirzio-Biroli to write an account of all this which he himself would deliver to Lord Halifax. He promised to divulge Hassell's name to no-one but the Foreign Secretary.

On returning to London, Bryans was surprised and put out to discover that in spite of having discoursed to Halifax on this very subject, he could not have instant access to the Minister. However, his path was smoothed by the intervention of Lord Brocket, a wealthy leading Conservative who wrote to Chamberlain on his behalf. Halifax saw Bryans on 8th January and accepted Pirzio-Biroli's letter. The Italian stressed the anxiety of the Opposition movement about the reaction of the British – the enemy – in the event of a change of régime in Germany. Bryans added that they were afraid that the Allies would take advantage of a revolution to attack the Siegfried Line. Halifax said that he would personally be against such an action if the revolution looked like being a genuine affair and producing a different régime in Germany in which it might be possible to place some confidence of honest dealing. According to his own record of the interview, Halifax emphasised that his own name must be kept completely out of the matter. If it ever came to the public notice, he would deny having said anything except that the Allies could not be satisfied with a patched-up peace. Having declared that 'it can do no harm and may do a lot of good,' Halifax agreed to Bryans making personal contact with Hassell and arranged for him to be provided with diplomatic travel facilities.[51]

One can only guess at the inflated account of his English connections which Bryans gave Pirzio-Biroli to pass on to his father-in-law. Hassell must have imagined that he had stumbled upon a direct route to the top of the British Government. A plan was worked out by which Bryans and Hassell could meet. It was arranged that Hassell's young son, who was asthmatic, should be taken by his mother to Arosa in Switzerland for treatment. Hassell would be able to visit them there from time to time. Bryans was to wait in Rome until he was summoned to Arosa, where he would play the part of a doctor visiting the sick boy. The meeting took place on 22nd February. On the 23rd, Hassell produced a document for Bryans to take back to London. In his own handwriting he enumerated what he called 'the principles considered to be essential for the re-establishment of permanent peace.' These included the restoration of an independent Poland and Czech Republic; a general reduction of armaments; re-establishment of free international economic co-operation; there should also be a recognition by all European states in common of the principles of Christian ethics; justice and law as fundamental elements of public life; social welfare as *leitmotiv*; control of the executive power of the State by the people; and liberty of thought, conscience and intellectual activity. 'All serious people in Germany,' he wrote, 'considered it as of the utmost importance to stop this mad war as soon as possible. . . . Europe does not mean for us a chess-board of political or military action or a base of power but it has "*la valeur d'une patrie*". . . .' Bryans asked Hassell to sign it. He compromised by signing a covering note addressed to Bryans.[52]

Bryans hastened back to London in triumph. He had actually got something in writing from the other side. He was considerably deflated to learn from Cadogan that Halifax was too busy preparing for the visit of Sumner Welles, Roosevelt's representative, to see him. However, he handed over Hassell's document in a sealed envelope, together with a further report from his Italian son-in-law. Cadogan recorded the visit in his diary: '28th February 1940. Lonsdale Bryans with his ridiculous stale story of a German Opposition ready to overthrow Hitler if we will guarantee not "to take advantage".' A week later Bryans was summoned to see Cadogan again. ('6th March 1940 . . . Lonsdale Bryans, whom I liquidated in as friendly a manner as I can do. . . .') Although at their previous meeting, according to

Cadogan, there had been a discussion about the means by which a written message could be conveyed to Hassell, Bryans was now told that this would not be possible because 'something similar was already transmitted by means of our official agents to the same sort of people on the other side.' The Foreign Office would facilitate his return to Switzerland to see Hassell and 'leave no frayed ends.' But it was made clear that the matter was now closed. On 11th March, Bryans received the word from Pirzio-Biroli that Hassell was ready to go to Arosa. The coded telegram indicated that Bryans' return 'with contract' was vital and urgent. Bryans took the telegram to the Foreign Office where, his narrative hints, he was not well received.[53] Cadogan again supplies the clue: '13th March 1940: Halifax and Van about Lonsdale Bryans, who is still trying to be busy. Settled to put kybosh on him.'

The Bryans-Hassell affair was clearly a case of the medium killing the message. Bryans was not the sort of person which any sensible government would have wanted to use for clandestine purposes. No doubt discreet enquiries were made about him, as he did indeed appear to have a wide acquaintance in London. A letter from Lord Brocket to Cadogan on 17th March rather puts Lonsdale Bryans into perspective. Lord Brocket wrote that he was aware that Bryans had brought back a communication of considerable importance (although he did not know the details). However, Bryans had asked him for money, not only to finance his clandestine operations but also to clear his personal debts. He was asking for the considerable (for those days) sum of £1,000. Brocket was unwilling to do anything about this but if Lord Halifax thought it was necessary he would do so. Cadogan replied that Bryans had been acting entirely on his own initiative and not that of the Foreign Office. Lord Brocket should not feel any obligation to relieve him of his debts.[54] No doubt Brocket's revelation strengthened the 'kybosh'. Cadogan's only reference to Hassell's paper was that it was 'on the face of it, interesting.' This was hardly an adequate reaction.

Bryans and Hassell met at Arosa on 14th April for the last time. According to Hassell's diary, Bryans told him that he had given his paper to Halifax who had shown it to the Prime Minister. Halifax had told Bryans that he was grateful for the communication, valued it highly and was in complete agreement with its contents. Bryans had, of course, no grounds whatever for making these statements. No doubt he felt he must give Hassell some good news. Nor could he admit that he had made no impact at all in London. Nevertheless, fifty years later, it is possible to deduce that the documents – Hassell's paper and Pirzio-Biroli's letter of 10th February – did reach Halifax. They lie side by side in a ragbag file entitled: 'Private Office papers from various sources 1940.' No doubt the contents were collected at the time Halifax left London to take up the ambassadorship in Washington in December, 1940. The documents appear in the list of contents as, respectively, 'Mr Hassell: Note on principles considered essential for the re-establishment of permanent peace' and 'Observations on German internal scene'.[55] It is an interesting experience to handle the original document, drafted over a few beers in the little Kursaal bar on that crisp Alpine night in February, and copied out next day in Hassell's bold hand – oddly reminiscent of Vansittart's. It is symbolic that an authentic document of the Opposition, addressed to the British Government and signed by one of the leaders, should be sunk without trace in the Foreign Office files.

By a curious chance, Arosa and Venlo touched briefly after the war. Hassell's daughter, Fey Pirzio-Biroli, was arrested by the Gestapo, together with other relatives of the executed Opposition leaders, after the 20th July bomb plot. She was held in a group of special prisoners of which Payne Best was one. Some months after the end of the war she wrote to Best that her mother had gone to Switzerland to retrieve certain papers which her father had hidden there. As later revealed, this Swiss cache concealed the first section of Hassell's diary notes up to the end of 1941.[56] They included a record of the encounters at Arosa.

The British no doubt felt they could well do without the freelance activity of Lonsdale Bryans: they had enough irons of their own in the fire. In addition to the tenuous contact maintained with Theo Kordt, seemingly on the part of Vansittart himself, other exchanges were being carried on in Switzerland. A former Chancellor of the Weimar period, Dr Wirth, living in Lausanne, had sent a letter to Chamberlain by hand of Dr Schairer, Goerdeler's friend, on 24 December 1939. Wirth suggested that Chamberlain should include in his forthcoming speech at the Mansion House on 9th January 'passages calculated to appeal to the more moderate sections in Germany.' A note on the file records that 'Makins is taking this into account in drafting PM's speech.' The question was raised by the Prime Minister's office whether to send a reply to Wirth. The department thought it better not to do so – Wirth would have read the speech and have seen that it contained what was in effect a reply.[57]

In the middle of February, 1940 Christie travelled to Switzerland where he had conversations, separately, with five Germans: Wirth; the industrialist Thyssen; Prince Max Hohenloe; Rauschning and his friend and informant 'Kn' (Ritter).[58] He had known the latter since they were both Air Attachés in Paris in the 1920s and it was Ritter who supplied Christie with much valuable intelligence before the war, particularly about air force matters. Rauschning, a former leader of the Danzig Senate, had been an early Nazi who repented and in 1936 fled to Switzerland. His book: *The Revolution of Nihilism*, published in 1939, was widely acclaimed as an exposé of Hitler and Nazism. The Foreign Office invited his opinion on German affairs from time to time. All had their contacts inside Germany. Wirth had a line to the military Opposition through Gessler, an intimate friend of Halder, who had served as War Minister during his Chancellorship. On his return to England, Christie compiled a long report from his German notes of the various conversations. It was not an easy task and he felt he had not made a success of it. Inevitably, as all these men shared the same basic views, it tends to be repetitious and a little entwined.

A summary of their views was that Hitler's prestige had sunk very much in spite of the victory in Poland. People were bewildered by frequent changes in decisions about war in the West. Those near the Führer found him highly irritable, nervous and unsure of himself, demanding from his own staff blitzkriegs and invasions in all directions. The Army was not eager for battle and the morale of the troops was poor: the cancellation of a January attack on Holland was received with jubilation. There was increasing animosity between the Army and the Party, particularly the SS, because of the disgraceful behaviour in Poland. The Army General Staff was solidly opposed on military and political grounds to any offensive in the West. Their views were backed by the industrialists, the agrarians and Church leaders. A serious military defeat or even diplomatic setback could cause a serious collapse of Hitler's prestige. However, the unarmed masses could do little against the militarily-equipped Blackshirts with their tanks, machine-guns and aircraft. 'The Opposition fully understood that the new Germany would have to make great sacrifices for peace,' Christie was told. All sides were much in favour of a federalised Germany. But they would hope for an assurance from the British Prime Minister that there would be no question of the French idea of a return to the small duchies and states of Napoleonic times, politically segregated from one another. Wirth believed that a new Germany could be created with a constitution which would contribute towards the peace of Europe. There was optimism among those interviewed (with the exception of Rauschning) that the generals could be persuaded to carry out a large-scale *putsch* which once started would be supported by the majority of the German people. Halder and the generals opposed to the offensive were gaining ground. However, there were other generals with guilty consciences about the fate of Austria, Czechoslovakia and Poland, who felt that the collapse of German power through a *putsch* would tempt the Allies to dismember the Reich and keep her in poverty. It was recommended that every effort should be made in official speeches and unofficial talks to let it be known that this was not the Allied intention. Tighten the blockade, already making itself felt, but continue to proclaim a willingness to negotiate, but only with a new government that represented a complete change of heart in Germany. It was stressed that when Hitler went, he would leave the country bankrupt and the new Germany would need wide financial and economic assistance from outside.[59]

A long letter from 'Kn' to Christie, addressed under cover to Vansittart and dispatched to London via the diplomatic bag, arrived just after Christie had left for Switzerland. Pending Christie's return, Vansittart passed it to Halifax, noting that 'the writer is of course very well-known to me and has provided a great deal of reliable information.' The letter set out much of what Christie was to hear verbally during his visit. 'Kn' concluded by saying that the military Opposition leaders were looking to an exchange of views and proposals between their representative and a representative of the British Government. He understood that Goerdeler was claiming that he was authorised to represent the German side. But a note by Vansittart at the bottom of the letter dismissed the idea of Goerdeler. Christie himself, who did not know Goerdeler well, did not want him now introduced into his own exchanges. 'Kn' pressed for Christie to be the British representative.[60]

Christie had a second meeting with Wirth before leaving Switzerland, the record of which, included in his Foreign Office memorandum, was to have a particular significance. Wirth confirmed what he had already said concerning the aims of the new government with which the Opposition would replace the Nazi régime. There would be a new federal Reich composed of the various states. Prussia would be broken down into its component states inside the federation. There was even a plan to replace Berlin by a new capital. The States of Poland and Czechoslovakia would be re-created. General disarmament in Europe was essential. They realised that the country would be in a state of bankruptcy; there must be a freeing of the currency and a return to general international trade, away from the narrow concepts of autarky. The Opposition, particularly the generals, were most anxious for a verbal message from the British Prime Minister that there would be no dismemberment of Germany. Christie undertook to 'discuss his proposals with my friends in London.'[61]

What is put together here from various sources for the first time is an authenticated account of a written document being produced from the British side to be shown to the Opposition. The authentication is in Christie's surviving notes. On 11th March, Vansittart wrote to Halifax: 'Christie has left for Switzerland this morning . . . and will carry out his instructions to the full and with complete discretion.'[62] This note of confirmation is evidence that the Foreign Secretary and therefore inevitably the Prime Minister were behind the operation.

The meeting between the two sides took place on 12th March just outside Lausanne. Christie, representing the British, had, as he recorded, taken Conwell-Evans with him 'as a witness.' On the German side were Wirth and 'Kn'. Christie told Wirth that he had 'something of considerable importance to communicate to him.'[63] He began by referring to a speech which Chamberlain had made on 24th February, i.e. after Christie's return from his previous visit to Switzerland. The Prime Minister had said: 'We do not wish the destruction of any nation.' Firstly, the independence of Poland and Czechoslovakia must be secured. There must be convincing evidence that promises would be kept: with the 'present German Government' there was no such security. It was for the Germans themselves to take the next step. If Germany could give convincing proof of her goodwill, there would be no lack of goodwill in other nations to help with the economic difficulties which would arise in the transition from war to peace. The Prime Minister had declared that the war aim involved neither the humiliation nor oppression of any other nation.[64] Wirth considered this a most effective response to the request for reassurance regarding the future of a new Germany which he had asked Christie to convey to 'friends in London.'

'I emphasised at once,' Christie wrote in his report to the Foreign Office, 'that the Prime Minister had had in mind the kind of conditions that Dr W. had assured me the German Opposition, including leading generals, would be willing to set up in a new Germany after the overthrow of the Nazi régime. . . .' Christie recalled that a list of these main conditions had been given in his report to London of his February conversation with Wirth:

> I had a copy of this excerpt from my memorandum in my hand and gave it also to Dr W. to read, which he did. Conwell-Evans is my witness that Dr W. entirely confirmed the statement in my memorandum as being a correct representation of what he had told me during our previous conversation.

Dr Wirth made only a slight amendment to what he had said at that time. Berlin might remain as the capital of the new Reich, provided that Prussia was sufficiently reduced territorially.

Christie then reproached Wirth for not having fulfilled the undertaking he had given him at their previous meeting that he would obtain from Germany a more concrete statement of confirmation which he would then send to Chamberlain through Halifax via the British Legation at Berne. Wirth acknowledged this and apologised. He had been waiting for the arrival of ex-War Minister Gessler, now expected the following day. Christie's note continues: 'I then handed to Dr W. to read the document which I told him had been given to me by Sir Robert Vansittart, but which had received higher approval. I had had it translated into German. . . .'[65] It is fortunate that Professor Ritter, writing while Wirth was still alive, had access to this document which had 'received higher approval', the text of which he reproduces in his book. Although hazy about the details of the meeting and unaware of the identity of the 'two Englishmen, friends of Vansittart' whom he mentions, his account of the receipt of the document tallies with the statement in Christie's notes that a translation had been made. Ritter writes: 'The document was not handed over but a translation was prepared for Wirth which is still in existence. . . . The translated text of this document is as follows

[This of course has been translated back into English for the English edition of Ritter's book]:

1. Assurance will be given that the British Government will not by attacking in the West use to Germany's military disadvantage any passing crisis which may be connected with action taken by the German Opposition.
2. The British Government declares itself ready to work with a new German Government which has its confidence to get a lasting peace and will give Germany the necessary financial aid.
3. Further assurances it cannot give without previous agreement with the French Government. If France's confidence is obtained then further assurances are possible.
4. In the case of French participation in the negotiations it would be desirable that the approximate date for the carrying out of this action inside Germany be communicated.
5. If the German Opposition should wish their action made easier through a diversion by the Western Powers, the British Government is ready within the bounds of possibility to meet that wish.[66]

Wirth welcomed the statement in the document which he said would be very helpful and valuable, particularly as Gessler would learn of it on the following day when he returned from Germany with a message from the generals. He also told Christie that he had not confided totally in his friend Dr Simon at the French Embassy, although he had told him 'a great deal'. After some more 'general conversation', Dr Wirth left to catch his train back to Lausanne:

He asked me, however, [wrote Christie] to permit his friend and confidant Kn who was already in an adjoining room, to make a few pencilled notes on the content of the document. We parted cordially after I had given him two copies of the PM's speech. . . . When W. had gone conversation continued with Kn. Nothing further, however, was said with regard to the document. He merely took down pencilled notes on the contents and then closed the subject.
Conwell-Evans went into the next room and burned the whole paper. . . .[67]

Christie's account of the burning of the document tallies with Ritter's statement that 'the document itself was not handed over,' only a translation. Furthermore Christie's reference to having given Wirth two copies of Chamberlain's speech is echoed, though inaccurately, by Ritter: '. . . they gave Wirth several copies of a speech which Chamberlain intended to make on 24th February and actually did make.' These mutual points of agreement in the two accounts support the authenticity of the terms of the British document.

'Kn' promised to have a long talk with Gessler when he arrived the following day from Germany to see Wirth. 'Kn wants, of course, to question G. more closely about the military aspect of the situation, the attitude of various generals and the prospect of a *putsch*,' noted Christie. 'He felt personally uncertain as to whether the generals, even after being encouraged and fortified by the PM's speech and the message in the document, would pluck up enough courage.' Gessler arrived on the 18th March. He stated, from personal conversation with Halder, that although Hitler was crying out for a land offensive, the generals had temporarily won. Gessler thought that the conditions were not yet ripe for a *putsch*. Wirth emphasised to Gessler that delay was dangerous. The Allies had made a generous offer to give them a fair chance and it should be seized.[68]

Confirmation that assurances were given is to be found embedded in a memorandum from Cadogan to Halifax on 19 March 1940. In the course of a conversation the French Ambassador had 'suddenly asked' Cadogan whether he could give him any indication in regard to the conversations which had been proceeding recently with Dr Wirth in Switzerland. It appeared that Wirth had told the French Embassy in Berne that he had been in touch with Col. Christie and that the initiative had come from the British side. Cadogan denied this, said it appeared to be the same old story of a *putsch*, probably nothing was to be expected of such a movement. He personally even doubted it was genuine. 'M. Corbin did not ask whether we had made any response to the request from Dr Wirth for assurances and I did not tell him that we had made any.' A note by Vansittart on the same page ('As a matter of fact Dr Wirth has told most of this – if perhaps not *quite* all – to M. Simon') reproduces Christie's notes so closely that it may be concluded that these were the basis of a report to the Foreign Office which no longer exists. Here we have the extraordinary state of affairs whereby the Head of the Foreign Office is denying formally to the French Ambassador that anything of consequence was afoot in Switzerland, while Christie was authorising Wirth to communicate the contents of the British document unofficially to his friend in the Embassy. There is no indication of what Wirth actually withheld from the French.

An interesting aspect of Christie's consultations in Switzerland on which he reported at such length is the reaction which this report provoked in the Secret Service. It casts light on both the attitude and the reliability of the Service. In a commentary on Christie's memorandum it was stated that it contained little more than pure speculation and was without much inside information: the SIS had often received such information but had withheld it from circulation. Obviously Christie was much resented, although no agent could have matched his German knowledge and contacts:

> The writer did not go with the whole object of collecting intelligence but also as a political agent and go-between. . . . Our representative lately in Switzerland says it passes his comprehension that Wirth should be regarded as a serious source and that it is very difficult to believe that Wirth is really in close touch with General Halder. . . . Moreover we find it difficult to believe that Halder is the leader of the disgruntled generals. . . .

'We have nothing to support the statement,' continued the SIS, 'about the intended attack on Holland in January.'[69] In fact, it had been ordered by Hitler on the 10th and called off on the 17th. The reason for the cancellation was the crash in Belgium of a German staff officer's plane, lost in bad weather on an internal flight near the border. The officer was carrying plans for the attack on the Low Countries. British and French General Staffs were informed by the Belgian Government and it is surprising that the Secret Service should know nothing about it.

It has been generally accepted by historians that because Gessler later denied having taken the British communication back to Germany, that the terms never reached the Opposition. Ritter, who would have had it directly from Wirth, wrote: 'The British disclosures were a day or two later communicated by Wirth to the former Defence Minister Gessler to be sent to Beck and Goerdeler,' but 'it seems never got to them.' He explains this in a footnote: 'Several witnesses assure me of this. Gessler wrote me to say that he knew nothing at all of it.'[70] In his notes Christie speaks of 'the message which he [Gessler] has promised to convey to them [the generals].' Hassell records meeting Gessler in Berlin just after he himself had had news that his own contact with Lonsdale Bryans had been interrupted: 'I saw Gessler yesterday,' he wrote on 22nd March. 'He has been to Switzerland on what appeared to be a similar mission. He

22. State Secretary von Weizsäcker and the British Ambassador, Sir Nevile Henderson

23. Susanne Simonis, "courier" for the Kordt brothers

24. Hitler signing the Munich Agreement; Erich Kordt, back to camera, on his right

25. At Croydon airport, Theo Kordt is present
at the return of the Prime Minister from Munich

26. Sir Nevile Henderson arriving at Downing Street
after the rape of Prague, March, 1939

27. Henderson, Cadogan and Halifax leaving the Foreign Office
on the eve of the war

28. Chamberlain's speech at the Mansion House, 9 January, 1940,
which incorporated a passage for the German Opposition

Confidential.

Enclosure in
Ge 140/2.

I. All serious-minded people in Germany consider it as of utmost importance to stop this mad war as soon as possible.

II. They consider this because the danger of a complete destruction and particularly a bolshevisation of Europe is rapidly growing.

III. "Europe" does not mean for us a chess-board of political and military action on a base of power but it has "la valeur d'une patrie" in the frame of which a healthy Germany in sound conditions of life is an indispensable factor.

IV. The purpose of a peace-treaty ought to be a permanent pacification and restablishment of Europe on a solid base and a security against a renewal of warlike tendencies.

29. First page of Hassell's Memorandum
to the British government,
delivered by Lonsdale Bryans
in February, 1940

30. Lord Vansittart
records *Black Record* for
Books for the Blind, 1941

31. Judge Roland
Freisler, President of the
People's Court in Berlin

32. Eugen Gerstenmaier
before the People's
Court (Helmuth von
Moltke seated behind)

33. Helmuth von
Moltke addressing
the People's Court

34. Judge Roland
Freisler trying
members of the
Opposition in the
People's Court

35. Ulrich von
Hassell, sentenced
to death by the
People's Court

36. Carl Goerdeler, sentenced to death by the People's Court

37. Adam von Trott, sentenced to death by the People's Court

38. Richard von Weizsäcker assists in his father's defence
before the U.S. Military Tribunal

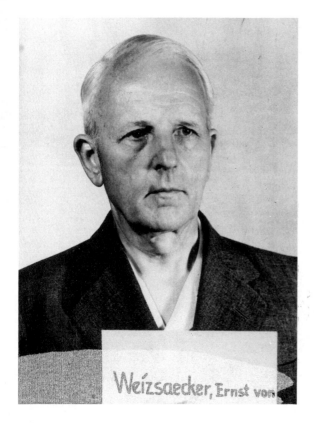

Weizsaecker, Ernst von

39. *left* Weizsacker's prison photogr
1948

40. Weizsäcker leaving
Lansberg prison

mentioned so many of the same things that I assumed he knew about the same events.'[71] Gessler was a leading member of the Opposition whose name was always included among the members of a Provisional Government. He was even considered a possible Head of State. He would have been only too anxious to convey the contents of such a document to Berlin and it seemed obvious that he did so. But it is possible to arrive at a reason for his later denial of having been in any way involved.

In the traumatic conditions in Germany immediately after the collapse in 1945, the subject of the Opposition was taboo. Public references were forbidden by the Occupation authorities. The Stauffenberg attempt – the only Opposition action to become publicly known inside and outside Germany – was thoroughly denigrated by the victors as the work of a handful of right-wing generals looking after their own interests. The full story of the Opposition had yet to emerge and was quite unknown to the mass of the German people. But those who had been lucky enough to survive recognised that their activities would be considered by the defeated nation as consorting with the enemy. They kept quiet. For members of the armed forces this was a particularly sensitive area. In 1938, Halder and Oster had despatched Major Hans Boehm-Tettelbach, a retired officer with business connections in London, as an emissary to Britain with the same mission as those others who came that summer. He saw Vansittart and Liddell Hart, among others. In two interrogations in 1945, Halder was asked about the major and denied knowing him until he was told that Boehm-Tettelbach (who was married to an American and whose sons were born in the USA) had written to Eisenhower at SHAEF HQ, describing the September, 1938 conspiracy and naming Halder as one of the leaders.[72] His aim in doing so may perhaps have been to support Halder who, though not a prisoner, was in Allied custody. Similarly Halder, in those first few weeks after the end of the war, thought it better to feign ignorance of Boehm-Tettelbach's activities in London for his sake. Halder referred to him on one occasion as his cousin. Halder told his interrogators that 'he would still greatly prefer if the story of this conspiracy was not given to the public. The reason for this is that he would not like the German people to know that he failed in his duty and loyalty as a high-ranking officer: "I can justify my action before God but I would like to be spared the task of having to justify it before my fellow-officers." '[73]

In a defeated and prostrate Germany there could only be misunderstanding and suspicion of past actions which seemed to smack of treason. A few years after the war Boehn-Tettelbach wrote to a friend that he and Halder had come to the conclusion that references to the Opposition movement should be dropped. They only served to stir up troubled waters.

It is therefore perhaps understandable that Gessler, the former War Minister, contacted by Professor Ritter in the early 1950s, should have made the statement which Ritter quotes: 'Gessler tells me that he never had dealings with any representative of an enemy country during the war.'[74] Certainly there is no evidence in Christie's notes that he and Gessler ever came face to face in March, 1940. What he reported from Germany was relayed to Christie through Wirth and 'Kn'. Nor did he receive the British document from Christie's hands. Nevertheless his statement can only be taken at its most literal.

The document which Christie had brought to Switzerland stressed the point of Britain's immediate reaction, in military terms, to the event of a *coup* against Hitler. Although this was vital information to the Opposition, it was only complementary to the more crucial question of the Allies' attitude to the form of government with which it was proposed to replace the Nazi régime, its intentions in the international field, and the terms which it would offer for the negotiation of an immediate peace. Cadogan had told Bryans that he could not be given anything in writing to take to his German contact, (Hassell), because 'something similar was already transmitted by means of our official agents to the same sort of people on the other side.' When Bryans quoted this to Hassell at their final meeting in April, the latter replied: 'Oh yes, we heard about it. But *that* is not the sort of thing we want.'[75] Cadogan's reference to 'agents' certainly suggests Christie and Conwell-Evans. Perhaps Hassell was playing down that exchange as being less important than his own far-reaching political exposition which had been taken to England. But the rather cryptic version of his response to Bryans which Hassell entered in his diary certainly contains a hint that the British document brought by Christie had got through:

> I replied that as far as the 'other channel' was concerned, I could not be completely sure what it was all about, but that I assumed it concerned a serious action known to me, and one which on our side had

reached the same group with which I was in contact. If my assumption was correct, I could only heartily welcome Mr X's [Bryans'] information as a kind of confirmation.[76]

The nature of Hassell's sharp retort to Bryans excludes the possibility that Cadogan's reference had been to yet another channel between the British and the Opposition which had been established some months earlier and was still in place. This, as will be seen, was the most serious, and held the greatest potential, of any contact the two sides ever had.

The plan was Oster's. It was formulated with the assistance of Dohnyani and with the approval and under the direction of General Beck. The Opposition would approach the British Government through the person of the most prestigious universal figure, the Pope. It was not a Catholic move – all three men were Protestants. It was a recognition of the Pope's position as a spiritual world leader, standing above the battle, and committed to no particular nation but to the cause of peace, for which he had demonstrated such a fervent desire. Moreover, from his years as Nuncio in Berlin before Hitler came to power and his subsequent ten years as Secretary of State at the Vatican, he was in a unique position to know the real situation inside Germany. From such prelates as Preysing of Berlin, Faulhaber of Munich, Galen of Munster and Frings of Cologne he would have learned not only of the persecutions of the régime, but also of the widespread opposition to it. These men had their own contacts with the Opposition. The Pope himself also had some acquaintance from these years in Germany with men who were now leading the anti-Nazi movement, such as Beck and Canaris. All that was required was that the Pope should stand between the two sides as a guarantee of integrity but taking no part in any negotiations or in advancing the cause of either side.

It was another instance of extraordinary times calling for extraordinary means. And the Opposition had just the man for the job. Josef Müller was eminently suited to initiate the Vatican connection. Indeed he had been recruited to the Abwehr with some such possibility in mind. Müller now learned that Oster's office was in effect the central directorate of the military Opposition, always, of course, under the eye of General Beck. Müller, Oster informed him, was to be given a single task and would not be involved in any other Abwehr assignments. That task was to use his connections in Rome to establish a line of communication to the British Government through – not the Vatican – but the Pope's own person. It was not his function to press for any official Vatican activity in the cause of peace. Nor was the Pontiff to be asked to take part in any negotiations between the Germans and the British, which he would inevitably have declined to do.[77]

The dangers were obvious. If it came out, the Papacy would be accused by the German Government of plotting its downfall, with dire consequences for Catholics both in Germany and in occupied countries. The British Government, on the other hand, would find itself accused of trying to treat with the Germans, i.e. the Nazis. In the eyes of the world the Pope would have abandoned his position as a purely spiritual leader and would be seen to have entered the world of politics and intrigue, involved with dissident elements in one country to conspire with the enemy against their own legitimate government. Above all, the possibility of any future rôle for the Vatican as a mediator between all nations in the cause of peace would have been destroyed.

As soon as the Polish campaign had ended, Müller arrived in Rome. Officially, he was there to monitor and report on political developments inside Italy. Müller was a well-known figure in the Eternal City. He was known personally to the Pope, who as Cardinal Secretary of State had at times invoked his assistance as Nazi pressures on the Church increased. Among the heads of religious orders he had a reputation for defending their members in Germany against Nazi persecution. He was close to Cardinal Faulhaber. He had even been married in St Peter's. Müller had an intimate friend in Rome in the person of Monsignor Kaas, former leader of the Central Party in pre-Nazi Germany. Now living in exile, he held the position of Superintendent of St Peter's Basilica. Müller confided the details of his mission. Kaas immediately put him in touch with Father Leiber, a German Jesuit who was a close aide and confidant of the Pope, whom he served for 34 years until the Pontiff's death. It was fortunate for the Opposition that a German held this privileged position. Fr Leiber conveyed to the Pope the nature of Müller's mission. Would the Holy Father act as an intermediary through whom the Opposition could, firstly, seek an assurance from the British Government that any hostilities would be suspended should a *coup* take place in Germany; and secondly, agree the nature of peace terms with a new government which had removed Hitler and his régime? With uncharacteristic swiftness, Pope Pius agreed to take on this rôle. According to Fr Leiber his response had been: 'The German Opposition must be heard in Britain.'[78]

Müller returned to Berlin with the good news of the Pope's agreement on 18th October. But it was not until 1st December that any indication of the German approach emerged from the British side – in a report by the British Minister, D'Arcy Osborne, to Lord Halifax. There had in fact been an exploratory approach to Osborne by Monsignor Kaas towards the end of October, but the succession of telegrams to the Foreign Office on the 28th, 30th and 31st show that Osborne failed to get the message. He thought he was being given information about a Nazi move towards the Pope, as his first despatch shows. The next day brought a complete contradiction: 'Have discreetly sounded Under-Secretary of State and believe that it is correct that Goering has *not* approached the Vatican.'[79] In fact, this was not as reliable a source as Osborne believed. The Pope deliberately kept the contacts with the Germans in Rome from the knowledge of his State Secretary. As far as Osborne was concerned, therefore, the first move by the Opposition towards the British was as reported in his despatch of the 1st December. This is confirmed not only by the terms of his own letter, but in a Cabinet summary in 1941 of all so-called peace-feelers, in which it was listed.[80]

The long interval between the Pope's acceptance of his rôle on 18th October, and the approach to Osborne, can be explained by the Venlo affair. Indeed, as Cadogan's diary shows, just about the time Müller was arriving back in Berlin with news of his successful contact with the Vatican, the British Government was already engaged upon its contacts with the 'dissident generals.' As the events of 9th November became known, the Pope must have been put on his guard. It is only surprising that the British, smarting from their self-inflicted wound, should have been prepared to consider another encounter with those claiming to be anti-Nazis. No doubt the involvement of the Pope in person set it apart from any possible tangling with Nazi secret agents or secret police. Another event which intervened between the Pope's agreement to co-operate, given in October, and the opening of approaches to the British at the end of November was the setting up of the *coup* which was intended to be delivered when Hitler launched the Western offensive on 12th

November. Had that succeeded, the Opposition might still have invoked the Pope's benevolent interest, but it would no longer have been clandestine.

Kaas's first move, as reported by Osborne on 1st December, seems to have been in the nature of simply drawing the idea across the British diplomat. He told Osborne that he had 'recently' been approached by representatives of German military sources who were anxious to discover whether the Pope could be invoked as an intermediary with the British Government. They were looking for an assurance of a 'fair and honourable peace' to be concluded with a government which could be trusted and which had replaced the Nazi régime. Kaas did not press Osborne on their behalf and rather played the rôle of a detached observer.[81] There is no record of London's reaction to this: perhaps they were still digesting it when Osborne followed up on 9th January with a further report, which reads curiously. Kaas, wrote Osborne, was irritated by the return to Rome of the 'purported representatives of certain German military circles':

> He said to me, and he will say the same to these German emissaries, that any talk of peace terms in present circumstances is altogether premature, that even were this not so, discussions would be impossible in the absence of any guarantees of the *bona fides* of the emissaries themselves as well as of their principals. And that even were these guarantees established there could be no assurance that the army circles in question would be able to carry out what they undertook, or, even if they could, were to be trusted to keep their word.[82]

There are only two ways in which Kaas's words, as they are reported by Osborne, make sense. Either he was playing devil's advocate to see whether Osborne would discount his pessimism; or he was simply reflecting upon the inevitable difficulties which must exist for the other side – the British – in evaluating such secret approaches, and Osborne misunderstood this to be an expression of his own opinion. It may be that the total secrecy enjoined on all the participants by the Pope caused Kaas to be too subtle and allusive in his communication with Osborne. Osborne's own language shows that he was misreading the situation. He wrote to Halifax that: 'Mgr Kaas strongly resents this endeavour to involve the Vatican in nebulous and dubious intrigue.' Kaas would never have imputed to his old friend Müller, whose reputation both as a devout Catholic and a fervent and articulate anti-Nazi was unassailable, an involvement in 'dubious intrigue.' Nor would Kaas himself have played his part to the end if this had been his opinion. It is probable that Kaas was also expressing a genuine concern about the risk the Pope was taking. This was echoed in Fr Leiber's statement after the war that 'the Pope went much too far.'[83] The theory that Osborne misread the signals coming from the other side is a tenable one. There are indications in later correspondence that Osborne was not fully aware of the significance of what he was dealing with. His attitude was consistently dismissive. Of course he had no background knowledge of the Opposition and its history from pre-war days and its contacts with Britain. It was shortly after this time that the Foreign Office came to the conclusion that Osborne was too cut off from knowledge of the march of events outside the Vatican and that he should in future receive regular briefings from London.[84]

Although Professor Deutsch, the historian and former Intelligence Officer, interviewed Leiber and Müller (the latter some thirty times) after the war, the chronology which he constructs does not fit the timetable revealed by the Foreign Office papers which were not available to him at the time. Given the distance of time and the lack of written records this is not surprising. But the impression that the contact between the two sides was made much earlier than it was suggests that talks were in progress for much longer than was actually the case. According to Leiber and Müller, the procedure was for short specific questions to be submitted to the Pope which he would then communicate to the British Minister, who would obtain a reply from London. No doubt many questions and answers were exchanged between the Pope and Müller via Leiber; and Müller and the Opposition leaders in Germany. The Pope must have wanted to inform himself of the *bona fides* of the German side. But as will be seen, Osborne's correspondence reveals no such continuing probing. The Pope did, however, have a set of short specific questions on his desk when he invited Osborne to see him on 12th January. It was the Pope's first direct approach to the British diplomat on the matter.

'I saw the Pope at 11.00 and talked to him for half an hour,' Osborne recorded in his diary. 'He gave me a personal message for Halifax and enjoined secrecy on me.' After giving Sir Percy Loraine, the British Ambassador to Italy, an account of this talk, the Minister retired to the Chancery to write 'a private letter, without draft' to the Foreign Secretary.[85] He explained that in response to the Pope's insistence on absolute secrecy (which he himself thought 'exaggerated') he was writing the letter in his own hand and was keeping no copy. It was being sent direct by Bag. The message from the Army chiefs, whose names the Pope knew but would not divulge, was that a great German offensive had been prepared which would be violent and unscrupulous, but it need never happen. The generals were prepared to replace the Nazi government with one with which it would be possible to negotiate but needed an assurance that the British Government would be prepared to conclude an honourable peace. Certain conditions were mentioned with regard to Poland, Czechoslovakia and Austria. The Pope said that the communication had been put to him but he had not been asked to put it forward (though as Osborne rightly noted, this was implicit in the communication). As a matter of conscience he felt he must pass on this information to the British diplomat, purely for information. 'He did not in the slightest degree wish to endorse or recommend it.' It is clear that the Pope was carefully dissociating himself from any rôle beyond that of 'Cupid's messenger'. Osborne's response to the overture was brusquely unforthcoming and shows him unaware of the nature of the situation in which he was involved. He told the Pope 'the whole thing was hopelessly vague and dangerously reminiscent of the Venlo affair.' The Pope's reply, as filtered through Osborne's language, was that he could answer for the good faith of the intermediary [i.e. Müller] but could not guarantee the good faith of the principals or whether they could effect the change of government or, even if they did so, they would be any more reliable than Hitler. The latter phrase sounds highly unlikely to have come from the Pope. If he had had any such doubts he would hardly have agreed to become involved in such delicate and dangerous exchanges. He would certainly never have made such a statement about General Beck. But it is not always easy to separate what the Pope actually said from what Osborne himself thought. It may well be that the circumstances in which he had to write his reports made them less detailed and lucid than they might have been.

With regard to guarantees, Osborne went on to tell the Pope, the Germans only had to read the speeches of Chamberlain and Halifax. The opening reference to the offensive which need never happen was 'a blackmailing touch reminiscent of Hitler.' The first step should be to effect a change of government and then talk peace. 'As it was, I did not see how, with the best will in the world on the part of His Majesty's Government, any such nebulous and uncertain proposition could be taken seriously or followed up.' In the face of this douche of cold water it is not surprising that the Pope drew back. He declined to press the matter further and said that he had acted purely on grounds of conscience. 'After he had listened to my comments on the communication he had received and passed on to me,' wrote Osborne,

> He said that perhaps, after all, it was not worth proceeding with the matter and he would therefore ask me to regard his communication to me as not having been made. This, however, I promptly declined as I said I refused to have the responsibilities of His Holiness' conscience unloaded on to my own. . . .

The Pope concluded that having thus salved his conscience 'he would not even expect any answer. But should you wish to send any sort of reply through him, I could ask to see him at any time.'[86] On 16th January Halifax reported on Osborne's letter to the Cabinet. The only conclusion noted was that the French should be informed.[87]

Osborne's attitude to the Pope in this interview seems almost curmudgeonly, quite apart from the nature of their conversation. And yet he often wrote warmly of Pius in his diaries, using such words as 'enchanting', 'easy', 'friendly'. But the diaries reveal an element in his life which could well have overshadowed the whole of the conduct of the approaches by the German Opposition, occurring as they did between November and the spring. Osborne suffered very greatly from cold. This is made quite plain in an entry in January, 1940: 'Chancery bitterly cold. So is this house. I hate cold more and more. It confuses and irritates me and makes me ill.' He refers to the cold weather (and it does seem to have lingered rather long that year) frequently in his journal. It was 'bad weather again' the morning he saw the Pope on the 12th. The fact that he had to hand-write his reports to Halifax in the 'bitterly cold' Chancery may have added to their asperity. Headaches too of unknown origin plagued him during the winter months.

The Minister was complaining of these afflictions in his diary on 25th January when the Bag arrived with a reply from Halifax to his report of 9th January. His Chief entirely approved the comments he had made to His Holiness. The French Embassy had picked up a Press report that the British Minister had been received by the Pope, continued Halifax, and had asked the Foreign Office 'whether anything of interest had passed between the Pope and yourself.' As it was government policy to keep the French Prime Minister informed of any peace feelers, the substance of Osborne's report had been passed by word of mouth to the Embassy for Daladier's personal information.[88] A note in his diary records that Osborne conveyed the contents of Halifax's letter to the Pope.

On 7th February the Minister was able to report to Halifax ('Personal and Secret') another interview with the Pope. This time it was, he reported, 'all very E. Phillips Oppenheim' (a popular writer of novels of political intrigue). The Maestro di Camera – Head of the Papal Household – had visited the British Minister the previous night and arranged that he should come to his office in the Papal apartments the following morning, but not formally dressed for an audience. No announcement would be made of his visit and he would be discreetly introduced into the Pope's apartment. Osborne duly presented himself the following morning. He observed that there were several pages of German typescript on the Pope's desk. His Holiness said he had been approached again by the 'reliable intermediary' but would still divulge no name on the German side, except to say that a well-known and important general was concerned, of sufficient importance to be taken very seriously. He would not name him as he did not wish inadvertently to be the cause of his death. The Pope then disclosed that the attack on the Low Countries had been called off because of the accident to the staff officer's plane through which the plans had fallen into Belgian hands. (Osborne did not believe this.) The Pope then proceeded to outline the nature of the Opposition's plans. They foresaw a period of civil war immediately after the overthrow of the régime and there would have to be some form of military government or martial law until control was secured and peace established. This administration would be replaced by a democratic, moderate, conservative government, decentralised and federal in nature. Poland and non-German Czechoslovakia would be independent. The new government would want to end hostilities and negotiate peace as soon as possible. The German side wanted the Pope to ascertain from the British Government whether the continued existence of the Reich, *plus* Austria, could be guaranteed as a basis of peace negotiations. According to his report, Osborne reiterated his previous objections and stated again that there was no guarantee 'that even if it succeeded, the German Government to be dealt with would be any more trustworthy or any less aggressive than the present one.' The Pope, he said, made no attempt to defend it or even to recommend it seriously. But any expression of partisanship was absolutely excluded from the Pope's rôle. There seems a touch of asperity in His Holiness's reply to Osborne. He disliked having to pass the message on and would no more expect an answer than on the previous occasion; 'but his conscience would not allow him to ignore it altogether lest there might conceivably be one chance in a million of its serving the purpose of sparing lives.'

But Osborne himself began to have second thoughts. He got the impression 'though I do not know from what, that the German initiative was more important and more genuine than I had believed on the first occasion.' The Pope's urgent insistence on absolute secrecy seemed to confirm the *bona fides* of the other side:

> He was very insistent that nothing should be put on paper except this letter which I have typed myself and of which I have kept no copy and he begged that its contents should only be communicated verbally by you or the Prime Minister to M. Daladier for his own secret information. If this was not possible he would prefer that you should regard the communication as not having been made or received.

The Pope also asked whether Halifax could personally give an opinion on the maintenance of German territorial integrity. Osborne concluded that the Opposition wanted a British guarantee against dismemberment by France. (This is exactly what Christie's contacts in Switzerland were raising with him at this very time.) If Osborne should have any communication to make to him – though he did not expect an answer – this should be made through his Maestro di Camera, as he did not even want the Cardinal Secretary of State to know of his communication through the British Minister.[89] At last, from London, an answer was forthcoming. After conferring with Halifax, Chamberlain jotted down some headings on a piece of paper, which the Foreign Office worked up into a draft reply. Sargent had one or two comments to make upon it. He felt that references to France called for the draft being shown to Daladier before the letter went to Rome. His second comment dealt with the expression 'Germany *plus* Austria' contained in Osborne's letter. Sargent advised that the stipulation should be made that Austria should decide for herself whether to enter any federal plan. This point was duly incorporated but the point about Daladier was not taken.[90]

Halifax's letter to Rome was dated 17th February. It began by stating that it was not proposed at the present stage to give M. Daladier any account of what passed. Osborne was instructed to get in touch with the Pope and convey to him 'an indication of our reaction to his message' which he could pass on to his interlocutors. If the 'principals in Germany' could convince the British Government 'they had the intention and the power to perform what they promised, the latter, together with the French Government, would be willing to consider any enquiries.' The British Government could not, however, broach the subject with the French 'on the basis of ideas emanating from undisclosed sources and so vague in character as those which have been conveyed to you.'[91] But the sources had been disclosed – to the Pope, who vouched for them personally. Evidently that was not enough. But if the names of Beck, Halder, Oster, Goerdeler, Hassell, Schacht *had* been disclosed, what difference would it have made? They were all names already known to the British and consistently rejected. Much of the 'vagueness' can be laid at Osborne's door. As to intention, surely this could not still be in doubt. Had it not been impressed upon the British continually since 1938? If progress was to be made, continued Halifax, 'a definite programme must be submitted and authoritatively vouched for.' But whose 'authority' would the British accept? As for a 'definite programme' they had had statements of principle, in writing, from Goerdeler and from Hassell. In examining any programme which was submitted and in 'framing their own conditions' the British Government would be looking above all for security for the future. In this connection the suggestion of a decentralised and federal Germany 'might be held to go some way towards a solution of this problem.' It would be useful if those who had made this suggestion could develop this or any similar idea in concrete terms.[92] What could have been more unequivocal on this point than the statements by Wirth and his other contacts in Switzerland which Christie was even then delivering to the Foreign Office?

The feeling that the Prime Minister and the Foreign Secretary were getting their lines of communication in a tangle perhaps inspired Sargent's minute, dated the same day as the letter to Osborne. Referring to contacts with Goerdeler and Thyssen in Switzerland and with the Pope, he recommended the one with the Pope as being the most circumstantial and inspiring the most confidence: 'I should be inclined for the present to restrict our answers to this one channel.'

It would be advisable to inform Daladier of the approach through the Pope 'so that he does not use the Thyssen channel at the same time as we are using the Papal channel.'[93]

Before Halifax's letter reached him, Osborne had already written reporting that he had escorted Lady Halifax and her son to a private audience with the Pope. The Pope had drawn him momentarily aside to say that the German military 'had confirmed their intention, or their desire, to effect a change of government.' Osborne's rather unceremonious reply had been 'Why didn't they get on with it?'[94]

The Pope's hint that intentions were firm on the German side was reinforced by a conversation which Osborne had with Monsignor Kaas a couple of days later. He came to luncheon on the 21st and was 'very interesting as usual.' (In his diary Osborne seems to use the word 'interesting' to represent the German approaches.) On the 23rd he reported on the meeting to London: 'Did Private letter for the bag all a.m.' Kaas had 'again referred to the hope of the German military circles' whose representative was still in Rome. It appeared that the Germans were still anxious to establish contact with the British Government in order to assure themselves that after the overthrow of the Nazi régime they would be able to negotiate a peace which would be neither destructive nor humiliating. The point which Kaas made which most interested Osborne, so he informed Halifax, was that 'these self-appointed and aspirant liberators of the German people' realised very well that their position would be very precarious if, after getting rid of Hitler, they should proceed to accept humiliating terms from the Allies. If this was all the Opposition would be able to offer their compatriots, their own days would be numbered. This proposition was surely self-evident. But Osborne put it to Kaas that this was 'a specious argument which . . . would provide for Germany getting away with the Hitler loot.'[95] Given Britain's part in letting Hitler get away with his 'loot' from the Rhineland to Poland, this impugning of the Opposition's intentions seems a little harsh.

But between the luncheon with Kaas and his report upon it there is a significant entry in Osborne's diary: 'Bag in. Interesting Private letter; dealt with it in the morning.' The British Government's communication of 17th February had at last arrived. There is no record of how the Minister 'dealt with it' but evidence can be found in his report of a later audience on 30th March. Osborne had asked the Pope whether he had heard anything further from 'the representative of the German military circles.' His Holiness had replied, reported Osborne, that he had heard nothing since he had communicated to them the contents of the letter 'which I had written to His Holiness on receipt of your letter to me.' (The Minister further disclosed in his report that he had destroyed Halifax's original letter 'in deference to the Pope's request for absolute secrecy.') Osborne told Halifax that the Pope had expressed the fear that 'the prospects of any favourable developments from the approaches made through his person were vitiated by the fact that other similar approaches had reached His Majesty's Government through other channels.' According to his understanding, His Majesty's Government were not very hopeful of any results from these communications nor enthusiastic about their receipt. Osborne agreed that this was probably so, particularly in view of the impossibility of establishing the *bona fides* of the German principals.[96] Osborne did not express any curiosity on his own part as to how the Pope could have been aware of other contacts between the Opposition and the British Government but the strong likelihood is that he had heard from Wirth, who had close contacts with the Vatican, about the talks with Christie. The Pope's words certainly indicate some displeasure that, having at great risk to his Office and to the Church, agreed to embark upon what he had believed was a unique and vital service in the cause of peace, he had discovered that he was only one of several in the field.

To give Osborne his due, however, he did briskly dispose of one of the Foreign Office's wilder flights of fancy in March, 1940 which claimed that Kaas was a tool of the Gestapo and the German seminarists – the clerical students of the *Collegio Germanicum* in Rome – were Gestapo agents. Kaas, he assured the Office, was strongly anti-Nazi but [sic] a good patriot. And the German students wore bright scarlet, not a garb best suited to subversive activity.[97]

But earlier, in the middle of March, unaware of the difficulties which the Opposition were experiencing at home in Germany, the Pope seems to have been optimistic about the possibility of a *coup*. Osborne in Rome and Cadogan in London severally reported to Halifax that the Pope had spoken to the French Minister at the Vatican and had 'referred darkly' to unforeseen developments – 'something unexpected might happen.' When asked whether this might mean the disappearance of Hitler, His Holiness refused to pursue the subject but said he might have more to say later.[98]

The Opposition under Beck's leadership meanwhile were compiling a long report using all the notes which Müller had brought back to Germany over the months, together with information which had reached them from London via the Pope. The purpose of this document was to prove to Halder and Brauchitsch that the conditions existed for the successful achievement of a *coup*. What was in the document – known as the 'X-Report' because that was the designation for Müller throughout – has been reconstructed by some historians from the testimony of surviving key figures. There is of course no detailed documentary evidence surviving; the X-Report fell into the hands of the Gestapo in September, 1944 and then disappeared.

However, an entry in Hassell's diary in the middle of March gives a clear indication that Halifax's communication had been received. Hassell was summoned to Beck's house, where Oster and Dohnanyi 'read me some extraordinarily interesting documents covering the conversations of a Catholic intermediary with the Pope. Following these conversations the Pope established contact with Halifax through Osborne.' Halifax was described as being 'cagey' but as having mentioned decentralisation and a referendum in Austria, the pre-requisite being, naturally, a change in the régime.[99] This is an accurate account of the British statement of 17th February. Curiously, Professor Deutsch claims in his book that the idea of self-determination for Austria came originally from Beck 'rather than the British;' that Beck felt that a union imposed by Hitler by force could not be maintained. Müller, he states, was instructed to introduce the concept into the Vatican exchanges, where 'it found its way on to Father Leiber's list of terms.'[100] But it is obvious, not surprisingly, that the concept was arrived at simultaneously by the Opposition leader and the British Government. Hassell had been specifically called in in the hope that he could get the X-Report to Halder and press its message upon him. The Chief of Staff was proving reluctant to meet his fellow-conspirators. There was a further meeting at Oster's house on 18th March, noted by Hassell: 'With Dohnanyi at Oster's home; we again discussed the matter of informing Halder of the Pope's action.' A few days later, Hassell heard from his son-in-law that Bryans could not come to Arosa again for the moment. It was the following day that Hassell encountered Gessler and learned of the latter's own excursion to Switzerland.[101]

On 5th April Hassell was summoned to Berlin from the country by an urgent message from Goerdeler that 'something had gone wrong.' This turned out to be a letter from Halder giving his reasons (which both Hassell and Goerdeler considered inadequate) for not taking action 'for the time being.' Later in the day, at Oster's house, he learned that the attack on Scandinavia had been ordered for the 9th April which meant that the attacking force must already be on the high seas. (On the evening of that same day, 3 April 1940, Oster sent two warnings of the invasion: one directed to the British through his friend Colonel Sas, the Dutch attaché; the other to the Holy See through a coded telephone call by Müller to a monsignor there.)

Oster and Dohnanyi now showed Hassell further notes from Müller about his mission in Rome:

> We discussed, without coming to a conclusion, whether Gessler's information had to do with this or with some unrelated action. It is still doubtful to me how my transactions with my conferee [Bryans] in Arosa fit into the picture. Did he fail to come again because Halifax 'gives up', or because the man had no authority, or because Halifax does not want to proceed along several lines at the same time?[102]

With Halder refusing to receive either Goerdeler or Hassell, the X-Report was finally served upon him by General Thomas. Unfortunately, as the latter was not privy to the Vatican affair he did not present it as persuasively as Hassell certainly would have done. However the Chief of Staff did take it to the Commander-in-Chief. Brauchitsch reacted in horror after he had read the document. This was treason. A soldier could not enter into contact with a foreign power in time of war. Halder should not even have shown it to him. The man who brought it should be arrested. 'Arrest me, then,' was Halder's reply.[103]

In his initial interrogation by American intelligence in June, 1945, after his liberation from Gestapo custody in the last weeks of the war, Halder made the first public reference to the existence of a contact between the Opposition and the Vatican. However, the very brief account is hopelessly garbled. One must assume some confusion on the part of the interviewers. Halder had just previously described the attempted *putsch* of September, 1938 and the same names were cropping up again. Halder is reported as saying that Hassell obtained a written statement of peace terms from the British Foreign Secretary and that this document had been brought to him by Hassell and General Witzleben (the latter had never had any connection with the Vatican affair). What is extraordinary, if the intelligence report is to be believed, is that Halder made no mention of either Thomas or Brauchitsch. They were still alive, while Hassell and Witzleben had already been executed. Was it deliberate muddling to protect the living? What the interrogation does confirm is that there *was* a document (the X-Report), that it contained material from the British, and that it was indeed delivered to Halder. At the time, he said, the military situation no longer justified him in making such an extreme break in his duties as an officer; and when the country was at war it was no time to bring about a change of political régime by such means.[104] Certainly Halder cannot be accused of personal cowardice. In an affidavit given at the time of the Weizsäcker trial in 1947, Hasso von Etzdorf, liaison officer between the Foreign Office and the High Command, described an extraordinary occasion in December, 1941, the first Christmas of the Russian war. In an address to officers, NCOs and men of Headquarters, the Chief of Staff had pointed to the Christmas tree in the middle of the square and declared: 'You will have to choose between these two symbols – the blazing flames of the Teutonic yuletide fire and the radiant Christmas tree. For myself I have chosen the symbol of Christianity.' In conclusion he had asked his audience 'to think of the man on whose shoulders rests the entire responsibility.' The implication was not misunderstood. There were cries of 'scandalous' and 'the man should be shot.'[105]

After the failure to activate Brauchitsch and Halder, Beck felt that it was most necessary to admit to the Holy See the collapse of the hopes about which they had appeared so optimistic. If nothing was said, the ghost of Venlo would walk again and contact with the West would be cut off for ever. It was also imperative for the Opposition to dissociate itself from the impending violation of the Low Countries. They had already testified that they did not identify with the acts of aggression of Hitler's Germany when they had given warning of the Scandinavian attack. Other nations must be made to understand that there was a decent Germany with which they could safely negotiate. Müller was dispatched to Rome with a final task to discharge. He arrived on 1st May. Through Fr Leiber he informed the Pope that there was no prospect of success for their plans; the generals had not been sufficiently impressed by the material which had come from Rome to act.

Would the Vatican exchanges have turned out differently if the Venlo affair had never happened? That disastrous venture was the only contact with the Germans to which the British ever whole-heartedly applied themselves. However many public denials were subsequently made, the evidence of Cadogan's diary proves that the British did indeed put forward ideas about terms – and without consulting the Cabinet who, when finally informed on 1st November (noted Cadogan), 'didn't like it.'[106] How seriously the contact was being taken is indicated by two entries in Cadogan's diary. On 24th October he wrote: ''C's' Germans have put two questions and I discuss with H[alifax] answer to give them and subsequently drafted it.' The draft was amended and approved by Chamberlain. On 1st November Cadogan noted: 'Had to re-draft (for the nth time) reply to Generals.'[107] The shock of the discovery by British statemen that they had been the dupes of the Gestapo could only have a lasting effect. Publicly, they had to dissociate themselves from any suspicion of peace talks. Replying to a Parliamentary Question some months after the débâcle, the Minister of State, R. A. Butler, declared:

> There was no question of these officers [Best and Stevens] conveying peace proposals on behalf of HMG. What they were authorised to do was to listen and report . . .[108]

But Stevens confided to the Chief of Intelligence of the Dutch General Staff that his instructions were to explore a basis for peace. The Gestapo interrogation of the two agents also recorded Best's orders to conduct negotiations for a peace treaty.[109] Schellenberg's indictment at Nuremberg made no mention of peace: the purpose of the Venlo affair was 'the kidnapping of enemy and neutral nationals to fabricate a pretext for the invasion of the Low Countries.' (And all in a single day!) In detailed evidence Schellenberg emphatically denied this charge and spoke of 'negotiations for peace of a very special nature.'

Had the time and effort expended on drafting messages to the Gestapo been directed to the approaches via the Pope, what might not the fortunate consequences have been? A strong, affirmative and supportive statement to the Opposition might even have won Brauchitsch over. It is difficult to see what the Allies had to lose by such encouragement. In the event of internal disorder following a *coup* in Germany it would have been to their advantage to stand aside. If a new democratic régime had been allowed to establish itself, the whole of Europe would have benefited. If the new régime had turned out to be 'no less aggressive than the present one' (in Osborne's words) – and it is impossible to accept that Chamberlain and Halifax believed this – then the war would have continued. Perhaps because the leading figure behind the approach to the Pope was General Beck, and because Colonel Oster had set up the facility for Müller to visit Rome as a member of the Abwehr, Kaas always spoke of 'military circles', despite the civilian participation. Nevertheless, the purpose of the Vatican initiative was not only to impress the British but to convince the military leadership. Hassell recorded in his diary on 30th October that Goerdeler had told him: 'Everything else was easy to arrange; the necessary number of determined generals is ready to proceed quickly and energetically if the order comes from the top. Herein lay the whole problem.'[110] Hitler never knew, when he destroyed Fritsch and replaced him with Brauchitsch, just how good a turn he had done himself.

— IX —

The Bitter End

If there are men in Germany also ready to wage war against the monstrous tyranny of the Nazis from within, is it right to discourage or ignore them? Can we afford to reject their aid in achieving our end? If we by our silence allow them to believe that there is no hope for any Germany, whether Hitlerite or anti-Hitlerite, that is in effect what we are doing.

George Bell
Bishop of Chichester

A whole nation is and remains our enemy and must be conquered whether it wants to be liberated or not.

Richard Crossman
Political Warfare Executive

O N the 10th May, 1940 the event took place which the Opposition had so eagerly desired before the war: Churchill succeeded Chamberlain as Prime Minister. But how different were the
circumstances now. By the end of May, Germany had secured the
surrender of Holland and Belgium and the battle was being lost
in France. Miraculously, the bulk of the British forces had escaped
to England from Dunkirk, though they had had to abandon their
equipment. The non-arrival of any German invasion force, the successes of the Battle of Britain in the air, together with Churchill's pugnacious leadership, extinguished any spirit of defeatism.
Chamberlain retired from political life at the beginning of October
and Eden took over as Foreign Secretary from Lord Halifax who
departed in December for the Embassy in Washington. The following month, January, 1941, Churchill ordered that any 'suggestions
or enquiries' about peace, coming from Germany, should be met
with 'absolute silence' and all British representatives in neutral countries were so advised.[1]

For the German Opposition, the fight against Hitler had become
immeasurably more difficult but it was not to be abandoned. German
forces were now at last engaged with the enemy in the West. And
Germany, having put itself in danger, had to be defended. The Army
could not be diverted from that function. Nor could units be moved
about as in 1938 and 1939, when they could be positioned for a
putsch. The only hope now was assassination and only very senior
officers had the slightest – and it was indeed a very slight – chance
of coming close enough to Hitler's person. Opportunities would
simply have to be seized as they arose. More than ever the Opposition must be ready to assume power and instant control. It was
essential therefore that they should keep the lines open to Britain. It

had to be made known that the intention to eradicate the Nazi régime had not been abandoned although it was impossible to say when the circumstances would arise which would make a *coup* possible. It was essential, as it had always been, for those who would constitute the new government to know what Allied attitudes would be.

Adam von Trott was chosen as the man best qualified to elicit answers from the other side. With the assistance of Weizsäcker and Canaris, he was able to travel to Switzerland and Sweden; to the German-occupied Low Countries and even to Turkey. A major and most reliable ally in his task was Dr Visser't Hooft, Secretary of what was later to become the World Council of Churches in Geneva, whom he had known since his student days. Indeed, it was Adam's membership of the Opposition which convinced the Dutch clergyman of the movement's genuineness and seriousness of purpose. Visser 't Hooft had already been raising with leading British and American churchmen with whom he had close ties many of those points of concern which the Opposition shared.[2] He had also established a unique relationship with resistance movements in occupied Europe and had held meetings at his home in Geneva attended by representatives from fifteen different countries, including Germany.[3] Since 1940 't Hooft had been transmitting, by secret methods, to the Dutch Government in London not only news about conditions inside Holland but also extracts from underground publications produced there. The trend of thinking among the resistance groups in the Netherlands was that, although the slightest compromise with Nazism was out of the question, and the restitution of all countries overrun by Hitler was a *sine qua non*, they looked to a reborn Germany taking an equal place in the new post-war Europe. The Netherlands Government reacted strongly against these ideas. Visser 't Hooft became increasingly concerned that there were serious misunderstandings developing between the government-in-exile and important sections of the Dutch people at home. The London government shared his concern and he was summoned from Geneva for consultations in February, 1942.[4] Adam von Trott seized upon the opportunity of this visit for a statement from the Opposition to be conveyed to the British Government.

The document which was to be taken to England was formal in tone and carefully constructed under five headings. It was compiled by Trott together with one or two other members of the Kreisau Circle. The memorandum stressed the danger to the whole of European civilisation entailed by the prolongation of the war. Germany shared with the West a common heritage and the Opposition felt it was vital that an attempt should be made for both sides to discuss these matters. The most urgent task in order to stave off catastrophe was the overthrow of the Nazi régime and its replacement by a government which would return the country to normal civilised standards. But such a government must be linked, outside Germany, to a larger movement against European nationalism, 'particularly in its military expression.' Those forces in Germany striving for this end were inspired by ideas which had crystallised in years of struggle against Nazism. But there were certain obstacles to the seizure of power: the 'dire necessity' of defence against the Soviet Union; the control of the entire national life by the Gestapo and 'the complete uncertainty of the British and American attitudes towards a change of government in Germany.' Without for obvious reasons giving details of names, dates and programme, continued the memorandum, it could be stated that support for the Opposition movement was drawn from a substantial part of the working class; from influential circles in the Army and administration; and from militant groups in the Churches. All groups were agreed on the principles of a federated Germany as an organic part of a federated Europe (including Britain) and close international co-operation with other continents. A free Czechoslovakia and a free Poland would be reconstituted. There should be progressive general disarmament, which was a social and economic concern for all peoples. Free access to raw materials should replace economic autarky. These principles were enunciated as a basis for wider and more detailed discussion. There should be a common recognition of past failure to deal with the historical, geographic, economic and psychological factors which had brought the world to its present situation. The Opposition, the authors declared, did not shirk the guilt and responsibility on the German side, but an exchange of views seemed fruitless if they were to be faced with a one-sided tendency to blame and judge. They hoped that their approach would be met 'with frank co-operation in the practical task of facing a common future beyond the catastrophe now confronting us all.'[5]

Visser 't Hooft was asked to deliver this communication into the hands of Sir Stafford Cripps, lately Ambassador in Moscow and now Lord Privy Seal. Adam was a close friend of the Cripps family, having been a fellow-student of John Cripps at Oxford. Copies were also to be given to the Master of Balliol, A. D. Lindsay; to Sir Alfred Zimmern, Professor of International Relations at Oxford; to Arnold Toynbee of the Royal Institute of International Affairs; and to William Temple, Archbishop of Canterbury. 'T Hooft put the original into Greek letters before starting his journey to England.[6]

The memorandum was handed personally to Sir Stafford Cripps by Visser 't Hooft shortly after his arrival in London in May. Learning that it came from Trott, Cripps expressed interest and promised to show it to the Prime Minister. When 't Hooft returned a week later to hear the result, Cripps told him that Churchill had studied the document carefully and had written on the bottom of it: 'Very encouraging.'[7] But Churchill had evidently not discussed it with his foreign policy advisers. No such sentiment was reflected in the Foreign Office. The matter first came to the notice of Central Department in the form of a report, based on a conversation between Visser 't Hooft and the Netherlands Foreign Minister, van Kleffens, which the latter sent to Eden. The Dutch Minister declared that he would not have anything to do with the Opposition group (adding, rather inconsequentially, that he thought Germany's fate would be better 'if really well-intentioned people succeeded in supplanting the Nazi régime, than under a continuation of that régime'). Eden, who was close to van Kleffens, commended his attitude which coincided with his own.[8]

If the Dutch Government did indeed share the Foreign Office attitude towards the Opposition, it was base ingratitude. A member of the Dutch resistance, writing after the war, described how he first met Adam von Trott in 1942, when he came to Holland to establish contact with the underground. Trott, he said, gave a full account, without naming names, of the elements of society which constituted the Opposition against Hitler. He offered as far as possible to keep the Dutch informed of any measures against them, and to use the influence of highly-placed members of the Opposition to alleviate the fate of those Dutchmen threatened with execution by the occupying power. In return he asked the resistance that they should keep their government in London informed of their contacts and of the existence of the Opposition and its intention to displace Hitler. Trott and Moltke kept in touch with the Dutch resistance through visits to Holland or through a trusted intermediary. There was little the Dutch could do in return, but, according to the writer: 'The one thing we could do and did do consistently was to keep our government in London informed of the existence and the work of the Kreisau conspirators.'[9] The baleful influence of the Foreign Office was still having its effect early in 1944. Colonel Stahle (executed by the Gestapo a few weeks before the end of the war as a member of the Opposition) warned the Dutch resistance that Hitler would soon be overthrown. They should prepare contingency plans for the event. Visser 't Hooft urgently transmitted to the Dutch Government in London a request from the resistance for permission to maintain this German contact. The reply was negative: the British Government were of the opinion that such approaches emanated from the German Secret Service.[10]

The burden of Adam von Trott's 1942 memorandum was also discussed at a meeting between 't Hooft and Kirkpatrick. The latter summarised it for the Foreign Office in three paragraphs. Both these secondhand reports – Kirkpatrick's and van Kleffens' – quite misrepresented its contents: the 'peace terms' (in fact the memorandum had not offered any) were 'quite ridiculous.' Harrison, of Central Department, thought all Christian bodies were too gullible in their response to approaches from 'decent German elements.' 'The point is that they must *do* something before we are prepared even to believe in their existence.'[11] This was a loyal regurgitation of Eden's speech in Edinburgh on 8th May.

A copy of the actual document finally reached the Department from Professor Marshall of Political Intelligence Department, who had received it from Arnold Toynbee. In the meantime, Cripps had been in touch with Eden. Harrison minuted that Cripps had asked how much the Foreign Office knew about Adam von Trott and Visser 't Hooft and what the attitude was towards the Opposition memorandum.[12] This was misinterpreted to mean that Cripps was asking for information about Adam, whom of course he knew well. Harrison procured a 'personal appreciation' of him from an Oxford contemporary. This was Richard Crossman, now head of the German section of the Political Warfare Executive. He had been a don when Adam was a Rhodes Scholar. He had also visited him in Germany before the war. (Crossman had once described him to the Head of SOE, Sir Duncan Wilson, as 'an extremely suspicious character.') Eden made use of Crossman's 'appreciation' in his reply to Cripps of the 18th, in which he gave his response to the communication from Germany:

We do not ourselves attach much importance as yet to these people, nor do we propose to respond to any overtures from them. Our view is that until they come out into the open and give some visible sign of their intention to assist in the overthrow of the Nazi régime, they can be of little use to us or to Germany.

Trott, Eden told Cripps, was a curious mixture of high-minded idealism and political dishonesty. He was 'not untypical of a number of young Germans in the Ministry of Foreign Affairs who had never quite been able to bring themselves to pay the price of their convictions and resign from the service of the Nazi régime.'[13]

Not surprisingly, Cripps replied with some asperity. He knew, he said, both Visser 't Hooft and Trott – the latter a good deal better than Eden's 'informant'. Adam had spent long periods staying with the family in the past. 'It is a complete failure to understand either him or what he stands for,' wrote Sir Stafford, 'that dubs him politically dishonest.' He had discussed with him at great length his attitude towards the Nazi régime:

> Any such superficial judgment as that indicated in your letter would lead to a grave misunderstanding as regards the outlook of himself and his friends. It is not a question of his bringing himself to pay the price of his conviction by resigning from the service of the Nazi régime, which would have been a very simple solution, like that of many émigrés. He paid the far higher price in risk in refusing to join the Nazi régime, but going back to Germany to fight for the things which he believed to be right.

At the Foreign Office, Harrison's comment was crushingly predictable: 'Sir S. Cripps is entitled to his own view of Adam v. Trott.'[14]

Crossman's own judgment of the memorandum, which he attributed to Adam's sole authorship, was that it was 'ingenuous in its politics and unaware of its intellectual and political dishonesty' but that it was probable that it truthfully represented a section of the German Foreign Ministry, the Army and the Church (all, presumably, suffering from the same mental disabilities as Trott). The memorandum itself was not weighed. Such discussion as there was confined itself to the personality of Adam von Trott. Cripps suggested that the MI6 representative in Berne, Elisabeth Wiskemann, should be asked to 'cool off' Adam, with whom she was in regular contact, on the grounds that he was 'too valuable.' Harrison did not agree: 'In fact, I do not think it is in our interest to do so since his value to us as a "martyr" is likely to exceed his value to us in post-war Germany.'[15]

Visser 't Hooft asked Sir Stafford Cripps what reply he could take back. He was told that there was no change in the Government's position that Germany should be defeated. There was to be no encouragement for the Opposition and no dialogue with it. When this message was transmitted to Trott he was, in the Dutch pastor's words, near to despair. He had felt that there were those in Britain whom he considered as comrades in the battle against Hitler and they had let him down. There was no recognition of any supra-national solidarity between those defending the same fundamental values.[16] The rare opportunity to contact a member of the British Government had yielded nothing, not even an expression of goodwill.

The German authors of the document had particularly requested that it should not be discredited by being wrongfully misused in the British Press, 'as has happened in the past:'

> Matters which may appear as sensational news on your side of the frontier are often of such a precarious character on ours that a minimum of sympathetic imagination should prevent giving publicity to them.[17]

The Foreign Office in fact was equally concerned that the memorandum should not become public, though for different reasons: 'It is really very dangerous,' minuted Harrison, 'for documents of the nature of this memorandum to be circulating in this country. . . . It can only be embarrassing if influential people are stimulated in this way to interfere in both our policy and political warfare towards Germany.' But they could not, he admitted, prevent the Dutchman from moving freely in various circles in Britain. Makins thought the solution was for MI6 to give advance information about 'the movement of such birds' so that arrangements could be made for dealing 'with those who succeed in reaching this country.'[18]

By coincidence, almost at the same time as Visser 't Hooft's mission to London, Bishop Bell of Chichester left England on a visit to Sweden in order to renew personal relationships with the Churches there.[19] The visit had been arranged some time previously by the Ministry of Information who thought it would be useful to maintain such links. A departmental note to Eden advising him of the tour mentioned Bishop Bell's known pacificism 'though not in the bad sense.' Bell was requesting a quarter of an hour with the Foreign Secretary before he left. Eden replied: 'I am not happy about this. I feel that I should know more of Bishop's views. Please speak.' However, the Bishop duly departed for Sweden and soon afterwards the British Minister, Victor Mallet, was reporting in the most enthusiastic terms of his progress.[20] Meanwhile a German clergyman, Dr Hans Schoenfeld, a director of the Ecumenical Council in Geneva who had known Bell since 1929, read of the Bishop's visit in the press. He hastened to Sweden to see his friend and quite unexpectedly arrived in Stockholm where Bishop Bell was staying with the British Minister. The Bishop was delighted to see him, but after some talk of Church matters, Schoenfeld introduced what was clearly the primary object of his visit. He wanted to inform the British prelate of a strong Opposition movement inside Germany, of which he himself was a member. The Catholic and Protestant churches were speaking up on behalf of the right to freedom, to the rule of law and to the unrestricted practice of their religion. They were allied to elements in military circles, the civil service and the trades unions. It was the aim of this movement to destroy Hitler. With the Nazi régime eliminated, they looked forward in due course to a new federation of European nations. There was trouble inside the Nazi Party and the possibility of a revolt against Hitler led by Himmler. But for the Opposition the essential was the elimination of Hitler, Himmler, the SS and the Gestapo. Would the British hold out encouragement to the leaders of the Opposition that they might hope for negotiations, after the overthrow, to end the war? Would the Allies be willing to make terms with a new German Government? After a further talk, Bishop Bell asked Schoenfeld to put down in writing everything he had told him. Meanwhile, he continued his programme of visits in Sweden.

Two days later, while visiting the Nordic Ecumenical Institute at Sigunta, Bishop Bell was astonished by the arrival of another old friend, Dietrich Bonhoeffer, who had spent some time in London in the 1930s as pastor to an Evangelical community. He had come straight from the heart of the Opposition in Berlin with a courier's pass issued on behalf of the Abwehr (for whom he worked) by Colonel Oster. The latter, together with Bonhoeffer's brother-in-law Dohnanyi, had planned this contact with the British visitor. Bonhoeffer, through Dohnanyi, had direct links with Oster and

Beck. Schoenfeld, through an Evangelical official at the Ministry of Foreign Affairs – Dr Eugen Gerstenmaier – was in close touch with the Kreisau Circle, and therefore Moltke and Trott. Yet neither of the two German pastors had any idea that the other was coming to Sweden to contact their old friend in the cause of the Opposition. Naturally, the unexpected arrival of this second visitor on the same errand strengthened the impression Bell had already gained from Schoenfeld. Bonhoeffer told the Bishop how he had been forbidden by the Gestapo to speak, preach or publish, but that he 'engaged by night in political activity.' Referring to the talks he had already had with Schoenfeld, Bell begged Bonhoeffer to understand that if he was to gain the ear of the British Government he must have the names of the leaders of the movement. It was a lot to ask. The fact that Bonhoeffer divulged them was sufficient proof of the desperate seriousness of those concerned with the approach to Britain. He named Beck and Goerdeler as the over-all leaders. He also named General Hammerstein; Leuschner, former President of the United Trades Unions; Kaiser, the Catholic Trade Union leader; Schacht, the former Reichminister; and certain generals – Kluge, Bock, Küchler, Witzleben. Bonhoeffer claimed that key positions were held by the Opposition in radio; in the main industrial concerns; in the water and gas supply industries. There were also close links with the State police. Schoenfeld then joined them at Sigunta and the Bishop was able to confer with his two friends together. Schoenfeld stressed that the Opposition had been developing for some time and had already been in existence before the war. They had full confidence in the strength of the German Army and were prepared to face the continuation of the war to its bitter end if the Allies should refuse to negotiate with a new government free of Nazism. But the continuation of the war on the present, or probably greater scale, would sentence still further millions to destruction, particularly in the occupied countries, and would be suicidal for Europe. Bonhoeffer on his side emphasised that whatever action was taken by the Opposition it should be understood by the world as an act of repentance. Whatever fate befell Germany must be accepted as Divine judgment.

The aims of the Opposition were made quite clear and although the two clergymen were acting quite independently of the Trott/ Visser 't Hooft approach (indeed the latter was still in London at this time) the points they listed were exactly the same as those in the Trott memorandum drawn up in April. Finally it was stressed that it would be useless to proceed, given the dangers, if the Allied governments intended to treat a Germany purged of Nazism in exactly the same way as they proposed to treat a Hitlerite Germany. The Bishop was therefore asked to obtain a response on this point. The two Germans also suggested that should there be any wish on the part of the British Government for preliminary private discussion, Adam von Trott, a friend of Sir Stafford Cripps' son, would be a very suitable person. A simple code was devised by means of which the Bishop should report, via Geneva, which of several possible anticipated responses he had secured from the British Government.[21] The Bishop took back with him to England a verbal message to Bonhoeffer's sister and her husband and a letter – signed 'James' – from Helmuth von Moltke for his friend Lionel Curtis. Most importantly, he took the written statement on the composition and aims of the Opposition in Germany which he had asked Schoenfeld to prepare.

Bishop Bell never saw Bonhoeffer again. The following year the pastor was arrested and after two years in gaol, where his saintly character impressed itself upon everyone, he was executed in the last days of the war. Shortly before his death he managed to pass a verbal message of farewell to the Bishop through a fellow-prisoner: Payne Best of the Venlo affair.[22]

After some delay due to bad weather, Bell arrived home on 11th June. He immediately set about transposing the contents of Schoenfeld's document into a memorandum for the Foreign Secretary. It set down in detail all the points which had been conveyed by the two Germans in their conversations with Bell. It was absolutely explicit about the composition of the Opposition in a national sense and the identity of its leading figures. It stated the intention to overthrow the Nazi régime and the aims of the government with which they would replace it. Bell listed these aims: (a) the renunciation of aggression; (b) abolition of the Nuremberg laws and co-operation in an international solution of the Jewish problem; (c) gradual retreat from the assaulted and occupied countries; (d) withdrawal of support from Japan and assistance to the Allies in ending the war in the Far East; (e) co-operation with the Allies in the reconstruction of areas destroyed or damaged by the war. Bell proceeded to sum up the principles upon which the Opposition based their hopes for the post-war world: the restoration in Germany of a state based on law and order in a federalised system of self-government in individual states;

the creation of economic interdependence among the nations of Europe for mutual advantage and as a guarantee against militarism; the establishment of a federation of free nations or states which would include a free Polish and a free Czech nation; establishment of a European army for the control of Europe under central leadership, into which the German Army would be incorporated. Having therefore placed all their cards on the table, the Opposition put two questions to the Allied governments. Would they be willing to enter into *bona fide* negotiations with a new government set up according to the guiding principles described? Could the allies declare clearly to the world that if the Hitler régime was overthrown, they would be willing to talk with such a German government on these terms with a view to reaching a peace settlement?

Having put together this long and detailed report the Bishop presented himself at the Foreign Office where he was advised to write to the Foreign Secretary. He did so the same day. After giving brief details of the events in Sweden, he stated that the British Minister, Mallet, had felt the matter sufficiently important for him to ask for a personal meeting with the Secretary of State. He then stated: 'The information is a sequel to the memorandum you have already seen, brought from Geneva by Dr Visser 't Hooft . . . and having to do with von Trott.' If the Foreign Secretary would receive him, he concluded, he would bring his papers with him. It would have been better, had he but known it, not to have prayed in aid the Trott memorandum.

Bell saw Eden on 30th June. He gave a detailed account of his experiences in Sweden and his conversations with the German pastors, whose integrity he guaranteed. He repeated all he had been told of the Opposition and listed the names which Bonhoeffer had given him. Eden professed much interest but was glad that the Bishop had warned the two Germans that the British Government was likely to be very reserved in its attitude. Opinion in Britain, he said, – advancing what in fact was his own personal opinion – tended to blame all Germans for tolerating the Nazis for so long. (Did Bell raise the question of Gestapo terror and concentration camps?) Perhaps the pastors were being used to put out peace feelers, suggested Eden. He had to be scrupulously careful not to give even the appearance of negotiations with the enemy and to be able to say so truthfully to the Americans and the Russians. In reply, Bell emphasised his belief in the reality of the Opposition and handed to Eden the memorandum prepared by Schoenfeld in Sweden, together with his own eight-page report. The two pastors, he said, would be waiting and hoping for some response. Eden promised to give the matter further consideration.

Meanwhile, on 13th July, Bishop Bell saw Sir Stafford Cripps. Here the atmosphere was rather different. Cripps spoke enthusiastically of Adam von Trott and gave an account of Visser 't Hooft's visit. Bell in turn showed him Schoenfeld's document which greatly impressed Cripps, who described it as far-reaching. Cripps said that he had been told to inform the Dutchman that on his return to Switzerland he might encourage Trott but only in terms of the defeat of Germany – the bitter end, in other words. The Bishop was doing no better with his own mission. Four days later he received from Eden a blandly negative reply: 'I have no doubt that it would be contrary to the interest of our nation to provide them with any answer whatever.' Bell saw the national interest differently. He had found much evidence on many sides in neutral Sweden that a sharp distinction between Nazis and Germans was being drawn elsewhere: 'It is the drawing of this distinction (with its consequences) by the Government in the most emphatic way which is so anxiously awaited by the Opposition.' Bell then quoted Churchill's first speech in the House of Commons as Prime Minister, when he had talked of waging war against 'a monstrous tyranny never surpassed in the dark and lamentable catalogue of human crime,' and he appealed to Eden:

> If there are men in Germany also ready to wage war against the monstrous tyranny of the Nazis from within, is it right to discourage or ignore them? Can we afford to reject their aid in achieving our end? If we by our silence allow them to believe that there is no hope for any Germany, whether Hitlerite or anti-Hitlerite, that is in effect what we are doing.[23]

Eden replied on 4th August:

> I realise the dangers and difficulties to which the Opposition in Germany is exposed, but they have so far given little evidence of their existence and until they show that they are willing to follow the example of the oppressed people of Europe in running risks and taking active steps to oppose and overthrow the Nazi rule of terror I do not see how we can usefully expand the statements which have already been made. . . . The longer the German people tolerate the Nazi

régime the greater becomes their responsibility for the crimes which that régime is committing in their name.[24]

Eden's letter was lacking in logic. Why should there be a 'rule of terror' if the German people tolerated the régime? If the resistance in occupied countries could receive support, why not in Germany? Did not the British tolerance of the Nazi régime over the years involve them, too, in some responsibility? Cadogan, Head of the Foreign Office, had admitted that Britain had continued 'to do business with Nazi Germany even after the evil nature of the régime was known.' Was there not a moral as well as a practical reason to support the Opposition?

Eden and his lieutenants in the Foreign Office had before them two solid, sober comprehensive statements of intent, already adumbrated before the war by Goerdeler and in the first months of the war by Hassell and by the Opposition approach through the Pope. The basic principles were unchanged although the progress of the war and the advent of the USA and the USSR into the conflict added new dimensions. A message to the Opposition need have contained no specific commitments. All that was required was a positive statement that if any government such as they had outlined took office after having got rid of Hitler and all the ramifications of the Nazi state, Britain would willingly extend a helping hand to the new democracy and gladly co-operate in finding a satisfactory way to terminate Hitler's war. Meanwhile, the fight against Hitler on the Allied side would be vigorously pursued. Was there any good reason why such an assurance should not have been sent? After the war, Wheeler-Bennett put about the entirely untrue statement that the Bell memorandum had been rejected 'after consultations between London, Washington and Moscow.'[25]

With his total faith in his friends Bell refused to accept defeat and carried the cause to the House of Lords, where he could bring it to public notice. He did this by putting down a motion for debate calling attention to Stalin's recent declarations on the Hitlerite State and the German people and asking whether the Government, in its war aims, made the same distinction. The Foreign Office got the message: 'It is necessary to bear in mind that the Bishop of Chichester is one of the leading proponents of the "good Germans" theory.' He had 'pressed his view particularly strongly after his return from Stockholm last summer.' He would obviously be using his motion to initiate a discussion on the necessity of making a clear public distinction between the German people and the Nazi régime. The attitude of the Foreign Office was that, firstly, this would arouse the wrath of Vansittart and his followers. (It is surprising that the crude and virulent anti-Germanism of which the former Head of the Foreign Office had become the public articulator should have been considered a factor in shaping Government policy.) Secondly, there was the fear of 'arousing the suspicions of our European allies.' But it was Stalin's statement which was the subject of the debate. As for the occupied countries, surely the knowledge that for many Germans, too, the Nazi régime was a hideous yoke which they sought to throw off would only have been a cause for hope. But there were those who would deny them that hope. The Head of the Political Warfare Executive, Bruce Lockhart, made his contribution to the discussion a brief one:

> The Nazi Party and its ancillaries now include virtually the whole nation. A clear-cut distinction between the German people and the Nazi Party is therefore hard to make and is perhaps better avoided.[26]

In such misconceptions was British propaganda to Germany grounded.

There was some attempt to persuade the Bishop to withdraw his motion but on 10 March 1943 the debate took place in the House of Lords. In his opening speech, Bell detailed the evidence of opposition inside Germany, with which he himself had been concerned before the war. He quoted Himmler's address to senior army staff (see above p. 42), which in itself was an answer to Eden's charge that the German resistance fell short of other resistance movements. Outside the concentration camps, declared the Bishop, 'there is an opposition continuous, very subtle, and determined.' He listed the forms of sabotage in the factories, and the work of the underground press. But the most steadfast *public* opposition was offered by the Churches. It was hard to exaggerate the significance in a totalitarian state of the forthright statements from the pulpit of Cardinal Faulhaber, Bishop von Galen, Bishop Bornewasser and Bishop von Preysing. There had been a declaration on human rights issued on behalf of the whole Catholic hierarchy. The Evangelical Bishop of Worms was an outstanding voice against the régime.

Bishop Bell insisted that he did not want to exaggerate the capacity of the Opposition in view of the forces ranged against it, but no wise statesman would ignore it. And he paraphrased the plea of the German pastors for outside support in the form of an unequivocal declaration that a Germany which had overthrown Hitler and all he stood for, had repudiated military domination and denounced Hitler's crimes and Hitler's gains, would be welcome to a proper place in the family of nations. He was careful to confine his testimony on behalf of the Opposition to those Church circles where it could be expected that he would have open contact, and to the public manifestations which he had quoted. To make mention of those elements of society inimical to Hitler of whose existence he could only have learned secretly, would have been a betrayal of his friends. He was not, the Bishop told the House, acquitting the whole of the German people of responsibility for the existence of the régime, but the chief blame for letting the Nazis seize control lay with certain powerful anti-democratic forces, partly in military and partly in industrial circles, who had sought only their own selfish ends. 'Nor in all honesty should we in Britain fail to recognise our own part in the general European and world responsibility.'[27]

While the diplomatic and religious elements in the Opposition were making use of their contacts abroad to convey to the Allies the principles upon which a new democratic German government would be founded, in Germany itself the military conspirators were straining to achieve the ultimate aim which alone would make such a government possible. As the war raged on, the task of eliminating Hitler seemed insurmountable. There was no possibility of breaching the wall of impenetrable security within which Hitler lived and moved. His killer would have to be someone who was officially admitted inside it. And the Führer's instant and random changes of plan were a further shield, as he himself was well aware, against the forward planning of any action. A major problem, almost insuperable at times, was the procurement of suitable explosive, for the possession of which high-ranking officers could have offered no possible valid justification. The use of a gun was out of the question at close quarters: the SS bodyguard had proved to be on the alert for any untoward movement, however innocent. The Stauffenberg attempt in July, 1944 was the only one which actually took place. Nevertheless, between 1940 and 1944 at least half-a-dozen attempts were carried out, only to be aborted at the last moment by circumstances outside the conspirators' control.[28]

At Army Group Centre, the headquarters of the campaign against Russia, Colonel von Tresckow, a professional soldier highly esteemed both for his military and personal qualities, dedicated himself to the task of destroying Hitler, whose enemy he had been since before the war. He drew into his orbit other like-thinking officers who could be counted on to assist his plans. These included Schlabrendorff, Bussche and Ewald von Kleist whose father had gone to London in the summer of 1938.

These specific attempts took place against a larger background of continuous activity in the military Opposition directed to 'converting' and enlisting as many key senior officers as possible. It was not easy, as Gisevius explained in the witness box at Nuremberg, to find and recruit generals who had the actual authority to order their troops to march.[29] For instance, there were generals in the provinces who could not give that order. There was also the difficulty enshrined in the whole concept of 'the generals', as Halder explained to his American interrogators at the end of the war. These could be thought of as a homogeneous group only in peace-time, when officers rose to that rank through very slow promotion and knew each other and were on friendly terms. The enlarging of the Officer Corps by the régime and the methods of war-time promotion destroyed this closeness. The few peace-time generals did not know personally the 'newcomers' and the age span ranged from 40 years to 80 years. In peace-time, said Halder, the basis of action by the Officer Corps could be agreed on by a small circle. There was unified leadership and a preparedness to act.[30] This, of course, had been the strength of the 1938 *putsch*.

In March, 1943, Beck, the presiding spirit of the Opposition, fell seriously ill. In June came the worst blow when the Abwehr came under Gestapo attack and Oster was placed under house arrest, while Dohnanyi, Müller and Boenhoffer were put in gaol. By the turn of the year Canaris's Abwehr no longer existed. But plans went ahead. Stauffenberg was appointed by the Opposition General Olbricht to direct the reorganisation of the Replacement Army, already in progress, to make it serve the purposes of the Opposition. Under the pretext of making preparations for dealing with possible internal unrest, Stauffenberg was able to assess the strength of the SS which might be met with in the immediate aftermath of a *coup*; to deploy units accordingly and to put them under the command of reliable anti-Nazis. The first twenty-four hours in the life of the new

Germany would be critical. Such key points as the radio station and the buildings of the Government district must be occupied at once. The exact date of the *coup* was inevitably lacking. Only Hitler would supply that. What was certain was that, with the lack of response from the democracies, the new government would be in the position of having to control possible civil disorder while ensuring that the frontier was securely held in the East.

At least no stone had been left unturned to prepare for the longed-for event in the form of careful staff work and forward planning. In other words, the conspirators *were* 'doing something.' What the British Government seemed to be demanding was something more colourful; in their own words 'a demonstration by the German people that they are brave enough to rise against their own authorities.'[31] Perhaps they had in mind the 'storming' of the Bastille, now cut down to size by history; or the 'storming' of the Winter Palace, the myth which Eisenstein created so dramatically on film. And, no doubt, after Himmler's divisions of Death's Head troops had piled them into heaps with their machine guns, the participants in such 'demonstrations' would have been accused of stupidity and lack of political judgment. A comment by the historian Elisabeth Wiskemann is à propos. She worked for MI6 during the war in Switzerland and Sweden. In both these countries, she wrote after the war:

. . . one was near enough to Germany to appreciate the extraordinary difficulties involved in getting rid of a firmly established terrorist dictatorship during a totalitarian war; and one was near enough to feel embarrassed by BBC exhortations in terms which were meaningless in an unfree country. . . .[32]

The German Service of the BBC was of course part of the propaganda arm of the Government, directed by the Political Warfare Executive. This in turn came under the control of the Foreign Office and all projects had to be submitted to check that they conformed with Government policy. Propaganda was therefore directed, under Eden, by those who like himself totally rejected what Orme Sargent called 'the dangerous doctrine of the good and bad Germans.'[33] The historian of the BBC, Asa Briggs, admits that broadcasts to Germany were handicapped by 'the Government's unwillingness to seek to create or encourage a German "resistance" or to hold out any definite hopes to the Germans in the future.'[34] Harrison of Central Department, who always discounted the existence of any viable opposition element inside Germany whenever any approaches were received from that quarter, now found a use for it: to promote disunity in Germany.[35] The policy was formalised in a paper by the Political Warfare Executive:

> Objectives: to encourage the growth of opposition by the Church, the Army, the landed gentry and the industrialists – the 'decent' people – or any individual leaders (i.e. Goering) and when such opposition emerges, to create fresh conflicts within it; to divide the people in support of these various elements of opposition and eventually to encourage revolt against their leadership.[36]

PWE obviously saw itself as creating an Opposition (which in fact already existed) and then only for negative purposes. But there is every indication in its endless and discursive policy papers that the department had never been 'filled in' by the Foreign Office on the history of the Opposition from its pre-war days and its contacts with the British; nor of its aims for the replacement of the Hitler régime in a regenerated Germany by a democratic government.

The British attitude to the post-war world was a long way from the European vision of the Opposition policy-makers. According to PWE what was needed was 'not exact plans for Europe but the expression of an Anglo-Saxon philosophy of life. . . .'

> [British] freedoms are based, not on continental theories of democracy or socialism, but on an innate sense of self-discipline and mutual respect of the responsible ruler and the responsible subject. Britain fights, not for any continentalisms or Orders, but for a decent way of life, which already exists here and in the Commonwealth.[37]

Propaganda to Germany should reflect this superiority: 'We should avoid at all costs making ourselves seem in any way commonplace and just like anyone else.'

The attitude of PWE towards the anti-Nazis was, and remained, a largely negative one:

> We must not compromise ourselves by suggesting that HMG is ready for peace with the 'decent Germans' but we might be able to deceive them into drawing false conclusions on this point.[38]

But the advent of the Soviet Union into the ranks of the belligerents added a new dimension to propaganda. Stalin appealed over the heads of the Nazi Party to the German proletariat itself:

> Every Hitler Youth who perishes in the woods of Russia, every destroyed tank, every smashed aeroplane, is a victory of the German people, deceived and enslaved by Hitler.[39]

PWE began to ponder whether the time might not be ripe to take a more positive line. Should the passage in Churchill's broadcast on 22nd June 1941 that 'any man or state which fights against Nazism will have our aid' be applied to Germans? Crossman requested a 'clear ruling' from the Foreign Office: 'Should the German people as distinct from the Nazis and the military hierarchy be included among those whose liberation will result from our victory?' The question was considered at a meeting of Bruce Lockhart; Strang, Head of German Department; Kirkpatrick, seconded from the Foreign Office to the BBC European Service, and Nigel Law, of the Ministry of Information. The matter was then referred upwards to the Foreign Secretary. The answer, relayed by Strang, was an emphatic 'no'.[40] Three years later, in 1944, Crossman wrote that one war – the war of liberation which began on the Normandy beaches – had ended in September and another had begun: 'A whole nation is and remains our enemy and must be conquered whether it wants to be liberated or not.'[41]

In August, 1941, a few weeks after that meeting in Whitehall, Weizsäcker and Burkhardt walked together along the deserted paths of the Tiergarten. The latter was in Berlin on a Red Cross Mission. He found his old friend on the verge of despair:

> The Americans must absolutely learn how matters stand within Germany, what great powers of interior resistance exist in Germany against this mob of gangsters which wields the power and is driving us and the world into an unimaginable catastrophe. . . .
> Can you not in Switzerland talk to the Americans better than we can here? If there was a faint ray of hope, a chance of mediation we could deal with this gang of criminals here, but we must have help, just as we ought to have been aided before the outbreak of war. Such régimes as this one . . . can only be abolished with help from abroad. . . .[42]

The attack on Pearl Harbour ended any hope of such mediation. When the Americans entered the war the official attitude to the anti-Nazi Opposition was unambiguous. Roosevelt was implacably hostile to the whole German race, without qualification. Nevertheless, although there were to be no dealings with the Opposition, it would be worth while keeping an eye on them. Allen Dulles of the OSS was sent into Switzerland in November, 1942 – just before the border with unoccupied France was closed by the Germans – for the purpose of monitoring and if possible establishing relations with oppositional elements in Germany. Dulles set up his office in Berne and very soon had made close personal contact with the Opposition, to whom his door was always open. But Dulles was not a mere secret service agent. A former diplomat, with a broad knowledge of European affairs, he had had the experience of working with the American delegation at the Paris Peace Conference after the First World War. He did not limit his attention to the conspirators in Germany, nor see the conquest of Germany as the ultimate end. It was essential to consider the political outcome of the war. To this end he extended his contacts to the occupied countries and his office in the Herren-gasse became a clearing house for European resistance movements. It was this forward-looking political thinking which the German Opposition had found so lacking in their contacts abroad. It had always been a matter of frustration that in their approaches they were always regarded simply as intelligence sources, although they steadfastly refused to communicate anything which might have been turned to the military advantage of Germany's enemies. This attitude, as Gisevius wrote, prevented the British from drawing any political advantage from the existence of a German underground. In Dulles, at last, 'a man had been found with whom it was possible to discuss the contradictory complex of problems emerging from Hitler's war.'[43] As an open-minded intelligence gatherer and adviser to the State Department, Dulles fulfilled the function so lacking in the British Foreign Office in pre-war years. He succeeded in engaging the confidence of the Opposition while at the same time remaining entirely objective about their activities and their hopes. Had there been a 'Dulles' in the Foreign Office in the 1930s the story of September, 1938 might have ended differently.

In the summer of 1940, Gisevius had been installed by Canaris in a counter-intelligence post as Vice-consul in the Consulate-General in Zurich. He was able to protect members of the underground from the Gestapo agents operating in Switzerland. He was able to travel freely to Germany, where he kept in close touch with the Opposition leaders, Beck and Goerdeler. He lost this facility when the Gestapo moved against the Abwehr in 1943 and was 'grounded' in Switzerland, returning to Germany only in 1944 to take part in Stauffenberg's *coup*. He soon became Dulles' foremost contact man with the conspirators in Germany. But long before Dulles arrived in Berne, Gisevius had attempted to establish contact with the British. In a Foreign Office paper prepared for Cabinet circulation under the heading 'Peace Feelers' it is recorded that information was received of conversations which had taken place between a 'neutral interlocutor' and

> a German connected with the German Consulate-General in Zurich alleged to be in touch with highly placed personages in Germany in the civil service, in the Army and in intellectual and business circles, including Dr Schacht. The German is known as Dr Gisevius and it is thought probable that this is his real name.[44]

Confirmation of this approach (evidently made through the Americans) is contained in the text of a cable from Dulles to Washington in July, 1944, four days after the failed attempt on Hitler:

> 512 [Gisevius] endeavoured to establish contact with Zulu [British Secret Service] through us as soon as the Breakers [Opposition] movement started to grow. London rejected this. . . .

Dulles further related that in July, 1943 the British had advised him to stop seeing Gisevius as they thought he was untrustworthy.

Dulles preferred to keep his distance from the SIS. In January, 1944 he told his chiefs in Washington:

> For a number of reasons I have not talked with Zulu about the Breakers situation at this particular time and pending further developments I recommend you also refrain from doing so on the basis of information in my messages.

One month before the 20th July bomb plot, Dulles finally agreed to the OSS London Office passing on to the British 'information re Breakers.' He had not done so before at his end '. . . since the British in Berne did not give us any information of their activists' operations within the Reich.'[45] Perhaps the truth was that the British had nothing to tell.

But it was not only information about the overthrow of Hitler which was reaching Dulles. Early in May, 1944, Gisevius and Waetjen came to him with 'an important oral message from Germany' which they had received from the generals in the Opposition group. In order to ensure that as large an area as possible should be occupied by the Allies, thereby halting the advance of Communism into Europe, the generals had drawn up certain proposals which they wished to submit to the Allies. These proposals were that the Allied forces should be allowed to make unopposed landings at or near Bremen and Hamburg. (Plans for landings on the French coast could not yet be formulated because Rommel was still an unknown quantity.) Three Allied parachute divisions would land in the Berlin region with the assistance of local German commanders. Hitler and the Party leaders would be isolated in Obersalzburg under the guard of trustworthy German units. The German forces in the West would surrender, but would then be allowed to reinforce the Eastern frontier, which would be held against the Soviet forces. Dulles was told that General Beck was involved in the plan.[46] That at least was an assurance that this was no military plot merely to save the Army. The full details of this approach were duly passed on to the British Foreign Office by the State Department on 24th May.[47] Also included were the names of some of the civilians involved – Goerdeler and Leuschner – together with the names of Oster and Beck. Familiar names all of them from before the war, as Central Department noted: 'This looks very bogus' (Harrison); '*very* bogus, and mostly old friends' (Roberts).[48]

The extension of Soviet domination was seen by the Opposition as a danger to the future of Europe of which they intended Germany, extricated from Nazi control, to be a worthy member. No doubt it was a fantastical idea that the Western Allies would range themselves alongside the Germans against their Soviet allies, but it was a measure of the deep (and justified) apprehension of the Opposition leaders. And it happened in the end, when the Federal Republic of Germany was invited to join NATO in 1955.

Stalin had not been slow to perceive Soviet self-interest in the cultivation of elements of resistance inside Germany. In comparison with the British and Americans, he was running a 'hearts-and-minds' campaign with an eye to the future. Moscow radio turned out some powerful stuff:

> The new Germany will be sovereign and independent and free of control from other nations. Our new Germany will place Hitler and his supporters, his ministers and representatives and helpers before the judgment of the people. . . . Our aim is a free Germany, a strong powerful democratic state. For people and Fatherland against Hitler's war! For immediate peace! For the salvation of the German people![49]

The message reaching Germany openly from the Soviet Union, was all the more seductive in the face of the stony silence maintained by the Western Allies on any plans they might have for the future either of Germany or of Europe. 'To give them a glimpse into our minds might drive them into the Nazi camp!' minuted Kirkpatrick.[50] Early in the war, the danger inherent in this policy of silence was vigorously expressed in a message received by the Dutch Foreign Minister in London:

> The Social Democrats in Germany complain that their work is considerably hampered by the fact that the German people have no idea of what Britain wants. They emphasise that slogans like: 'until the bitter end,' 'extirpation of Nazism' and the like are inadequate for launching an anti-Nazi campaign, let alone a revolution. . . .

It was felt vitally necessary that the German anti-Nazi movement should be understood and helped if a defeated Germany were not to slide towards Communism, thus constituting a new danger to the world.[51] As late as April, 1944 attitudes had not changed although the problem remained, as Adam von Trott testified in an urgent message to Allen Dulles:

> Constructive thoughts and plans for the post-war reconstruction of Germany are coming steadily from the Russian side, while the democratic countries make no proposals whatever concerning the future of Central Europe. Socialist leaders in Germany stress the necessity of filling this vacuum as quickly as possible.[52]

Gisevius told Dulles that he was convinced that the Russians would enter Germany with a carefully assembled and thoroughly indoctrinated group of Germans which they would hope to put forward as the government of Germany. Faced with probable Anglo-American opposition, they would at first confine their function to the Soviet Zone. However, since it would be the only German organisation of its kind, having the prestige of Soviet backing and having been well-established in the public eye – or ear – through its activities by radio during the war, it would probably become more and more accepted as a government. Britain and the US would have nothing comparable to offer.

In reporting these views of the Opposition, as he had been requested to do, Dulles took the opportunity to raise once again the importance in this context of enlisting the help of the anti-Nazi element wherever it could be identified:

> I feel we should prepare quietly and without formality in Switzerland, France and elsewhere certain individual Germans who have maintained close contact with Germany and who would be suitable to advise on certain phases of German matters and possibly serve on technical administrative committees which any occupying authorities in Germany will find absolutely essential. . . . If we do nothing of this nature, the ready-made Russian–German committee may monopolise the field.[53]

It should be realised, he wrote, that unless some interest was shown in working along the lines indicated by Gisevius, or by adopting some other programme intended to achieve similar results, there was a grave danger 'that anti-Nazi elements, who might render real service . . . will find no practical alternative except to throw in their lot with the Russians.'[54]

Conscious of what might happen in the aftermath of war, with the victors insisting that every German was a Nazi and must be treated as such, Dulles sounded Washington 'as to measure of protection which can be held out to those who retain their official positions and render service to us.' The question was put to the President. The most that Roosevelt would concede was that nothing should be given in writing, but a general statement could be made that 'in the event that they should become involved in future trials, reports of such activities would be offered in evidence' (a principle which was not subsequently adhered to).[55]

That it should be the Americans who were taking such initiatives was a cause of some concern in certain quarters. As the war entered its final months, Dr 't Hooft expressed this concern in a letter to Elisabeth Wiskemann in December, 1944. The provision which the British had made for political contacts in Switzerland with representatives of Continental countries did not seem to him fully adequate to the situation. He feared that opportunities were being missed:

> I tried to make it clear that we would like to pass on information and suggestions to the British Government but that, so far, we had not met with much response. On the other hand, we did get a considerable response from the American Government. Now, we do not want to deal only with the American Government for we are convinced that there are in Britain even more persons who would play a helpful rôle in this connection than in America, which is further away from the realities of the European continent. . . .

Miss Wiskemann passed the letter on to the Foreign Office in London. The Minister, Richard Law, had met Visser 't Hooft a short time before, as it happened, and had been much impressed by him. He told Central Department that he had exhibited 'a wide knowledge of "good" Germans who might be useful to our administration in Germany. . . .' Arnold Toynbee supported the Minister. He had met Visser 't Hooft early in the war and had been much impressed by his objectivity. Law drafted a reply (which has not survived) but it was not sent. Only the Foreign Secretary could have stopped it. It was an action of which Harrison of Central Department wholeheartedly approved. Visser 't Hooft, he minuted, was known particularly to have been in touch with 'the civilian side of the Opposition which was associated with the attempted *coup* of July 20.' (So much, incidentally, for the Foreign Office claim at the time that the *coup* was a purely military act by disaffected generals.) Harrison concluded:

> In view of Dr V. H.'s acknowledged contacts with oppositional circles in Germany, I should be very reluctant to see our own official contacts with him extended. I am glad therefore to see that the draft letter to him from Mr Law did not issue. . . .[56]

But as Dulles was aware, such people needed to be identified and recruited well before the war wound down into chaos. As D-Day approached, the American Embassy had enquired of the Foreign Office whether they had a 'white list' of genuine anti-Nazis who might be useful in the future. The British reply, given by telephone, was so preposterous that it can only be seen as a put-down of the Americans. The Foreign Office knew of no such list. However, from time to time PWE heard, from sources such as POW interrogations, of individuals who appeared to be anti-Nazi. They had for example recently heard of a school-teacher somewhere in Würtemberg who had shown some courage in resisting Nazi attempts to interfere with German education and who might at some future date prove useful![57]

As an alternative to the provincial school-teacher, the Foreign Office might have offered the Americans the names of a member of the Abwehr and his wife who had defected to the British some weeks earlier, in February, 1944. Erich Vermehren was stationed in Ankara on the staff of his friend and fellow-Oppositionist, Paul Leverkühn, Abwehr representative in Turkey. The appointment had been engineered for the Vermehrens, at the request of Leverkühn, by Adam von Trott. What had prompted the action of the Vermehrens was the disastrous penetration of the Solf circle in Berlin by Gestapo agents (see above p. 48). One of those arrested, Otto Kiep, was a close friend of the Vermehrens. A former Consul-General in New York, Kiep had nominated Erich for a Rhodes scholarship at Oxford. When, soon after Kiep's arrest, the couple were summoned to Berlin, they had no illusions about the fate which awaited them. They approached British Intelligence who flew them to Cairo, where they told their story and revealed their background in the Opposition. They were both Catholics: Elisabeth was a relative of the redoubtable Bishop von Galen. Her parents had been in trouble for distributing copies of his sermons. All this was duly telegraphed to London. But it was not at all what London wanted to hear. A telegram was dispatched to Cairo by return:

> In our view biographical details contained in your tel. suggest opposition of long standing to Nazi régime. Can only discount propaganda value of V's statement and should not be released.[58]

Long-standing opposition to Hitler was not an acceptable substitute for a dramatic conversion of committed Nazis.

The Vermehrens were in due course flown to London where they were interviewed by Political Intelligence Department. They freely identified names and aims of the Opposition and urged the British to make contact through Trott. The Foreign Office briskly dismissed all this talk of opposition as simply a matter of Germans wanting 'to work their passage home, help to accelerate Hitler's downfall and claim for Germany proportionately mild treatment.' Kirkpatrick wrote to Harvey: 'You will not be surprised to see that I do not think there is any money in this German opposition.'[59]

The Foreign Office was prepared to go to extraordinary lengths to prevent the existence of anti-Nazi opposition inside Germany becoming publicly known. This might encourage the idea of the possibility of an alternative to the ultimate goal of unconditional surrender at whatever cost. There is a well-documented example of this policy in the experience of Visser 't Hooft in September, 1944. He already had a black mark against him through his involvement with the Trott memorandum two years earlier. After the disaster of 'Operation North Pole', when agents parachuted into Holland from Britain had been captured and 'turned', 't Hooft was virtually the only trustworthy conduit of communication in both directions between the government-in-exile and the Dutch resistance. As the Allied armies advanced on the Continent, up-to-date contact was vital. In September the Netherlands Government in London presented a request to the Foreign Secretary to grant permission for Visser 't Hooft to visit London 'in connection with his important work in Switzerland' and the valuable information he could provide about conditions in Holland. The response from the Foreign Office was unexpected. The request had been 'carefully considered' but as France was an 'operational area' and there was no air service between Switzerland and Britain, it would not be possible for Dr 't Hooft to come to England for 'some considerable time.' Within an hour of the receipt of this message, the Dutch Prime Minister instructed his Foreign Minister to raise the matter again 'most insistently': Dr 't Hooft was one of their main channels to the underground movement:

> In view of recent instructions sent to the underground which might have to be revised in view of the slower nature of [the Allied] advance in Holland, it was really essential to consult Dr 't Hooft personally in London.

It was very much hoped that the decision would be reviewed and facilities made available. But the Foreign Office refused to budge. It should be suggested to the Netherlands Government that they send someone out from London to Switzerland instead. Having declared that it was impossible to travel *from* Switzerland to London, the

Foreign Office did not explain why it would be possible to travel in the reverse direction.[60]

What consideration could be so important as to override the necessity of contact with the Dutch resistance, awaiting the critical moment to rise against the German occupiers? It was fully set out in a Central Department minute by Harrison:

> [Visser 't Hooft] is known in the past to have been in touch with German oppositional groups, in particular the civilian side of the opposition which has probably been eliminated as a result of the purge following the attempted *coup* of July 20. When he came to this country in 1942 he brought with him a memorandum from a group of Germans which included Adam von Trott, liquidated [sic] a week or so ago.
>
> I have an uneasy feeling that if we allow Visser 't Hooft to come to this country . . . he may supply information to the Archbishop of Canterbury, but also to men like the Bishop of Chichester, which it may be inconvenient for them to have, e.g. stories of continued oppositional movements in Germany, especially in Church circles. I should hope therefore that it may be possible to find administrative or technical difficulties which would prevent Visser 't Hooft coming to this country.[61]

It was a part of the Foreign Office's case that revelations about opposition activity in Germany would generate calls for a 'soft peace'. But peace, hard or soft, was a matter not for the British public but for the Allied governments, to whom revelations of the existence of German opposition would hardly have been news; and who were firmly pledged to the policy of unconditional surrender. Furthermore, if peace was the Foreign Office argument, why did they continue to block the entry of those connected with the Opposition even after the war was over? There is no clearer example than that of the widow of Helmuth von Moltke.

Moltke was, like Trott, one of the legendary figures of the Opposition and his unwavering fight against Nazism has already been described. When, in January, 1945 the OSS in Berne reported to the British Secret Service that they had learned that Moltke had been condemned to death, they suggested that the British might try some sort of delaying action on the grounds that his mother was British (she was a South African Scot). 'Our experience here,' advised Dulles, 'is that if some stir is created, Germans at this stage may consider person more valuable alive than dead.'[62] But there was to be no British attempt to stay the hangman's hand. Eden had made clear in July, 1944 that 'I cannot admit that we have any obligation to help those concerned in the recent plot.' Apparently this non-obligation extended to the widow and the orphan. At the end of the war, the tragically widowed Countess von Moltke was living, in great privation and not a little danger, on the estate at Kreisau, once the scene of those meetings at which a new Germany and a new Europe had been envisioned. Kreisau was now in that area of Germany which had been ceded to Poland. In addition to her three small children, she had under her protection another Opposition widow, Countess Yorck, and her children. Through the good offices of Allen Dulles, now moved from Berne to Berlin, Freya von Moltke managed, in August, 1945, to get a letter to Lionel Curtis. As an old family friend and godfather to her eldest child, Curtis pressed the Foreign Office vigorously for permission for the family to join him in England. He would assume full financial responsibility for them. The matter fell to the attention of a member of Central Department – Con O'Neill – who had been a guest of the Moltke family at Kreisau before the war. In a Foreign Office minute, he had once written of Helmuth von Moltke in terms of the highest esteem (though admittedly only to discredit Adam von Trott by contrast). But there was to be no help for Helmuth's family from that quarter now. While acknowledging that as an opponent of Hitler Moltke had helped others to safety, O'Neill had no hesitation in advising that the request that his widow and children should come to England 'can only be granted if a complete exception is made to all rules and regulations. They have no right whatever to be given refuge in this country.' The fact that his mother was British; that he had been a member of the English bar; that his child had an English godparent; that he had an outstanding record of opposition – these were not sufficiently cogent reasons, insisted O'Neill, to make an exception. Harvey agreed: 'I am sure it would be wrong. Her husband was only half English and she is wholly German.' O'Neill drafted a letter for Cadogan to submit to the Foreign Secretary, Ernest Bevin, which prevailed even against the personal appeal of such a distinguished advocate as Lionel Curtis.[63]

The Departmental exchanges are characterised by an extraordinary harshness, almost vindictiveness, towards the Countess. The Foreign Office were willing that she should go direct to South Africa, if she could get out of Poland. Or, if the Poles would allow her to leave and the Soviet Union would allow her to cross their zone, she could be admitted to the chaos and misery of the British Zone, to take her chance there. But she must not come to Britain. It was perhaps fatal to the Countess's cause that in his letter to the Foreign Office, Lionel Curtis had stressed 'the valuable information this heroic woman could give us to all that led up to the attempt on Hitler in July, 1944.' In addition to the letters received by his friends in England during the war, all Moltke's papers had been preserved by his wife at Kreisau. These constituted a unique archive of the Opposition and were a testimony to the potential of the movement which the British had always rejected. And of course Helmuth von Moltke himself had been especially active in his efforts, through his English friends, to initiate and sustain contact with Britain in the hope of advancing the cause of the internal war against Hitler. Harvey warned that if the Moltke family were allowed in, questions might be asked in the House. Certainly the Foreign Office would not have wanted to be put into the position of having to justify their refusal.

Six months later, the Foreign Office noted that Fabian von Schlabrendorff, who had been a major emissary of the Opposition to Britain before the war, was living with his wife and three children in extremely impoverished circumstances. The US Occupation authorities, according to his wife, treated them with suspicion and something close to hostility because he was classed as a 'militarist'. Schlabrendorff was simply a war-time soldier, a lawyer by profession. In the same village was living the widow of Colonel Hansen, who had taken over Canaris' work for the Opposition after the Gestapo had caused the removal of the Admiral from the Abwehr. The same charge of 'militarist' was made against her executed husband and she too was living 'in great grief and poverty' because she was refused a pension and his bank account was blacked.[64] The Opposition was without honour in what had virtually ceased to be their own country.

Churchill's statement to Schlabrendorff at Chequers in 1949 that he had been misled about the extent of the Opposition inside Germany seems to be borne out at least by one paper prepared for the Cabinet by Harrison in June 1944 entitled: *German 'Dissident' Groups*. The word 'Dissident', framed as it was by quotation marks, suggested passive disagreement rather than active resistance. 'There are undoubtedly in Germany a considerable number of individuals,' conceded the report, 'who are genuinely anti-Nazi.' But

> The indications are that these individuals are in fact less concerned with active steps in eliminating the Nazis than in stepping into the Nazis' shoes, when the Nazis have been eliminated. . . .[65]

What indications? A couple of days before the 20th July *putsch*, a *German Morale Report* prepared by Central Department stated that there was no indication that the Nazi leaders would not fight on to the bitter end; meanwhile there was no sign of any other potential leaders emerging in Germany. (The Foreign Office knew exactly who the leaders were; they had 'emerged' long ago.) 'It is by no means certain that the High Command . . . are today in a position to take action even if they wished to do so.' Two days later Harrison was hastily taking up his pen again; explanations seemed to be called for. Reports of a possible *coup* had circulated so frequently during the war, he wrote, that they had come to be regarded with great scepticism.[66]

But the conspirators had always considered it essential that the Allies (and, as has been seen, the occupied countries) should be given time to consider in advance the steps they would need to take at the critical moment of Hitler's assassination. Only the Führer should be taken by surprise. But inevitably there were false alarms, such as those already described. In July, 1944 the Opposition took every possible step to alert the Allies. This was done through contacts in Lisbon, Madrid, Berne and Stockholm by civilian members of the conspiracy, thus contradicting the charge that the attempt was merely the act of a small military clique. As Harrison admitted, shortly before the *coup* the British received information from an exceptional German source, via a British agent in Lisbon, that the conspirators in Germany, 'who included General Beck,' had decided to move against Hitler without waiting for encouragement from outside and that Hitler would be murdered before the end of July. The message was discounted as of little importance.[67] Otto John, who as a director of Lufthansa travelled often to Madrid, had good contacts with the British and American embassies there. He was sent by his fellow-conspirators General von Tresckow and Colonel Hansen of the Abwehr, to make known to the Allies the imminence of the *coup* and to prepare a direct line of contact to General Eisenhower at SHAEF.

The efforts of the Opposition to ensure that the Allied governments would not be taken unawares were wasted on the British. Confirmation of the fact that their messages had fallen on deaf ears is contained in a passage in Cadogan's diary. The Head of the Foreign Office wrote on 21st July: 'Papers full of attempt on Hitler's life. Don't know what it means. Not very much, I think.'[68] The American Government, however, did not have to rely on the newspapers. Dulles had already cabled, a week before the attempt: 'There is a possibility that a dramatic event may take place up North [i.e. Germany], if Breaker's courier is to be trusted. 512 [Gisevius] has gone north for discussions with Tucky [Beck].'[69] By the 21st July, Dulles had been able to supply his Chief in Washington with details of the *coup* and many of those taking part. On 24th July he received a cable in return: 'We wish to extend our congratulations on the fine scoop you scored with your Breakers information.'[70]

After the failure of the 20th July became known, the press in the West lined up solidly behind Hitler in condemning the conspirators. They were dismissed as a group of disaffected generals who had wanted to be rid of Hitler simply because they felt they could prosecute his criminal plans more efficiently without him. The attempt would also stand them in good stead with the victors – 're-insurance', the Foreign Office called it. The *Daily Telegraph* declared positively, without any grounds for doing so, that 'there was not a scrap of evidence' that the plotters were actuated by hostility of long-standing towards Hitler and his policies: 'We are thus in the presence of no more and no less than a candid confession of military defeat by professional soldiers.' (If so, it was a premature one. By the end of the year thousands of American soldiers were lying dead in the snows of the Ardennes; General Eisenhower was demanding that 'every appropriate weapon' should be brought to bear on the problem of breaking the German will to resist; and Churchill was warning a complacent Foreign Office: 'We have not defeated them yet.') The *New York Times* described the conspirators as gangsters using the weapon of the underworld: the bomb. The *Herald Tribune* declared that the American people, who held no brief for aristocrats and least of all for those given to the goose-step, would not feel sorry that the bomb had spared Hitler that he might liquidate his generals himself. Even Churchill, in an unconsidered remark in Parliament which he later regretted, spoke about people in high places in Germany murdering one another, or trying to.[71]

In Cabinet, Eden took a rather different line from the public derision when he admitted that 'there seemed little doubt that there had been and still was a movement of considerable force in Germany behind the generals.' There was a discussion among Ministers of what line the Foreign Secretary should take in the House of Commons. The general opinion was that 'at this stage the less said the better.'[72] Although Eden informed the House on the 25th July that too little was yet known about the incident to pronounce upon it, in fact the Americans had already sent London all the information they had had from Dulles. Nevertheless, on 26th July, the Foreign Office Political Intelligence Department in its weekly bulletin had no hesitation in declaring:

> As to what actually happened, or indeed when it happened, almost nothing is known. . . . The only evidence we have consists of German public statements. . . .

There was to be no suggestion anywhere that the attack was anything more than, in the words of the *Daily Telegraph*, 'an attempt to replace the swastika with the jackboot.' It was to rebut such a charge that General Beck had insisted, from the beginning, on building up a depository of documents as evidence of Nazi crimes. This would be produced in court if Hitler was taken alive or communicated to the nation if he was assassinated. Alas, it was put to different use when it fell into the hands of the Gestapo after 20th July.

Goerdeler was on the run for three weeks. Political Warfare Department noted that 'Himmler's offer [a million marks] for Goerdeler's head will keep the story going.'[73] Mr A. P. Young, the industrialist who had worked so closely with him before the war as a courier to the Foreign Office was deeply distressed at his plight. Like Bishop Bell, he tried to find ways to help. He was in touch with influential friends in America, who at first seemed to hold out some hope. He wrote at great length to Eden, recalling the 'X documents' he had brought from Switzerland in 1938 and his visit to Eden at the time. He poured out his great admiration and affection for Goerdeler and stressed the invaluable contribution he could make to Germany after the war. Eden's reply, acknowledging his letter, betrayed no feeling whatsoever and merely stated the facts: 'You will no doubt now have seen the announcement issued by the German News Service on the 11th September that Dr Goerdeler has been sentenced to death by the German People's Court.' A. P. Young recorded later that he heard from A. J. Cummings of the *News Chronicle* that 'Winston Churchill was interested in Goerdeler's plight and had requested to see all the relevant papers.'[74]

A week after the *putsch*, Bishop Bell wrote to Eden in some distress. He felt certain that Catholic and Protestant clergy would be in grave danger. Would it be possible to let it be known in Sweden, perhaps through the Swedish friend who had been privy to the 1942 conversations, that there was a readiness to help, if help were needed? Could a way be found through which Evangelical Church leaders might get in touch with him? 'I cannot help seeing some connection between the present revolt in Germany and the movement towards a revolt of which I learned in such a confidential way two years ago,' he wrote. Eden's response was swift. He sent the letter straight to Central Department, writing across it with his usual red ink: 'I see no reason whatever to encourage this pestilent priest. Perhaps you will advise me as to reply.' Cadogan and Roberts hastened to obey. Cadogan's phrase: '. . . would not be in the national interest' (whatever that meant, in the circumstances) was amended by Roberts to: '. . . would raise serious difficulties.' Eden added the words: '. . . and I cannot agree. It is important that rules forbidding contact with enemy nationals should be strictly adhered to.'

Within a week Bell wrote to Eden again. One senses the feeling of outrage which was driving his pen as he recalled everything which he had pressed upon Eden in May, 1942. The letter begins without preamble:

> The hue and cry for Goerdeler following the death of Beck, shows me very clearly how closely linked is the attempt on Hitler's life of July 20 with the plan for a revolt of which I brought you evidence in the summer of 1942 from Sweden. Beck and Goerdeler were the names given to me of the men who would be at the head of the rising against Hitler which was then in view, and to help forward which, support was desired from HM Government. I was told then that under the leadership of Beck on the military side, and Goerdeler on the civil side, with others closely in touch, there was an organisation ready in every Ministry, officers in all the big towns, trades-union leaders, and generals on the various fronts and at home, who were ready to act once the signal was given. . . .

Would it not be possible for the Government to consider 'the taking of steps to help the principal leaders of the revolt (not yet killed) to escape from Germany?' Bell then named Goerdeler, Leuschner, Kaiser and Generals Hammerstein and Witzleben. It would make an immense difference if some of these men could be rescued from Germany. It might be a formidable task but if it was possible to help British prisoners-of-war to escape it should not be entirely inconceivable. (It was not. The Americans helped Gisevius to escape from Berlin.) Bell's second suggestion was that an appeal should be made over the heads of Hitler and Himmler to those people in Germany who had proved the reality of their hatred of Hitler:

> You will remember that the question to which they wished an answer in the summer of 1942 was, 'Is it any use our trying to overthrow Hitler? Or are all Germans equally to be destroyed by the Allies?'[75]

The letter finished abruptly on that note, without any of the usual courtesies.

This letter, too, was handed by Eden to his trusty lieutenants: 'More from this pestilent priest and I fear I must reply.' Roberts drafted the reply, which was initialled by Harrison and Harvey and approved by Eden. This correspondence, it said in effect, must now cease:

> Apart from the practical difficulties, I cannot admit that we have any obligation to help those concerned in the recent plot, who had their own reasons for acting as they did and were certainly not moved primarily by a desire to help our cause. . . .[76]

After five months of physical and mental torture, shackled hand and foot in the Gestapo prison, Goerdeler was hanged on 2 February 1945.

Eden cannot be allowed the last word. That belongs to the men of 20 July who left to posterity their reasons for acting as they did. Let a few speak for the many. General von Tresckow declared that it had to be proved to the world that the German resistance was prepared to stake its all, even if they failed. Claus von Stauffenberg was of the same mind: 'Something must be done, but he who has the courage to do it must do so in the knowledge that he will go down in German history as a traitor. If he does not do it, however, he will go down as a traitor to his conscience.'[77] For his brother

Berthold, 'the worst thing is knowing that we cannot succeed and yet we have to do it, for our country and our children.'[78] General von Tresckow told his friend Schlabrendorff: 'Hitler is not only the arch-enemy of Germany, he is the arch-enemy of the whole world. In a few hours' time I shall stand before God. . . . I think I shall be able to uphold with a clear conscience all that I have done in the fight against Hitler.'[79] Peter Graf Yorck von Wartenburg wrote to his wife and mother from prison: 'I assure you that not a single ambitious thought, no lust for power has influenced me in what I have done. It was solely my feeling for my country. . . . I am dying for my country. . . . We wished to light the torch of life and now we stand in a sea of flames.'[80]

On the eleventh anniversary of the tragic attempt, the newly-created British Embassy in Bonn produced a paper on the Plot, reviewing its impact on German opinion in the ensuing years. The writer concluded:

> It should, however, not be forgotten that those who participated were a small minority acting from widely divergent motives, not always in line with democratic principles or Western interests.[81]

The Foreign Office line was still firmly in place.

Would the bloody conflict which was now reaching its bitter end have been avoided if those 'voices from Germany' which Halifax was to regret having ignored had been listened to in good time; and had the diplomatic weapons of the Western democracies been turned on Hitler as the Opposition had urged? These were questions which the Foreign Office, after the war, preferred not to have raised, let alone answered.

— X —

Trials and Errors

The work of these people in their opposition was not only *not* supported by foreign countries but was actually made more difficult. . . . This evidence is of the utmost importance in carrying on the defence and as much as I can, I will fight for this evidence.

German Defence Counsel
International Military Tribunal
Nuremberg

It appears that after carefully weighing all the evidence and pointing out that it was chiefly in favour of von Weizsäcker, the majority of the Judges reached the judgment, nevertheless, that he was guilty.

Foreign Office Memorandum

IN 1945, there being no longer in existence any German state which they could represent, German diplomats abroad were being repatriated from their host countries at the Allies' request. As public servants, they automatically came under suspicion. Von Weizsäcker was at the Embassy in the Vatican. As his home in Berlin had been destroyed, he wanted to go to his mother-in-law's house at Lindau. But this was in the French Zone. Occupation regulations on the movement of Germans inside Germany necessitated special permission. Weizsäcker confidently sought assistance from influential quarters abroad. Through the British Minister at the Vatican he stated that he was sure that 'if Mr Churchill or the similar highest authorities in the United States were apprised of his request, there would be no doubt of its being granted in view of all that was known of him in London and Washington.'[1] The Vatican, aware of his efforts on behalf of the persecuted Churches during the Nazi régime and of his interventions with the German military authorities in Rome during the war, made its own approach to London on his behalf. The Papal Nuncio, Monsignor Godfrey, wrote to Sir Orme Sargent that Baron von Weizsäcker had intimated to the Holy See that 'he believes that his attitude towards Nazism and the war is known to the British authorities and for that reason he ventures to hope that his request may be favourably received.'[2]

This misplaced confidence in the past was shared by another notable member of the Opposition. Theo Kordt was to be repatriated from Switzerland to the contiguous zone of occupied Germany, which happened to be the French Zone. He too had lost his home and he and his wife wished to go to his mother-in-law's house in the Rhineland – the British Zone. Permission would be needed. Kordt, too, looked to those Englishmen who, before the war, had known of his opposition to Hitler's foreign policies and his efforts to confound them: Lord Halifax, R. A. Butler, Vansittart, Christie. Kordt's first approach, in August, 1945 was to R. A. Butler, Minister of State at the Foreign Office in 1939. If he was unable to help, wrote Kordt, he would be obliged if Butler would regard this letter as unwritten.[3] It would appear that that is exactly what happened, as in October Kordt addressed further appeals, to Lord Halifax and Lord Vansittart. In a telegram to Halifax at his Embassy in Washington, he set out the nature of his difficulty, adding that 'my feelings regarding war and its instigators are well known to you and have not altered.' Halifax took no special steps to help. He merely forwarded Kordt's telegram to Cadogan in London with a note: 'You will know if it is desirable or possible to comply with his request.' It was a month before Cadogan replied, enclosing a copy of a letter he had written to Vansittart on the same subject.[4]

Vansittart, too, had received a telegram from Kordt. He referred it to the Foreign Office from which he was now retired. But this was the Vansittart of *Black Record*, not of the secret meetings in Kensington. The Foreign Office, he suggested, might want to act deeming it better that Kordt should be back in Germany rather than remaining in Switzerland where 'he would inevitably do some propaganda.' No doubt this was a coded reference to the possibility that Kordt might talk about his relations with the British Foreign Office. He himself, wrote Vansittart, had seen little of Kordt and that mainly in the last weeks before the war. From his 'limited experience of the man' he would say that he did not want war with the West. However:

> What he really wanted was a German maximum, without war with *us*. His real game was to get a free hand in expansion to the limit, including Russia. I tried in vain to explain to him that nobody in their senses would ever agree to let Germany have a free hand anywhere, but Kordt was riddled with the notion of expansion. . . . I think he hated the Nazi Party for personal and public reasons. But of course he would have accepted their conquests. . . .[5]

This unrecognisable version of his relationship with the man who had striven against not only German aggression but British appeasement and was now seeking to reach the only roof available to himself and his family, was penned by Vansittart from the comfort of his country house, Denham Place.

The Foreign Office expended much time and effort in an attempt not to help. It was three weeks before Cadogan replied to Vansittart. It took him some time to get to the point, which was that the only way of getting Kordt and his family back to the British Zone was to arrange this as a subsequent move with the authorities in the French Zone. 'We should be very reluctant to raise this issue by taking up a particular case.' He did not explain why the French should raise any difficulties about the Kordt family passing through their Zone. If Vansittart felt obliged to say anything to Kordt, continued Cadogan, it should be that 'no immediate arrangements can be made for his and his family's return to the British Zone in preference to the resettlement of other displaced persons in a similar position.' Vansittart was grateful for this reply: 'The last thing I should wish to do would be to intervene in favour of Kordt to ask for any exception to be made in his case. . . . I would greatly prefer not to answer him myself.' Perhaps it would be possible for somebody at the Foreign Office 'to cause a brief reply to be sent to him.'[6]

This was an early indication of the attitude inside the British Foreign Office towards Weizsäcker and the Kordt brothers which was to prevail after the war. But if the British thought that these ghosts from the past had been laid, they were much mistaken.

Erich Kordt's homecoming took a very different form. He had been banished to Tokyo by Ribbentrop in April, 1941 and a year later was further removed into outer darkness to a non-political post in China. The end of the war found him in Shanghai, where his diplomatic duties were restricted to trade matters. This brought him into contact with an intelligence officer for the US Foreign Economic Administration, E. A. Bayne. The two men became friendly and Bayne began to learn something of Kordt's background. Realising the importance of this from the intelligence point of view, he interviewed Kordt at his home in the German Embassy late in September, 1945. (Problems of shipping space delayed the repatriation of German diplomats from the Far East.) As a result, Bayne asked him to put his story on paper. Kordt found this a painful task, as he explained to Bayne in a letter dated 2nd October which accompanied his manuscript: 'Thinking about things of the past calls up many bitter memories for me.' One concern was close to his heart. He had written about matters upon which, in other circumstances, he had pledged secrecy. He knew little of the fate of his friends in the Opposition and although he had agreed to mention names, he asked the American for his 'word as a gentleman' that the material should not be made public: 'The efforts of my friends were considerable, even if all endeavours failed, and I feel I must protect them against cheap contempt which easily attaches itself to failure.' Kordt also handed to Bayne a series of notebooks in which he had recorded, as cryptically as he could for his own safety and those of others, a distillation of the development of 'the evil in Germany.' In a further letter of 23rd October, he again pleaded for caution in using the notes and reserved editorial control.[7]

On 13th October Bayne sent Kordt's material from Shanghai to the Chief of the Enemy Branch of the Intelligence Service of the FEA in Washington. A covering memorandum related the circumstances of his contacts with the German diplomat. Referring to the importance of Dr Kordt's knowledge of pre-war and war-time European and world politics, Bayne referred particularly to his knowledge of German-Russian affairs and German-British relationships, 'much of which is not known by the United States Government.' He urged the removal of Kordt to the United States for reasons of personal security and for obvious purposes of further interrogation.

Bayne enclosed Kordt's *curriculum vitae*; a list of some 40 members of the Foreign Ministry whose anti-Nazi credentials were beyond question (including Weizsäcker and Schmidt, Hitler's interpreter): and a long, detailed account of Kordt's own diplomatic career. The latter included accounts of all Erich's and Theo's activities vis-à-vis the British Foreign Office and the meetings with Vansittart and Conwell-Evans. Most particularly, he described Theo's clandestine visit to Sir Horace Wilson and subsequently to Lord Halifax to deliver the Opposition's critical message in September, 1938.[8]

Bayne also delivered copies of the material to the office of the US Chief of Counsel for Prosecution of Axis Criminality, Robert H. Jackson. He handed them to an aide who sent them with a memorandum to the Chief of Counsel: the material had been delivered by Bayne for whatever purposes it might be needed but also to determine whether Kordt should be brought immediately from Shanghai to Nuremberg as a potential witness. Jackson's reaction was brief and to the point. He circled Kordt's name with his pen and wrote: 'Bring him here. R.H.J.'.[9]

Kordt was flown to the United States under an assumed name. He was briefly reunited after seven years with the confidential secretary,

Hilde Waldo – now living in California – who had witnessed some of the comings and goings in Cornwall Gardens (and whose exit from Germany had been facilitated by Vansittart). She had already given Bayne an account from her own knowledge of the Kordt brothers' oppositional activities.[10] Kordt was then flown from Washington to Nuremberg, furnished with a certificate issued by Riddelberger, Chief of the Division of Central European affairs in the State Department, to the effect that he was under the charge of the War Department. As a key figure in the anti-Nazi Opposition he would probably be used as a witness in the War Crimes Prosecution. Because of information he had given, the State Department had an interest in him and his disposition after he had given his testimony.[11]

After his arrival at Nuremberg, where he was housed with other witnesses in spartan conditions, Kordt produced a paper for Bayne under the heading *Notes on the Foreign Office Conspiracy against the Nazi Régime*. In this he detailed the efforts of the diplomats at the Wilhelmstrasse to encompass Hitler's downfall, in association with others outside such as Goerdeler, Canaris, Oster, Halder and his brother Theo. Kordt was in a position to supply, from the inside, an exposé of the perfidious activities of Ribbentrop. He also set out the difficulties which beset the conspirators in trying to carry out their plans in a police state. Nevertheless, had the leadership of the régime been destroyed, he had no doubt that 'the machinery of the opposition in the Ministry of War, the Foreign Office and the Police Headquarters of Berlin would have been sufficient to carry through the first stage of a *putsch*.'[12] Kordt could not himself speak for events after he had left for the Far East in 1941, but he arranged for the history to be continued in a separate account by a friend, a former officer, Dr A. Scheidt, who provided Bayne with an account of the 20th July attempt. Later, his brother Theo filled in the details of an earlier chapter when he supplied Bayne with a copy of an account he had written for a member of the British Secret Service on the subject of *The Anti-Nazi Crisis in 1938–9: Events and Personalities in London.*[13]

Meanwhile, Bayne, now returned to civilian life, pursued his own investigations with a view to writing an account of the events recounted by the Kordts. To this end he addressed himself to Lord Halifax at the British Embassy in Washington. In a letter to the Ambassador's Private Secretary dated 8 April 1946 he referred briefly to the 'attempts to influence British policy by members of an anti-

Hitler conspiracy working chiefly through Theo Kordt' who was in close contact with Sir Horace Wilson, R. A. Butler, Philip Conwell-Evans and Sir Robert Vansittart. The conspiracy, of which Erich Kordt was also a member, 'as was probably known at the time,' was headed by General Beck and supported by many in the German Foreign Office and the General Staff. Bayne wanted to know whether Lord Halifax could substantiate the statements made by the Kordt brothers and others, 'the internal coherency of which makes them extremely credible.'[14] The reply was brief. The Ambassador, wrote the Secretary, 'does not feel that he is able to give you much help.' The buck was neatly passed with the suggestion that Bayne's best course would be to write to Lord Vansittart, whose address was thoughtfully provided.

Vansittart's reply was longer but managed to avoid any confirmation of the Kordts' activities in London, while at the same time undermining their records as opponents of Hitler. Although both were anti-Nazi, wrote Vansittart, 'neither of them, so far as I know, ever did anything to demonstrate the fact':

> For instance, a considerable effect might have been produced, if Theo had dissociated himself from a war which he knew to be vile, unjust and aggressive and had decided to stay in London. Of course, he did not. Both of them, indeed, to the best of my knowledge, continued to do their best for Germany in official positions. . . .
> I understand that there is some prospect of their being re-employed in Germany. It may well be that no better material can be found. . . .[15]

This vicious letter finally reached Bayne in Shanghai where he was now in US government service. Evidently he passed on Vansittart's remarks to Erich Kordt, who replied from Nuremberg on 14th August that he was astonished at the suggestion that Theo should 'have saved his skin by staying in London.' Apart from the fact that his brother would have considered this cowardly if nothing more could be achieved there, Erich distinctly remembered that it was 'Bob' (i.e. Vansittart – German letters were censored) who had urgently asked him to make himself available in some neutral country. He and his brother could rightly be accused of not having succeeded and their failure was fatal; but they could refute the reproach of not having 'demonstrated' for the easy benefit of the Gestapo. He was at a loss to understand Vansittart's reference to 'one of them' being 'an advocate of expansion eastward.' Both 'the Ks', wrote Erich, had had only one aim: to finish the Nazi régime and to impede the outbreak of war.[16] Erich passed on to Theo the gist of Vansittart's accusations, which he too could not understand. 'Bob' had never, throughout their many discussions, given any hint that he disagreed with Theo's intention to continue the struggle. And how to explain the arrangement for maintaining contact using the verse of Horace as a password to facilitate the visits of Conwell-Evans in 1939/40? Politically, he and Vansittart had been united in the desire to prevent or to shorten 'the insane war.'[17] Such ill-feeling was baffling and unexpected. It had never occurred to Theo that the failure of his former British colleagues to help with his repatriation had been due to animosity. His attitude to them was quite different. When complying with Bayne's request for an account of his experience in 'the crisis years of 1938/9,' he had shown himself particularly sensitive to the British position regarding their pre-war (and wartime) contacts:'

> I would be very grateful to you if you would be good enough to regard it as strictly confidential since I do not know whether my British friends would like a discussion of those negotiations, at least at the present time. . . . At least it would be decent to ask for their consent before making any use of it. . . . It is for that reason that I refrained from showing these recollections to any person not immediately pertinent to it. My desire is quite the same as Erich's: I want to serve the idea of truth which appears to me more important than anything else. . . .[18]

In his book *Nicht aus den Akten* Erich Kordt stated that, rightly or wrongly, the brothers decided after the war to keep silent publicly about the confidential discussions in which British personalities had participated. What was the point of opening old wounds? But when 'in a grotesque distortion of the facts' former State Secretary von Weizsäcker was arraigned as one of the chief instigators of Hitler's aggressive war, it became, he wrote, a 'moral duty' to speak out.[19]

The prospect of unwelcome revelations on a wide scale loomed large as the date approached for the opening in December 1945, of what the Foreign Office accurately described as 'war crimes demonstrations' at Nuremberg. The British found the Americans accommodating. Not normally averse to levelling criticism at past British policies, they did not want to give the defendants (of whose guilt no-one was in doubt) an opportunity of obscuring the issues by counter-attacking the record of other countries. The Chief American Prosecutor, Robert H. Jackson, agreed with the points raised with him by the Chief British Prosecutor, Sir David Maxwell-Fyfe, when the indictments were being drawn up:

> I think it is desirable to avoid discussion of the ideology or political background of this war. We should hold closely to our single point, which is regardless of the merit of the policies involved. . . . I think the indictment should avoid argumentation.

The two lawyers would eliminate from the final version of the documents controversial statements 'upon which the defence would inevitably concentrate.'[20]

The plea of 'public policy' had already been raised with Maxwell-Fyfe by Dean against the possibility of 'prominent British subjects' being called. He suggested a common policy should be followed by the four prosecutors 'since we do not want to be alone in the position of honestly admitting that it is against public policy for this or that man to attend.'[21] Ribbentrop made an application for Philip Conwell-Evans as a witness on his behalf. Unaware of the latter's early defection from a sympathetic interest in Nazism, Ribbentrop no doubt believed that he had in his old friend a strong defence witness to testify to his lasting desire to establish a close alliance between Britain and Germany.[22] When the application came before the Tribunal for a ruling, Maxwell-Fyfe jumped all over it. Who was this Professor Conwell-Evans? *He* had never heard of him. Why, he wasn't even in *Who's Who*, where all persons of consequence appeared. His evidence 'would not help the Tribunal and is not relevant to the issue before the Court.' Application refused.[23] Neither Christie (who *was* in *Who's Who*) nor Conwell-Evans took any part in the proceedings at Nuremberg. But then they were really witnesses for the prosecution – of the Foreign Office.

But the British had no control over German witnesses. Hans Bernd Gisevius, leading member of the Opposition and one of its few survivors, took the stand on behalf of the former Reichminister of Economics and President of the Reichsbank, Hjalmar Schacht. The problem of 'avoiding discussion of the political background of the war' now became a live issue.

A handwritten pencil note on a document among some personal papers of Leith-Ross, Economic Adviser to the Government, records that he had learned from Montagu Norman (Governor of the Bank of England) that 'HMG did not want to put Schacht on the list of war criminals', but that the Americans had insisted as they 'wanted to make a play with economic preparations for war.' Norman 'did not think there was any risk of his being hanged.'[24] Schacht was of course well known in Britain. Montagu Norman was godfather to his son. He had had clandestine discussions with Leith-Ross. Even the Prime Minister had received him secretly. On 21 December 1938 Chamberlain told the Cabinet that although the Press said he had not seen Schacht – then on a visit to London – he had in fact talked to him for an hour and 'had discussed conditions in Germany at length. Schacht had made it quite clear that he was quite out of sympathy with the present régime in Germany.'[25] As has been seen, as early as 1936 Schacht was writing personally to the British Foreign Secretary, Eden, warning him against Hitler. Certainly he had begun by supporting Hitler when he came to power, believing that he himself would then be able to call the tune in the financial direction of the State. His disillusion with Hitler brought him into contact with Opposition circles and he became an active member.

In the course of his testimony for the defence, Gisevius gave a detailed account of the activities of the Opposition and of Schacht's part in them.[26] His account raised various questions which were unwelcome to the prosecution and which indeed presented difficulties for himself. Dr Dix, Schacht's counsel, introduced the subject of the Opposition's contacts abroad. In reply, Gisevius stated that co-operation with foreign countries before or during the war was a very controversial subject: 'If I am to talk about it, then it is at least as important for me to state the reasons which led these people to carry on such discussions with foreign countries as it is to give times and dates.' Counsel was sure the Tribunal would permit this. But the President (Lord Justice Lawrence) disagreed: 'I think the Tribunal thinks you are going into too great detail over these matters . . . which seem to me not very important.' But Counsel felt that the gravity and intensity of the activities of these conspirators should be substantiated in detail.

PRESIDENT: But you have touched upon them since 10 o'clock this morning.

DR DIX: If the Defendant Goering and others had time for days to describe the entire course of events from

> their point of view, I think that justice demands
> that those men, represented in this courtroom by
> the Defendant Schacht, who fought against that
> system under most dreadful conditions of terror,
> should also be permitted to tell in detail the story
> of their Opposition movement.

The President 'hoped that he would deal with it as shortly as possible and without unnecessary details.' Gisevius responded that there were very detailed and weighty discussions with foreign countries in order to try everything possible to prevent the outbreak of war, or at least to shorten it or keep it from spreading.

> I owe it to my conscience and above all to those who participated and
> are now dead, to state here that those matters which I have described
> weighed very heavily upon their consciences. We knew that we would
> be accused of conspiring with foreign countries.

The President replied 'that we are not really here for the purpose of considering people who have, unfortunately, lost their lives.' But Gisevius insisted that there were relatives still alive who might become the subject of unjust accusations to the effect that those whom they had lost were guilty of high treason: 'Our friends who did these things rejected the accusation of high treason because we felt that we were morally obliged to take these steps.'

Gisevius then recounted the steps which had been taken in 1938, when London was informed of 'the existence of an opposition group which was resolved to go to any lengths.' In the name of this group the British Government was continuously informed of what was happening and that it was absolutely necessary to make it clear, to the German people and the generals, that every step across the Czech border would constitute for the Western Powers a reason for war. Then, without naming the principals involved, Gisevius related the 'unusual step' by which the British Government was warned that Hitler's ambitions extended beyond the Sudetenland to the whole of Czechoslovakia and that 'if the British Government on its side were to remain firm, we could give the assurance that there would be no war.'

It was at this session in the witness box that the first public reference was heard to the Vatican connection in the winter of 1939/40 which General Halder had revealed in his interrogation. Gisevius spoke of the Pope's personal efforts to confirm to the British that there existed a trustworthy group in Germany with whom talks could be undertaken. A sort of 'gentleman's agreement' had been reached as a result of which the Opposition believed they could assure the generals that 'in the event of the overthrow of the Hitler régime, an agreement could be reached with a decent civil German government.' He then recounted the reception which Halder had received when he took the report of the negotiations to Brauchitsch. Lord Justice Lawrence felt that *one sentence* 'about some negotiations with the Vatican' could be properly given but all other details were unnecessary.

Dr Dix returned to the dangerous subject of foreigners when Schacht himself took the stand.[27] But now it was the American member of the Tribunal who tangled with the defence counsel. Again, the subject was the support given to Hitler by other countries. Schacht declared that, although the Nuremberg rallies were Party functions and not State occasions, the Diplomatic Corps had attended 'in large numbers, with great ostentation and seated in the front rows.' Mr Justice Jackson found this statement 'objectionable.' The conduct of the Ambassadors of other countries was 'utterly beyond probative value.' Dr Dix thought otherwise. It was of prime importance to know who, throughout the 'oppositional activities' of Gisevius and his friends, gave them moral, spiritual or any other support and who did not support them:

> I, the Defence, maintain that this opposition group . . . not only received no support from abroad, but that foreigners rendered opposition more difficult. . . . It was of decisive value for the attitude of these men of this oppositional group what position the foreign countries took to this régime; . . . This evidence is of the utmost importance to me in the carrying on of the defence . . . and as much as I can, I will fight for this piece of evidence.

Counsel wished to refer to the honours accorded the régime abroad and to the representatives and State visitors who came from overseas to pay their respects. Dr Dix had just begun with the British Labour Party delegation of 1935, when Lord Justice Lawrence intervened to rule that specific details of visits should not be given. Mr Justice Jackson took the objection further and with some heat:

This thing is entirely irrelevant. . . . I cannot understand how it constitutes any defence for mitigation for Schacht to show that the foreign powers maintained intercourse with Germany even at a period of its degeneration.

Schacht replied to the court's objections by claiming that the stream of visitors conveyed respect and recognition for the Führer which enhanced his stature in the eyes of the people and made it difficult for the Opposition to disseminate a contrary view. Cadogan had been making essentially the same point, when, in 1939, he deprecated the revelation of any evidence that the British Government had been pursuing appeasement while 'the real nature of the régime was already known.'[28] And in 1947 Sir Duncan Wilson, formerly head of SOE, in a report on *German Reactions to the Nuremberg Trials*, recorded that 'the Allies were considered to have some responsibility for maintaining diplomatic relations with the régime after its criminal nature had been established.'[29]

The Americans lost the battle for Schacht. The Tribunal found that the case against him of planning aggressive war could not be established beyond reasonable doubt and he was acquitted.

With the conclusion of the trials of the major war criminals the Americans – the only nation which could afford to do so – embarked on a series of trials under the categories of industrialists, the Army (the High Command) and selected civil servants. They set up their own so-called Military Tribunals and used the same facilities at Nuremberg. The Americans created a legal basis for these trials by relying on Control Council Law No. 10 (which had been the foundation of the Nuremberg trials), reinforced by various executive orders, US Military Government ordinances and general orders. The other Powers took no part in the indictment or presentation of the cases. The American flag was displayed in the courtroom and the Court Marshal opened each day's proceedings with a request for God's blessing on the United States.

There were twelve separate proceedings of which No. 11 – known as 'The Ministries Case' – dealt with the central political and economic administration of the Third Reich in Berlin. Twenty-one civil servants were arraigned, of which former State Secretary von Weizsäcker was one. He had to share the dock with former Nazi officials, and members of the SS and the Gestapo. The defendants were charged upon eight counts covering planning of aggressive war and initiating aggressive war; crimes against humanity, slave labour, and membership of criminal organisations. In Weizsäcker's case these were eventually reduced to two: Count I: participation in the planning, preparation, initiation and waging of wars of aggression; Count V: war crimes and crimes against humanity from 1938–45. The case lasted from 20 December 1947 to 14 April 1949.

The Tribunal consisted exclusively of American citizens; three judges from, respectively, Michigan, Oregon and Iowa. Only one of the three was a Federal judge: the other two were members of State judiciaries. Not one of them knew any German and the standard of simultaneous translation of the Court proceedings was so low that it is difficult sometimes to follow the transcripts coherently. One of the defence team wrote to the *New York Herald Tribune* that the translations bore only a very remote resemblance to the meaning of the original document and sometimes stated the direct opposite.[30] Halder was astonished when testifying to be asked at one point if he could put the verb a little earlier in his sentences as this would make it much easier to translate!

The Chief Prosecutor was General Telford Taylor. In his opening statement he declared that the defendants from the Foreign Ministry stood 'on the top rung of dishonour' and had so perverted diplomacy that no German diplomat would be trusted for decades to come. 'The broad sweep of the Nazi conspiracy has already been seen at Nuremberg . . . and everywhere is the hand of Baron von Weizsäcker.' After the opening he took no further part in the proceedings but handed over to his Deputy, Robert F. Kempner. Kempner was a former member of the Department of Political Police in the Prussian Ministry of the Interior. He had left Germany in 1936 and had been an American citizen since the end of the war. He was therefore in a better position than any of the prosecution team to be aware of the danger of taking official documents issued during the Nazi régime at their face value. Having virtually no witnesses against Weizsäcker to call, Kempner based the prosecution case almost exclusively on documents. A large staff spent over two years working over a mountain of captured German Foreign Office archives, held by the Allies at the Document Centre in Berlin. The defence was allowed only two representatives for two months to work on these papers. (The defence computed their research at the Document Centre as the equivalent of five working months against the prosecution effort of 160 working months.)[31]

With the help of Weizsäcker family connections in Switzerland, efforts were made to engage an American counsel. General William Donovan, formerly of the OSS, was approached but he demanded a colossal fee and unlimited expenses. In the end a Washington attorney, Warren Magee, who had some experience of Germany and of denazification procedures, was approached. He would not accept without a preliminary meeting with the German counsel so Dr Helmuth Becker, by a special dispensation of the Court, travelled to Zurich to meet him. Dr Becker brought with him supportive letters from the Vatican. A handwritten letter from Pope Pius XII at Easter, 1946, extended his blessing and promise of prayers to Weizsäcker and his wife.[32] On the 23rd August that year, Monsignor Montini (later Pope Paul VI), the Secretary of State, acknowledged Weizsäcker's farewell letter of respect and gratitude on leaving Vatican City to return to Germany. His Holiness's best wishes accompanied him, and his prayers for God's protection of his family. These documents and the assurance by Becker of wide-reaching foreign support decided the American to take the appointment as Chief Counsel for the defence. He was duly appointed by order of the Court on 29 December 1947. Fortunately, the Court had blundered. In fact, according to an agreement between the Powers when the International Military Tribunals were set up, no outside lawyers were permitted to defend. The defence team was considerably strengthened by the advent of an American attorney as co-counsel with Dr Becker. As a diplomat, much of Weizsäcker's defence would have to be obtained abroad. But Germans were not allowed to travel outside Germany, or even to move freely between the Zones of Occupation.

Magee was a match for his fellow-Americans on the other side. He found that there was only one telephone for the defence team, while each American prosecuting counsel had one on his desk and one for his secretary. Magee got some changes made. There was a law library at Nuremberg to which only the prosecution had free access: the defence had to request individual books in writing. Magee insisted on being supplied with a complete catalogue of the contents.[33] It was also due to the presence of Magee that the Tribunal in the Ministries Case became the first of the US Military Courts to grant the German defence access to documents. Even so, as Magee pointed out in his opening address, there was still no question of equal access to both sides.

Before the engagement of the American lawyer, the defence had already been able to make some important contacts abroad. Dr Becker's wife was French and was therefore able to travel to Rome, where she spent many hours with Fr Leiber, the Pope's confidential assistant who had acted in the Opposition approaches to the Pontiff in the winter of 1939/40. Dr Becker himself was allowed to go to Baden-Baden, headquarters of the French Zone, to meet Carl Burckhardt, now Swiss Minister in Paris, who came as a guest of the Military Governor, General Koenig. The two men held their conference on a bench in the park.[34] But the really weighty evidence on Weizsäcker's behalf had to come from Britain, and only the Foreign Office could provide it.

Weizsäcker and the Kordt brothers had assumed that their known efforts against Hitler would now stand them in good stead in calling on former British colleagues for support for the defence. Dr Becker wrote to Ivone Kirkpatrick as the closest colleague of the late Sir Nevile Henderson, informing him that Weizsäcker stood accused of participation in the planning, preparation, initiation and waging of wars of aggression. Dr Becker asked for 'written testimony dealing with the strenuous efforts of Baron von Weizsäcker to maintain the peace of the world and the concepts of decency and honour among nations in the face of so many odds and at great personal risk.' It would be difficult to give the Court a true picture of his almost superhuman efforts without the help of those with real inside knowledge who could cite specific instances. Kirkpatrick replied that he had some difficulty in complying with this request. From 'second-hand reports at the time' he believed that Weizsäcker was 'unsympathetic to the Nazi régime.' But Kirkpatrick also managed to be precisely damaging:

> Unlike some of his colleagues, von Weizsäcker never made in my hearing any remark derogatory to the Nazi government or their policy. On occasions, when his official duties compelled him to do so, he defended Hitler's policy with skill and vigour. I left Germany in December 1938. I am therefore not in a position to give any evidence in regard to the conduct of Baron von Weizsäcker immediately before the war.[35]

The implication that because he had left Berlin he knew nothing further of Weizsäcker was, to put it at its mildest, disingenuous. He did not mention that he had left Berlin to become adviser on German affairs at the Foreign Office and had unique access to evidence of the State Secretary's efforts to engage the British in taking a firm stand against Hitler.

Theo Kordt, meanwhile, had taken on the big guns. On 17 December 1948 he wrote to the former Foreign Secretary on Weizsäcker's behalf. On 31 January 1948 Halifax (who had been advised by the Foreign Office to be 'cautious') replied: 'Before the war, so far as my information went, he was in general out of sympathy with the National. Socialist Government and the policy that this Government was pursuing. I have no doubt that those who adjudicate on the charges brought will examine them with thoroughness and fairness.'[36]

Something of the disappointment with which this tepid response was received is to be found in a letter which Theo addressed to Halifax on 24th March. As a former diplomat of a great Power he quite understood, he wrote, the professional reluctance of Foreign Offices to give details of very secret negotiations before at least 30 years have elapsed, but at present he considered it even more important to give full evidence. He was glad, he went on, that Halifax 'had no doubt that those who adjudicate on the charges will examine them with thoroughness and fairness.'

Kordt felt that perhaps his own observations would be considered untimely and unwise but 'I think that people who know about the truth are obliged by their conscience to do what they can to prevent a monstrous development.'[37] It was a good thing, perhaps, that his brother Erich persuaded Theo not to send this letter.[38]

Kordt also wrote at some length to R. A. Butler, the former Minister of State, whom he had known well while at the Embassy. He recalled the occasion when they had walked together in St James's Park on Ascension Day, 1939 and how he had confided in the Minister that Weizsäcker was the personification of the opposition within the Foreign Office and the protector of those engaged in anti-Nazi activity. Butler had in turn revealed to Kordt that the British had changed their policy and entered into negotiations with the Soviet Union. Kordt went on to recall that he had been returning to Berlin that same afternoon and had indicated to Butler that this information would be passed on to Weizsäcker to assist him in his fight against the nefarious intentions of Hitler and Ribbentrop. Kordt concluded his letter by declaring that he was unhappy about the way evidence on behalf of Weizsäcker, including his own, was being rejected by the Court. He now ventured to ask Butler if he could let him have 'a statement which reflects the truth as far as it is known to you.'[39] Butler merely replied:

> I am afraid I have not enough intimate knowledge of Dr Weizsäcker's activities to give you a very convincing reply. All I can say is that it appeared that Dr Weizsäcker was out of sympathy with the National-Socialist Government. I hope you are keeping well.[40]

The most moving appeal of all had been sent long before. On 12 April 1946, while he was still in the Vatican City, Weizsäcker wrote personally to his erstwhile opposite number in the British Foreign Office – Sir Alexander Cadogan. He had just learned that as a result of a law published in the US Zone, he was to be 'classified among a certain category of men who are *ipso facto* defendants, threatened by draconian sentences.' They were obliged to prove their innocence. He himself would prefer not to talk about his lasting endeavours for international understanding and peace. However, 'grotesque as it may appear, I am bound by law, for my family's sake and for my own reputation to ask those, especially non-Germans, who know something about me, if they are prepared to lend me their aid.' He now ventured to ask Cadogan 'for a word which you might deem fit.' As regards collaborations with the British Embassy during that period (1938–1939) Mr Kirkpatrick could furnish this. He expressed his reluctance to bother Cadogan and hoped he would not take amiss 'this appeal to you as a former colleague.'[41]

Cadogan, by this time British representative at the United Nations in New York, forwarded the letter to the Foreign Office with a covering note to Strang asking for advice. He had known Weizsäcker at Geneva – up to the end of 1933. 'I don't think I could give him any testimonial that would do him much good.' This was pretty devious. It was obvious that this was not the relevant period. Weizsäcker himself had specified in his letter 'the decisive period 1938–1939.' Cadogan capped it all by saying: 'I don't know what the Foreign Office know about him'![42] As Permanent Secretary at that time Cadogan *was* the Foreign Office.

Oliver Harvey forwarded Cadogan's letter to Strang, now on the staff of the British Commander-in-Chief in occupied Berlin. 'Our own opinion of him,' he wrote in a covering letter, 'is that he preserved from the time of his service in the German Navy the typical nationalist outlook of a German Naval Officer.' Up to the time of Munich he was genuinely anxious for a peaceful solution and did all he could in that direction. After Munich, 'according to Kirkpatrick who knew him at that time,' continued Harvey, he appeared to have resigned himself to the on-coming war and collaborated, possibly against his better judgment, with Ribbentrop. Kirkpatrick summarised his character by saying that he was probably fundamentally opposed to Nazi policy but had neither the background nor the character to offer any effective opposition during the time in which he was Secretary of State. Harvey concluded by saying that there was unlikely to be any question of Weizsäcker being tried as a war criminal, though it could not be ruled out. Eventually a message was passed to Weizsäcker, by that time held in Nuremberg, simply that his letter to Cadogan had been received.[43]

Early in 1947 Cadogan received an appeal on Weizsäcker's behalf from his niece, Camilla, who had married into the Stauffenberg family. Her uncle's reply is couched in terms more consonant with an affidavit than a family communication. It suggests that the contents were meant for other eyes besides those of Camilla von Stauffenberg – perhaps the defence who would certainly have been aware of her appeal. It would surely have been unnecessary for Cadogan to inform his niece that 'at the beginning of 1934 I went to China, returning to London in the summer of 1936 and remaining there throughout the war.' The most likely possibility is that it was intended as an 'on the record' statement for the Foreign Office. Why else place a copy of a family letter on file? Sir Alexander wrote:

I remember hearing that von Weizsäcker was not in sympathy with the Nazi Government but that, so far as I remember, was pure hearsay, and I know of no facts to show that that was his attitude – still less that he was working with the underground. And I do not remember receiving any definite report from Nevile Henderson on the subject. You will understand that, without any facts to go upon, there is no testimony which I can give, however willing I might be, personally, to believe any evidence to show that he was anti-Nazi. But I am writing to the Foreign Office to ask them to search their archives, in case these contain any documentary evidence that could and should be used in von Weizsäcker's favour.[44]

But this was not a needle-in-a-haystack problem. There would be no need to mount a great search of the archives. The files of 1938–1939 were studded with references to Weizsäcker's initiatives. The documentary evidence of the Kordt brothers' activities, in which they had always acknowledged Weizsäcker's authority, have already been detailed. (And had not Cadogan himself recorded in his diary Theo Kordt's clandestine visit to Downing Street in August, 1938?) There were also on file references to Weizsäcker by name, in connection with advice which he conveyed to the Foreign Office.

On 13 June 1939 Kirkpatrick wrote a minute which distilled the essence of a conversation held between Burckhardt and Makins at Basle, following visits by the High Commissioner to Warsaw, Berlin and Danzig. The main point was that made by Weizsäcker to Burckhardt when they met in Berlin. Kirkpatrick wrote: 'Great Britain should continue to show an absolutely firm front. This is the course advocated by Baron von Weizsäcker and by most well-disposed Germans.' Kirkpatrick concluded his minute:

> If it is decided to print or circulate this report I would suggest that the name of Baron von Weizsäcker should be excised and that he should be called 'a high German official.'

This minute was initialled by Sargent, Vansittart, Butler and by Cadogan who noted 'This was discussed with S. of S. today.' A further note records that on the Secretary of State's instructions a copy of Makins' paper was sent to the Prime Minister and to the Embassies in Berlin, Warsaw, Stockholm, Rome and Moscow.

Kirkpatrick added a rider to his previous minute later that day:

> I drew attention to the fact that Baron von Weizsäcker had expressed the opinion that the best chance for peace now was for His Majesty's Government to show a firm front and to leave only a very small loop-hole for negotiation. . . . It is worth noting that in September last Baron von Weizsäcker had a similar conversation with M. Burckhardt. . . .

A minute by Sargent follows: 'This at all events shows that Weizsäcker is consistent in his advice that the only thing which will make Hitler see reason is the maintenance of a firm front. . . .' Cadogan commented: 'This is worth noting' and Halifax initialled the minutes.[45] There was also the incident, recorded in Cabinet Minutes, of how Weizsäcker had sent a message from Danzig on 22 August 1939 to the British Government to take advantage of Ribbentrop's absence in Moscow to bring pressure to bear directly on Hitler.[46]

These papers clearly record the fact that the Head of the German Foreign Office was giving advice to the British Government on how to resist Hitler's aggression. That in itself was powerful enough defence material, mentioning him, as it does, by name. But there was even stronger evidence: the acknowledgment in writing that the Government was not only receiving such advice but acting upon it. The incident has been related of the argument in Central Department when Vansittart insisted on protecting his sources (the Kordt brothers) from the indiscretion of Sir Nevile Henderson. The insistence of Vansittart at that time that Henderson did not, and must not, know of the existence of the Foreign Office sources in the Opposition makes a nonsense of Cadogan's excuse to his niece that he had never received any definite report from Nevile Henderson of Weizsäcker's possible connection with 'the underground.' Sargent had chosen to carry the argument further by the unusual method of a personal letter to Vansittart on Foreign Office writing paper. (Did he feel that what he had to say should not be on file?) If Henderson was not fully briefed, argued Sargent:

> . . . he may well misunderstand some of our actions which may be the direct result of the advice we have received. For instance, in the early days of last September [1938] Weizsäcker's advice was, through Burckhardt, to send a strong warning to Hitler. It was largely on this advice that the Cabinet decided to instruct Sir N. Henderson at Nuremberg to deliver the famous message to Hitler. If you remember, Sir N. Henderson demurred, and eventually won the day, but if he had known that we were acting on Weizsäcker's advice, it is possible that he would not have taken so strong a line about it.[47]

If there had been no other evidence of the State Secretary's actions and attitudes, this categorical statement that the British Government had acted on his advice given in order to avert war and maintain peace would have demolished his case before it came to Court, had it been communicated to the Americans at a high level. But to have revealed all this would have cast light on aspects of pre-war policy which the British strove to conceal, above all from the dreaded Americans.

Nevertheless, there was some concern in the War Crimes Section of the Foreign Office. One member expressed the view that 'it is absolutely wrong that Weizsäcker should be prosecuted for war crimes.' Another made the point equally forcefully in a minute to Patrick Dean: 'It seems monstrous that von Weizsäcker should be tried on these charges and by a bench of backwoods Middle West judges who have got the job because they are useless at home. Is there nothing we can do?' Dean's reply distilled in one word the Office attitude: 'Nothing.'[48]

Not surprisingly, Burckhardt raised his voice in an attempt to get the case withdrawn. As Weizsäcker's friend and confidant he knew exactly what efforts he had made for peace. The records show, without any details, that he wrote to R. A. Butler, that his letter was passed to the Secretary of State (now Ernest Bevin) and according to the Private Secretary was then passed to Germany, but there is no indication of its ultimate destination.[49]

The German members of Weizsäcker's defence team had only been able to write letters to England and await the dusty answers. The American counsel, Magee, was able to go there and he arrived in London in April, 1948. 'Kordt and the counsel for the defence have been as busy as bees trying to collect evidence,' noted Sir Orme Sargent, who had succeeded Cadogan as Head of the Foreign Office.[50]

Magee must have suspected, from the tone of the reply he received from Christopher Steel, that he might not achieve very concrete results. Steel had served in the Berlin Embassy under Nevile Henderson. Now he was back there as Political Adviser to the Military Governor. Steel had consulted the Foreign Office about his response to Magee. He would like, he wrote to London:

> to give what I know to have been the general opinion of the Ambassador and the Embassy of Weizsäcker: namely, that he loathed Ribbentrop and the Nazi gang and seemed to be hanging on in the hope of preventing the Foreign Ministry from getting into worse hands. I should like to give them a statement on these lines because Weizsäcker behaved well to us and I honestly think he did his best. But first I must know the Office's attitude to all this.

Patrick Dean gave it to him. While indicating that the State Secretary strongly disliked Ribbentrop and the Nazis:

You should add that you cannot testify that to your own personal knowledge he put into words or action what you believe to have been his personal feelings and that you therefore regret that you can cite no definite positive instance of anti-Nazi behaviour on his part.

Steel adhered to these directions. He wrote to Magee that the British Embassy had felt that Weizsäcker was genuinely anxious to avoid war: 'On the other hand, he did not translate his feelings into any action that I knew of.'

Magee secured a clutch of declarations from Butler, Kirkpatrick and Steel. Kirkpatrick managed to be not quite so derogatory as he had been in his letter to Dr Becker. Butler was personally in a position to provide what the defence really wanted: an example of action on the part of the State Secretary. The Minister, it may be remembered, had been on the receiving end in London of Weizsäcker's message, telephoned by Burckhardt from Berne in September, 1938. But he ended his affidavit with the words: 'I have no evidence as to the manner in which he translated his sentiments into action.'[51] (Cadogan once described Butler as 'a most baleful man, craven pacifist, muddle-headed appeaser and nit-wit.')[52]

Although Magee was not able to meet Halifax, the former Foreign Secretary supplied an affidavit which handsomely redeemed his earlier non-committal reply to Theo Kordt. It also completely contradicted what his former colleagues were writing to Weizsäcker's defence counsel. Halifax testified that though he himself had never had any personal contact with him, State Secretary von Weizsäcker was frequently reported to him, by his Foreign Office advisers and by the British Ambassador, as being a convinced opponent of Nazi ideals and policies, and as *using his official position* in the Ministry of Foreign Affairs to hinder, so far as lay in his power, the execution of the policy pursued by Ribbentrop.[53]

Halifax's testimony had the added distinction of being the only one of the four documents supplied to Magee which was a legal affidavit sworn before a Commissioner of Oaths. For whatever reason – and we must forebear to speculate – Steel and Kirkpatrick had merely had their signatures attested by the Head of the German Department; Butler by the Head of the Conservative Party Secretariat, neither of whom were Commissioners. In due course, their 'affidavits' were rejected by the Court as not being legal documents. They were obliged to replace them with properly sworn testimony.

In forwarding Kirkpatrick's – now legal – document to Magee, the Foreign Office sank to a new low:

> There is one small matter, the question of the fee for the affidavit. While we have no wish to be niggling, we understand that it is customary in such cases for the affidavit fee to form part of the costs of the party on whose behalf it is made. The sum involved is 10/6d and if you can let me have this I will see that the account is duly settled.[54]

Meanwhile, Magee had embarked on another journey, to Rome. The prosecution, having learned that the defence had received a personal communication from the Pope supportive of Weizsäcker, declared publicly that if the Vatican were familiar with the contents of the documents submitted against Weizsäcker, such a communication would not have been made and they sent the Vatican what purported to be damaging material. Magee moved quickly. Through the good offices of the Pope's representative in Germany, a private interview with the Pope was arranged for him on 27th April. This extraordinary gesture was not only proof of Weizsäcker's personal standing with the Pope, but an acknowledgment of the Church's indebtedness to him for assistance and protection both in Rome, where he intervened with the German military authorities and thwarted the Gestapo, but particularly in Germany under the Nazi régime. But the Pope would also have had to be assured of Weizsäcker's absolute integrity. This was, after all, a man on trial as a war criminal. It was a delicate matter. The Pope could hardly gainsay the prosecution's communication. He asked Magee for advice as to how best the matter could be handled. Magee pointed out that His Holiness had received a letter from Frau von Weizsäcker advising him of the process against her husband and asking for his assistance. He might now answer that letter in positive terms.

The following day, as he was preparing to leave for Germany, two uniformed members of the Papal Guard presented themselves at Magee's hotel bearing the Pope's letter to Frau von Weizsäcker. Dated 2 May 1948, it read:

> We were pleased to accept your letter written some time ago in which you appealed for help in view of the situation of your husband. Your esteemed family may be sure of our participation as well as our prayers, that in all things may God's blessing reign over it.[55]

A copy of that letter adorns the wall of Warren Magee's office today.

Before the trial opened, while Weizsäcker was still living freely at home in Lindau and the American prosecutors were preparing their case against him, incriminating publicity was spread in the press, even to the extent of reproducing a document purporting to link Weizsäcker with the deportation of Jews to Auschwitz. He was also accused of persecution of the churches. The result of this publicity was to alert many interested people and the defence received an avalanche of support in the form of affidavits.[56] Their very sources provided incontrovertible evidence of Weizsäcker's innocence. Not only was evidence of his involvement in the Opposition given by surviving members such as Gisevius, Schlabrendorff, Halder, Schoenfeld, Kessel, Selzam, Etzdorf. More cogent perhaps were the voices of the widows of the 20th July conspirators: Dohnyani, Canaris, Haeften. Clarita von Trott declared that, knowing the principles for which her husband had sacrificed his life, it was almost unbearable to her to know that Herr von Weizsäcker, whom he had respected so much, should be one of the defendants in the trial. Numerous statements by former colleagues (themselves exonerated by denazification courts) created a picture of the extraordinary way in which the Foreign Office was forced to function under the eyes of Ribbentrop's informers. Kempner subsequently derided these witnesses as 'a mutual insurance society.' General Halder also described how, when he took over from Beck as Chief of Staff, the latter advised him to maintain continuous contact with Weizsäcker as he himself had done. Halder did so and kept the State Secretary informed of the *putsch* planned in September, 1938. Schlabrendorff testified in Court and spoke at length and in detail about the Opposition, much as Gisevius had done at the major trial in Nuremberg. And he too had already told his story in his book: *The Secret War Against Hitler*. The prosecution dismissed the Opposition as an 'unresisting resistance. . . . The testimony of von Weizsäcker's witnesses and dozens of affidavits on this point are extremely nebulous and padded with hearsay and *ex post facto* wishful thinking.' Weizsäcker himself, it was said, had merely maintained 'some professional and social contacts with anti-Nazis.'

The churches, which had owed so much to Weizsäcker's protection before and during the war, were represented by clerics and lay people of high standing from all denominations who were eager to discharge their debt to him. The International Red Cross and other charitable organisations testified to his efforts on behalf of prisoners of war. From Rome came evidence of religious orders which had been hiding Jews: Weizsäcker had stood between them and the Gestapo. Visser 't Hooft also provided a lengthy account of how he had used his influence to ameliorate the lot of prisoners-of-war and internees.

Diplomatic contributions came from Scandinavia, Belgium, France, Switzerland and Portugal. François-Poncet, former French Ambassador in Berlin, who had been transported to Germany for 22 months during the war, sent an affidavit. The other ambassadors of that time – the British, the Italian and the American – were all dead. But Attolico's widow, who had been close to her husband in his work, spoke in his name of the 'fierce, silent and strenuous battle to prevent war' which the two diplomats had fought together. The former German Chancellor, Heinrich Brüning, now teaching at Harvard University, counted himself among Weizsäcker's supporters. The Primate of Norway, Bishop Berggrav, had known Weizsäcker since 1931, when he had been Minister in Oslo. They had remained close friends. The Bishop had led the resistance in Norway, mostly from the cell in which he had been kept in solitary confinement under the German occupation. Not only did he give a detailed affidavit but by permission of the King of Norway he was permitted to give evidence in person. He spoke of his visit to Berlin in December 1939 when he had seen the State Secretary before leaving for an ecclesiastical conference in London. Weizsäcker had entrusted him with a personal message to Halifax regarding possible peace terms; he had stressed that efforts for peace should not even now be abandoned. The Bishop had repeated to Halifax Weizsäcker's words: 'Constant dripping wears away a stone. It may not be in vain.' A note of Bishop Berggrav's visit was put on record by the Foreign Secretary. At the end of his evidence the Bishop, who had suffered so much under the Germans, with the permission of the Court had approached the dock and warmly shaken Weizsäcker by the hand.

The affidavits for the defence were assembled in various document books under such headings as 'Efforts for Peace'; 'Help to the persecuted'; 'Motives for staying in Office'; 'War between Germany and the United States'; 'Assistance to the persecuted Church'. They are far too numerous to name and too lengthy to cite. All those who testified for Weizsäcker were either in some way victims of Nazism themselves or had worked for those who suffered under Nazism. If

Weizsäcker had been guilty, if only to the extent of being a fellow-traveller, he would have been anathema to them. The weight of their combined testimony seems irresistible. But the American tribunal and its prosecutor managed to resist it.

But perhaps the most powerful and the most conclusive evidence was that submitted by Weizsäcker's old friend and collaborator, Carl Burckhardt. His standing was unassailable. He was a former League of Nations diplomat; head of the International Red Cross during the war, and now Swiss Minister to France. His affidavit consisted of some twenty or more pages of his secret diary in which he had recorded many meetings with Weizsäcker, both before and during the war, in which the State Secretary had been able to speak without inhibition and reveal his real situation and his motives. Much of this confirmed the material concealed in British Foreign Office files. Burckhardt's diary also revealed the details of his mission to Berne at the time of the Czech crisis on Weizsäcker's behalf and how he had spoken on the telephone to Butler.[57] This major defence material met with an odd fate. Because Burckhardt failed to appear in Court for cross-examination, the Tribunal declined to consider 'what purported to be extracts from his diary.' In subsequently setting aside the verdict of guilty on Count I, the Tribunal admitted that there had been a number of conferences about this evidence with counsel on both sides. They recalled that they had been informed that Burckhardt's government would not permit the submission of the whole diary because it contained references to living persons, nor would they allow him to be cross-examined. The material from the diary was therefore received only for what, 'under the circumstances, it might be considered to be worth.' The Tribunal now pleaded 'language difficulties' and counsel's failure to express himself accurately, or their own misunderstandings during the conference. They therefore now wished to express their regret both to Dr Burckhardt and his government for comments which might have been unjust.[58]

But the prosecution had one witness on whom they had made sure they could rely: Friedrich Gaus, formerly Chief of the Legal Division of the Foreign Office and Ribbentrop's right-hand man on legal matters. He had been held at Nuremberg during the major trials and had been interrogated twice. When he was applied for as a witness on Ribbentrop's behalf, defence counsel was informed that it had been found that, unfortunately, Gaus was having exceptional difficulty with his memory as a result of his long imprisonment.[59] After his interrogations by the Americans he had made a written public declaration repenting of his errors and urging his fellow-Germans to do the same.

In March, 1947, during the preparation of the case against Weizsäcker, Kempner visited Gaus, then in the fourth week of solitary confinement. In May the following year, Weizsäcker's defence team acquired a copy of the stenographic transcript of Kempner's interrogation. This showed that Gaus had been threatened with being handed over to the Russians who, he was told, were 'interested in him.' Kempner's approach was on the lines of: 'I have documents before me. . . . We have it in black and white: you were Ribbentrop's evil spirit.' Ribbentrop was dead, but those who had worked with him 'are not any better in our opinion, and our attitude is not so severe as the Russians. Who are these persons in the Foreign Ministry who are most guilty? Is it any use sparing those people? What sort of court would you rather face . . . a Russian? You must think it over. The only thing that can save you is telling the truth.' The sort of truth which was required was indicated: 'What about von Weizsäcker? What are the worst things – write them down. Am I making myself clear? Just get down to it and then we shall see.'[60]

Gaus was released from solitary confinement and ensconced in a room close to Kempner's office where, according to Magee, he produced affidavits on demand 'like a slot machine.' The defence produced the copy of Kempner's interrogation in court and showed that when questioned about Weizsäcker, Gaus had replied: 'Oh, I do not believe he did anything wrong.' Now he was testifying that the former Secretary of State had approved acts of aggressive warfare, as charged. In the light of this proof of intimidation and manipulation of the witness, it was demanded that his evidence should be struck from the record. This disgraceful action on the part of the American prosecution was duly reported in the American press.[61]

There is no doubt that the most powerful defence witnesses were Erich and Theo Kordt. While the prosecution manipulated dubious documents – and Kempner, having himself been a civil servant under the Nazi régime, would have well understood their dubiety – the Kordt brothers were first-hand witnesses. In 1946, Theo Kordt had urged upon the American diplomat, E. A. Bayne, discretion in writing about connections between the British and the German Opposition which he and his brother had revealed to him. Now circumstances had changed. Nothing was to be withheld which could be of help to Weizsäcker. British sensibilities could no longer be taken into consideration.

Their evidence, which has already been quoted from in earlier chapters, gave a first-hand account of British diplomatic activity, particularly in the last two years of peace, and the difficulties which they, and the State Secretary, had had in making any impact in London. Vansittart of course figured in their story. In his own evidence, Weizsäcker had summed up their efforts: 'In August and September 1938, the interaction of the resistance movement and political action in London was not as perfect as had been intended. . . . From the spring of 1940 onwards, in London, the German resistance movement was only discouraged instead of being encouraged. . . .'[62]

Within a fortnight of Theo Kordt's testimony the egregious Kempner was taking steps to discredit him. He sent the British MP Sydney Silverman a copy of a telegram from the German Embassy in London to Berlin on 29 April 1939. Signed by Counsellor Kordt, this was a report on British reactions to a major speech by Hitler the previous day. Kordt, asserted Kempner, had 'encouraged Hitler in steps against Poland.' He added pointedly that Kordt was now a lecturer in international law at Bonn University, 'an institution supervised by the British Occupation forces.' Silverman passed the correspondence to the Foreign Office, who were not impressed. 'Not by any stretch of the imagination' could the telegram be read as 'a belligerent incitement to the otherwise peaceful Hitler.' It was a routine Embassy report. The prosecutor Kempner, it was noted, was disliked equally by Americans, British and Germans and was a byword for aggressiveness and relentlessness. Silverman returned with a new charge: that Kordt had made a false statement at his denazification by not stating that he had been in Japan in 1942. Investigation of the records revealed that it was of course his brother Erich who had been there. The Foreign Office saw no grounds to interfere with his University appointment. Nevertheless, Kempner told Silverman that he could not understand how the education of youth and the setting up of a new Constitution could be entrusted to people like Kordt. Silverman told the Foreign Office that he considered this charge 'unanswerable.' They agreed and did not answer![63]

Kempner's smear campaign went rather better with his approach to Lord Vansittart. On 12th August His Lordship supplied the prosecution with an affidavit deliberately intended to discredit the Kordts

as witnesses and to contradict Weizsäcker's evidence. It is so poison-
ous that it must be quoted at length. Although claiming that he 'did
not see much of these men' before the war in London, he seemed to
know a lot about them:

> I had reason to regard them both as unreliable and essentially time-
> servers, plausible and therefore the more dangerous. They served
> Hitler and Ribbentrop until the Nazi tyranny was clearly beaten. Till
> then they remained on the winning side and never showed any real
> intention of breaking with the Nazi tyranny. . . . It would have been
> easy for [Theo Kordt] to remain in Britain to fight the Nazi tyranny,
> he went out and became German Minister [sic] in Berne. . . . During
> my conversations with the Kordts I never had any impression that
> they really intended to take action against the régime or that they
> were associated with any persons or groups who would do so. . . . I
> see no reason to believe that the Kordt brothers used their official
> positions in the German Foreign Service to sabotage Ribbentrop's
> policy. . . .

Vansittart then added the irrelevant jibe that he was 'astonished to
hear that Erich Kordt was entrusted with an important position in
German youth education at Munich University.' Having disposed
of the Kordts, His Lordship then turned on Weizsäcker. He weighed
his words with care:

> I always considered, and I still consider, Baron von Weizsäcker the
> chief executant of Ribbentrop's policy. I can recall nothing that made
> me believe or suppose that Baron von Weizsäcker used his official
> position to hinder these calamitous courses. To the best of my recollec-
> tion he was never mentioned or reported to me as being a convinced
> and active opponent of Nazi policy. . . .

This farrago of lies and character assassination was properly sworn
before a notary public.

Ten days later, Vansittart struck again with a further declaration.
He had 'now seen some of the allegations put forward by Herr Theo
Kordt on behalf of Baron von Weizsäcker.' An attempt was being
made, he stated, to build up an unwarrantable legend which, in the
interests of history, must be refuted. The whole basis of his own
attitude to Germany had been the conviction that there neither
existed nor would exist any real effective opposition:

Had I ever sought hopefully for any Resistance Movement in Germany I should still have counted on none in the German Foreign Office. Had I entertained any such illusions, I should still have counted on nothing from the Kordt brothers. . . . Neither the German Foreign Office in general nor the Kordt brothers in particular did anything. Any subsequent pretensions on their part to subtle heroism are therefore mythical. Neither can I recall any active recalcitrance on the part of Weizsäcker.

Goerdeler, whom Vansittart had so viciously denigrated in 1939, was now praised as sincere and courageous, and as having given his life while the Kordts 'remained comfortably in Nazi service.' It was, pursued Vansittart, 'an impertinence to speak of the maintenance of a trusting collaboration between the German Opposition on the one hand and the British Government on the other.' The only communications he received from Theo Kordt were at the end of the war 'asking for some personal advantage. I ignored them.'[64] (This was a reference to the appeal for help to return to the Rhineland.)

The prosecution introduced the Vansittart material as rebuttal of evidence given by Weizsäcker and the Kordt brothers. During the rebuttal period the Tribunal judges went to London on holiday and left another judge to preside over the rebuttal testimony. But a Court order limited the prosecutors to what they could put in the rebuttal and what witnesses they could call. The prime witness they had up their sleeve was Otto John, one of the conspirators of the 20th July attempt. Magee had himself interviewed him on behalf of the defence in England, where he had been working for the British Secret Service after escaping from Germany in 1944. Now Magee found that he was going to 'pull a switcharoo' and state that Weizsäcker was not a party to the 20th July attempt – literally true, of course, as he was in Vatican City at the time, but false in its implications. When John was brought into Court, Magee pointed out to the judge that this was a violation of the Court Order as he was not named in it. It was contempt of Court; and he was withdrawing his client from any further proceedings with regard to the rebuttal, and promptly did so. When the Tribunal judges returned, Magee was 'yanked into Chambers' and reprimanded for his action, but replied that he would not be party to contempt of Court by the prosecution.[65]

Theo Kordt moved fast to counter Vansittart's vicious statements. He wrote to Lord Halifax, enclosing copies of two letters. One was from himself to Halifax on 29 July 1947 and the other the latter's reply on 9th August. The reason for that exchange had been the denazification process of Erich Kordt in Munich in the US Zone of Occupation. Although he was already covered by a certificate issued by the State Department in Washington, the Court had requested 'additional testimony of active resistance for the years 1938–9.' Kordt had reminded the former Foreign Secretary that 'the information I gave you and Sir Robert Vansittart on Hitler's plans and moves in those terrible years of crisis came all from my brother Erich.' He then detailed specific occasions. He also recalled how he himself had been 'in close (sometimes daily) contact' with Sir Robert Vansittart. In the interests of justice, would Lord Halifax be good enough to confirm that Erich, 'under whose instructions on behalf of the Opposition I did all the steps known to you,' had given proof of 'active resistance to the criminal Nazi policy.' Lord Halifax had replied promptly:

> Of course I remember very well the information that came to me through Lord Vansittart in those days before the War, and that he said reached him from your brother. You will no doubt have been in communication with Lord Vansittart direct. I cannot doubt that in so acting your brother took very great risk and in so doing gave very practical evidence of his active opposition to the criminal policy of Hitler.[66]

Now, a year later, Kordt was writing again for help. The former Foreign Secretary did not disappoint him. On 30 September 1948, he sent an affidavit stating that he had received the letter of 29 July 1947, had replied to it on the 9th August; and that:

> The facts stated in Kordt's letter to me and contained in my reply thereto, I hereby confirm as true. This affidavit is furnished in reply to the declarations of Lord Vansittart and to refute his statement.[67]

The conflict of evidence between Lord Halifax and Lord Vansittart was pointed up by the distinguished periodical *Die Zeit*, which concluded that Vansittart should be obliged to submit to cross-examination by the defence. The article was passed to London by Control Commission Headquarters in Berlin. Whitehall expressed the hope that Berlin was not proposing to try publicly to resolve the conflict: 'Clearly the less said about the matter the better.' A minute by the Foreign Office Legal Department heartily endorsed this attitude: 'I entirely agree that the less said about all this the better. The Nuremberg tribunal's ideas of evidence are quaint. It is no part of our business to sort out differences of opinion for them.' Alas for Weizsäcker, the differences were of *fact*.[68]

Magee meanwhile had hastened to England where he secured an affidavit from Bishop Bell on 1st October, handwritten on Victoria Station and sworn on the spot.[69] (The lawyer was empowered by the Court to administer the oath.) The Bishop, who had already testified in Court, was willing to do so again, feeling it was his duty, as he said at the beginning of his affidavit, to answer Vansittart's declarations. He rejected the latter's statement that the existence of an Opposition in Germany was an unwarrantable legend. 'Lord Vansittart is better informed and certainly knows of "very active recalcitrance on the part of Weizsäcker" from his "reliable British and German sources".' Perhaps because, as he said to Magee, 'these judges might think: what would an English bishop know about these things,' he established his own credentials by referring to his meeting with Schoenfeld and Boenhoffer and the secret information they had given him about the Opposition and its plans against Hitler and the participation of the German Foreign Office. 'I passed that information on,' he concluded, 'in personal interviews with Mr Anthony Eden and Ambassador Winant of the United States.'[70]

So incensed was Theo Kordt by Vansittart's behaviour that he took the extraordinary step of writing an open letter to him which was published in certain German papers. He did so on the grounds that Kempner had disseminated the gist of Vansittart's affidavits to the German and foreign press. No doubt, he wrote, His Lordship would be prepared to come to Nuremberg and defend his assertions in Court and resolve the contradiction between these and the statement of his former Chief, Lord Halifax. He reminded him that when they first met for confidential discussions in London it had been at his – Vansittart's – instigation. Kordt went on to review their relationship, including the details of their last dramatic meeting on the eve of war and the continuing connection through 'our friend Philip' [Conwell-Evans] into 1940.[71]

It was Kempner's predilection for leaking to the press which did for him in the end. The prosecution had two documents from the captured German archives concerning the transfer of French Jews which had been arranged between Laval and Hitler. Because foreigners were involved, these documents went through the Foreign Office. Weizsäcker was on the distribution list and had initialled them. These documents were still secret and had not yet been produced in evidence in Court. But Kempner had copies sent to leading newspapers in Germany, Switzerland and the United States.[72] Two recipients of these communications, in New York and Washington respectively, sent them to Magee. He thereupon called in the representatives of the international press in Nuremberg, told them the story and suggested they ask the US Military Governor in Berlin, General Clay, what he thought of an American prosecutor mailing abroad matter not yet used in evidence and prejudicial to the German defendant. The result was an enquiry by the Inspector-General. His report went to Clay and Kempner was ordered to make an apology in open court. Clay also ordered that at the conclusion of the case Kempner should be dismissed from the prosecution staff and was to leave Occupied Germany and never return.[73]

The defence did have one special name to conjure with. Churchill, now Leader of the Opposition, had promised Magee that he would try to make some gesture towards Weizsäcker. He sent a copy of the report in Hansard of his speech during the Debate on the King's Speech on 28 October 1948, with permission for the defence to use the relevant portion of it in their summing up. Churchill had been speaking warmly about progress in rehabilitation in Germany and had criticised the process of court cases dragging on far too long. He continued:

> My attention has been drawn to the case of Baron Weizsäcker. I was asked to make some affidavit about him, as many people in this country have been asked. I was not able to do so, because I had never met Weizsäcker, never being brought officially into contact with his work.

He was, explained Churchill, a permanent official in the Foreign Office under Ribbentrop, in a similar capacity to that of Sir Alexander Cadogan 'and now, after 3½ years, he is being tried.' He was using this as an illustration to show 'the kind of deadly error which, in my opinion, is being committed at this time.' Elwyn Jones and Sydney Silverman interrupted on the grounds that the case was *sub judice* but Churchill pointed out that the trial was being held under United States jurisdiction.

I have just as much right to express an opinion about it as people in England had to express opinions about the Dreyfus case although it was taking place under foreign jurisdiction.[74]

Churchill's intervention arrived in time to be included in Dr Becker's closing statement.

Weizsäcker was initially found guilty on Count I – the initation, planning and waging of aggressive war – by a majority verdict of two to one. The dissenting Judge Powers found 'the necessary evidence was conspicuous by its absence.'[75] Eventually, as a result of defence motions alleging errors, the verdict was set aside. Given the evidence, it could never have hoped to succeed.

Weizsäcker was also found guilty on Count V – atrocities and offences against civilian populations. Again, the evidence from scores of witnesses was in his favour. The prosecution could not do much more than offer certain documents concerning the deportation of French Jews. Again Judge Powers dissented. He could see no justification for holding Weizsäcker (and his fellow-defendant from the Foreign Office, Woermann) guilty of the persecution of the Jews as alleged:

> The deportation of these Jews was in the hands of the SS or the occupying forces in France. The Foreign Office . . . had a limited right of objection as to Jews of foreign nationality. They seem to have exercised that right where it was available. Where it was not available, they had no grounds for objection. To convict them, is to punish them for the acts of another department of government, which they did not order and which they were powerless to prevent.[76]

But the Americans were not going to allow Weizsäcker to 'escape conviction' (as they had described Schacht's acquittal). He was sentenced to seven years' imprisonment, reduced after various defence motions to five years.

When Magee wrote to Kirkpatrick in April, 1949 informing him of the dissenting opinion and the intention to appeal, Kirkpatrick replied that 'he had not seen the evidence or the proceedings of the trial.'[77] Impossible to believe that a case which touched the Foreign Office so closely and was being conducted by the Americans was not being carefully monitored. There was after all a British liaison officer at Nuremberg Court. But there is no need to speculate: in September, 1949 the Foreign Office wrote:

We have been somewhat surprised at the judgment of the Nuremberg Tribunal in von Weizsäcker's case and have privately tended to share the views of Judge Powers, who entered a dissenting judgment. . . . Our surprise at the verdict and sentence has been based . . . upon the opinion expressed by the court on which they based their judgment. It appears that after carefully weighing all the evidence and pointing out that it was chiefly in favour of von Weizsäcker, the majority of the Judges reached the judgment nevertheless, that he was guilty.[78]

It was not the imprisonment for years of an innocent man which the Foreign Office deprecated, so much as the incompetence of the American judges. The 'Von Weizsäcker Trial' file listed in the Foreign Office index is not, alas, to be found. No doubt it still exists somewhere in the weeders' limbo.

There had been virtually no coverage in the British Press of the trial, apart from the indictment and the verdict and sentence. Perhaps after the major international trials it was felt that readers had had enough; perhaps the idea of an American tribunal trying civil servants was not very titillating.

The conclusion of the trial produced a special article in *The Times* entitled: 'Nazi Diplomacy: Share of Guilt in Hitler's Campaigns.' The verdict from Printing House Square was that 'the only step [Weizsäcker] took to discourage Hitler was to try to send a round-about message through Switzerland to the British Government requesting them to send someone to Berlin to make an impression on Hitler.'[79] *The Economist* did better. British opinion was reconciled to the major war crimes trials only by the feeling that, however arguable their legal basis, justice and commonsense demanded that the guilty should be brought to book. To what extent justice and commonsense predominated over legal hair-splitting in the majority verdict of the American tribunal was open to question. After summarising some of the nature of Weizsäcker's actions, the writer concluded:

> The risks he ran for peace are not to be rewarded by seven years' imprisonment. The sentence may still be reduced or annulled, and although the trial was an exclusively American concern, von Weiz-säcker's fate cannot be a matter of indifference to Britain. . . . Some elder statesmen may now be reproaching themselves for not having paid more heed to his warnings, and if so it would be a sign of grace in them to raise a voice on his behalf.[80]

But grace was not abounding in these quarters.

However, English voices were raised. In the letter columns of *The Times* there was some powerful support for Weizsäcker. Professor Gilbert Murray wrote:

> No-one having read the full extracts from the proceedings can avoid feeling the deepest misgivings. . . . The good name of the Allies cannot but gain from a careful reconsideration of the evidence.

The publisher Victor Gollancz, quoting from the dissenting judgment, passionately objected to the verdict:

> Weizsäcker was sentenced by an American court. But English voices, if there are only enough of them, can still avail to move the world.

Bertrand Russell supported Gollancz's letter 'with all possible emphasis':

> All the evidence so far as I have been able to obtain it, goes to show that he was actively engaged, at great personal risk, in trying to mitigate Nazi crimes. If any person associated with the German Government of that time deserved acquittal, he deserved it. I earnestly hope, for the sake of the victors' reputation for justice, that the sentence will be revised and his immediate release ordered.

There was one tantalisingly cryptic letter from the pen of Henry M. Andrews (whom a little research reveals as the husband of Rebecca West):

> There are reasons – some objective, some connected with certain personalities associated with this trial – why in this case justice has not been and will not be manifestly seen to have been done. . . .[81]

Foreign Office comments on the trial verdict, already quoted, were contained in a reply to a letter from the British Legation in Vatican City. This letter, dated 20 August 1949, had enclosed a copy of an appeal which Bishop Bell had addressed to President Truman when Weizsäcker was convicted. Now, four months later, the Bishop had sent a copy of this to the British Minister at the Legation though there is no indication of why he had done so. Perhaps he was trying to enlist support from those who had served with the former

Ambassador von Weizsäcker in Vatican City. The Bishop had begun by addressing an 'urgent appeal' to the President for reconsideration of the sentence and for the release of the prisoner. He referred to all those aspects of Weizsäcker's work for peace, at the risk of his life, of which he himself was aware; and of his continuing care for the churches. The condemnation of Weizsäcker, he wrote, had come as a great shock to those who knew the facts:

> We cannot understand how, in the face of the evidence which was given on his behalf, and in the face of the admissions of the Tribunal itself, it could have been possible to condemn him.

After detailing some of Weizsäcker's resistance activities, Bell went on:

> It is also known that he was instrumental in warning the British Government and other governments about Hitler's intentions before the war broke out. . . . Unfortunately they were disregarded. . . .[82]

It does not seem to have occurred to the Bishop that he was impugning the judgment of an American court to the President of the United States.

The Foreign Office reply to the Vatican Legation shows no flicker of guilt for its own rôle in placing the former State Secretary behind bars, nor compassion for his situation. They had not known of Bell's letter to the President but they were 'not in the least surprised.' In spite of the evidence to the contrary in their own papers, the letter then stated:

> The experience of people here who knew von Weizsäcker personally does not agree with the Bishops' [sic] statement that he did all he could to prevent war, using his position for this purpose. It is rather that although he was genuinely opposed to the Nazis he was a weak man who allowed himself rather too readily to be used as a tool. It is perfectly true that an affidavit was made by Viscount Halifax, but if he took the advice given to him by us he did not go as far as the Bishop. Affidavits were also given by Sir Ivone Kirkpatrick and Christopher Steel but they were very guarded. . . .

With regard to the Bishop's reference to warnings given before the war, the Foreign Office made short work of this:

This is probably true if one substitutes for the word 'warnings' the word 'intimations', and it is doubtful whether von Weizsäcker was risking his life in giving such intimations since there were many people who anyhow guessed at them.[83]

Why Weizsäcker's life should not have been at risk because other people were 'guessing' along the same lines is not immediately apparent.

But this was not the only approach made towards President Truman. The faithful Theo Kordt renewed his pressure on Lord Halifax in a letter in December, 1949. As a teacher of international law, he wrote, he had now made a profound and detailed study of the Weizsäcker case. He felt bound to associate himself with the statement of Herr Arnold, Minister-President of the new region of North Rhine-Westphalia created by the British Occupying Power – 'personally known to you as a man of honour and integrity. Herr Arnold had stated publicly that the Weizsäcker case was a new Dreyfus case – this time on an international level.' There had been an alarming deterioration in the international sense of justice and he was deeply disturbed if the case should remain, in spite of dissenting judicial opinion and support from figures of international standing, without any possibility of legal review. Weizsäcker had acted on a principle 'which may be of utmost importance in times to come.' He had put the supranational interest above the national interest: the prevention of aggressive war. The Foreign Office had lost more victims through Nazi tyranny than any other department of State. 'All those who gave their lives, most of them personal friends of mine, considered Weizsäcker as their example and their spiritual leader.' Kordt concluded: 'Some time ago you let Warren Magee know that you hesitated to write to President Truman on behalf of the Weizsäcker case. My friends and I would be greatly obliged to you if you could see your way to re-examine that provisional decision.'

On 4th January, Halifax wrote to President Truman, enclosing Kordt's letter. The appeal had come to him with the claim, 'based on what I know to have been his [Kordt's] own willingness to incur grave danger in the cause that he believed right – namely, trying to check the Nazi movement to war.' He continued:

It is not for me to do more than express my own personal belief that from all I have ever heard, reconsideration of Weizsäcker's case, if you felt able to give it, would be both justified on merits and would exercise a powerful effect in those German quarters, where the conviction prevails today that in his case justice has been miscarried.'

Truman replied that he was 'looking into the matter to determine what steps should be taken to insure that justice prevails in his case.'[84]

A year later, in 1951, after a review of sentences by the US High Commissioner for Germany, McCloy, the sentence on Weizsäcker was reduced to 'time served,' but the verdict against him was not reversed. He was, however, allowed to leave Landsberg Prison in October, 1950. He died in Lindau in August, 1951. Theo Kordt gave Halifax the credit for making it possible for Weizsäcker to spend the last months of his life in freedom with his family, although there is no evidence that Truman responded to the British diplomat's approach.

Kordt expressed his thanks to Lord Halifax when he called on him in London in 1953, after his appointment as Ambassador to Greece. He sent a note of the meeting to his brother. He learned from Halifax that during the trial he too had received a document from the prosecution purporting to prove Weizsäcker culpable for the deportation of Jews. Kordt replied that Kempner had done a great deal of damage to the reputation of the United States Tribunal and Halifax agreed. He had not known of Vansittart's attempts to discredit Weizsäcker and the Kordt brothers; which in the end, Kordt told him, had not even been mentioned in the judgment. The talk turned to the historian Sir Lewis Namier and his book *In the Nazi Era*. Namier had made it look, said Kordt, as if the initiative for the meetings in times of crisis – sometimes daily – had come from his side; whereas Lord Halifax knew it was Vansittart himself who had requested them, through Conwell-Evans. Halifax found Namier one of those who always appeared to have predicted everything correctly – after the event. He was thus able 'to join meritoriously statemanship and history.'[85]

One member of Ernst von Weizsäcker's defence team was his younger son Richard, then a young law student home from the wars. That young lawyer has now entered upon his second term as the internationally respected and admired President of the Federal Republic of Germany. Forty years after the trial has come an acknowledgment of his father's innocence from a quarter which cannot be gainsaid. In March, 1990, after Czechoslovakia had regained its independence, the newly elected President Vaclav Havel made the generous and imaginative gesture of inviting the German President for a State visit on the anniversary of Hitler's march into Prague which had extinguished that independence and at which Weizsäcker had been accused of conniving.

In conversation with some British journalists at the time, Havel spoke of Tomas Masaryk, founder and president of that first Czechoslovakian Republic. Masaryk was an excellent man: a profoundly moral man who had endowed the new State with virtuous ideas. He had been a kind of national symbol, exercising an almost spiritual influence. If there was anything comparable today, declared the President of Czechoslovakia, it was the presidency of Richard von Weizsäcker.[86]

— XI —

Not in the Public Interest

I have now made an examination of the documentary material available in the official files of the Foreign Office. . . . For various reasons it may be judged wiser not to publish some of the documents concerned. . . .

John Wheeler-Bennett
Foreign Office memorandum

I must confess to a slight feeling of doubt as to how good a case we could make for ourselves. . . .

Con O'Neill
Member of the Foreign Office

S URELY the Foreign Office could now relax. There were no more trials to come and even posterity was being taken care of, as some revealing exchanges in Parliament indicated. In June, 1944 the forthcoming publication of *Documents on British Foreign Policy 1919–1939* was announced in the House of Commons by the Minister of State, Mr Richard Law. The Conservative Member for Wallsend, Miss Irene Ward, had a question for him. During the years leading up to the war, she said, she had many opportunities of discussing in foreign countries the kind of information that was being sent in to the Foreign Office and was quite frequently told by responsible people that they felt utterly depressed at the reception given to their information. The Foreign Office did not welcome reports from outsiders and these reports were ignored and not given the consideration which they deserved. Would the collection of documents include unofficial as well as official papers? Would there be an answer to the question that had vexed so many minds: how did we get into this war? 'Is that question going to be answered fairly, squarely and completely? I want to know whether, when the papers are published, we shall really get the whole story.' The answer, in a nutshell, was no. Although the Minister spoke at some length, the crux of his reply was contained in one sentence:

> It is the purpose of these documents, when they are published, to show to the world and to the historians of the future what *was* our foreign policy; it is not the intention to try to explain how that foreign policy was arrived at, or how the foreign policy which in fact we had, might have been improved.[1]

The manipulation of the facts of pre-war foreign policy in order to protect British prestige had first come up for consideration in the

Foreign Office during the war. In August, 1941, the Foreign Secretary, Eden, called the attention of the Cabinet to certain dangerous trends. There was a school of thought, which would become much stronger at the peace, which maintained that British pre-war policy was indirectly responsible for Hitler's rise to power from 1925–1933 and for giving him a 'free run in Europe' from 1933–1939. Large blocs of influential opinion here and abroad held the view that Britain encouraged Hitler and only turned against him when it became obvious that this policy would directly endanger British interests. The source of the trouble, Eden stated, was the existence in the United States of many 'more or less distinguished' German émigrés, some of whom were collaborating with US intelligence organisations. 'Although these people are no doubt anti-Nazi, it would be too much to expect that their version of events before 1939 would be favourable to this country.'[2] No doubt Eden had in mind Heinrich Brüning, the former Chancellor, who always maintained that it was the failure of the British and French Governments to strengthen his hand which led to the downfall of the Weimar Republic and the emergence of the Nazi Party. Although this claim was always resisted, Foreign Office files record the concerted opinion of the very highest economic and foreign policy advisers in 1931 that urgent moral and material support should be given to Brüning, otherwise 'in the near future the Nazis would sweep the board. . . .'[3]

Eden's proposal to the Cabinet was that the British should present their own version of events by publishing a selection of Anglo-German diplomatic documents covering the period from 1925 to 1939: that is to say, from the Treaty of Locarno to the German march into Prague. Professor Woodward, the official historian to whom the task of assembling the collection would fall, pointed out an advantage which could be gained in the long run by judicious selection:

> The trend of post-war politics in Great Britain might well lead to a demand for publication of documents on lines, and for reasons, which I should myself deprecate most strongly (e.g. a 'grand inquest' into pre-war diplomacy). The present 'controlled' publication should go a long way to avoiding the risk of an uncontrolled or 'unsatisfactorily controlled' publication. . . .[4]

The Head of the Foreign Office, Cadogan, shared the feeling that although 'an accurate and official account of HMG's foreign policy before the war' had been 'forced upon us by circumstances outside our control,' i.e. the Americans, there was more to gain than to lose by what he euphemistically called 'controlled publicity'.[5]

But even the promise of benevolent censorship was not enough to reassure some of those who had been involved in the events under review. Caveats began to be entered right, left and centre. Few felt able to share the cheerfully insouciant attitude of Vansittart, the consistent enemy of appeasement:

> Every friendly foreigner accepts the tradition that we are *naif*. . . . Here we are playing to perfection. It is – particularly in view of what has happened – the only convincing answer to that other and fictitious rôle – a quite incompatible one, which our enemies always try to foist upon us – of *perfide Albion*. Every continental called us *naif* for years because we couldn't see the storm coming. In these papers we disappoint nobody and disarm many.[6]

Not surprisingly, the events of September, 1938 provided a few stumbling blocks. Lord Cranborne, Under-Secretary of State at the time of Munich, having declared stoutly that 'our case is overwhelming and should be given to the world,' rather then spoilt the effect of this ringing declaration in a private letter to Eden, handwritten from home ('My dear Anthony . . . Yours, Bobbety') expressing reservations about the account of the meeting between Hitler, Sir Nevile Henderson and Sir Horace Wilson on 26 September 1938:

> That is a really dreadful document. Our readiness to bully and batter the Czechs, and to do anything, however contemptible, to avoid a war makes one blush, and is bound to create a deplorable impression, both in the US and in occupied countries themselves. Would it be very disingenuous to leave it out?[7]

Woodward (described by the Minister of State in the House as 'an impartial historian who can be trusted to take an entirely objective view') also had a suggestion to make: 'I think it may be desired to cut, from the Prime Minister's account of his conversation in Hitler's flat, the PM's words – "The Czech Government might be mad enough to refuse the [Munich] terms".' Makins had had the same thought. Cadogan minuted: 'Yes, that should certainly be changed' and Woodward agreed.[8] This piece of suppression was rationalised by reference to the fact that the account of the meeting between

Hitler and Chamberlain had been recorded by the German interpreter, Dr Schmidt, and therefore need not be relied upon. That Chamberlain himself had never disputed Schmidt's account or made any alterations in the wording was regarded as a minor consideration.

Vansittart made a characteristic contribution to the debate:

> Throughout the world people, particularly in the USA, conclude that HMG were animated by knavery. In my view the slithering out of the guarantee of the new Czech frontiers *was* near to knavery, but only the German dirty linen is here washed in public . . . so here again a good time is had by all but the Germans.[9]

Woodward had another impartial and objective thought with respect to Hitler's reoccupation of the Rhineland in 1936. It was 'better not to invite controversy by printing documents which are not essential to the record of our exchange with Germany.'

The Lord Chancellor, Lord Simon, who had been Foreign Secretary from 1931–1935, inclined to the view that the publication of documents would be unwise because of 'the risk of domestic controversy of a partisan kind and of unsettlement of mind in occupied countries.'[10] It seems, however, that his misgivings were of a more personal kind. Woodward wrote to the Cabinet Secretary, Sir Edward Bridges:

> I was sure I could persuade the Lord Simon that his stock would not go down and might even rise a little by the publication of some of his despatches. The poor man has even tried bribery on me – last All Souls Day he asked me whether I had any ex-pupils I would care to suggest for livings in the gift of the Lord Chancellor.[11]

Then the Air Ministry gave the boat a rock. They pointed to a despatch from the Air Attaché in 1933 which had remarked upon 'the similarity of Hitlerism to Bolshevism.' Roberts, Grey and Woodward agreed that the collection would have to be gone through 'for passages which might offend our new ally.'[12] Whatever the Foreign Office was endeavouring to produce, it was not history. Publication of the Anglo-German documents was finally abandoned by Cabinet on 27 January 1944.

But in the Foreign Office the consciousness of a need for exculpation remained. The following month the Office weighed the possibility of a short book, explaining British pre-war foreign policy, which could be distributed on the Continent after liberation. Woodward felt that he could produce a book on the origins of the war in which 'he could treat awkward periods such as these without causing any embarrassment.'[13]

With the right kind of support, the idea could be put about that nothing had been withheld. The historian Sir Lewis Namier assured his readers that within the Foreign Office during the critical years 'there was no lack of sound knowledge of European affairs, or of sane insight into them. And the willingness which they have shown to allow all their material to see daylight does them honour now'![14]

After the First World War, the new government of Germany decided that all the secrets of German diplomacy during the previous half-century should be published whether favourable to Germany or not. Secret and confidential documents 'which in the ordinary course would slumber till the scholars of the future broke the seals' should now be published: 'A government and a people which thus reveals its secrets displays unbounded confidence in the power of the truth to reconcile and heal.'[15] But truth could have other, more unpleasant, side effects as the Foreign Office was well aware.

The first event which set the alarm bells ringing in Whitehall was the interrogation in the first weeks of peace of the former Chief of Staff, General Halder.[16] He had been, as they knew, a leading member of the Opposition. The interrogation was carried out by an American Intelligence unit: Halder had been one of a party of some one hundred 'special' prisoners who had been rescued by American troops from their Gestapo escorts in South Tyrol.

Wind of this interrogation reached Christopher Steel, Political Officer on the staff of the British Commander-in-Chief in Berlin. 'The first three pages of the report strike me as very dangerous,' he wrote to London on 11 August 1945. Apparently Halder had spelled out Germany's military weakness at the time of the Czech crisis in 1938 – 'nothing less than catastrophic', according to the former Chief of Staff at that time. Twenty-one divisions against the Czechs' well-equipped thirty-five and a West Wall that was little better than a building site, with only five divisions to man it. Munich, General Halder was claiming, was an enormous and wholly undeserved triumph for Hitler's methods of bluff. 'Never in history,' he had declared, 'has a nation been more betrayed than the Czechs by the British at Munich.' He had gone on to describe the *putsch* which had been prepared in September, 1938 and which he insisted had been wrecked by Chamberlain's sudden arrival in Germany. 'He is on strong ground,' wrote Steel, 'as all the people he names as his confederates were, I think, exterminated after the 20th July.'

Halder had further referred to various contacts between the Opposition leaders and the British Government in the winter of 1939/40, notably the one conducted through the offices of the Pope. Halder had testified therefore that there was an active anti-Nazi element in Germany comprising both military and civilians which had been in touch with the British in the interests of peace.[17] The possibility that this information might leak out, particularly to the American Press who would use it as anti-British propaganda, caused considerable alarm in the Foreign Office. The lengths to which they were prepared to go to prevent unwelcome facts emerging is revealed in an exchange of minutes in Central Department. American Intelligence units, it was agreed, were working 'far outside their terms of reference.' They were 'wasting time and manpower on factitious and vexatious interrogations.'

- Most of this work is undertaken by busy-bodies who are merely inquisitive if not mischievous as well, and serves no reasonable military or political object any longer. . . .
- The best thing to aim at would be to discredit Halder in the course of an interrogation of our own. . . .
- I really don't think we can complain about the first allegation relating to the Munich crisis. After all, it may have some truth in it. . . .
- As regards the allegations of peace-feelers in the winter of 1939/40, this again emanates from the same circle of conspirators. It is again easy for them to say that had these worked as they hoped, the war would have lasted only a few weeks, Hitler would have been overthrown and we would all have been happy ever after. . . .
- With regard to the allegation [about the Vatican] I think no tactics could be worse than to display anxiety about it before it is published, as it never may be. I suggest we do nothing, but wait and see.

And if defensive action had to be taken the Foreign Office knew how best this could be done:

- It is quite likely that the same type of mischievous evidence will crop up in the course of the war crimes demonstrations, unless the mouths of witnesses are stopped by GPU–Gestapo methods of court management.[18]

It is pleasing to record that Halder's interrogator on this occasion was no American busy-body but a British Intelligence officer, later to become a member of the House of Lords – Nicholas Kaldor. He had hoped, he has said, that the Halder material might have been leaked to the public during the General Election in July, to the discredit of the Conservative Party.[19] Halder's three interrogations of June, July and August did become available to the *Daily Worker*, which published two articles by 'Frank Pitcairn' (the *nom-de-plume* of Claud Cockburn, the well-known left-wing journalist) under the title: 'How the Tories saved Hitler in 1938.'[20]

Michael Foot MP put down a question to the Prime Minister asking if he would arrange for the publication of evidence about events leading up to the war elicited from generals such as Halder and Keitel. The Foreign Office was asked to advise on the Reply. The Prime Minister, Attlee, was informed that 'the full statement of Halder is a mischievous document and probably deliberately so.' The Foreign Office had decided that it would be inexpedient to pick on individual pieces of evidence for publication. Michael Foot's question was so answered.[21] However, soon afterwards, the reports of General Keitel's interrogation were carried by all Paris newspapers. The Soviet News Agency, Tass, declared that the French had done this deliberately as a gesture of disapproval of the British Prime Minister's refusal to publish.[22] As a result of this publicity the Halder affair was raised again in the Foreign Office. The general was now in Britain and 'could easily be re-interrogated.' There were conflicting views:

> Many people who should know have always held the view – and this includes General Ismay – that it would have been to our military advantage to make war at the time of Munich. This is a very controversial subject and I am not at present inclined to press for further interrogation of Halder with a view to forcing out of him disclosures contradictory to his earlier investigation, and then to publish interrogation No. 2 in order to controvert interrogation No. 1. . . . I can imagine nothing more unwise than any attempt to rig a statement on Halder to justify our part in Munich.[23]

How the former Chief of Staff was to be 'forced' to change his story completely was not divulged! By 'OGPU-Gestapo methods'?

The case for appeasement and for the abandonment of Czechoslovakia had been based on the insistence of the British Government that the Germans possessed overwhelming military superiority. As has been shown, evidence to the contrary both from the German Opposition and the British Military Attaché in Prague had been rejected. Now the German Chief of Staff at the time, General Halder, was demolishing the British case. But the myth had to be maintained. On 26th November the Foreign Office anxiously sought reassurance from the Director of Military Intelligence. Certain German officers, it was explained, had been claiming during interrogation that at the time of Munich Germany was comparatively unprepared for war and could not have resisted united action by the Allied Powers. This was of course a very controversial subject raising as it did the whole question of British policy. Wide political considerations were involved. The writer asked for an 'objective review' of the argument in the light of 'up-to-date intelligence.' The reply came within a few days, hardly an interval which would have allowed for detailed research. The Director merely gave Halder the lie by stating that 'Germany had 51 divisions at the time of Munich,' adding for good measure that compared with the Allies' 'German equipment was more up-to-date, and German industry and the German nation as a whole better organised and prepared for war.' This latter statement completely belied all the inside intelligence from Opposition sources before the war.[24]

The Foreign Office thanked the Director: 'What you say fits in with our own judgment of the Germans' confidence in the strength of their hand.' But the Foreign Office had been completely misled. Far from checking German Army records (by that time – November, 1945 – in Allied hands) the Director or his staff had obviously been content simply to refer to the Chiefs of Staff report to the Cabinet in April, 1938, concerning the strength of the German Army. That report, which had been so welcomed by Chamberlain as a support for his policy, had given that precise figure of 51 divisions. Halder's statement was in due course to be confirmed by both Keitel and Jodl in the dock at Nuremberg.

Not long afterwards, confirmation of much of what Halder had claimed reached the Foreign Office in the form of a document forwarded by the Consul-General in Zurich. It was a copy of the typescript of a memorandum by General Thomas, subsequently published, in part, in a Swiss paper. It was Thomas who had joined with Schacht, Gisevius and Oster in a last-minute attempt to stop the war. He had pressed upon Keitel evidence of military weakness. He had delivered the 'X Report' of the Vatican exchanges to

Brauchitsch. He had ended the war in Gestapo hands together with the other eminent prisoners rescued by the Americans. But the Foreign Office was not impressed by the revelations in his article: 'He seems a slippery customer though at times surprisingly naïve.' However, it was felt that there was a fair proportion of truth in Thomas's report. The inclusion of Schacht among Hitler's opponents was interesting and the general rather confirmed Halder's statement about Munich. But O'Neill summed up: 'What an unpleasant – and stupid – man the author is. His smugness is gigantic and his claims to be an anti-militarist and a good European are manifest rubbish. . . .'[25] As usual, the Foreign Office protested too much.

In February, 1946, another Parliamentary Question was put to the Foreign Secretary (now Ernest Bevin): when did he propose to make arrangements for publication of documents in the possession of His Majesty's Government relating to the resistance of anti-Nazi Germans to the Hitler régime? The Foreign Office was required to advise. 'The piecemeal publication of documents whose value and veracity would be hard to assess without considerable research was undesirable.' They could have stopped there, but no opportunity of demolishing the legend of a German Opposition could be ignored. Hitler's suppression before the war of all democratic elements had resulted in the elimination of any well-organised opposition. There were of course, continued the memorandum, a considerable number of individual German opponents of all classes and parties to the Hitler régime, *a number of whom* were placed in concentration camps. It was a masterpiece of understatement. The verb 'placed' was an inspired touch.[26]

The publication in Germany of accounts of the Opposition by the few leading figures who survived the war brought the Foreign Office on to the defensive again. Hans Bernd Gisevius and Fabian von Schlabrendorff had been early and active anti-Nazis. Both had participated in attempts on Hitler's life and the latter had also been one of the emissaries of the Opposition who came to London in 1939. Now they had written accounts of the Opposition from the point of view of their own participation in it. The diary of Ulrich von Hassell, with its extraordinary commentary on the Hitler years, had been posthumously published also. These books revealed the existence of a very real anti-Nazi element in Germany which had been striving against Hitler and for peace long before the war began.

In 1949, the Research Department of the Foreign Office produced a compilation covering 'all known members of the Opposition, families and other witnesses' traced up to 1948. The list, which runs to over 200 closely typed pages, was based on the Hassell diaries, Schlabrendorff's book *Offiziere gegen Hitler,* and *Deutscher Widerstand* by the Opposition journalist Pechel. Gisevius' book, *To The Bitter End,* was rejected. Other sources cited were newspaper cuttings and military intelligence reports. Biographical notes were made up from quotations from the three German authors. But one source conspicuously lacking from the compilation was the archives of the Foreign Office. Nowhere is there any mention of direct contact between members of the Opposition and the British Government, the Foreign Office or leading British figures. The Kordt brothers do not even make it into the list. Weizsäcker is dismissed as 'at best a very feeble resister.' Trott's activities in Washington, London and Switzerland are ignored. An account of the 1942 memorandum delivered in London by Visser 't Hooft is omitted (although a copy of this had been received at the time by the Head of Research Department, Arnold Toynbee). The simultaneous Schoenfeld-Bonhoeffer document and its transmission to the Foreign Secretary is likewise omitted. The two Opposition clergymen are merely recorded as having put forward 'peace feelers' to the Bishop of Chichester. Kleist's visit to London is not mentioned but the elderly landowner is misplaced (as Lieutenant von Kleist) in the dramatic events in the Bendlerstrasse on 20th July. Schwerin, so active in London in 1939, does not even rate a mention. Hassell's reference in his diary about his contacts with an Englishman is quoted at length and his Italian son-in-law has an entry. But the nature of his memorandum on the political future is not included. Moltke is included for his Kreisau Circle but not for his communications with Britain. There is no entry for Wirth; Gessler's entry makes no mention of contacts in Switzerland with the British representative, Christie. Halder and Gisevius receive short shrift and the 1938 *putsch* is glossed over as a non-event. Goerdeler is allotted no less than four pages, all of which manage to exclude his special relationship with the British Government and Foreign Office and his efforts with his colleagues to prevent or curtail the war.[27]

By withholding all evidence of activity abroad and of the political programmes for Germany and for Europe put forward both before and during the war, the Foreign Office Research document reduced the rôle of the Opposition to a conspiracy to eliminate the leader who was dragging Germany down into military defeat. This 'A to Z' of the Opposition therefore is incomplete, untrue, misleading and unhistorical. Had it been simply an 'in-house' project (perhaps to give work to idle hands) this would have been of no great consequence. It was, however, directed at important targets. Copies were distributed inside the Foreign Office to the Political, Education and Information sections of the department responsible for German Internal Affairs. In Berlin, at the Headquarters of the British Control Commission, the recipients were the Heads of the Political and Intelligence Divisions, and the Education Adviser to the Commander-in-Chief. There was an even wider distribution. The document reached the Chief of Intelligence of the US Military Government and the Director of Intelligence of the US Army.

But there were other publications coming out of Germany which were to cause particular concern to the Foreign Office. These were the diplomatic memoirs by former State Secretary von Weizsäcker and by Erich Kordt. Weizsäcker's book (written in Landsberg gaol), though diplomatically restrained, nevertheless made clear the efforts made to engage the co-operation of the British in defeating Hitler's policies of aggression. No such restraint was displayed by Erich Kordt. In his book *Nicht aus den Akten* he told the full story, incorporating his brother's experiences in London, and revealing their particular relationship with the British Foreign Office.

Strang, Makins, Passant, O'Neill and Wheeler-Bennett reviewed the situation. Wheeler-Bennett went straight on to the offensive:

> Recent publications by former members of the German diplomatic service contain fallacious – and in some cases mendacious – statements regarding the peace feelers put out by the German Government during the war. In addition, these works contain a further claim in respect of 'opposition' and 'resistance' overtures by members of the German Foreign Office and others, both before and during the war. . . .

Much material existed in the archives, he said, to produce a counter-blast.[28] It is difficult to know what had sprung so readily to mind. Much of what was there would merely confirm what the Germans had recorded. However, Passant, Head of Research Department, passed Wheeler-Bennett's suggestion to O'Neill, who was now on the staff of the High Commissioner in Berlin. Passant put his finger on what was in fact the salient point emerging from these various German accounts:

> The further implication is that, but for the refusal of His Majesty's Government to listen to these overtures, war might either have been averted or ended at an earlier date.

What did O'Neill think?[29]

Given his position as Political Director at the headquarters of the British Zone of Germany, it is indeed astonishing to find O'Neill writing, in 1951, that his knowledge of the Kordt and Weizsäcker books (published in 1948 and 1950 respectively) was 'incomplete'. He had his reservations about Wheeler-Bennett's proposal:

> I must confess to a slight feeling of doubt as to how good a case we could make for ourselves. . . . So far as I recollect, the important peace feelers were put out from sources hostile to the then German Government, and indeed conspiring against it. . . . They were turned down, or not replied to, and probably this was the right thing to do. But it may be harder today in the light of subsequent events, to persuade the public that HMG was right in ignoring these advances. . . .
> Such damage as the Kordt brothers' views may do is confined to a relatively small circle in Germany. It has not occurred to the German public as a whole to criticise us for not supporting the conspirators against Hitler. . . .[30]

Professor Woodward had also been consulted. He was in favour of rebuttal because 'this is one of the spheres in which a myth is developing in Germany and may develop in America.' But it might be impractical, because the papers might be unsuitable for publication.[31] This is exactly what Wheeler-Bennett discovered.

Originally, Wheeler-Bennett had distinguished, more exactly than his colleagues, between 'peace feelers' and Opposition 'overtures'. The Opposition, not being a government, had no power to offer peace. What they had done was to set out the conditions which they would propose, when they became a government, for the settlement of legitimate aspirations, the re-ordering of Germany itself and the pacification of Europe. Through their 'overtures' they sought to obtain the reaction from the other side, both before and during the war. If this was positive, they would be able to reassure the generals who must carry out the overthrow of the régime; and they would have a programme which they could confidently present to the nation as the foundation of a new era of government. Major documentary evidence which the files would yield were Goerdeler's paper, requested by the Foreign Office in December, 1938; the British side of the exchanges with the Vatican in 1939–1940; the Trott memorandum delivered by Visser 't Hooft and the Bonhoeffer/ Schoenfeld memorandum delivered by Bishop Bell, in 1942. This was hardly material for inclusion in a government publication intended to prove the 'mendacity' and 'fallaciousness' of German claims.

In June, six months after his original memorandum, Wheeler-Bennett wrote to Passant again. He reiterated his opinion that 'indiscriminate and piecemeal' revelations now being made in Germany and elsewhere could result in 'wrong ideas as to our willingness to entertain peace offers from Nazi Germany and our unwillingness to receive them from the "Resistance Movement":'

> The writings of von Weizsäcker and Erich Kordt, both of whom claim to have been members of the German 'Resistance Movement' . . . contain statements as to their efforts to bring about a peaceful settlement as between His Majesty's Government and a new Government in Germany, which are not only tendentious but also, in some cases, deliberate perversions of fact. . . .

Publications had also appeared in France and America which were 'detrimental to the interests and prestige of His Majesty's Government.' But the idea of the White Paper had run into difficulties. One *could* be compiled but 'for various reasons, it may be judged wiser to suppress [altered to: "not to publish"] some of the documents. . . .'[32]

Passant passed these various advices to Sir William Strang, saying that it was 'important for the reputation of the country that "legends" on this subject should not be allowed to grow up in Germany.' Sir William found it 'hard to come to a conclusion'. Would Mr Wheeler-Bennett be willing to prepare the necessary documentation without a definite commitment to publication? Mr Wheeler-Bennett, consulted, most emphatically would not. Strang wrote to Makins: 'Have you a view about this? I am divided in my mind.' Makins replied: '. . . We could wait and see if there is really much substance in the activities of the few individuals who are concerning themselves in this matter in Germany and elsewhere.' Relieved, Strang responded: 'That is what I feel also. Let us *not* proceed.'[33] So, nine months after it was originally mooted, the project was, with a sigh of relief, abandoned. It would have been quite obvious to Strang and Makins that no such official refutation of the German diplomats' account was possible. But there were always the useful expedients of *suppressio veri* and *suggestio falsi*. When a member of the Foreign Office, seconded to write a chapter for the Royal Institute of International Affairs Survey, submitted his draft to his superiors for clearance, certain alterations were suggested. The word 'resistance' in connection with the Germans should be avoided. And it was better to omit any reference to the Kordt brothers having been particularly concerned with the Opposition inside the German Foreign Ministry.[34]

Vibrations from these publications however had already been troubling Vansittart's retirement. The Kordt brothers must have begun to seem like a couple of Banquo's ghosts. Miss Lambert, assistant editor of the Documents on British Foreign Policy, asked Vansittart to set the record straight concerning references to him in Kordt's book *Nicht aus den Akten*.[35] (The Foreign Office had still not, in 1950, yet acquired a copy but Miss Lambert had been lent one, apparently by Wheeler-Bennett.) Vansittart replied: 'Erich Kordt seems to have written up for himself rather a nice part in the extract you have sent me. . . .' He had, wrote Vansittart, met the author once or twice in London and his brother Theo 'three or four times in all.' The reason for Erich Kordt's visit to London in June, 1939 (concerning the Nazi-Soviet negotiations) had merely been concerned with getting a Jewish lady out of Germany. This lady was in fact the Kordts' confidential secretary, Hilde Waldo, and Vansittart did indeed arrange her entry into Britain. But by the date in question she had already been in England for several months.

Vansittart completely turned on its head the warning about the Nazi-Soviet Pact which Kordt had come to London specifically to deliver. The Kordts had been *against* any Western agreement with Russia but 'our representatives were already negotiating in Moscow and I tried to make it plain that here also we would not be deterred.' The next time he had met Erich, there was 'some show of over-dramatised secrecy and naturally some political talk. It had not much real importance for there was no prospect of the Kordts or their friends ever taking action. . . . I never took the Kordts seriously though I thought them pretty sly, as I made plain in my affidavit at Nuremberg – at which they both took mortal offence.' Vansittart concluded with what was obviously a reference to the appeal for assistance at the time of the repatriation from Switzerland. Theo Kordt had sent him a telegram 'asking me to do him some service in Germany but I did not answer for I felt that the Allies were certainly under no obligation to him.'[36]

Miss Lambert thanked him for replying so fully: 'On the basis of your recollections we can now rest assured that we have not missed anything of importance in the Foreign Office records.' They were hardly assiduous researchers. Evidence against Vansittart's falsification was all there, most particularly concerning the Nazi-Soviet Pact. But perhaps it was easier just to rely on the word of the former Head of the Foreign Office – and who can blame them – and much less trouble. Weizsäcker's memoirs had also appeared in Germany, continued Miss Lambert, but the Foreign Office was still waiting for a copy. She gathered it was 'a long and rather tedious attempt at self-vindication, probably much on the lines of the evidence he gave at his trial.' Her comments must be given in full:

> My own impression, for what it is worth, is that anyone really brave enough to stand up to Hitler was liquidated, so that the time-servers and re-insurers now have a clear field and are taking full advantage of it. That is one reason why we are anxious to make our British Documents as complete as possible; they do supply a certain corrective for people who really want to know the facts.

Finally, she wrote, when a copy of Erich Kordt's book became available Vansittart might care to look through it as there was a reference to the Kordts having been in touch with him after the outbreak of the war.[37]

Vansittart rose swiftly to the allegation of a war-time contact. This was quite untrue, he replied, 'and if the allegation is made in the Kordts' book it shows what slippery customers they both are. . . . When Theo Kordt was leaving London he muttered something about wishing to keep in contact from his post in Switzerland, but nothing whatever happened. . . . I have looked through Weizsäcker's memoirs. They are really not worth reading . . . and pretty poor stuff on the whole.'[38] Later, Miss Lambert had another chance to look at the Kordt book and reported to Vansittart that it included the text of a letter claimed to have been addressed to him by Theo Kordt on 16 February 1940. It would seem 'only too probable, if the letter is genuine, that you never received it. . . .'[39]

At this point the figure of Conwell-Evans emerges from the shadows. At the time of Weizsäcker's trial the Kordts had tried in vain to contact him both at home and at the Travellers' Club. In 1951 he was no longer living at the celebrated address in South Kensington but had moved to Bayswater. He was evidently still on friendly terms with Vansittart, who seems to have consulted him – as his go-between at the time – about the letter. Conwell-Evans reminded Vansittart that he *had* brought a letter from Theo Kordt in February, 1940. But the letter printed in Kordt's book was dated 16th February and, according to Christie's diary, he was in Paris on that date and could not therefore have been given it. On the evidence of this slight confusion of dates, Vansittart felt able to dismiss the matter. He sent a copy of his reply to Conwell-Evans to Miss Lambert. There is so much verbal juggling that it is difficult to elucidate the facts of the matter. 'You must certainly not take seriously the twisting efforts of the Kordts to rehabilitate themselves,' he told his friend. 'It is really a matter of no consequence.' The Kordt letter was 'full of falsehood, such as the suggestion that the brothers, who served Hitler to the end, were engaged as early as 1940 in trying to put someone in his place or to overthrow him.' Conwell-Evans should get in touch with Namier, 'in case he attaches any importance to these belated attempts at whitewash.' Vansittart concluded his letter: 'I cannot be bothered with these creatures any more.'[40]

A memorandum by Theo Kordt among his papers describes how during the last meeting in Berne with Conwell-Evans he drafted a message to Vansittart which he worked over with the former again and again until he knew it by heart. A roughly-typed version of the letter, attached to this memorandum, matches the published version except for the omission of some paragraphs in the latter. Perhaps the full version was too much for Conwell-Evans to memorise. The typescript is headed 'March, 1940' and a note penned in ink across the top indicates that it was intended to be inserted in a manuscript. In a letter to his brother in July, 1947, Theo mentions 'the letter which I sent to Vansittart through Philip [Conwell-Evans] in March, 1940, of which you have a copy. . . .'[41]

Whatever the precise truth of the matter, the correspondence generated succeeds in confirming in the official records that Vansittart and Theo Kordt were indeed in contact through Conwell-Evans in the early months of the war. It is sad that the latter, who had had so many good friends inside the German Foreign Office and who had urged upon the British Government their efforts to negate Hitler's policies, should after the war have severed his friendship with them. But perhaps pressure had been brought to bear upon him at the time of the Nuremberg trials.

However, Vansittart was forced to speak up on behalf of one member of the pre-war German Embassy, because the request came through Christie. Eduard von Selzam was an old friend of the latter: they had met in the years when they were both at their respective embassies in Washington. Selzam's wife was American and he had been the Opposition's contact with American diplomats both in London and Berne. He had also been a source of information for Christie, as Vansittart well knew. Indeed there is evidence on at least one occasion of a secret conversation in the Foreign Office.[42] In connection with his denazification process, Selzam wrote a letter to Vansittart which he sent to Christie for forwarding. Christie replied that he had done so and had 'added some reminders about your communications to me, passed on to him.' He had also spoken to Vansittart on the telephone 'but not with much success, I am afraid.' Vansittart had claimed that he had been 'so harassed with seeing people from other legations and embassies in those days that he could not remember half of them or who was who.'

> I am sorry that his reply is so brief and rather vague [wrote Christie] but I am enclosing it for what it is worth. I should be unhappy if it was not for the fact that you've got so many first-class people nevertheless in other countries, with whom you worked intimately and who remember your gallant efforts. . . .[43]

Vansittart's support was compressed into one lukewarm sentence:

> Thank you for your letter in regard to Selzam. I remember that, as you say, he did what he could to keep us informed during the latter part of the inter-war period. You are at liberty to make any use that you think fit of this letter.[44]

As those who knew the contents of the official files would not divulge the facts, and as those who knew the facts did not have access to British official records to substantiate their claims, it was easy to have the German versions of events dismissed as attempts at self-justification. The Foreign Office had nervously characterised the accounts emerging from the German side as the foundations of 'myths' and 'legends'. Namier declared that such memoirs should be treated with the greatest reserve and nothing should be accepted unless it was confirmed by some independent and more scholarly authority. But where was this independence? Where was the scholarship? Not among British historians. Namier dealt with what he contemptuously described as 'this mushroom growth of memoirs' (mostly through book reviews) in Goebbels-like language: 'laboured yet frantic apologia'; 'muffled heroes'; 'soaking the reader with blubbering sham-pacification'; 'Nazi self-justification'. The 'crafty' Weizsäcker's opposition to Hitler's policy of aggression existed 'only in retrospect at Nuremberg.' As for the rest:

> We must take leave to doubt whether von Trott, his colleagues in the Kreisau circle, Beck, von Schlabrendorff, von Hassell and the rest . . . would really, once in power, have led a Germany essentially different from that of the Nazis.[45]

In his book *The Lost Days of Hitler* Trevor-Roper conceded that no doubt many Germans 'quietly grumbled about the Nazis.' But –

> As for the 'democratic opposition' . . . it is a creature as fabulous as the centaur and the hippogriff. Who of these 'democrats' ever concerted a programme or approached the Allies with concrete proposals? A few high-minded aristocrats, a few disappointed officials and dismayed parsons. . . .

Trevor-Roper further informed his wide readership that the 'Generals' Plot' showed that the Army leaders regarded the war as lost and 'were at last prepared to break their alliance with the Party'. A small section of the German people – the East German aristocracy – 'ignoring or overriding the fumblings and hesitations of more timorous conspirators', having accepted the Nazis as junior partners now sought by this desperate blow to undo their disastrous error.[46] Or, as Wheeler-Bennett put it:

> What they plotted to do was no mere attempt upon a wicked ruler . . . it was an attempt to conserve as much as possible of what [Germany] already held and, perhaps, a little more.[47]

His blood-boltered verdict on their failure has already been quoted. Wheeler-Bennett's attitude to the Opposition, after his defection to Eden's camp, can be traced in the papers which, during the war, he fired off to Central Department from New York, where he was on the staff of the British Information Service. No doubt he was grateful for the fact that his enthusiastic endorsement of their aims in December, 1938 had 'gone by'. In April, 1943 he volunteered a long paper on Adam von Trott the burden of which according to O'Neill was a complaint that 'he did not quite succeed in being an Englishman.'[48] He accused Trott of 'considerable ambition and a certain confused mysticism which had absorbed something of the stuff of which Nazis are made.' He had 'seen a certain amount of him during his American visit,' but this was at the request of Lord Lothian, the Ambassador.[49] A month later Ambassador Lord Halifax forwarded to Eden a lengthy screed entitled *On what to do with Germany* in which Wheeler-Bennett expatiated on the merits of unconditional surrender and offered advice of his own – that the Allies should 'stand outside' while the blood-letting between Germans and Germans inside the country went ahead: 'Total occupation of Germany should not be effected until a beneficial degree of liquidation has been achieved.'[50] In February, 1944 an effusion entitled *The 'Other' Germans* included attacks on German émigrés in America, including Brüning, whose confidence he was still enjoying. It would be some time, concluded the author, before Germany was 'deloused'. Professor Marshall, of Research Department, condemned 'this vitriolic little paper' as 'hardly worthy of its distinguished author.'[51]

Wheeler-Bennett's abandonment of Trott was total. Although they had first met in Germany in 1935, for some reason he had always denied this.[52] His only published reference to a pre-war encounter is of some 'conversations' in England in the summer of 1939 in which he imputes to Trott 'a certain confused political mysticism . . . a false sense of realism and a belief in power politics and his own part in them.'[53] The author was not of course obliged to explain why, that being so, he had, a few months later, so warmly recommended the young man to the former Chancellor Brüning while he was on his mission to the United States. He simply omitted to mention the fact.

Wheeler-Bennett had privileged access to Foreign Office papers but his loyalty was to the Foreign Office, not to historical fact which, where it concerned the German Opposition, he often chose to disdain. By slanderous comments upon its leaders and by imputations against the spirit, the motivations and the efforts of the anti-Nazi movement he managed, with Namier, to put down markers for students of the Opposition. Their writings have subsequently been challenged by scholars of the Opposition. But as Anthony Howard wrote of Wheeler-Bennett even as late as thirty years after the outbreak of the war: 'At least in British books on the period it is his view that has prevailed.'[54]

The attempt to silence the voices of the Opposition after the war is the greatest tribute which could have been paid to them. It was an acknowledgment that if they had been heeded and responded to with goodwill, and their warnings acted upon, the consequences for the benefit of all might have been immeasurable. There had of course never been any certainty that the Opposition would have succeeded in overthrowing Hitler, so heavily were the odds stacked against them. But that made it even more imperative that the West, particularly Britain, should have backed them with the diplomatic weapons so powerfully and so readily to hand, above all in September, 1938. Wheeler-Bennett claimed that the British and French Governments were being asked to 'gamble with the fate of their countries.' But where was the gamble? An attempted *coup* involving so many top military men would, even if it had failed, have further undermined Germany's ability to fight a major war. It would in any case have negated the boast of internal solidarity vital to a dictatorship dedicated to aggression. There might well have been civil war in Germany, initially at least. This would hardly have constituted a threat to Britain and France; quite the contrary. If failure had left Hitler a wounded beast, he would have savaged his German attackers (as he did in 1944). 'The dire consequences would have been borne by us alone,' wrote Schlabrendorff. 'England and France, far from being in danger, would have been in a much stronger position than before.'[55] These were not questions which the Foreign Office was prepared to have debated in the aftermath of war, if it could be avoided.

The attempt of the 20th July, 1944 was a public act and could not be denied, but it was presented on the Allied side as merely a unique act of doubtful motivation. Yet the tragic failure was only the ultimate manifestation of years of frustrated endeavour by brave and honourable men and women of all classes and political beliefs and religious creeds to root out the evil which they had always known could never be confined within their own country. Eden had said of the July plot that those who carried it out 'were not moved primarily by a desire to help our cause.' But if 'our cause' was the destruction of Hitler and the Nazi régime, this had been the cause of the Opposition in Germany long before the Allies had drawn their swords. The Opposition had always foreseen in all its desolation the ultimate catastrophe to which Hitler would bring Germany and Europe, and possibly the world. They had tried to inspire those in power in other countries with the same nightmare vision. For the British to have admitted this would have called in question their entire policy towards opposition inside the Third Reich. The Foreign Office was never going to let that happen.

Abbreviations and Glossary

Abwehr	Military Intelligence: espionage, counter-espionage and sabotage.
Case XI	Trials of War Criminals before the Nuremberg Military Tribunals under Control Council Law No. 10: The United States v. Ernst von Weizsäcker. (US Government Printing Office, Washington)
DBFP	Documents on British Foreign Policy 1919–1939 (HMSO, London)
DGFP	Documents on German Foreign Policy 1918–1945. Series D 1937–1945. (HMSO, London)
IMT	Trials of the Major War Criminals before the International Military Tribunal, Nuremberg, 14th November 1945–1 October 1946. (Tribunal Secretariat, Nuremberg)
Kristallnacht	The pogrom of 9 November 1938 – 'night of the broken glass.'
NA	National Archive, Washington, DC.
OKH	Oberkommando des Heeres – High Command of the German Army.
OKW	Oberkommando der Wehrmacht – High Command of the Armed Forces. Hitler's staff as Supreme Commander.
OSS	Office of Strategic Services: US war-time intelligence organisation.
SA	Storm Troopers: first Nazi paramilitaries.

SHAEF   Supreme Headquarters, Allied Expeditionary Force

SS   Political police. Most powerful arm of Nazi Party paramilitary force.

Wehrmacht   The Armed forces of the Third Reich.

Notes

Note: Public Record Office documents are referred to by group and file number.

Introduction

1 *The Times*, 17 October 1938.
2 *The Times*, 16 November 1945.
3 FO 371/21658.
4 CAB 106/311.
5 FO 371/22946.
6 *Hansard*, Cols. 571–2, 12 October 1939.
7 Fabian von Schlabrendorff: *The Secret War Against Hitler*, p. 98.
8 Hans Herwarth von Bittenfeld: *Against Two Evils*, p. 276.
9 FO 371/46778.
10 FO 371/39062.
11 Ibid.
12 *Hansard*, Col. 1762, 9 June 1944.
13 *The Times*, 30 September 1954.
14 *DBFP*, Preface to Vol. I, Third Series.
15 FO 370/2347.
16 Schlabrendorff, op. cit., pp. 103–4.

I Whitehall and Wilhelmstrasse

1 FO 800/309.
2 FO 800/214.
3 *Case XI*, Doc. Book 1a. Burckhardt affidavit.
4 Martin Gilbert: *Sir Horace Rumbold*, p. 449.
5 Lord Vansittart: *The Mist Procession*, p. 374.
6 CAB 21/540.
7 FO 371/16681.
8 FO 371/17761.

9 Ed: John Harvey: *The Diplomatic Diaries of Oliver Harvey 1937–40* 23 February 1938.

10 Ed. David Dilks: *The Diaries of Sir Alexander Cadogan 1938–45.*

11 FO 371/18828.

12 Vansittart Papers 2/43. Churchill Archive Centre, Cambridge.

13 Vansittart, op. cit., p. 400.

14 Ian Colvin: *Vansittart in Office*, pp. 147/8.

15 Unpublished Cadogan Diaries, Churchill Archive Centre, Cambridge. 24 May 1937.

16 Interview with Lady Vansittart, 18 August 1984.

17 CAB 140/149.

18 *DGFP*, Series D, Vol. I, pp. 169/70, 176.

19 FO 800/269.

20 Dilks: *Cadogan Diaries*, op. cit., p. 67.

21 FO 371/26532.

22 PREM 4/23/2.

23 Ed. Louis P. Lochner: *Goebbels Diaries*, pp. 171, 267.

24 FO 794/10.

25 CAB 27/627.

26 CAB 21/540.

27 FO 800/315.

28 *New Statesman & Nation*, 25 September 1954.

29 T 188/288.

30 FO 371/16681.

31 *IMT*, Vol. X, pp. 110/111.

32 PREM 1/330.

33 *Case XI*, Trial transcript, p. 10016.

34 FO 370/1489. Ernst von Weizsäcker: *Memoirs*, pp. 307/8.

35 *Case XI*, Trial transcript, p. 7761.

36 *DGFP*, Series D, Vol. IV, Introduction.

37 CAB 21/240.

38 T. P. Conwell-Evans: *None So Blind*, p. 174.

39 *Case XI*, Trial transcript, p. 10016.

40 Weizsäcker, op. cit., p. 177.

41 Weizsäcker, op. cit., pp. 164–5.

42 Carl J. Burckhardt: *Meine Danziger Mission 1937–9*, pp. 63–68.

43 FO 371/26528.

44 *Case XI*, Trial transcript, p. 12008.

45 *Memorandum* by Erich Kordt to E. A. Bayne, January 1946: *Notes on the Foreign Office Conspiracy against the Nazi Régime 1933–41* (Courtesy Mrs Martha C. Johnson).

46 *Memorandum* by Erich Kordt to US State Dept., Shanghai, September 1945. NA RG 238 Entry 51 Box 24.

47 FO 371/23006.
48 Erich Kordt: *Memorandum* to State Dept., op. cit.
49 T 5061/232/383.
50 A. Beverley Baxter: *Men, Martyrs and Mountebanks*, pp. 61–63.
51 *Case XI*, Trial transcript, p. 9491.
52 FO 371/23005.
53 *Case XI*, Trial transcript, pp. 10016–18.
54 *Case XI*, Burckhardt affidavit, op. cit.
55 *Case XI*, Trial transcript, pp. 10016–18.

II *The Other Germany*

1 Heinrich Fraenkel: *Vansittart's Gift Goebbels: The Left News*.
2 FO 371/21662.
3 FO 371/17364.
4 Sebastian Haffner: *Germany: Jekyll and Hyde*, p. 155.
5 FO 371/18884.
6 Fabian von Schlabrendorff: *Revolt Against Hitler*, p. 35.
7 FO 371/17705.
8 FO 371/20728.
9 PREM 1/330.
10 FO 371/21664.
11 FO 371/24389.
12 CAB 120/753.
13 Haffner, op. cit., p. 152.
14 Joachim C. Fest: *Hitler*, p. 764.
15 FO 371/20731.
16 FO 371/20733.
17 FO 371/20729.
18 *The Times*, 27 September 1937.
19 FO 371/21661.
20 Ibid.
21 FO 371/23006.
22 FO 371/23005.
23 FO 371/21732.
24 FO 371/21664.
25 FO 371/21665.
26 FO 800/269.
27 FO 371/21665.
28 FO 371/21666.
29 FO 371/23015.
30 FO CAB 67/627.

31 Ulrich von Hassell: *The von Hassell Diaries*, pp. 20, 21, 25.
32 *IMT*, Vol. XII, p. 327.
33 J. W. Wheeler–Bennett: *The Nemesis of Power*, pp. 426, 432.
34 FO 371/22963.
35 FO 371/20733.
36 FO 371/23002.
37 CAB 21/540.
38 FO 371/23010.
39 FO 371/20733.
40 Heinrich Fraenkel: *Help Us Germans to Beat the Nazis*.
41 Lutz Papers Box 2, Hoover Institution on War, Revolution and Peace, Stanford, California.
42 FO 371/26528.
43 Ibid.
44 FO 371/30928.
45 FO 800/313.
46 FO 371/21661.
47 Inge Scholl: *Six Against Tyranny*.
48 FO 371/24391.
49 Fraenkel, op. cit.
50 FO 371/22975.
51 NA RG 331 091.1–2 SHAEF.
52 *Daily Mail*, 23 February 1945.
53 Fraenkel, op. cit.
54 FO 371/23010.
55 FO 371/23006.
56 NA 103.918/7–1244.
57 FO 371/24391.
58 Balfour and Frisby: *Helmuth von Moltke*, p. 219.
59 US Strategic Bombing Survey 1947.
60 Balfour and Frisby, op. cit., p. 219.
61 US Strategic Bombing Survey 1947.
62 Balfour and Frisby, op. cit., p. 220.
63 Haffner, op. cit., p. 153.
64 Haffner, op. cit., p. 150.
65 FO 371/26532.
66 FO 800/398.
67 Balfour and Frisby, op. cit., p. 322.
68 FO 800/317.
69 FO 371/23098.
70 Haffner, op. cit., p. 182.

III Warnings

1 FO 371/39226.
2 FO 370/2160.
3 PREM 4 97/11.
4 Ibid.
5 Harold C. Deutsch: *The Conspiracy Against Hitler in the Twilight War*, pp. 74–77.
6 Ibid., pp. 96–7.
7 PREM 1/435.
8 FO 898/181.
9 J. Wheeler-Bennett: *The Nemesis of Power*, p. 479.
10 S. Payne Best: *The Venlo Incident*; Case XI trial transcript, pp. 5058–86, 5269–99.
11 E. N. van Kleffens: *The Rape of the Netherlands; Netherlands Parliamentary Committee of Inquiry* (The Orange Book).
12 PREM 4 97/11.
13 FO 800/270.
14 H. B. Gisevius: *To the Bitter End*, p. 360.
15 FO 371/22979; Louis P. Lochner: *What about Germany?*, p. 13.
16 *IMT*, Vol. II, pp. 286 ff.
17 *IMT*, Vol. II, pp. 291 ff.
18 FO 800/270.
19 J. Wheeler-Bennett, op. cit., p. 447(n).
20 *IMT*, Vol. IV, pp. 242–3; Vol. X, p. 515.
21 FO 371/6749.
22 FO 371/22979.
23 Lord Templewood: *Nine Troubled Years*.
24 FO 371/16681.
25 FO 371/21736.
26 FO 371/20733.
27 Ibid.
28 Interview with Lady Vansittart, 6 August 1984.
29 Lord Vansittart: *The Mist Procession*, pp. 497–8.
30 Interview with Lady Vansittart, 6 August 1984.
31 Christie Papers, Churchill Archive Centre, Cambridge.
32 FO 371/21737.
33 Vansittart, op. cit., p. 498.
34 FO 371/15946.
35 FO 371/15936.
36 Vansittart, op. cit., p. 498.
37 FO 371/21708.
38 Lochner Papers, Box 1, Hoover Institution on War, Revolution and Peace, Stanford, California.

39 FO 371/23006.
40 FO 371/22965; T. P. Conwell-Evans: *None So Blind*, p. 176.
41 FO 371/22963.
42 Ed. David Dilks: *Cadogan Diaries*, p. 155.
43 *Diaries*, op. cit., p. 156.
44 *Hansard*, Vol. 346, Col. 33.
45 *Hansard*, Vol. 346, Col. 140.
46 FO 371/21708.
47 CAB 27/624.
48 Last Will & Testament of Graham C. Christie, Somerset House, London.
49 Theo Kordt: *Kordt Papers*, Record of a visit to Lord Halifax, 15 November 1953.
50 Theo Kordt: *Memorandum for MI6, 1946*. Courtesy of Mrs Martha C. Johnson.
51 Interview with Lady Vansittart, 6 August 1984.
52 Theo Kordt, op. cit.
53 Interview with Miss Hilde Waldo, Santa Monica, California. 7 June 1987.
54 Interview with Herr Reinhard Spitzy, Hinterthal, Austria. 10 October 1988.
55 FO 371/20733.
56 FO 371/22963.
57 FO 371/22975.
58 FO 371/24386.
59 FO 371/22963.
60 FO 371/23006.
61 FO 371/21708.
62 FO 371/21666.
63 FO 371/20733.
64 Ibid.
65 Ibid.
66 FO 371/21666.
67 Conwell-Evans, op. cit., p. 102; Christie Papers 1/21A.
68 FO 371/20733.
69 Vansittart Papers, VNST 1/20. Churchill Archive Centre, Cambridge.
70 Ian Colvin: *Vansittart in Office*, pp. 154–5.
71 PREM 1/330.
72 FO 371/20728.
73 Ibid.
74 Ibid.
75 FO 371/21660.
76 FO 371/23002.

77 FO 371/16681.
78 FO 371/23006.
79 Ibid.
80 Ibid.
81 *Hansard*, Col. 1757, 9 June 1944.

IV *Dialogues with the Deaf*

1 T. P. Conwell-Evans: *None So Blind*, p. 51; William L. Shirer: *The Rise and Fall of the Third Reich*, p. 291.
2 *IMT*, Prosecution Document, PS–386.
3 FO 371/21661.
4 H. B. Gisevius: *To the Bitter End*, p. 254 ff.; *IMT*, Vol. II, p. 203; Fabian von Schlabrendorff: *The Secret War Against Hitler*, Appendix IV.
5 *IMT*, Vol. XII, p. 642.
6 FO 371/21662.
7 Ibid.
8 Ibid.
9 Private communications to Hon. David Astor.
10 Ed: Claire Nix: *Heinreich Brüning: Briefe und Gespräche 1934–45*, pp. 176–9.
11 Nix, op. cit., pp. 184–6.
12 Nix, op. cit., p. 188 [note 3].
13 Conwell-Evans, op. cit. pp. 91–2. Christie Papers 121/A; Kordt Papers.
14 FO 371/21660.
15 PREM 1/308.
16 Conwell-Evans, op. cit., pp. 132/3.
17 FO 371/21708.
18 *IMT*, Vol. XIV, p. 141. Doc. No. 3037-PS.
19 FO 371/46749.
20 Ibid.
21 FO 371/21698.
22 FO 371/21713.
23 FO 800/309.
24 Brigadier H. C. T. Stronge CBE, DSO, MC: *Personal memorandum relating to the state of morale and general readiness for war of the Army of the Czechoslovak Republic at the time of the Munich Crisis in September 1938 and the period immediately preceding it.* Imperial War Museum.
25 CAB 27/646.
26 *History of The Times*, Vol. IV, Part II, p. 935.
27 *IMT*, Vol. X, p. 509.

28 *IMT*, Vol. XX, p. 606.
29 FO 371/21578.
30 FO 371/22957.
31 NA RG 243 2a. (52a) 30 June/1 July 1945.
32 Peter Hoffmann: *The History of the German Resistance 1939–45*, p. 77.
33 FO 371/22957.
34 Ibid.
35 FO 371/21708.
36 FO 371/21736.
37 Ian Colvin: *Vansittart in Office*, pp. 211 ff.
38 FO 371/21732.
39 FO 800/420.
40 *DBFP*, 3rd Series Vol. II, pp. 687–9.
41 FO 800/314.
42 Schlabrendorff, op. cit., pp. 94–9.
43 *DGFP*, Vol. II, p. 706.
44 FO 371/21732.
45 *Cadogan Diaries*, p. 91.
46 FO 371/21737.
47 Conwell-Evans, op. cit., pp. 139–40.
48 Conwell-Evans, op. cit., p. 140.
49 CAB 23/94.
50 Colvin, op. cit., p. 232.
51 Conwell-Evans, op. cit., p. 142.
52 FO 371/21734.
53 FO 800/314.
54 Gisevius, op. cit., p. 320.
55 Theo Kordt: *The Anti-Nazi Crisis in 1938–39. Events and Personalities in London: Memorandum for MI6* (courtesy of Mrs Martha C. Johnson).
56 *DGFP*, Series D, Vol. I, pp. 605–9.
57 *DGFP*, Series D, Vol. I, pp. 676–8.
58 *Case XI*, Trial transcript, pp. 7380 ff.
59 *Case XI*, Trial transcript, pp. 12015 ff. Theo Kordt: *Memorandum*, op. cit.
60 *Case XI*, Trial transcript, pp. 12015–9.
61 *Cadogan Diaries*, pp. 94–5.
62 *Case XI*, Trial transcript, pp. 12015–9.
63 CAB 23/95.
64 *Case XI*, Trial transcript, p. 12018.
65 *Case XI*, Doc. Book 1a, Burckhardt affidavit.
66 FO 371/21805.
67 FO 371/21736.
68 PREM 1/265.

69 PREM 1/265.

70 Ibid.

71 FO 800/314.

V *The Impossible Had Happened* . . .

1 FO 800/314.

2 FO 371/21737.

3 *DGFP*, Series D, Vol. II, pp. 765–80.

4 Erich Kordt: *Nicht aus den Akten*, p. 253.

5 T. P. Conwell-Evans: *None So Blind*, pp. 141–2.

6 Op. cit., pp. 142–4.

7 FO 800/314.

8 FO 371/21736.

9 CAB 29/95.

10 *Cadogan Diaries*, pp. 95, 96.

11 FO 371/21737.

12 FO 371/21739.

13 FO 371/21736.

14 Ibid.

15 PREM 1/266A.

16 FO 800/314.

17 Ed. John Harvey: *The Diplomatic Diaries of Oliver Harvey 1937–40*, 10 September 1938.

18 FO 371/21765.

19 Harvey, op. cit. 14 September 1938.

20 *The Times*, 12 September 1938.

21 CAB 23/95.

22 FO 800/314.

23 FO 370/2292.

24 FO 371/21736.

25 J. Wheeler-Bennett: *George VI*, pp. 346–7.

26 *Case XI*, Trial transcript, p. 12019.

27 *Case XI*, Trial transcript, p. 1843; Halder Interview, June 30/July 1, 1945 2a (52a), NA RG243 US Strategic Bombing Survey; *IMT*, Vol. XII, pp. 218–9; Gisevius, pp. 317–27; Erich Kordt, op. cit., 277–8.

28 CAB 23/95.

29 *DGFP*, Series D, Vol. II, pp. 786–98.

30 Erich Kordt: *Memorandum*, January 1946 (courtesy Mrs Martha C. Johnson).

31 Kordt, op. cit.

32 PREM 1/266A.
33 CAB 27/646; FO 371/21741.
34 *IMT, XXVIII* Doc. No. 1780-PS.
35 *Case XI*, Trial transcript, pp. 7384 ff; Erich Kordt: *Wahn und Wirklich-keit*; Erich Kordt: *Memorandum*.
36 William L. Shirer: The *Rise and Fall of the Third Reich*, p. 399.
37 FO 371/21665.
38 *DGFP*, Series D, Vol. II, pp. 966–8.
39 FO 370/561.
40 FO 371/21664.
41 Ulrich von Hassell: *Von Hassell Diaries*, p. 13.
42 FO 371/21664.
43 Conwell-Evans, op. cit., pp. 147–8.
44 NA M.1270 Roll 22.
45 FO 371/21665.
46 *Command Paper* 5848 No. 1.
47 *IMT*, Vol. XII, pp. 218–9; Gerhard Ritter: *The German Resistance*, pp. 109–110; H. B. Gisevius: *To the Bitter End*, p. 325.
48 Erich Kordt: *Memorandum*.
49 Kordt, op. cit.
50 FO 371/21745.
51 *Nazi Conspiracy and Aggression*. Supplement B, pp. 1557–8.
52 Kordt, op. cit.
53 *Nazi Conspiracy and Aggression*, p. 1557/8.
54 FO 371/21664.
55 Ibid.
56 Ibid.
57 *The Times*, 8 June 1971. Letter from Ivan Maisky.
58 *Case XI*, Trial transcript, p. 1005, p. 7722; *Wahn und Wirklichkeit*, pp. 131–2; *DGFP*, Series D, Vol. II, pp. 786–98; Paul Otto Schmidt: *I was Hitler's Interpreter*, p. 111.
59 *DBFP*, Third Series, Vol. II, No. 1227.
60 CAB 23/96.
61 PREM 1/331A.
62 FO 370/561.
63 FO 371/21665.
64 Ibid.
65 Ibid.
66 Ibid.
67 *Hansard* (Munich Debate), House of Lords.
68 Hjalmar Schacht: *Account Settled*, p. 125.
69 Gisevius, op. cit., p. 326.

VI *Voices from Germany*

1 Erich Kordt: *Memorandum* to US State Dept. NA RG 238 Entry 51, Box 24.
2 *Case XI*, Trial transcript, p. 12030.
3 Kordt, op. cit.; *Case IX*, Hilde Waldo affidavit; Interview with Hilde Waldo, Santa Monica, California, 6 June 1987; *Case XI*, Weizsäcker Document No. 434.
4 FO 371/22963.
5 FO 371/22965.
6 *Nazi Conspiracy and Aggression*, Supplement B, p. 1558.
7 FO 371/21659.
8 FO 371/21665.
9 A. P. Young: *The 'X' Documents*, p. 148.
10 FO 371/21665.
11 Young, op. cit., pp. 148–56.
12 FO 371/21659.
13 *Focus: A footnote to the History of the Thirties*.
14 Unpublished Cadogan Diaries. Churchill Archive Centre, Cambridge.
15 Young, op. cit., p. 152.
16 FO 371/22961.
17 FO 371/21665.
18 FO 371/21659.
19 FO 371/21665.
20 *Cadogan Diaries*, p. 129.
21 FO 371/21665.
22 FO 371/21659.
23 Ibid.
24 FO 371/22961.
25 FO 371/22963.
26 Young, op. cit., p. 156.
27 CAB 27/624.
28 Ibid.
29 CAB 27/627.
30 FO 371/23006.
31 Keith Feiling: *Life of Neville Chamberlain*, p. 396.
32 Winston S. Churchill: *The Second World War*, Vol. I, p. 307.
33 FO 371/23006.
34 FO 371/23025.
35 *Case XI*, Trial transcript, p. 12031 ff.
36 CAB 23/99.
37 FO 371/21805.

38 CAB 23/98.

39 *Hansard*, Col. 2415, 31 March 1938.

40 H. B. Gisevius: *To the Bitter End*, p. 362.

41 FO 371/22963.

42 FO 371/22974.

43 FO 371/22973.

44 FO 371/22990.

45 FO 371/22974.

46 David Astor: 'Why the revolt against Hitler was ignored,' *Encounter*, Vol. 33, June 1969.

47 FO 371/22974.

48 Ibid.

49 Ibid.

50 FO 371/22991.

51 FO 800/316.

52 CAB 23/95.

53 FO 371/22974.

54 Gräfin Marion Dönhoff, *Die Zeit*, 1979.

55 FO 371/22109.

56 David Astor: 'Adam von Trott: A Personal View;' *The Challenge of the Third Reich*, pp. 26–8; Christopher Sykes: *Troubled Loyalty*, pp. 240–50; William Douglas Home: *Half-Term Report; DGFP*, Series D, Vol. VI, No. 674.

57 *Daily Express*, 28 May 1956; *Manchester Guardian*, 28 May 1956.

58 *Manchester Guardian*, 4 June 1956.

59 PREM 1/328.

60 FO 370/2082.

61 Fabian von Schlabrendorff: *The Secret War Against Hitler*, pp. 95–98.

62 FO 371/23020.

63 FO 371/23021.

64 *Case XI*, Trial transcript, pp. 9800–9816.

VII *Milestones to Catastrophe*

1 FO 370/2393.

2 Erich Kordt: *Memorandum* to US State Dept. NA RG 238, Entry 51, Box 24; Erich Kordt: *Nicht aus den Akten*, pp. 301–2; Theo Kordt: *The Anti-Nazi Crisis in 1938–39: Memorandum for MI6; Case XI*, Trial transcript, p. 12033.

3 FO 371/22963.

4 FO 371/22944.

5 Joseph E. Davies: *Mission to Moscow*, pp. 440–41.

6 *Case XI*, Trial transcript, pp. 7756–7.
7 CAB 27/627.
8 FO 371/22972; T. P. Conwell-Evans: *None So Blind*, pp. 192–3 (A note in Christie's Papers (129B) says information came from 'Kn' and was handed to Halifax).
9 FO 371/22972.
10 *Case XI*, Trial transcript, pp. 12034–5.
11 Erich Kordt, statement 21–22 June 1946. NA M 1019 (R37).
12 FO 371/22973.
13 Ibid.
14 Ibid.
15 FO 800/269.
16 FO 371/22973.
17 Ibid.
18 Erich Kordt: *Nicht aus den Akten*, pp. 313–6; Case XI Trial transcript, pp. 12035; 7395.
19 CAB 23/100.
20 FO 371/23686.
21 *DGFP*, Series D, Vol. VIII, p. 61.
22 Erich Kordt: *Nicht aus den Akten*, p. 316; *Case XI*, Trial transcript p. 12035; 7395. Erich Kordt: *Memorandum* to State Dept., op. cit.
23 *DGFP*, Series D, Vol. II, pp. 618–20.
24 *Case XI*, Trial transcript, pp. 12050 ff.
25 *DGFP*, Series D, Vol. VI, pp. 971–2.
26 *Case XI*, Trial transcript, pp. 12047–53.
27 FO 800/316.
28 FO 371/23025.
29 *Cadogan Diaries*, p. 195.
30 *Case XI*, Trial transcript, p. 9860.
31 FO 800/316.
32 PREM/22A.
33 FO 371/23686.
34 Ibid.
35 CAB 23/100.
36 Ibid.
37 FO 371/23026.
38 FO 371/22977.
39 *Case XI*, Trial transcript, pp. 12052ff.
40 *IMT*, Vol. XI, p. 1086.
41 FO 371/55511; H. B. Gisevius: *To the Bitter End*, pp. 355–6; *Schweizer Monatshefte* 25 (1945).
42 Gisevius, op. cit., pp. 368–73; *IMT*, Vol. XII, pp. 224–5.

43 *Nazi Conspiracy and Aggression*, Vol. VI, pp. 997–8; *IMT*, Vol. XX, p. 572.
44 Gisevius, op. cit., pp. 369–71.
45 FO 371/22980.
46 Erich Kordt: 'Was war inevitable after Munich?' (Kordt Papers).
47 *IMT*, Vol. X, pp. 196–9; P. O. Schmidt: *Hitler's Interpreter*, p. 152.
48 William L. Shirer: *The Rise and Fall of the Third Reich*, p. 152; Sir Nevile Henderson: *Failure of a Mission*, Appendix VIII.
49 Schmidt, op. cit., p. 153.
50 FO 370/2436; Birger Dahlerus: *The Last Attempt*.
51 Ulrich von Hassell: *The von Hassell Diaries*, pp. 67–70.
52 FO 371/22980.
53 Dahlerus, op. cit.
54 *DGFP*, Series D, Vol. VII, No. 458.
55 *Case XI*, Trial transcript, pp. 12056–9; Theo Kordt: *Memorandum*, op. cit.; Erich Kordt: *Nicht aus den Akten*, pp. 337–8.
56 Gisevius, op. cit., p. 372.
57 Shirer, op. cit., p. 598.
58 FO 371/22981.
59 *IMT*, Vol. X, pp. 200–1; Schmidt, op. cit., pp. 157–8.
60 Henderson, op. cit., pp. 287–8.
61 Ernst von Weizsäcker: *Memoirs*, p. 21.
62 Hassell, op. cit., p. 71.
63 *Case XI*, Doc. Book 9, No. 391; Kordt Papers.

VIII Underground Channels

1 Fabian von Schlabrendorff: *The Secret War Against Hitler*, pp. 105–6.
2 Walter Warlimont: *Inside Hitler's Headquarters 1939–45*, pp. 34–6; *IMT*, Vol. XX, p. 572.
3 Warlimont, op. cit., p. 37.
4 Quoted in Harold C. Deutsch: *The Conspiracy Against Hitler in the Twilight War*.
5 *IMT*, Vol. XX, p. 573.
6 Hans Bernd Gisevius: *To the Bitter End*, p. 383.
7 Franz Halder: *Kriegstagebuch*, pp. 117–8.
8 Gisevius, op. cit., p. 384.
9 Deutsch, op. cit., pp. 227–33.
10 Gisevius, op. cit., p. 386.
11 *Case XI*, Trial transcript, p. 9592.
12 *Case XI*, Georg Bruns affidavit, Doc. No. 13; Interview Dr Georg Bruns, Lindau, Germany, 14 September 1985.

13 *Case XI*, Trial transcript, pp. 12064–6; Theo Kordt: *Memorandum: The Anti-Nazi Crisis in 1938–39*.

14 *Case XI*, Doc. Book 9, No. 433.

15 *Case XI*, Trial transcript, pp. 12067–9; Theo Kordt, *Memorandum*, op. cit.

16 Christie Papers, Churchill Archive Centre, Cambridge.

17 Deutsch, op. cit., p. 257.

18 Erich Kordt: *Nicht aus den Akten*, pp. 386–9.

19 Kordt, op. cit., pp. 370–2; *Case XI*, Trial transcript, p. 12070.

20 Kordt, op. cit., p. 374.

21 *Case XI*, Trial transcript, p. 12070.

22 Op. cit., p. 12075.

23 Erich Kordt, op. cit., pp. 380–2; Kordt Papers.

24 FO 800/325; FO 371/23097.

25 FO 371/23098.

26 FO 800/322.

27 *Cadogan Diaries*, p. 228.

28 FO 800/397.

29 CAB 23/94.

30 FO 800/317.

31 FO 371/23097.

32 FO 371/24362.

33 Erich Kordt, op. cit., p. 341; Letter Erich Kordt to E. A. Bayne (Kordt Papers).

34 Ed: Claire Nix: *Heinrich Brüning: Briefe und Gespräche 1934–45*, p. 299, p. 360 (n2).

35 FO 371/34449; Christopher Sykes: *Troubled Loyalty*, p. 308.

36 Maurice Bowra: *Memories 1898–1939*.

37 NA Box 5226 862.2011.

38 Sykes, op. cit., p. 314.

39 FO 371/24363.

40 Ibid.

41 Ibid.

42 Ibid.

43 *Cadogan Diaries*, p. 249.

44 FO 371/24363.

45 FO 371/26542.

46 J. Wheeler-Bennett: *The Nemesis of Power*, p. 487.

47 J. Wheeler-Bennett: *Special Relationships*, p. 152.

48 *Encounter*, Vol. 33, 1969, p. 95.

49 *New Statesman*, 23 May 1969, p. 724.

50 J. Lonsdale Bryans: *Blind Victory*, pp. 15/16.

51 FO 800/326.

52 Ulrich von Hassell: *The Hassell Diaries*, pp. 109–11.
53 Bryans, op. cit., pp. 73–4.
54 FO 800/326.
55 FO 800/398.
56 Hassell, op. cit., p. 329.
57 FO 371/24386.
58 FO 371/24389.
59 Ibid.
60 FO 371/24405.
61 FO 371/24389.
62 Ibid.
63 Christie Papers 1/35.
64 Broadcast from Birmingham Town Hall: *The Times*, 26 February 1940.
65 Christie Papers 1/35.
66 Gerhard Ritter: *The German Resistance*.
67 Christie Papers 1/35.
68 Ibid.
69 FO 371/24389.
70 Ritter, op. cit., p. 159.
71 Hassell, op. cit., p. 120.
72 NA XE 138 356. I 8c 002 Boehm-Tettelbach.
73 NA RG 243 2a (52a) Halder interview, 30 June/1 July 1945; NA M.1270, 27 October 1945; *Nazi Conspiracy and Aggression*, p. 1558.
74 Ritter, op. cit., p. 212 (n.2).
75 Bryans, op. cit., pp. 73, 80.
76 Hassell, op. cit., p. 124.
77 FO 1019–60, Müller statement, 16 January 1946; Deutsch, op. cit., pp. 116–7.
78 Deutsch, op. cit., pp. 120 ff.
79 FO 371/23099.
80 FO 371/26542.
81 FO 371/23100.
82 FO 371/24405.
83 Deutsch, op. cit., p. 121.
84 FO 371/24957.
85 Diaries of Sir Francis D'Arcy Osborne (unpublished), Egerton MSS 3845, British Library.
86 FO 371/24405.
87 CAB 65/2.
88 FO 371/24405.
89 Ibid.
90 Ibid.

91 FO 371/24405.
92 Ibid.
93 Ibid.
94 Ibid.
95 Ibid.
96 FO 371/24407.
97 FO 371/24962.
98 FO 371/24957; FO 371/24407.
99 Hassell, op. cit., p. 117.
100 Deutsch, op. cit., p. 297.
101 Hassell, op. cit., pp. 117–20.
102 Hassell, op. cit., pp. 122–3.
103 Deutsch, op. cit., pp. 311–2; Gisevius, op. cit., pp. 442–3.
104 Halder: Interview, op. cit.
105 *Case XI*, Defence Document No. 140.
106 *Cadogan Diaries*, p. 228.
107 Cadogan, op. cit., pp. 226, 228.
108 *The Times*, 22 February 1940.
109 E. N. van Kleffens: *The Rape of the Netherlands*; Case XI Prosecution
    Doc. No. NG–4672; trial transcript pp. 5058–86, 5269–99.
110 Hassell, op. cit., p. 81.

IX The Bitter End

1 FO 371/26542.
2 W. A. Visser 't Hooft: *Memoirs*, p. 151.
3 Visser 't Hooft, op. cit., p. 178.
4 Visser 't Hooft, op. cit., Chapter 21.
5 FO 371/30912.
6 Interview with Dr Visser 't Hooft, Geneva, 12 November 1984.
7 Visser 't Hooft, op. cit., p. 157; *Encounter*, Vol. XXXIII, 1969.
8 371/30912.
9 *Encounter*, Vol. XXXIII, p. 91.
10 Visser 't Hooft, op. cit., p. 160.
11 FO 371/30912.
12 Ibid.
13 Ibid.
14 Ibid.
15 Ibid.
16 Visser 't Hooft, op. cit., pp. 157–8.
17 FO 371/30912.
18 Ibid.

19 Account taken from transcript of a lecture by Bishop Bell: *The Church and the Resistance Movement in Germany* given at Bonn and Göttingen Universities, 15–16 May 1957. World Council of Churches Archive, Geneva, Box XII, No. 5.

20 FO 371/33055.

21 FO 188/460.

22 Private Papers.

23 Bell, op. cit.; Letter: Bell to Eden, 25 July 1942.

24 Bell, op. cit.; Letter: Eden to Bell, 4 August 1942.

25 *New York Review of Books*, September 1969, p. 37.

26 FO 371/30928.

27 *Hansard*, House of Lords, Debate 10 March 1943, Cols. 535–49.

28 A detailed account of the assassination attempts is to be found in *The History of the German Resistance 1933–45*, Peter Hoffmann.

29 *IMT*, Vol. XII, p. 215.

30 Halder: Interview, 7 August 1945 CSDIC (VIC) GRGG. 332(c) (courtesy of the late Lord Kaldor).

31 FO 371/34444.

32 *The Spectator*, No. 6181, 13 December 1946, p. 636.

33 FO 371/30928.

34 Asa Briggs: *The History of Broadcasting*, p. 427.

35 FO 371/30928.

36 FO 898/182.

37 FO 898/181.

38 Ibid.

39 FO 371/26532.

40 Ibid.

41 CAB 118/50.

42 *Case XI*, Defence Book II, Supplement 2, Doc. No. 169c.

43 H. B. Gisevius: *The Bitter End*, p. 476.

44 PREM 4/100/8.

45 NA RG 226. OSS. Entry 138, Box 2, 25 July 1944; 28 July 1944; 26 January 1944.

46 NA RG 226. OSS. Entry 138, Box 2, Folder 76.

47 NA 740, 0011 EW 1939/2635.

48 FO 371/39087.

49 Allen Dulles: *Germany's Underground*, p. 171.

50 FO 371/39087.

51 FO 371/26508.

52 Dulles, op. cit., p. 138.

53 NA RG 226. OSS. Entry 99, Box No. 18, Folder 83.

54 NA RG 226. OSS. Entry 138, Box No. 2, Folder 72.

55 Ibid.

56 Visser 't Hooft, op. cit., p. 162.
57 FO 371/39151.
58 FO 898/192.
59 FO 371/39087.
60 FO 371/39332.
61 FO 371/39088.
62 NA RG 226. OSS. Entry 138, Box 2, Folder 72.
63 FO 371/46787.
64 FO 371/55511.
65 FO 371/39087.
66 FO 371/39062.
67 Ibid.
68 *Cadogan Diaries*, p. 647.
69 NA RG 226. OSS. Entry 138, Box 2, 12 July 1944.
70 Ibid., Folder 75.
71 *Hansard*, 2 August 1944, Col. 1487.
72 FO 371/39062.
73 FO 371/39077.
74 A. P. Young: *The X Documents*, pp. 209–14.
75 FO 371/39087.
76 FO 371/39063.
77 Hoffmann, op. cit., p. 374.
78 Annedore Leber: *Conscience in Revolt*, p. 139.
79 Fabian von Schlabrendorff: *Revolt Against Hitler*, p. 145.
80 Leber, op. cit., p. 186.
81 FO 371/118 198.

X Trials and Errors

1 FO 371/46834.
2 Ibid.
3 Kordt Papers: Letter: Theo Kordt to R. A. Butler, 3 August 1945.
4 FO 371/46852.
5 Ibid.
6 Ibid.
7 Letters: Erich Kordt to E. A. Bayne, Shanghai, 2 October 1945, 23 October 1945 (courtesy of Mrs Martha C. Johnson).
8 NA RG 238, Entry 51, Box 24.
9 Ibid.
10 Interview with Hilde Waldo, Santa Monica, California, 19 June 1987.
11 *Case XI*, Weizsäcker, Document No. 496.

12 Erich Kordt: *Memorandum* (courtesy of Mrs Martha C. Johnson).
13 Theo Kordt: *Memorandum* (courtesy of Mrs Martha C. Johnson).
14 Letters: E. A. Bayne to Major J. G. Lockhart and reply from British Embassy (courtesy of Mrs Martha C. Johnson).
15 Letter: Lord Vansittart to E. A. Bayne, Kordt Papers.
16 Letter: Erich Kordt to E. A. Bayne, 14 November 1946, Kordt Papers.
17 Letter: Theo to Erich Kordt, 22 August 1946, Kordt Papers.
18 Letter: Theo to Erich Kordt, 20 April 1946, Kordt Papers.
19 Erich Kordt: *Nicht aus den Akten*, pp. 316–7.
20 FO 1019/82.
21 FO 1019/60.
22 FO 1019/39.
23 *IMT*, Vol. VIII, p. 168.
24 T 188/288.
25 T 188/226.
26 *IMT*, Vol. XII, pp. 187–305.
27 *IMT*, Vol. XII, pp. 469 ff.
28 FO 371/23105.
29 FO 371/66559.
30 *New York Herald Tribune* (European edition).
31 *Case XI*: Opening statement for the Defence.
32 *Case XI*: Document Book 9: document no. 439; document no. 455.
33 Interview: Warren Magee, Washington USA, June 1985.
34 Interview: Dr Helmuth Becker, Berlin, June 1986.
35 FO 371/70793.
36 FO 371/70796.
37 Letter: Theo Kordt to Lord Halifax, 24 March 1948, Kordt Papers.
38 Information from Frau Lore Kordt.
39 Letter: Theo Kordt to R. A. Butler, 24 December 1947, Kordt Papers.
40 FO 371/70796.
41 FO 371/57660.
42 Ibid.
43 Ibid.
44 FO 371/70796.
45 FO 371/23020.
46 CAB 23/100.
47 FO 371/22973.
48 FO 370/1505.
49 FO 371/70795.
50 FO 371/70799.
51 *Case XI*, Weizsäcker Documents Nos. 391, 390, 261.

52 Unpublished Cadogan Diaries, Churchill Archive Centre, Cambridge, 21 March 1940.
53 *Case XI*, Weizsäcker Document 408.
54 FO 371/70799.
55 Interview, Warren Magee, Washington; *New York Times*, 10 November 1948; *Case XI*, Weizsäcker Document No. 438.
56 *Case XI*, Closing Statement for the Defence, pp. 27191–264.
57 *Case XI*, Document Books I (a)(d).
58 *Nazi Conspiracy and Aggression*, Chapter XIV, p. 956.
59 FO 1019/39.
60 *Case XI*, Weizsäcker Doc. No. 460, Interrogation of Friedrich Gaus, 6 May 1947 by Dr Kempner, prosecutor.
61 *New York Herald Tribune*, 12 May 1948.
62 *Case XI*, Trial transcript, p. 7709.
63 FO 371/70786; FO 371/77063.
64 *Case XI*, Prosecution Doc. No. NG-5786 and NG-5786A.
65 Interview: Warren Magee.
66 *Case XI*, Weizsäcker Document No. 496.
67 Ibid.
68 FO 371/70786.
69 Interview: Warren Magee.
70 *Case XI*, Weizsäcker, Document No. 497.
71 Kordt Papers; Erich Kordt: *Nicht aus den Akten*, p. 317n; *Frankfurter Hefte*, November 1948; *Die Zeit*, December 1949.
72 *New York Times*, 17 October 1948.
73 Interview: Warren Magee.
74 *Hansard*: Vol. 457, Cols. 255–6, 28 October 1948.
75 *Nazi Conspiracy and Aggression*, Vol. XIV, p. 893.
76 Op. cit., p. 913.
77 FO 371/77014.
78 FO 371/77020.
79 *The Times*, 18 April 1949.
80 *The Economist*, 23 April 1949, p. 739.
81 *The Times*, December 8, 10, 12, 19, 1949.
82 FO 371/77020.
83 Ibid.
84 Harry S. Truman Library, Independence, Missouri, by courtesy of the Librarian.
85 Record of visit to Lord Halifax by Theo Kordt, 15 November 1953, Kordt Papers.
86 *The Independent*, 20 March 1990.

XI *Not in the Public Interest*

1 *Hansard*, 9 June 1944, Cols. 1755–64.
2 FO 371/30945.
3 FO 371/15213.
4 FO 371/26579.
5 PREM 4 6/13.
6 FO 371/26579.
7 Ibid.
8 Ibid.
9 Ibid.
10 FO 371/30945.
11 CAB 103/21.
12 FO 371/26579.
13 FO 371/34478.
14 Sir Lewis Namier: *Europe in Decay: The Road to Munich*, p. 72.
15 FO 898/531.
16 NA RG 243, European Survey No. 52.
17 FO 371/46790.
18 Ibid.
19 Interview and correspondence with the late Lord Kaldor, February–September 1985.
20 *The Daily Worker*, 12/13 September 1945.
21 FO 371/46719.
22 FO 371/46781.
23 Ibid.
24 Ibid.
25 FO 371/55511.
26 Ibid.
27 FO 371/76732.
28 FO 370/2168.
29 Ibid.
30 Ibid.
31 Ibid.
32 Ibid.
33 Ibid.
34 FO 370/2199.
35 FO 370/2082.
36 Ibid.
37 Ibid.
38 Ibid.
39 Ibid.
40 FO 370/2154.

41 Kordt Papers.
42 PREM 1/331A.
43 *Case XI*, Weizsäcker Document No. 494.
44 Ibid., No. 495.
45 *Times Literary Supplement*, 27 March 1969.
46 H. Trevor-Roper: *The Last Days of Hitler*, p. 260.
47 *New York Review of Books*, September 1939, p. 37.
48 FO 371/39066.
49 FO 371/34449.
50 Ibid.
51 FO 371/39137.
52 Henry O. Malone: *Adam von Trott zu Solz*, p. 159(n).
53 J. W. Wheeler-Bennett: *The Nemesis of Power*, 442/3.
54 *New Statesman & Nation*, 23 May 1969, p. 724.
55 Fabian von Schlabrendorff: *The Secret War Against Hitler*, p. 89.

Bibliography

Ashton-Gwatkin, F., *The British Foreign Office* (Syracuse, USA, 1950).

Avon, Earl of, *Facing The Dictators* (London, 1962).

Balfour, Michael & Frisby, Julian, *Helmuth von Moltke* (London, 1972).

Baxter, Beverley, *Men, Martyrs and Mountebanks* (London).

Bayne, E. A., 'Resistance in the German Foreign Office', *Human Events*, No. 14, April, 1946.

Bielenberg, Christabel, *The Past Is Myself* (London, 1968).

Birkenhead, Earl of, *Halifax* (London, 1965).

Bohlen, Charles, *Witness To History* (New York, 1973).

Boveri, Margret, *Treason In The Twentieth Century*, trans. Jonathan Steinberg (New York, 1963).

Bowra, Sir Maurice, *Memories* (London, 1966).

Briggs, Asa, *The History Of Broadcasting* (Oxford, 1970).

Brüning, Heinrich, *Briefe und Gespräche 1934–45*, ed. Claire Nix (Stuttgart, 1974).

Bryans, J. Lonsdale, *Blind Victory* (London, 1951).

Burckhardt, Carl J., *Meine Danziger Mission 1937–39* (Munich, 1960).

Bull, Hedley (Ed.), *The Challenge Of The Third Reich* (Oxford, 1986).

Butler, Sir John, *Lord Lothian* (London, 1960).

Cadogan, Sir Alexander, *The Diaries Of Sir Alexander Cadogan*, ed. David Dilks (London, 1971).

Chadwick, Owen, *Britain And The Vatican During The Second World War* (Cambridge, 1981).

Churchill, Winston S., *The Second World War* (London, 1954).

Clay, Lucius D., *Decision In Germany* (London, 1950).

Colvin, Ian, *Vansittart In Office* (London, 1965).

Colvin, Ian, *The Chamberlain Cabinet* (London, 1971).

Conwell-Evans, T. P., *None So Blind* (London, 1947).

Dahlerus, Birger, *The Last Attempt* (London, 1947).

Davies, Joseph E., *Mission To Moscow* (London, 1942).

Deutsch, Harold C., *The Conspiracy Against Hitler In The Twilight War* (Oxford, 1968).

Dirksen, Herbert von, *Moscow, Tokyo, London* (London, 1951).

Dulles, Allen, *Germany's Underground* (New York, 1947).

Feiling, Keith, *Life Of Neville Chamberlain* (London, 1946).

Bibliography

Fest, Joachim C., *Hitler* (London, 1977).

FitzGibbon, Constantine, *The Shirt Of Nessus* (London, 1956).

Fraenkel, Heinrich, *Help Us Germans To Beat The Nazis* (London, 1941).

Fraenkel, Heinrich, *Vansittart's Gift To Goebbels* (London, 1940).

Gilbert, Martin, *Sir Horace Rumbold* (London, 1973).

Gilbert, Martin & Gott, Richard, *The Appeasers* (London, 1963).

Gisevius, Hans Bernd, *To The Bitter End* (London, 1948).

Haffner, Sebastian, *Germany: Jekyll and Hyde* (London, 1940).

Halder, Franz, *Kriegstagebuch* (Stuttgart, 1962).

Hart, B. H. Liddell, *The Other Side Of The Hill* (London, 1951).

Harvey, John (Ed.), *The Diplomatic Diaries Of Oliver Harvey 1937–40* (London, 1970).

Hassell, Ulrich von, *The Von Hassell Diaries 1938–44* (London, 1948).

Henderson, Sir Nevile, *Failure Of A Mission* (London, 1940).

Herwarth von Bittenfeld, Hans, *Against Two Evils* (London, 1981).

Hinsley, F. H., *British Intelligence In The Second World War, Vol. One* (Cambridge, 1979).

Hoffman, Peter, *The History Of the German Resistance 1933–45* (London, 1977).

Home, William Douglas, *Half Term Report* (London, 1956).

Jacobsen, Hans-Adolf (Ed.), *July 20, 1944* (Bonn, 1969).

Jacobsen, Hans-Adolf & Zimmerman, Erich (Eds.), *Germans Against Hitler* (Bonn, 1960).

Jansen, J. B. & Wahl, Stefan, *The Silent War* (New York, 1943).

John, Otto, *Twice Through The Lines* (London, 1972).

Kelly, Sir David, *The Ruling Few* (London, 1952).

Kleffens, E. N. van, *The Rape Of The Netherlands* (London, 1940).

Kordt, Erich, *Nicht Aus Den Akten* (Stuttgart, 1950).

Kordt, Erich, *Wahn Und Wirklichkeit* (Stuttgart, 1948).

Leber, Annedore, *Conscience In Revolt* (London, 1957).

Lochner, Louis P. (Ed.), *The Goebbels Diaries* (London, 1948).

Lochner, Louis P., *What About Germany?* (London, 1943).

Malone, Henry O., *Adam von Trott zu Solz* (Berlin, 1986).

Mosley, Leonard, *On Borrowed Time* (New York, 1969).

Muggeridge, Malcolm (Ed.), *Ciano's Diary 1939–43* (London, 1947).

Murphy, Robert, *A Diplomat Among Warriors* (New York, 1964).

Murray, Williamson, *The Change In The Balance Of Power* (Princeton, 1984).

Namier, L. B., *Diplomatic Prelude 1938–9* (London, 1948).

Namier, L. B., *In The Nazi Era* (London, 1952).

Namier, L. B., *Europe In Decay: The Road To Munich* (London, 1950).

Nicolson, Harold, *Diaries & Letters, 1939–45* (London, 1967).

Payne Best, Sigismund, *The Venlo Incident* (London, 1950).

Pechel, Rudolf, *Deutscher Widerstand* (Zurich, 1946).

Prittie, Terence, *Germans Against Hitler* (London, 1964).

Rauschning, Hermann, *Germany's Revolution Of Destruction* (London, 1939).

Ritter, Gerhard, *The German Resistance* (London, 1958).

Roon, Ger van, *German Resistance To Hitler* (London, 1971).

Rose, Norman, *Vansittart: Study Of A Diplomat* (London, 1958).

Rothfels, Hans, *The German Opposition To Hitler* (London, 1970).

Rothstein, Andrew (trans.), *Soviet Foreign Policy During The Patriotic War: Documents And Materials* (London, 1946).

Schacht, Hjalmar, *Account Settled* (London, 1949).

Schlabrendorff, Fabian von, *Revolt Against Hitler* (London, 1966).

Schlabrendorff, Fabian von, *The Secret War Against Hitler* (London, 1966).

Schmidt, Paul Otto, *Hitler's Interpreter* (London, 1951).

Scholl, Inge, *Six Against Tyranny* (London, 1955).

Selby, Sir Walford, *Diplomatic Twilight* (London, 1953).

Shirer, William, *The Rise And Fall Of The Third Reich* (London, 1972).

Spier, Eugen, *Focus: A Footnote To The History Of The Thirties* (London, 1963).

Spitzy, Reinhard, *So Haben Wir Das Reich Verspielt* (Vienna, 1988).

Strang, Lord, *Home And Abroad* (London, 1956).

Sykes, Christopher, *Troubled Loyalty* (London, 1968).

Taylor, A. J. P., *New Statesman and Nation* (22 September 1954).

Taylor, A. J. P., *The Origins Of The Second World War* (London, 1961).

Templewood, Lord, *Nine Troubled Years* (London, 1954).

Trevor-Roper, Hugh, *The Last Days Of Hitler* (London, 1956).

United States Strategic Bombing Survey (Washington, 1945).

Vansittart, Lord, *Black Record* (London, 1941).

Vansittart, Lord, *Lessons Of My Life* (London, 1943).

Vansittart, Lord, *The Mist Procession* (London, 1958).

Visser 't Hooft, W. A., *Memoirs* (London, 1973).

Warlimont, Walter, *Inside Hitler's Headquarters* (London, 1964).

Wark, Wesley K., *The Ultimate Enemy* (London, 1958).

Weizsäcker, Ernst von, *Memoirs* (London, 1951).

Wheeler-Bennett, J. W., *George VI* (London, 1958).

Wheeler-Bennett, J. W., *The Nemesis Of Power* (New York, 1969).

Wheeler-Bennett, J. W., *Special Relationships* (London, 1972).

Young, A. P., *The 'X' Documents* (London, 1974).

Index